Natural Gas Vehicles

Natural Gas Vehicles

by

John G. Ingersoll, Ph.D.

Published by
THE FAIRMONT PRESS, INC.
700 Indian Trail
Lilburn, GA 30247

Library of Congress Cataloging-in-Publication Data

Ingersoll, John G., 1948-
  Natural gas vehicles / by John C. Ingersoll.
  p. cm.
  Includes bibliographical references and index.
  ISBN 0-88173-218-4
  1. Natural gas vehicles--United States. 2. Motor vehicle industry--United States. I. Title.
TL228.I54   1995   333.79'68-dc20   95-38382
                                                      CIP

Published by The Fairmont Press, Inc.
700 Indian Trail
Lilburn, GA 30247

Printed in the United States of America

10 9 8 7 6 5 4 3 2 1

ISBN 0-88173-218-4   FP

ISBN 0-13-231846-6   PH

While every effort is made to provide dependable information, the publisher, authors, and editors cannot be held responsible for any errors or omissions.

Distributed by Prentice Hall PTR
Prentice-Hall, Inc.
A Simon & Schuster Company
Upper Saddle River, NJ 07458

Prentice-Hall International (UK) Limited, London
Prentice-Hall of Australia Pty. Limited, Sydney
Prentice-Hall Canada Inc., Toronto
Prentice-Hall Hispanoamericana, S.A., Mexico
Prentice-Hall of India Private Limited, New Delhi
Prentice-Hall of Japan, Inc., Tokyo
Simon & Schuster Asia Pte. Ltd., Singapore
Editora Prentice-Hall do Brasil, Ltda., Rio de Janeiro

DEDICATION

*To the American people who, presented with a new beginning,
can regain control of the economy and national security,
left for so long to the mercy of oil suppliers in faraway lands,
and restore the quality of the ambient air natural resource
for a healthy environment in which to live and work.*

Contents

ACKNOWLEDGEMENTS

The author wishes to express his thanks to the many individuals who have, through their knowledge, questions and insight over the years, contributed in one way or another to making this publication possible. These individuals include teachers, colleagues in academia and the industry, students and clients. The author would also like to express his sincere gratitude to the people who have assisted him in the arduous task of processing this manuscript, notably Alberto Schroth and Mike Dombrower in preparing the art work.

While every effort has been made to provide accurate and up-to-date information, changes in the arena of natural gas vehicles occur very rapidly as this is a young and dynamic industry. Hopefully, the message of this book transcends the ephemeral and addresses the more permanent issues. It is also hoped that those who favor different approaches will nonetheless expose themselves to the message of this publication and subject their views to the ultimate test: can they be implemented in practice? Admittedly, what must be done is hard to describe and even harder to do. And yet the message is plain and simple: natural gas vehicles represent the wave of the future in land transport.

Introduction

"A major revolution in the habits of the American people is now under way as the use of natural gas spreads swiftly from one section of the country to another." This is how the author of "The Eternal Flame", an article in the October 1951 issue of National Geographic, described the impact natural gas was beginning to make on American life. Now, some 44 years years later, we are standing at the threshold of the final phase of that revolution in the habits of the American people as natural gas emerges as the transportation fuel of choice in the country.

The last four and a half decades have witnessed the spreading of the use of natural gas in just about every facet of every day life except driving. Industry relies heavily on natural gas as the premier feedstock material for a multitude of products and as an energy source. Natural gas has become the fuel par excellence for clean electricity generation by the utilities. Hot water generation, and heating and cooling of commercial buildings relies on natural gas driven equipment. Natural gas conditions space, provides hot water, dries clothes and supplies the energy for cooking in homes all across America. Natural gas is about ready to enter a new utility: the powering of motor vehicles.

In the early days of the automobile industry and through the 1930s, manufactured gas in Europe and natural gas in the United States was used to fuel a significant number of automobiles. The rapid expansion in the availability of crude oil and its derivatives gasoline and diesel fuel after World War II practically eliminated the importance of other automotive fuels. Nevertheless, natural gas vehicles never disappeared from the roads of America. In the mean time, technological developments, particularly with regard to on-board storage as well as extremely low emissions, and an abundant domestic supply have made natural gas a realistic prospect for a motor fuel.

Technological innovation, of which the replacement of gasoline and diesel fuel vehicles by natural gas vehicles constitutes such an example, is not driven by technology alone. A confluence of other factors must be present for technological innovation to occur. Economic viability is of paramount importance. Unfortunately, gasoline and diesel vehicles represent a mature and well entrenched technology that enjoys a significant cost advantage. For even though natural gas as a fuel costs half as much as gasoline or diesel fuel today, this cost differential may not on its own be sufficient to overcome the added cost of modifying parts of the present fuel infrastructure and automobile manufacturing process. Additional factors are necessary.

It seems that we are fast approaching the time when overriding factors will make the transition form gasoline and diesel vehicles to natural gas vehicles inevitable. These factors comprise the much broader and more fundamental goals for the country of *economic vitality, environmental quality* and *national security.* Therefore, as we consider the steps necessary to implement the substitution of current motor vehicles with natural gas vehicles, it only makes sense to develop a strategy that does the best job in supporting these and other related goals.

A multitude of ancillary factors that are instrumental in this transition have been also evolving over the years. The expansion of the natural gas pipeline distribution system to every corner of the country reduces immensely the cost of transitioning from the gasoline/diesel fuel infrastructure to the natural gas fuel infrastructure. Natural gas is now available in most homes and business in the country. Refueling at home or place of work is a more economical and more practical solution to the traditional public gasoline station or even the public natural gas station alternative.

Any technological innovation creates new opportunities, generates new business, and produces economic vitality, while old business are slowly overtaken and eventually disappear. The implementation of natural gas vehicles is no different in that respect. However, this implementation is not the result of government fiat or policy, but rather the natural outcome of evolutionary socioeconomic forces. Governments, of course, respond to these forces either in a positive fashion by developing appropriate policy or in a negative fashion by obstructing the natural process through counterproductive legislation.

Several forces are currently at work shaping our energy policy in general and the implementation of natural gas vehicles in particular. These forces include global economic growth, environmental issues, a changing economic structure, and continuing improvements in energy-efficient technologies.

The need for economic growth dominates much of the policy discussions. The economy of the nations of the world becomes more and more interdependent. This gives rise to a host of important implications with regard to resource use, environmental quality and international trade. Most of the growth in these areas will come from developing countries in the future. The US depends heavily on imported oil that must be shared in the future with several other nations. In fact motor vehicles in the US use annually as many barrels of petroleum products as the number of barrels of imported crude oil. This imported oil adds more than $60 billion annually to the trade deficit of the US with the rest of the world. In addition, the US must maintain a military presence in certain parts of the world, particularly the Persian Gulf, to guarantee the free flow of oil. Last but not least, gasoline or diesel are not the cleanest of fuels.

Environmental issues such as acid rain, photochemical smog, urban ozone, global warming are taking center stage in energy use and energy policy. Motor vehicles are responsible for a good deal of these issues. The US was first to experience automobile pollution dating back to the 1940s because of its large vehicular population. Starting in 1965 and continuing to 1990 the Clean Air Act and its Amendments have sought to mandate reduction in motor vehicle emissions by more than a factor of ten. Thus, the carbon monoxide emissions have been reduced from a pre 1968 level of 84 g/mi (grams per mile) to a 1996 and beyond standard of 3.4 g/mi (96% reduction). Likewise, nitrous oxide emissions have been reduced from 4.1 g/mi to 0.4 g/mi (90% reduction) and non-methane organic gas emissions from 10.60 g/mi to 0.25 g/mi (97% reduction).

Despite these drastic reductions in automobile emissions, the air pollution problem in the US is nowhere near to being eliminated. Part of the reason is the increase in the number of motor vehicles by almost a factor of three in the last 30 years. Moreover, these emission standards do not apply to all vehicles. But even more important, the catalytic converters that maintain the emission levels low in new vehicles become gradually much less effective because of minute amounts of contaminants found in the gasoline fuel — picked up in the refining process. Thus, an automobile fueled with gasoline may be producing after 50 thousand miles 3 or 4 times as much pollutants as when new and may revert after 100 thousand miles to the pre-control emissions.

The internal combustion engine powering motor vehicles today has been considered as the culprit of motor vehicle air pollution. Hence, the misguided attempt to legislate electric vehicles into existence has originated. It is the opinion of this author that the gasoline and diesel fuels are the true culprits. Gaseous fuels such as natural gas and hydrogen have the potential to reduce emissions to negligible amounts or at the very least to amounts below the so called *assimilative capacity* of the environment. For example, the compressed natural gas 1994 Chrysler minivan, classified as a light duty truck with a 3.3 liter V-6 150 hp engine, has average emissions, over a 100 thousand mile life, of 0.30 g/mi for carbon monoxide (91% reduction over the 1996 standard), 0.04 g/mi for nitrous oxides (90% reduction) and 0.05 g/mi for non-reactive organic gases (98% reduction). Incidentally, this is the first vehicle to be certified as ultra low emission vehicle by the California Air Resources Board. Thus, natural gas vehicles offer another factor of ten or better reduction in emissions from the 1996 federal emission standards (1993 California standards) for gasoline vehicles.

Despite reductions in the emissions of gasoline vehicles in the US over the last 25 years, unhealthy air in most major metropolitan areas of the country is still a reality that cannot be overlooked. This unhealthy air may be causing lost productivity because of illness as well as damage to property in excess of 1% and possibly as high as 2% of the gross national product annually.

The economic structure of the United States has been undergoing significant changes in the last 15 years. The industrial structure is changing toward a more service oriented economy. Industry is turning away from energy intensive products such as automobiles. The balance of trade is shifting as more energy intensive energy products are imported. Meanwhile, all major corporations are downsizing as a means to stay competitive in the domestic and the global markets. Finally, the consumer end-product demand shows changing patterns toward new technology.

The number of passenger-miles accommodated by automobiles as a percent of the total passenger-miles travelled in the country has been diminishing for more than twenty years now after peaking around 1973. At the same time the percent of passenger-miles representing air travel has been increasing and is currently substituting automobile travel following a logistic growth. The last decade or so may have witnessed the birth of yet a new mode of transportation that is destined to become the dominant in the second half of the 21st century. This mode, which represents new technology in its infancy, is what we may call telecommuting.

The significance of all these developments is that the number of motor vehicles in the US will reach a maximum of about 260 million in the next 40 to 50 years irrespectively of the population growth of the country.

Improvements in the efficient use of energy continue in every sector of the economy. The transportation sector is no exception. The average fuel efficiency of all motor vehicles in the US has been increasing at a rate of about 0.5 mpg per year in recent years. Since the late 1970s, when the CAFE standard was enacted, the average fuel efficiency of motor vehicles in the US has increased by more than 50 percent. The current average of 21 mpg will rise to the maximum of 27 or 28 mpg in about 10 years. In the mean time, additional voluntary or mandatory improvements in efficiency will have to be instituted that will bring the average fuel efficiency of new vehicles to 40 mpg. Natural gas alone as a fuel can boost vehicle fuel efficiency, because of its very high octane rating, by at least 15% through high compression ratio engines and by another 5% through a lean fuel-air mixture with either improved engine design or appropriate emission controls or inclusion of small amount of hydrogen in the fuel. Numerous other technological innovations can readily attain the 40 mpg goal by the year 2005.

The rest of the world and particularly the developing countries may have a 20 to 30 year lag behind the US in attaining the peak in motor vehicle population. The more than 500 million vehicles in the world, of which one-third is in the US today, may double in the next 15 years especially if countries like China become heavily industrialized. Already several major cities in the world have air pollution problems that make the Los Angeles smog problem pale by comparison. Lack of emission controls and poor maintenance of vehicles in developing countries present a serious environmental threat. If gasoline and diesel remain the fuels of choice for the vehicles in these countries, the air quality prognostication cannot be anything but very bleak 20 years hence. Natural gas vehicles offer the only cost effective alternative for these countries to avoid disaster and rely also less on imported oil.

The implementation of natural gas vehicles offers a tremendous opportunity for economic development and technological innovation in the US starting now and for several decades to come: more than $100 billion in trade balance and budget deficit reduction annually; increased national security; another $100 billion each year in increased productivity because of healthier citizens; clean air all across the country; and the expansion of existing as well as the creation of new industries of at least $50 billion annually to support the transition initially in the domestic arena and later on a global scale. Last but not least, the US has the ability to propel itself into a leadership position with regard to a badly needed globally sustainable transportation development.

The fundamental reason for writing this book has been the desire to make the case for natural gas as the only practical, virtually emission free, very efficient, and domestic alternative fuel in the US to replace gasoline and diesel fuel. It appears that the information on this subject is at best not readily available and at worst incomplete and not always accurate. Consequently, the targeted readership for this book covers a very wide spectrum of individuals including: policy makers and other officials in the federal, state and local governments; executives, administrators and engineers in utilities, oil companies, motor vehicle manufacturing companies and automotive component suppliers; members of environmental organizations and groups; college and university students;

private vehicle fleet operators and related businesses; and last but not least the general public.

This book consists of ten chapters and three appendices. The first chapter examines the historical aspects of the evolution of the automobile and automotive fuels. In the second chapter a comparison is made of the properties of current automotive fuels as well as alternative motor fuels with special emphasis placed on natural gas. The third chapter addresses in detail natural gas with regard to the production aspects, including relevant technology, consumption by sector of the economy, and future reserves and resources to meet the increased demand in the transportation sector. The fourth chapter discusses the minimum requirements of natural gas fuel storage on-board a vehicle and describes the latest technological advances in the vehicular storage of natural gas. Chapter five examines the evolution of the present automobile infrastructure, presents the current state of the natural gas infrastructure, examines the advantages of natural gas delivery systems vs. gasoline and other liquid fuels, and discusses in depth the latest developments of natural gas refueling technology.

Chapter six is devoted to the types of automotive pollution and its effect on health and the climate, the description of the legislative measures on emissions control by federal and state governments through the year 2000, the technological fixes offered by automobile manufacturers, and a detail examination of the huge reduction in emissions from natural gas vehicles vs. other fuels including even electricity. The seventh chapter examines in great length the natural gas pricing system from production to customer delivery, evaluates the incremental cost of natural gas vehicles and reduced costs associated with vehicle maintenance and estimates the cost savings resulting from the use of natural gas fuel. Chapter eight addresses the dynamics of technological change processes on the basis of the logistic substitution, and borrows from the competition of biological systems to develop a predictive substitution model of natural gas vehicles for gasoline and diesel fuel vehicles. Chapter nine reviews the on-going developments in other low polluting fuel technologies such as electricity and hydrogen and develops a framework in which natural gas is the first practical element in the long term implementation of clean transportation technologies. Chapter ten examines a variety of physical and economic issues that guide society in developing appropriate transportation and other technologies employing natural gas, challenges the notion that higher gasoline prices are the solution to clean air, refutes the need for zero emission vehicles, examines future trends in automobile efficiency, considers the availability of natural gas as a global transportation fuel, and concludes by developing a path for an efficient and timely implementation of the transition to natural gas fuel. The appendices contain listings of selected suppliers of natural gas vehicles, components and fueling equipment, an outline of the 1990 Clean Air Act Amendment and areas affected by it, and conversion tables of physical units from the engineering system to the metric system.

It is hoped that this book will help catalyze action at all levels of society to bring about a timely transformation of our present land transportation system to one that relies totally on domestic fuels and to one that results in the regaining of clean and healthy air across the country in a practical and above all affordable fashion.

Chapter 1

Petroleum and the Automobile

EVOLUTION OF THE AUTOMOBILE IN THE UNITED STATES

The invention of the steam engine at the beginning of the eighteenth century was instrumental in the launching of the industrial revolution. Steam driven machines could enable humanity to produce many times over what has been possible since the beginning of civilization on the basis of human and animal labor alone. The invention of the internal combustion engine during the second half of the nineteenth century was destined to revolutionize human affairs once more in an even more profound way. The ensuing transportation revolution through the use of mechanized modes of travel on land and in air would allow humanity to increase further its productivity. The average speed of an automobile is ten times higher than the average speed of walking, the traditional mode of transport since the beginning of civilization. Consequently, the automobile would allow human interaction to expand to a territory some one hundred times larger than that accessible by walking, which historically represented the village or small town settlement. Incidentally, the advent of the airplane with an average speed ten times higher than the automobile affords humanity an interaction territory of some ten thousand times larger than the size of the typical community most people lived in as late as one hundred years ago.

Nicholas Otto devised the thermodynamic cycle which became the basis of the four-stroke internal combustion engine in 1877[1]. The first practical high speed gasoline engine operating on this cycle was developed by Gottlieb Daimler and August Maybach within the next six or seven years and was used to self-power a carriage formerly drawn by horses. This first "horseless carriage" assembled by Karl Benz and Gottlieb Daimler sometime in 1885 or 1886 was to usher us ultimately into the automobile age. The pneumatic tire was manufactured by John Boyd Dunlop in 1890. The Diesel cycle and the motor based on it were developed by Rudolph Diesel between 1893 and 1897. By 1891 there were already factories producing cars on a regular commercial basis in France. Words like *automobile, garage, chauffeur, chassis* are reminders of the early lead established by the French in the automotive field, building on the basis of German technology.

The first demonstration of a gasoline-powered vehicle in America took place in Springfield, Massachusetts in September of 1893 by the brothers Charles and Frank Duryea[2]. Over the next several years excitement swept among a lot of tinkerers, each trying to produce a viable version of the horseless carriage. Between 1900 and 1908 no less than 500 American companies were formed to manufacture automobiles. Most of them dropped out or entered another line of business, but that still left 290 survivors by 1910. As late as 1917, after many shakedowns and mergers, there were 23 carmaking companies in Detroit alone, which by that time had been established as the automotive manufacturing capital of the nation.

America was on its way of becoming the preeminent automobile manufacturing country in the world for decades to come. In 1901, Ransom E. Olds, the Lansing, Michigan carmaker who has moved to Detroit, introduced his little curved-dash Oldsmobile shown in Figure 1-1, the world's first low priced car to be produced in any quantity. By 1904, the production of this vehicle exceeded 5,500 units, a more than ten-fold increase since its introduction, and represented more than one-third of the total American made gasoline powered cars. A year earlier, the Ford Motor Company was founded in Detroit by Henry Ford, who was to become to the gasoline-powered vehicle what James Watt was to the steam engine some 150 years earlier[3]. In 1909 also in Detroit, the

(a)

(b)

FIGURE 1-1. Ninety four years in the evolution of the automobile product by Oldsmobile, the oldest American motor vehicle nameplate still in production: (a) The 1901 Curved Dash; and (b) The 1995 Aurora with automatic climate control, dimensional audio system, remote entry, 50 mi "limp-home" engine mode, solar control glass, leather/wood trim, seat/mirror memory, power accessories.

SPECIFICATIONS	Curved-Dash	Aurora
Capacity/Safety	Two persons	Five persons/Dual Air Bags-Side Imp.
Frame	Angle steel	Unibody, front/rear crush zones
Wheelbase	66 inches	113.8 inches
Suspension	Side Springs	Indep. 4-Wheel, Coil spring front/rear
Steering	Tiller	Magnetic Variable-Assist
Brakes	Friction	ABS, full-range traction control
Wheels	28-inch wood artillery	16-inch cast alloy, 44 psi/low rr tires
Motor	7 hp horizontal	250 hp transverse, 100k mile tune-up
Transmission	All-spur gear, 2-speed	4-speed automatic, normal/sport shift
Fuel	5 gallons gasoline	20 gallons
Price	$650 (1901)	$31,900 (1995)

FIGURE 1-1.   (Continued)

Cadillac Automotive Company, founded some seven years before and having established a reputation for unparalleled quality and reliability, became the flagship of the fledgling General Motors Corporation, the company which was to become 13 years hence the largest automotive manufacturer in the world and remain in that position to this day. The ground was laid for the automobile industry whose main development took place after the First World War. The petroleum industry rose to importance accordingly.

The explosive growth of the automobile in the United States since the beginning of the twentieth century is summarized in Table 1-1, where historical data have been included of annual sales as well as of the registration number of passenger cars, trucks and buses[4][5][6][7]. The two decades from 1900 through 1920 were the formative years of the American automobile industry which has dominated the world ever since. It is interesting to note that by the late 1920s the United States accounted for almost 80% of all the vehicles on the roads around the world. Even today one out of three vehicles in the world is in the United States. The impact of the automobile on the American society has been immense throughout the years, but this subject is outside the scope of this book. Suffice it to mention two relatively recent consequences of the automobile to the American scene. First, the dependency of the country on imported oil to power its automobiles, a reality developed in a short period of time some 25 years ago. Second, the gradual deterioration of the air quality in several large metropolitan areas start-

TABLE 1-1. Historical Data on the Annual Sales and Total Registration of Automobiles in the United States from 1900 to the Present

Year	Factory Sales (1,000)			Registrations (1,000)		
	Total	Passenger Cars	Trucks Buses	Total	Passenger Cars	Trucks Buses
1900	4	4	—	8	8	—
1910	187	181	6	469	458	10
1920	2,227	1,906	322	9,239	8,132	1,108
1930	3,363	2,787	575	26,750	23,035	3,715
1940	4,472	3,717	755	32,453	27,466	4,987
1945	725	70	656	31,053	25,793	5,242
1950	8,003	6,666	1,337	49,162	40,334	8,828
1955	9,169	7,920	1,249	62,694	52,136	10,558
1960	7,869	6,675	1,194	73,941	61,724	12,217
1965	11,057	9,306	1,752	90,358	75,258	15,100
1970	8,239	6,547	1,692	108,400	89,200	19,200
1975	8,985	6,713	2,272	132,900	106,700	26,200
1980	8,067	6,400	1,667	155,800	121,600	34,100
1985	11,359	8,002	3,357	172,000	132,000	40,000
1990	9,769	6,050	3,719	189,000	144,000	45,000

Notes. Prior to 1930 buses are included with passenger cars. Taxis are included in passenger cars. Registration includes publicly owned vehicles and excludes military vehicles.

ing in the late 1940s because of the emissions generated form the vast numbers of automobiles on the roads.

It is the contention of the author that both of these problems are not inherent to the automobile, but rather a consequence of the fuel employed currently to power it, whether it is gasoline or to a smaller scale diesel fuel. Moreover, it will be demonstrated in subsequent chapters that there exists today a fuel that is abundant domestically and one that reduces air pollution by an order of magnitude compared to gasoline. This fuel is none other than natural gas. It is, therefore, the objective of this book to show that natural gas as a motor fuel is the logical succession to gasoline and diesel fuels in the years to come. Moreover, natural gas may become the ultimate motor fuel or it could be viewed as the interim or transition fuel during the next fifty years, depending on technological developments in that time period. It is anticipated that the internal combustion engine could be either augmented in efficiency through a hybrid propulsion system or be replaced with an even more efficient one, such as a fuel cell. It is also envisioned that the universal utilization of an entirely pollution free fuel generated from domestic renewable energy sources in the form of either methane, the main constituent of natural gas, or hydrogen, will eventually become the motor fuel of choice.

DEPENDENCY OF CURRENT MOTOR FUELS ON CRUDE OIL

The automotive fleet in the United States consists currently of about 145 million passenger cars and 45 million trucks and busses. The fuels of choice for this automotive fleet have traditionally been hydrocarbon based fuels, namely motor gasoline and diesel fuel. Both of these fuels are derived from the refining of crude oil, which comprises essentially the feedstock fuel. The fuel consumption required to operate the 190 million passenger cars, trucks and buses is on the order of 8 million barrels per day (bbl/d). Motor gasoline comprises 7 million bbl/d and diesel fuel the remainder 1 million bbl/d[8]. It is worth noting that in 1992 over 98% of the total motor gasoline used in the US was unleaded gasoline. While the total amount of motor gasoline produced has remained fairly constant during the last 15 years, the percent of unleaded gasoline has increased very rapidly. In 1977 it stood at 27.5%, in 1980 it increased to 46.6%, by 1985 it reached 64.5% and then by 1990 it had attained a 94.5% market dominance. It appears that by 1995 unleaded gasoline will comprise over 99% of the motor gasoline marketed in this country.

Increased concerns over automotive generated air pollution in the last decade have resulted in the introduction of two additional fuels into the market. Ethanol is marketed as a gasoline additive to reduce carbon monoxide emissions. Some 1.1 billion gallons of ethanol were produced in 1992 (0.075 million bbl/d), up from 600 million gallons six years ago [9][10]. All of this ethanol is derived from agricultural feedstock with corn in the mid-west being the most predominant one. Ethanol is mixed with gasoline at a minimum content of 10% and is marketed under the name of gasohol. In essence ethanol serves as an oxygenating agent in the gasoline in order to reduce the carbon monoxide emissions. The significance of alcohols as alternative fuels will be examined in a later chapter. Suffice it to say that the maximum amount of ethanol that can be produced ultimately in the US from corn feedstock is on the order of 3 to 5 billion gallons per year[11]. In addition, compressed natural gas (CNG) has been expanding its usage in recent years to power motor vehicles. In 1992 some 500 million standard cubic feet (scf) were used for this purpose[12]. Other automotive fuels used in a small to very small scale include propane derived from natural gas liquids, methanol derived from natural gas reforming and electricity.

The fuel consumption of passenger cars accounts for about 55% of the total fuel use even though passenger cars comprise numerically more than 76% of the US automotive fleet. This is due to the fact that passenger cars are by nature lighter (smaller weight) and more efficient, thereby requiring less fuel per mile driven. The average fuel efficiency of passenger cars stands at about 21 miles per gallon (mpg)[13]. It is interesting to note that since 1973 passenger car fuel efficiency has risen from about 13 mpg to the present 21 mpg, an improvement of almost 60%[13]. However, the fuel consumption has remained virtually the same during the same period of time, because the gains in fuel efficiency have been offset by an almost equal increase in the number of passenger vehicles on the road. It is also interesting to note that the average fuel consumption is about 500 gal per year for passenger cars, and more than twice as much for trucks and buses[13].

Thus, motor gasoline is unquestionably the dominant motor vehicle fuel at the present time accounting for some 86% of the total amount of motor fuels, while diesel fuel accounts for 13.5% and ethanol for 0.5%, in terms of energy content. Consequently, of the automotive fuels currently in use in the US 99.5% are derived from crude oil and 0.5% from biomass.

CRUDE OIL AND THE US ENERGY SUPPLY

In 1990 the US produced 67.853 quadrillion BTU (quads) of energy and consumed 81.292 quads of energy for a net importation of 13,439 quads of energy[14]. On the production side, coal contributed 22.456 quads, natural gas 18.362 quads, crude oil 15.701 quads, natural gas liquids 2.175 quads, and nuclear, hydro and other renewable electric power the remainder 9.289 quads. On the consumption side, coal accounted for 19.101 quads, natural gas for 19.242 quads, crude oil for 33.553 quads, and nuclear, hydro and other renewable electric power 9.314 quads. Thus, the current hydrocarbon consumption in the US, described in more familiar units, consists of 16 million barrels of petroleum per day and almost 20 trillion standard cubic feet of natural gas per year.

While all of the natural gas consumed is essentially produced in the US, the petroleum used consists of 9 million bbl/d of crude oil and natural gas liquids produced in the US (56%) as well as a net 7 million bbl/d of crude oil and petroleum products (44%) imported from all around the world, as indicated in Figure 1-2[15]. Figure 1-3 shows the level of petroleum imports in the US from selected countries. Of the imported crude oil and petroleum products, some 73% originates from five countries and another 14% from five more countries as follows, in order of decreasing contribution: Saudi Arabia (24%), Venezuela (15%), Canada (14%), Mexico (11%), Nigeria (10%), Algeria (3%), Angola (3%), Virgin Islands (3%), Colombia (2%) and UK (2%)[15]. Moreover, the imported 7 million bbl/d of crude oil and petroleum products (44%) consist of 3 million bbl/d from non-OPEC countries(19%), 2 million bbl/d from Arab-OPEC (12.5%) and 2 million bbl/d from other OPEC countries (12.5%).

It is interesting to note that the crude oil production of the 48 contiguous states in the US has been continuously declining during the last twenty years as shown in Figure 1-4. The decline of the total US production of crude oil was, however, arrested for a period of about 10 years between 1976 and 1985 as the production from Alaska was coming on line until it reached its maximum production of about 2 million bbl/d by 1988.

In the last few years domestic crude oil production has dropped significantly. The average daily production of crude oil in 1992 was about 7 million bbl/d, down from 9 million bbl/d in 1985. Even the output from Alaska has declined a little and is currently about 1.8 million bbl/d. Thus, the average decline in production of crude oil for each year in the period between 1986 and 1992 has been about 0.3 million barrels per day, on the average. Whether this decline can be arrested or not remains to be seen. The continuing recession since the early 1991 has reduced temporarily the consumption of petroleum products. This occurrence has been beneficial in that the imports of crude oil have not increased despite the decline of domestic production, thereby keeping unchanged the portion of the trade deficit due to oil imports. On the

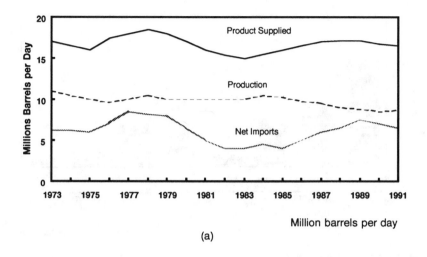

(a)

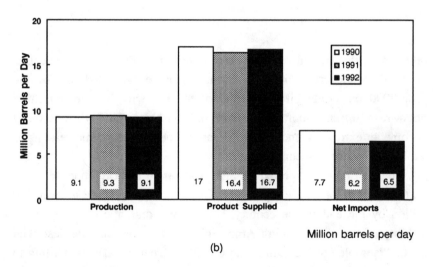

(b)

FIGURE 1-2. Petroleum overview of product supplied, production, and net imports in the US: (a) Historical trend 1973-1991; and (b) Recent trend 1990-1992 (Source: Energy Information Administration, US DOE).

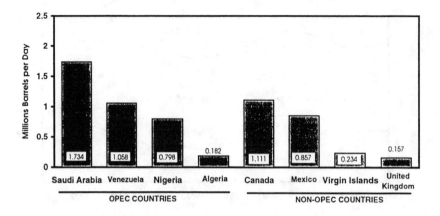

Million Barrels per day

FIGURE 1-3. Imports of crude oil (10^6 bbl/d) to the US from selected countries in 1992 (Source: Energy Information Administration, US DOE).

other hand, the present recession has masked the severity of the decline in the domestic crude oil production. It can be estimated that by the year 2000 the crude oil production of the US will drop to 5 million bbl/d, resulting in imports of over 10 million bbl/d. This will obviously become an extremely undesirable situation both for economic reasons as well as for national security concerns.

The cost of the imported oil and products to the US trade deficit is on the order of $60 billion per year. This cost may increase to over $80 billion by the end of the century, barring any dramatic changes in the stability of the oil producing Arab regions. This cost may be described as the "tangible cost" of importing crude oil. There is also, according to several authors, an "intangible cost" associated with importing crude oil which arises from the need to maintain US military presence in the Persian Gulf and elsewhere in the world. This intangible cost is given a wide range of values from a minimum of $10 billion per year to a conservative maximum of $40 billion per year[16][17].

It is worth noting that the present hydrocarbon fuel consumption of passenger cars, trucks and busses is of the same magnitude as the

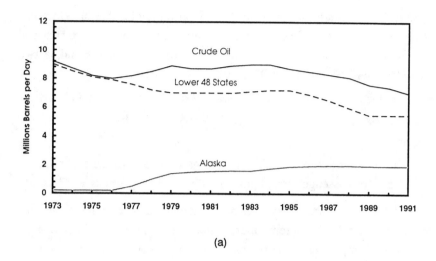

(a)

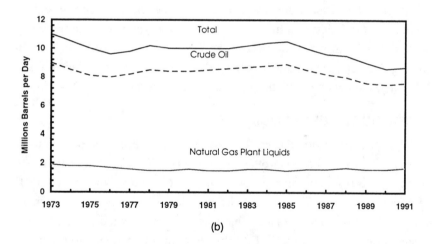

(b)

FIGURE 1-4. Liquid Hydrocarbon Production (million bbl/d) in the US from 1973 to 1992:(a) Crude Oil; (b) Total Including Natural Gas Liquids (Source: Energy Information Administration, US DOE).

amount of petroleum imported to the US on an annual basis. While this is an enormous rate of consumption, there exists a way to reduce and ultimately eliminate the need to import petroleum. To this end, a two step effort will be necessary. This effort will consist of:

I.   The further increase in fuel efficiency of passenger cars and particu-
     larly light trucks and vans (under 10,000 lb weight) sold in the US;
     and

II. The switch of automotive fuels from gasoline and diesel fuel to natur-
     al gas for passenger cars, light trucks, vans, heavy trucks and buses.

Both of these steps ought to be implemented in parallel. Given the relatively short life of automobiles, which is on the order of ten years, a fast rate of implementation of this two step effort is possible within a time frame of about three decades. It is therefore realistic to expect that, if the proper measures are taken on the part of the government and on the part of the industry, a highly efficient natural gas based transportation system can be in place throughout the US by the year 2020. In the following chapters, the case will be then made regarding the technical feasibility and the economic viability of such a transportation fuel system.

AUTOMOBILE FUEL EFFICIENCY

The fuel of choice during the early days of the automobile industry appears to have been none other than ethanol. This is clearly indicated in the advertisement of the *"Automobile Club de France"* of 1902 reproduced here in Figure 1-5. The petroleum industry was still in its infancy. The availability of gasoline was very limited and its distribution system was not yet in place. Ethanol, by contrast, derived from the fermentation of sugars and starches was a well established industry and a relatively abundant supply of it was available. It is reported that in 1908, when Henry Ford began the production of the famous "Model T", which was to establish the automobile as we now know it, he consulted with Thomas Edison whether to use gasoline or ethanol as the fuel for the new model vehicle. Edison advised Ford to choose gasoline. In retrospect it would have been impossible to have had the subsequent expansion of the automobile in the US, first, and the world, later, if Edison and Ford had made a different choice.

FIGURE 1-5. Advertisement of the French Automotive Club in 1902 clearly indicating the use of ethanol as the automotive fuel of choice at the time (French poster 1902, Musee des Arts Decoratifs, Paris).

American automobiles have been traditionally larger in size, have more powerful engines and possess accessories for higher passenger comfort than automobiles anywhere else in the world. The result has been a lower fuel efficiency, which has always been tolerated because of the relatively low price of motor fuels compared to the prices anywhere else in the world. Table 1-2 summarizes historical data on the fuel con-

TABLE 1-2. Historical Data on Fuel Consumption by Vehicle Type: 1940 to 1990

Year	Fuel Consumption[1]				Avg. Miles Per Vehicle[2]		
	All	Cars	Buses	Trucks	Cars	Buses	Trucks
1940	22.3	16.8	0.4	5.1	9,100	18,600	10,600
1945	20.5	13.3	0.7	5.0	9,100	20,900	10,800
1950	36.3	25.0	0.7	10.6	9,100	20,900	10,800
1955	48.3	34.3	0.7	13.3	9,400	17,700	10,700
1960	62.8	42.0	0.9	19.9	9,400	16,000	10,600
1965	71.1	51.1	0.9	19.9	9,300	15,200	11,600
1970	92.3	67.8	0.8	23.6	10,000	12,000	9,900
1975	109.0	76.4	1.1	31.4	9,400	11,100	10,400
1980	115.0	71.9	1.0	41.9	8,800	11,500	11,900
1985	121.3	69.3	0.8	51.0	9,200	8,200	12,700
1990	131.6	72.4	0.9	58.1	10,300	9,100	13,900

Note. Fuel includes gasoline and all other fuels under state motor fuel laws. Excludes non-highway fuel usage and federal purchases for military use.
1. Billions of gallons per year. 2 Rounded to the nearest one-hundred miles.

sumption and average annual miles driven by vehicle type, i.e., passenger car, buses and trucks in the US[18][19][20]. Table 1-3 presents data on the evolution of the fuel efficiency and the average annual fuel use per vehicle type. It is interesting to note that in the last twenty years fuel consumption for passenger cars has remained virtually the same. The fuel consumption of buses has also remained constant over the years. However, buses account for a very small fraction of the total fuel consumption. Finally, truck fuel consumption has increased by almost 2.5 times from its level twenty years ago due to an almost equal increase of the number of trucks on the road.

The average miles driven annually per passenger car have remained constant at about 10,000 mi/y in the last 50 years. During the same period, the corresponding number of mi/y for buses has been reduced by more than a factor of two, while the number of mi/y for trucks has increased by more than 30 percent. Moreover, the average fuel efficiency of cars is roughly twice that of trucks, and the fuel efficiency of trucks is twice that of buses. In addition, the average motor fuel consumption of passenger cars is currently about 500 gal/y, while the average fuel consumption of trucks is more than 2.5 times higher than that of passenger cars. Last but not least, the fuel efficiency of passenger

TABLE 1-3. Average Fuel Use and Fuel Efficiency by Vehicle Type: 1940 to 1990

Year	Average Fuel Use[1]				Fuel Efficiency[2]		
	All	Cars	Buses	Trucks	Cars	Buses	Trucks
1940	680	594	3,050	1,095	15.29	6.10	9.68
1945	617	517	4,300	1,020	14.95	5.48	9.08
1950	728	603	3,752	1,257	14.95	5.57	8.57
1955	759	644	3,021	1,278	14.53	5.85	8.37
1960	777	661	3,040	1,330	14.28	5.26	7.96
1965	775	656	2,844	1,347	14.15	5.35	8.60
1970	854	760	2,172	1,257	13.52	5.54	7.85
1975	819	716	2,279	1,217	13.52	5.75	8.99
1980	737	591	1,926	1,243	15.46	5.95	9.54
1985	705	525	1,407	1,302	18.20	5.84	9.79
1990	696	505	1,436	1,305	21.00	5.36	10.62

Note. "All" refers to the average fuel use per vehicle in the country.
1. Gallons per year. 2. Miles per Gallon.

cars has increased by more than 55% in the last twenty years. By contrast, the fuel efficiency of buses has remained virtually the same in the last 50 years. Lastly, the fuel efficiency of trucks has increased by about 35% since 1970. It is worth noting that the fuel efficiency of cars and trucks reached its minimum in the early 1970s and has been steadily increasing ever since.

What has prompted the increase in passenger car fuel efficiency in the last twenty years can be attributed to the following two factors:

I. The rise in the price of motor fuels since the first energy crisis in 1973;

II. The passage of the Corporate Average Fuel Economy (CAFE) standards in the mid 1970s.

In 1973 the price of gasoline was $0.388 per gallon and in 1980 it has risen to $1.191 per gallon, both in current dollars[21]. This was a three-fold price increase, while in the same period the consumer price index had a two-fold rise[22]. The CAFE standards, on the other hand, required a more than two-fold increase in passenger car fuel efficiency from a little over 13 gpm in 1973 to 27.5 gpm today. While higher fuel prices were initially the catalyst for the public to purchase more fuel efficient cars, the CAFE standards have been responsible for the sustained gains in fuel efficiency of passenger cars in the last decade and will continue to do so through the end of the century. Incidentally, the price of gasoline is today roughly the same as it was ten years ago, while the consumer price index is today three times higher than what it was in 1973. Thus, the price of gasoline in constant dollars is today the same as what it was twenty years ago.

The fuel efficiency of trucks has also shown improvement in the last twenty years. However, these improvements are not nearly as impressive as those of passenger cars. Presumably, the initial impetus to acquire more fuel efficient trucks due to higher fuel prices has all but vanish. Moreover, there exist no standards for trucks, similar to the CAFE standards, to provide a gradual and continuous fuel efficiency improvement.

If one conclusion can be derived from the preceding observations, this is that automotive fuel efficiency standards constitute a far more effective as well as a much less disruptive mechanism, compared to artificial motor fuel price increases, in order to promote automobile fuel efficiency. The question of higher fuel efficiency standards will be addressed in a later chapter. Suffice it to observe for now that petroleum is responsible for a $60 billion to $100 billion deficit annually and that the supply of domestic crude oil is steadily diminishing, thereby making the US more dependent on foreign oil. In addition, poor air quality affects the health of millions of Americans with a comparable financial burden to that of the trade deficit. The health issue will be examined in a later chapter as well.

It would appear that the US is headed toward a new energy crisis alongside a potential environmental crisis both on a local scale, i.e., air quality in large metropolitan areas of the country, as well as on a global scale, i.e., greenhouse effect and stratospheric ozone depletion.

It is our thesis that natural gas has the potential by becoming the transportation fuel of choice in the US to:

A. Avert any new energy crises;

B. Eliminate the dependency of the US on foreign energy supplies;

C. Improve dramatically the balance of payments;

D. Produce a much cleaner air in all major cities across the country;

E. Slow down substantially and possibly permanently the making of a global environmental disaster;

G. Become the precursor of hydrogen, a potentially even cleaner transportation fuel.

In subsequent chapters, it will be demonstrated why and how natural gas has the technological, economic, demographic and sociological potential to become the next transportation fuel, initially in the US and ultimately in the entire world.

REFERENCES

1. H. Gollwitzer, Europe in the Age of Imperialism: 1880-1914, pp. 19-30, Harcourt, Brace & World, Inc., London, UK, 1969.

2. J. B. Rae, American Automobile Manufacturers: The First Forty Years, pp. 28-36, Chilton, Philadelphia, PA, 1959.

3. R. Lacey, Ford: The Men and the Machine, Little, Brown and Company, Boston, MA, 1986.

4. Statistical Abstract of the United States 1963, p. 567, US Department of Commerce, Bureau of Census, Washington, D.C., 1993.

5. Statistical Abstract of the United States 1970, p. 544, US Department of Commerce, Bureau of Census, Washington, D.C., 1993.

6. Statistical Abstract of the United States 1985, p. 597, US Department of Commerce, Bureau of Census, Washington, D.C., 1993.

7. Statistical Abstract of the United States 1992, p. 606, US Department of Commerce, Bureau of Census, Washington, D.C., 1993.

8. Energy Information Administration, Monthly Energy Review- June 1992, pp. 56-59, US Department of Energy, Washington D.C., 1992.

9. Energy Information Administration, Estimates of US Biofuels Consumption 1990, US Department of Energy, Washington, D.C., 1991.

10. D. Greising and P. Hong, Business Week, p. 31, July 20, 1992.

11. Energy Information Administration, <u>Natural Gas 1992 – Issues and Trends</u>, pp. 13-14, DOE/EIA-0560(92), US Department of Energy, Washington D.C., 1993.

12. M. Brower, <u>Cool Energy</u>, pp. 101-104, The MIT Press, Cambridge, MA, 1992.

13. Energy Information Administration, <u>Monthly Energy Review – June 1992</u>, *loc. cit.,* p. 17.

14. Energy Information Administration, <u>Monthly Energy Review – June 1992</u>, *loc. cit.,* pp. 6-9.

15. Energy Information Administration, <u>Monthly Energy Review – June 1992</u>, *loc. cit.,* pp. 44-55.

16. H. Broadman and W. Hogan, "Is an Oil Tariff Justified? The numbers say 'Yes'", *Energy Journal,* July 1988.

17. A. B. Lovins and H. Lovins, *The New York Times,* December, 3, 1990.

18. <u>Statistical Abstract of the United States 1963</u>, *loc. cit.,* pp. 538-539.

19. <u>Statistical Abstract of the United States 1970</u>, *loc. cit.,* pp. 548.

20. <u>Statistical Abstract of the United States 1992</u>, *loc. cit.,* pp. 614-615.

21. Energy Information Administration, <u>Monthly Energy Review – June 1992</u>, *loc. cit.,* p. 108.

22. Energy Information Administration, <u>Monthly Energy Review – June 1992</u>, *loc. cit.,* p. 20.

Chapter 2

Natural Gas as a Vehicular Fuel

PRESENT AUTOMOTIVE FUELS

Gasoline and diesel fuel are presently the established automotive fuels in the US and the rest of the world. Both of these fuels are derived from crude oil through appropriate refining processes. The major products of a crude oil refinery can be divided into three major components: fuels for transportation, fuels for energy production and nonfuel products[1]. Fuels for transportation include gasoline, jet fuel, diesel fuel and marine fuel. Fuels for energy production include heating fuel, which is similar to diesel fuel but is used to heat residential and commercial buildings, and residual fuel used by the utilities for power generation. Nonfuel products include materials used in the petrochemical industry to produce polymers, rubbers, chemicals, textiles, solvents, lubricants, specialty oils and waxes. The typical breakdown of the products derived from each barrel of crude oil, on an energy content basis, is given in Table 2-1[1][2]. Only about 90% of the input energy emerges in the products, while the remaining 10% is consumed at the refinery to make the types of products required by today's market.

Gasoline includes hydrocarbon blends from butane or C_4 (four carbon atoms in the molecule) to C_{12} (twelve carbon atoms in the molecule). Typically, a barrel of crude oil will yield upon distillation, i.e., separation of products through differentiation of their boiling points,

27

TABLE 2-1. Typical Petroleum Product Distribution Resulting from the Refining of a Barrel of Crude Oil in the United States on an Energy Content Basis

Product		Percent of Initial Energy Content
A.	Fuels for Transportation	60
	Gasoline	40
	Jet Fuel	9
	Diesel Fuel	11
B.	Fuels for Energy Production[1]	25
	Distillate Fuel Oil	15
	Residual and Heavy Oil	10
C.	Nonfuel Products	5
	Total Output Products	90
	Refining Process Energy	10
	Total Input Energy (Crude Oil)	100

1. Fuel oil is the heavier portion of distillate oil, the lighter portion being diesel fuel, and is used for residential building heating and power production in gas turbines. Residual oil is used in electric power generation, industrial steam generation, process heating and steamship operation.

about 20 % of gasoline. Since more gasoline is normally desired, it is necessary to resort to both cracking and alkylation processes. Cracking entails the breaking down of heavier molecules into smaller ones of the gasoline type with the aid of heat and appropriate catalysts. Alkylation entails the combining of the gaseous and lighter molecules into larger ones under elevated temperature and pressure and in the presence of appropriate catalysts. Important parameters of gasoline as a fuel include its calorific value or energy content both per unit mass and per unit volume, volatility and octane number. The typical numerical values of these parameters for gasoline are summarized in Table 2-2. The mass and volume calorific values are indicative of the ability of the fuel to be stored conveniently on board a vehicle. The volatility of the fuel has been traditionally important in terms of vehicle performance with regard to cold engine start and fuel vapor — air mixture combustion sustainability. In more recent times, the volatility of the fuel has been also crucial in terms of the type of emissions generated in the exhaust gases as well as the fuel evaporation from the tank in warm weather. The octane number of gasoline is indicative of the fuel's ability to prevent the

TABLE 2-2. Pertinent Physical Properties of Isooctane, Motor Gasoline, Diesel Fuel and Liquefied Propane as Transportation Fuels

Property	Isooctane	Gasoline[1]	Diesel Fuel	Propane[2]
Formula	C_8H_{18}	C_4-C_{12}	C_{14}-C_{22}	C_3H_8
H/C Atom Ratio	2.25	2.03	1.63	2.67
Molecular Weight	114	—	—	44
Density @ 15°C (lb/gal)	5.76	6.23	7.35	4.84
Heating Value (BTU/lb)	19,100	18,455	17,465	19,960
Energy Density(BTU/gal)	110,015	115,000	128,440	96,610
Air/Fuel Stoichiometry				
Mass Ratio	15.1	14.7	13.9	15.7
Octane Number	100	86-92	N/A	105
Cetane Number	N/A	N/A	40-55	N/A
Energy of Stoich. Mix.[3]				
BTU/lb st. mix.	1,186	1,175	1,172	1,196
BTU/ft³ st. mix.	94.6	95.0	96.9 93.0	
Lat. Heat Vap. (BTU/lb)	133	150	116	183
Boiling Temp. (°F)	257	85-400	365-640	-44[4]
Vapor Pressure (psi)[5]	8	8-15	0.2	206[6]
Flammability Limits				
Lower (% vol.)	1.4	1.4	1	2.2
Higher (% vol.)	7.6	7.6	6	9.5

1. Gasoline refers to unleaded blends. 2. Propane is in liquefied state. 3. Energy of stoichiometric mixture is expressed per lb or ft³ of fuel-air mixture. 4. The critical temperature of propane is 206°F and the critical pressure is 616 psi. 5. Vapor pressure is based on the Reid measuring procedure. 6. Fuel under pressure.

occurrence of premature ignition of the fuel-air mixture in the engine cylinders. The octane number affects therefore the engine compression ratio and consequently the engine efficiency as it will be discussed in a later section. Isooctane, a hydrocarbon with eight carbon atoms (C_8) in its molecule has excellent anti-knocking ability and is assigned the value of 100 for its octane number. Normal heptane, a hydrocarbon with seven carbon atoms (C_7) in its molecule and with a very poor anti-knocking ability is assigned the value of 0 for its octane number. The octane number of a gasoline is then defined as the percentage of isooctane required in a blend with normal heptane to match the knocking behavior of the gasoline being considered. Gasoline octane determination tests are performed under two sets of engine operating conditions and are characterized as motor octane number (MON) and research octane number (RON)[3]. The octane number of gasoline is typically given as the arithmetic average of these two octane numbers. Presently unleaded gasoline has an octane number ranging from 86 (regular) to 92 (premium). Until recently, an organic lead compound (tetra ethyl lead) was employed at a rate of 0.05 grams of lead or higher per gallon to boost the octane number of gasoline. This gasoline was then character-ized as leaded gasoline. In the late 1970s the phasing out of leaded gasoline began, because of concerns of lead poisoning to the environ-ment. By 1992, over 98% of the marketed gasoline was of the unleaded type. However, the compression ratio of vehicles running on unleaded gasoline had to be reduced by more than 10%, from well above 10:1 to a little less than 9:1, because of the 10% or so lower octane rating of the unleaded gasoline. Lead was also eliminated from gasoline because of its poisoning effect on the long term effectiveness of the materials in the catalytic converter of vehicles controlling the composition of the exhaust gases.

Diesel fuel is blended from both distilled and cracked crude oil fractions up to C_{22} type hydrocarbons[1][4]. There exist normally three grades of diesel fuel in the US classified as No. 1-D, No. 2-D and No. 4-D. Diesel fuel No. 1 is a volatile distillate fuel for engines requiring frequent speed and load change such as cars, trucks and buses. Diesel No. 2 is a lower volatility distillate fuel for engines in industrial and heavy mobile service such as off-the road vehicles, tractors, farm machinery and locomotives. Diesel No. 4 is a fuel for low and medium speed engines such as marine engines and stationary power generators. Typical compression ratios of diesel engines range from 12:1 up to 22:1 and the corresponding parameter characterizing the ability of the fuel to ignite quickly after being injected into the cylinder is the cetane number. Hexadecane (C_{16}), which has a high ignition quality (short chemical ignition delay), has been assigned a cetane number of 100, whereas hep-tamethylnonane (a C_{16} isomer) has been assigned a cetane number of 0. The cetane number of a diesel fuel is determined by comparing it to a blend of hexadecane and heptamethylnonane which has the same igni-tion quality. The cetane number is the percentage by volume of hexade-cane in the blend. Table 2-2 summarizes the relevant properties of diesel fuel as well.

Jet fuel comprises blends of the higher boiling fractions C_8 to C_{15} hydrocarbons[1][5]. There are two general types of jet fuel designated as Jet A or JP-5 and Jet B or JP-4. The first designation is the commercial one, while the second one is used by the US military. The Jet A fuel is a kerosene used by the world's airlines as well as the US Navy. The Jet B fuel is a heavy naphtha-kerosene blend, whose importance diminished in the period 1960-1975 both as a commercial fuel as well as a fuel used by the US Air Force, accounting presently for only a few percent of the total jet fuel market. Incidentally, the jet fuel supply in the US is on the order of 1.5 million barrels per day of which 87% is kerosene[2].

Natural gas plant liquids refer to natural gas liquids recovered from natural gas in processing plants and, in some situations, from natural gas fields facilities. Natural gas plant liquids consist by definition of hydrocarbons C_2 and above such as ethane, propane, normal butane, isobutane, isopentane, natural gasoline, and other higher hydrocarbons. The production of 1.5 million barrels per day of natural gas plant liquids combined with about 0.3 million barrels per day of natural gas liquids generated at crude oil refineries, is marketed as liquefied petroleum gas (LPG). This LPG, predominantly of propane and butane composition, constitutes a major supplementary source of petroleum transportation fuels and nonfuel products[2]. Liquefied petroleum gas represents, on an energy content basis rather than volume, more than 15% of the daily petroleum production in the US. Liquefied petroleum gas is employed as fuel for tractors, trucks, and buses as well as a remote domestic fuel for heating, cooking, and drying. The more reactive components of natural gas plant liquids such as ethylene, propylene and butylene serve as the feedstock for the petrochemical industry's output of polymers, rubbers, chemicals, textiles and films. Table 2-2 contains the pertinent properties of propane as a transportation fuel. It is important to note that LPG in general and propane in particular, despite their sizable production along with natural gas, will never be adequate to substitute more than about 10% to 15% of gasoline and diesel fuel. Consequently, propane alone or in conjunction with butane and higher natural gas liquids does not have the potential to become a universal alternative transportation fuel, although it does have the potential for specialized niche markets.

Finally, it is worth noting that the crude oil refining capacity of the United States has been constantly declining from the peak of 18.1 million bbl per day in 1980 to about 15.2 million barrels per day at the present time and an 86% utilization factor[6]. Environmental considerations favor the refining of imported crude oil outside the US and the subsequent delivery of finished products to the country rather than transporting crude oil to the US and refining it locally. As the amount of crude oil produced domestically diminishes so will the refining capacity of the country. Thus, the on-going gradual reduction of refining capacity in the United States facilitates immensely the switching of the traditional automotive fuels to natural gas from an economic point of view. Switching to natural gas as a motor fuel does not entail the closing down of refineries, which represent a significant investment. On the contrary, the natural gas fuel substitution will require the utilization of certain refining capacity as it is explained in a later chapter.

ALTERNATIVE AUTOMOTIVE FUELS

The perceived decline in crude oil reserves during the 1970s resulted in two types of responses to deal with the problem. The first response was to institute measures to utilize more efficiently the existing resources. The second response was to investigate the development of substitutes or alternative automotive fuels. The impact of implementing energy efficiency measures in the US, particularly in the transportation sector, will be examined in a later section. In the remainder of this section, consideration will be given to the alternative automotive fuels that have emerged as the most likely candidates in the last decade.

The broader interpretation of the term "alternative automotive fuels" includes conventional fuels utilized in an alternative application such as powering vehicles as well as substitute fuels with properties and origin unrelated to conventional fuels[7]. However, the distinction is not as straightforward as it may appear. For example, alcohols such as methanol or ethanol are considered substitute fuels. Methanol, however, may be manufactured from either natural gas or biomass through appropriate processes. Hence, methanol in the former instance is a conventional automotive fuel, but in the later instance is a substitute fuel. There exists, obviously, a large number of potential fuels that can be employed in the future as automotive fuels. In view of the massive investment represented by present day processing, distribution and conversion equipment, and given the long time required for development of new technologies, the next alternative fuel to gasoline and diesel fuel will have to be a conventional fuel. Such a fuel will, therefore, be fossil-based and as such will be a non-renewable fuel. With continuing depletion of the fossil-based source of this conventional fuel, a progressive substitution may take place of the origin of the fuel, the conversion equipment and possibly the type of the fuel itself.

In the last twenty years, the following four fuels have emerged as potential contenders of becoming the alternative automotive fuel of the future: ethanol, methanol, natural gas and hydrogen. Electricity may be viewed as a fifth potential "alternative automotive fuel", albeit of a different nature than the other four fuels. The major limitation of electricity as a universal automotive fuel at the present time is the lack of adequate battery technology to provide comparable vehicle range as the chemical fuels do[8]. Consequently, electric powered vehicles can only occupy niche applications rather than replace gasoline powered vehicles in a large scale in the foreseeable future, i.e., in the next twenty years. This issue will be addressed in a later chapter. Hydrogen is another fuel whose potential is limited at the present time because of cost and technological considerations. Given that hydrogen has to be generated either from fossil fuels or from the electrolysis of water and given that the internal combustion engine has a relatively low efficiency, it is not cost effective to use hydrogen to replace gasoline in a present day automobile. Moreover, the vehicle range, which is comparable to that of an electric vehicle, becomes an issue because of limitations in storage[9]. Thus, hydrogen as an alternative automotive fuel belongs to the long term fuels and as such will be examined in conjunction with electricity in a later chapter. This leaves as immediate alternative fuels the two alcohols, ethanol and methanol, and natural gas. The pertinent properties of these three potential alternative transportation fuels are shown in Table 2-3. Notice that the properties of methane are shown instead of those for natural gas since the composition of the latter varies, even though it consists typically of 95% methane. The pertinent properties of hydrogen have also been included in Table 2-3 for comparison purposes.

TABLE 2-3. Pertinent Physical Properties of Ethanol, Methanol, Methane and Hydrogen as Alternative Transportation Fuels

Property	Ethanol	Methanol	Methane	Hydrogen
Formula	C_2H_5OH	CH_3OH	CH_4	H_2
H/C Atom Ratio	3	4	4	—
Molecular Weight	46.1	32.0	16.0	2.0
Density @ 15°C (lb/gal)	6.58	6.60	3.54[1]	0.59[2]
Heating Value (BTU/lb)	11,486	8,560	21,550	51,620
Energy Density (BTU/gal)	75,575	56,500	76,290[1]	30,455[2]
Air/Fuel Stoichiometry				
Mass Ratio	9.0	6.5	17.3	34.5
Octane Number	101	100	129	60[3]
Energy of Stoich. Mix.[4]				
BTU/lb st. mix.	1,157	1,148	1,183	1,454
BTU/ft^3 st. mix.	93.0	88.5	86.0	107.3
Lat. Heat Vap. (BTU/lb)	369	469	219	193
Boiling Temp. (°F)	173	147	-259	-423
Vapor Pressure (psi)[5]	2.3	4.6	3,600[5]	3,600[6]
Flammability Limits				
Lower (% vol.)	4.3	7.3	5.3	4.1
Higher (% vol.)	19	36	15	74

1. Methane properties at boiling point (liquid state). The density of methane at room temperature and 1 atm is 0.042 lb/ft^3 (gaseous state) so that the energy density is 122 BTU/gal. 2. Hydrogen properties at boiling point (liquid state). The density of hydrogen at room temperature and 1 atm is 0.0054 lb/ft^3 (gaseous state) so that the energy density is 37 BTU/gal. 3. RON exceeds 130. 4. Energy of stoichiometric mixture is expressed per lb or ft^3 of fuel-air mixture. 5. Vapor pressure is based on the Reid measuring procedure. 6. Gaseous fuel under pressure.

In the remainder part of this section, the general features of ethanol and methanol will be presented along with those of alternative gasolines. Natural gas will be addressed in subsequent sections.

Ethanol can be directly blended with gasoline, reacted with isobuty-lene to form the oxygenated fuel additive ethyl-tert-butyl ether (ETBE) or burned as a neat fuel.

A gasoline-ethanol blend in the US consists of 90% gasoline and 10% ethanol and is marketed under the name of gasohol. Gasohol is also designated as an E10 motor fuel. The energy of combustion of gasohol per unit volume of stoichiometric mixture in the vapor state is 96 BTU/ft^3,i.e., nearly the same as gasoline[10]. Therefore, gasohol produces almost identical power as gasoline. Because ethanol has more than twice as high a latent heat of vaporization as gasoline, the temperature of the air/fuel mixture and the degree of vaporization of the fuel will be reduced. This will result in a lower charge temperature and an increasing amount of fuel entering the engine cylinder. Consequently, gasohol should provide better power than gasoline at stoichiometric combustion and the fuel economy should be higher than that predicted from the lower heating value given in Table 2-3. The octane value of gasohol is about 87 to 93, an increase of less than 1 point from the that of the gasoline blend used (regular to premium gasoline). The volatility of gasohol is higher than that of gasoline, even though ethanol has a lower volatility (Reid vapor pressure) than gasoline. Thus, the Reid vapor pressure of gasohol is about 0.5 to 1.0 psi greater than that of gasoline. The relatively lower volatility (lower vapor pressure) of pure ethanol tends to produce lower evaporative emissions than gasoline. However, the relatively higher volatility of an ethanol-gasoline blend increases the evaporative emissions compared to gasoline. This is clearly undesirable as it increases the smog formation potential of the fuel, even though it reduces the carbon monoxide formation potential. It should be pointed out that it is not until ethanol reaches a concentration point above 70% that the vapor pressure of the blend becomes less than the vapor pressure of gasoline.

Another potential problem with an ethanol-gasoline blend is the separation of ethanol and gasoline in the presence of water. Thus the presence of any amount of water in the tank, will lead to the combination of that water with ethanol and the separation of gasoline. This effect is unacceptable in terms of the performance and function of the engine.

It is worth noting that the present production of ethanol in the US of 1.1 billion gallons per year is sufficient to be blended with about 10% of the gasoline consumed in the country annually. Even at the maximum projected production in the US of 3 to 5 billion gallons per year no more than 30% to 50% of gasoline can be blended to produce gasohol — however, the maximum ethanol production will be 80% to 100% sufficient, if gasohol is used only in the winter months as an oxygenated gasoline to reduce carbon monoxide emissions.

ETBE is a relatively new high octane, oxygenated fuel additive made by the chemical reaction of ethanol with isobutylene. The pertinent properties of ETBE are given in Table 2-4. Currently, the EPA allows a 12.7% ETBE blend with gasoline to form the ETBE oxygenat-

TABLE 2-4. Pertinent Physical Properties of Ethyl Tertiary Butyl Ether (ETBE) and Methyl Tertiary Butyl Ether (MTBE) to Produce Oxygenated Gasoline as an Alternative Transportation Fuel

Property	ETBE	MTBE
Formula	$(CH_3)_3COC_2H_5$	$(CH_3)_3COCH_3$
Molecular Weight	102.2	44.1
Density @ 15°C (lb/gal)	6.26	6.18
Heating Value (BTU/lb)	15,615	15,056
Energy Density (BTU/gal)	97,750	93,046
Air/Fuel Stoichiometry		
Mass Ratio	12.1	11.7
Octane Number	110	108
Energy of Stoich. Mix.[1]		
BTU/lb st. mix.	1,191	1,185
BTU/ft^3 st. mix.	96.3	93.9
Lat. Heat Vap. (BTU/lb)	108	138
Boiling Temp. (°F)	158	131
Vapor Pressure (psi)[2]	4.3	7.7
Flammability Limits		
Lower (% vol.)	1.5	1.6
Higher (% vol.)	8.0	8.4

1. Energy of stoichiometric mixture is expressed per lb or ft3 of fuel-air mixture. 2. Vapor pressure is based on the Reid measuring procedure.

ed gasoline. The energy of combustion of the ETBE oxygenated gasoline per unit volume of stoichiometric mixture in the vapor state is almost the same as that of gasoline. Even at the maximum recommended blend of 22% ETBE and 78% gasoline, the stoichiometric energy of combustion is 95.2 BTU/ft^3[10]. The octane number of the 12.7 % ETBE blend at 111 is in fact higher than that of either one of the two components[10]. The latent heat of vaporization of ETBE is similar to that of gasoline and therefore ETBE-gasoline blends are not expected to have cold start problems. Moreover, the lower vapor pressure of the ETBE compared to gasoline lowers engine vapor lock and allows the addition of more low-cost butanes in gasoline. Furthermore, the lower vapor pressure of the ETBE/gasoline mixture compared to gasohol improves the evaporative emissions problem. Finally, ETBE reduces in part the problem of water mixing with the fuel as it allows up to 0.4% water presence without gasoline separation.

It should be noted that if the current ethanol production in the US was used to produce ETBE, some 2.6 billion gallons of ETBE could be manufactured annually. This amount of ETBE would be sufficient to be blended with some 18% of the current gasoline consumption. At the maximum feasible production rate of ethanol from biomass in the US, the produced ETBE could be close to 12 billion gallons annually. This is sufficient to be blended with almost 90% of the present gasoline consumption all year around. All the isobutylene required in the manufacture of ETBE can be supplied form natural gas plant liquids and refinery products. Consequently, the production of ethanol from biomass in combination with portion of the natural gas liquids can replace some 0.8 million bbl/d of crude oil. This amounts to a 10% substitution of crude oil and petroleum product imports by using entirely domestic fuel sources.

Ethanol may be used directly as a motor fuel in three ways: i. Anhydrous ethanol or 100% ethanol, designated in the US as E100 motor fuel; ii. Anhydrous ethanol mixed in a relatively small percentage of gasoline, typically 5 to 15%, and designated as E95 to E85 motor fuel, respectively; and iii. Hydrous ethanol consisting of 95% ethanol and 5% water. Hydrous ethanol is the fuel used in Brazil to power 90% of all the new cars, while the remainder operate on a 20% ethanol/80% gasoline blend. Incidentally, Brazil produces annually some 4 billion gallons of ethanol derived from the fermentation of cane sugar.

The direct use of ethanol — in the aforementioned three ways — as a motor fuel has advantages and disadvantages as well. As it has been already mentioned in conjunction with gasohol, the high latent heat of vaporization of ethanol results in a lower burning temperature in the engine cylinder, thereby improving fuel power utilization and fuel efficiency. Even though the stoichiometric energy density of ethanol is slightly smaller than that of gasoline, it is compensated by the higher vapor density of ethanol in the air/fuel mixture. The octane number of ethanol is over 100, thereby allowing the increase in engine compression ratio for higher fuel efficiency. It has been reported that a 5% fuel efficiency increase has been obtained with the use of ethanol versus gasoline[11]. On the negative side of ethanol, the high latent heat of vaporization will make a cold start difficult. This problem can be alleviated, however, with either the addition of more volatile compounds, hence the need of E95 to E85 mixtures, or the use of a small electric heater to warm a small amount of a E100 fuel. Exhaust gas in any ethanol burning engine may contain other undesirable compounds such as aldehydes as it will be discussed in a later chapter. Hydrous ethanol is less expensive than anhydrous ethanol. It offers some advantages in the engine operation, one of which is lower temperature, and some disadvantages, one of which is the difficulty of a cold start.

However, the major problem or rather obstacle in the universal use of ethanol (E100 to E85) as a motor fuel is that at best it can replace ultimately no more than 2% of the gasoline consumed currently in the US. Given that it takes about one metric ton of corn to produce 100 gallons of ethanol, the entire corn production of the US, which amounts to about 45% of the total agricultural output of the US in tonnage, will be sufficient to produce no more than 20 billion gallons of ethanol annually.

Another potentially serious problem in the fermentation of sugars and starches to produce ethanol is the required energy input. As it turns out, only ethanol from sugar cane is a net energy producing operation in that the wastes generated after the removal of the sugar possess sufficient heat content to be used to generate all the electricity and heat input required for the fermentation process itself[12][13]. Thus, one unit of cane sugar energy input results in 1.3 units of energy output in the form of ethanol. In the case of corn, one unit of energy input results in 0.6 energy units in the form of ethanol[14]. The use of agricultural wastes, which invariably have a high content of non-fermentable material (lignin) as well as the use of wood to generate process heat and electricity will probably give an ethanol output of 0.9 to 1.0 energy units for each unit of corn starch energy input. At the present time all the deficit energy inputs in corn fermentation are from fossil fuels, including petroleum products. In the future, the large scale production of ethanol from corn could be augmented by the use of any type of agricultural wastes for a more efficient process. Finally, it should be pointed out that corn cultivation and subsequent conversion of corn starch to ethanol, even with the input of fossil fuels, may be desirable, if the final ethanol product is more valuable to society than pure gasoline.

The conclusion, however, remains the same. While ethanol can not provide a solution to the problem of importing oil, it has the potential for some significant reduction in the imports, if it is used in combination with natural gas liquids to optimize the utilization of the latter as transportation fuels. The proposed optimization scheme may consist of two elements: i. The use of ETBE as an oxygenated gasoline additive from ethanol and components of natural gas liquids; and ii. The increase of total ethanol production to possibly 6 billion gallons per year from the currently projected production of 3 billion gallons per year by employing surplus and/wastes of other crops, such as sugar cane, sugar beet and fruits, in addition to corn surplus. The fossil energy deficit to produce this ethanol may be explicitly supplied by propane, a natural gas liquid product, to insure the net benefit of eliminating some 1 million bbl/l of crude oil imports through the proposed scheme of combining domestically produced biomass and natural gas liquids. This approach becomes viable during the transition period of one to two decades as gasoline is being substituted gradually with natural gas as an automotive fuel. After that transition period biomass ethanol may be used as a feedstock in the petrochemical industry as well as a component of a possible substitute for the kerosene based jet fuel.

Methanol can be directed blended with gasoline, reacted with isobutylene to form the oxygenated fuel additive methyl-tert-butyl ether (MTBE) or burned directly in a manner entirely analogous to ethanol. However, a major difference between ethanol and methanol is that the former is currently produced from biomass, while the latter will have to be produced from fossil fuels. In particular, natural gas offers the most attractive source for methanol production on the basis of economical and environmental considerations[15].

A standard composition of gasoline/methanol blends has not been established in the US yet, but it may typically consists of as little as 10% methanol or as much as 85% methanol. These two fuels will be designated as M10 and M85, respectively. Thus, the designation M100 implies a pure methanol fuel. The energy of combustion of methanol/gasoline blends per unit volume of stoichiometric mixture in the vapor state varies from a high of 95 BTU/ft^3, i.e., nearly the same as gasoline, to a low of 91 BTU/ft^3, i.e., about 5% less than gasoline. Methanol has almost three times as high a latent heat of vaporization as gasoline. Consequently, the comments made on ethanol blends regarding the temperature of the air/fuel mixture, the degree of vaporiation, charge temperature and amount of fuel entering the engine cylinder, power at stoichiometric combustion and the fuel economy are also true for methanol blends, but to an even higher degree. The octane value of methanol/gasoline blends are slightly lower than that of similar ethanol/gasoline blends. The volatility (vapor pressure) of methanol and gasoline blends follows the same trend as that of ethanol and gasoline blends as a function of the methanol content of the blend. However, the evaporative emissions of methanol/gasoline blends may be even more undesirable than those of comparable ethanol/gasoline blends from a health point of view as methanol is a more toxic substance than gasoline and ethanol. This point will be addressed in a subsequent chapter. Finally, methanol/gasoline blends will separate in the presence of water in the tank, leading to an unacceptable performance and function of the engine.

MTBE is a high octane, oxygenated fuel additive made by the chemical reaction of methanol with isobutylene. The pertinent properties of MTBE are given in Table 2-4. Because MTBE is very similar in function, use and performance to the already described ETBE, there is no need to repeat the same information here. It should be also noted that MTBE in a mixture with gasoline does not reduce the vapor pressure nearly as much as ETBE does.

Methanol may be used directly as a motor fuel as neat methanol or 100% methanol, designated in the US as M100 motor fuel. The direct use of methanol as a motor fuel has advantages and disadvantages as well. As it has been already mentioned in conjunction with ethanol, the relatively very high latent heat of vaporization of methanol results in a lower burning temperature in the engine cylinders, thereby improving fuel power utilization and fuel efficiency. However, the stoichiometric energy density of methanol is almost 10% smaller than that of gasoline and it is not entirely compensated by the higher vapor density of methanol in the air/fuel mixture. The octane number of methanol is close to 100 allowing the increase in engine compression ratio. It has been reported that a 5% fuel efficiency increase has been obtained also with the use of methanol versus gasoline[11]. On the negative side of methanol, the high latent heat of vaporization will make a cold start even more difficult than ethanol. This problem has been alleviated, however, by restricting the fuel content to only 85% methanol or M85 and by adding more volatile compounds, such as butane, to the fuel. Exhaust gas in any methanol burning engine may contain a very undesirable compound, formaldehyde. This issue will be discussed in a later chapter.

Regarding the supply of methanol from natural gas by steam reformation, it should be noted that it requires 40,000 scf of natural gas to produce 1 metric ton of methanol[16]. Thus, if all gasoline consumed currently in this country were to be replaced with an M85 blend, some 600 million tons or 200 billion gallons of methanol would need to be produced annually. The required natural gas input for this methanol production would be 24 trillion scf per year. By comparison, the current production of methanol in the US, mainly as a chemical feedstock, is only 1% of that amount. It is highly unrealistic to expect that such a large production of a liquid synthetic fuel is ever going to materialize.

It is instructive to discuss at this point the main developments in the evolution of the traditional motor fuels gasoline and diesel fuel. The Clean Air Act Amendment (CAAA) of 1990 mandates the introduction of oxygenated and reformulated gasolines in areas of the country which do not meet the air quality standards. The Environmental Protection Agency (EPA) is directed by CAAA to determine these areas.

Oxygeneted gasolines are required in the winter time in order to reduce carbon monoxide (CO) emissions. Low temperatures and high altitudes increase CO vehicle exhaust emissions due to inefficient combustion. Increasing the oxygen content of gasoline improves combustion and reduces CO emissions. Thus, the EPA specified that oxygenated gasoline contain no less than 2.7% oxygen by weight. Moreover, the EPA has identified 39 areas in the country that are required to use oxygenated gasoline. These carbon monoxide non-attainment areas have been selected on the basis of having CO values in excess of 9.5 parts per million (1988 and 1989 data). The length of the CO control period for each of the 39 CO non-attainment areas is determined by the EPA and is not to be less than four months per year (typically 1 November through 28 February). The gasoline consumed in all the CO non-attainment areas represent about 30% of the total gasoline used in the country. Oxygenated gasoline can be produced by adding either alcohol oxygenates such as methanol, ethanol, and tertiary butyl alcohol (TBA) or ether oxygenates such as MTBE, ETBE and tertiary amyl methyl ether (TAME). Oxygenated gasoline was introduced in the 1992-1993 season and contains either MTBE or ethanol as the most economical additives. Based on the EPA oxygen requirements in oxygenated gasoline, the minimum additive content must be 15% for MTBE or 7.7% for ethanol (either one by volume). Natural gas is the feedstock for MTBE and biomass (i.e., corn) is the feedstock for ethanol. The latter is subsidized by the federal government as an agricultural product at a rate of $0.10 per gallon. However, the federal subsidy applies to gasohol fuel (minimum 10% ethanol by volume). Hence, more ethanol must be used in oxygenated gasoline than necessary. All other additives are not nearly as cost effective at the present time.

Reformulated gasoline (RFG) was mandated by the CAAA in order to reduce vehicle hydrocarbons and toxic emissions in ozone non-attainment areas. The EPA has identified nine areas that have the highest ozone problems. These areas include some 22% of the population of the country. There exist additional ozone non-attainment areas which may opt to participate in the RFG program. These additional areas include almost 30% of the population of the country. The goals of the RFG program, which may affect more than 50% of the population of the country, are as follows:

Phase I. Between 1995 and 1999, the typical or baseline vehicle summer volatile organic compound (VOC) emissions and the year-round toxic emissions must be 15% less than those of the 1990 baseline vehicle and 1990 gasoline.

Phase II. By 2000, the baseline vehicle summer VOC and year-round toxic emissions will be 20 to 25% lower than emissions from the same vehicles using 1990 gasoline.

In either phase of the RFG implementation there will be no increase in nitrous oxides (NO_x) emissions. The reformulated gasoline will be introduced year-round after January 1, 1995. Initially, the EPA will certify gasoline as RFG if it meets the following requirements : i. A minimum of 2% oxygen by weight; ii. A maximum of 1% benzene by volume; iii. Adequate detergents to prevent accumulation of deposits in engines and vehicle fuel systems; iv. No heavy metal content. After 1998 a much more complex composition of RFG will be required by the EPA in order to meet the Phase II goals. The gasoline producers can attain the reductions in VOC and NOx through a combination of the following: A. Reduced fuel volatility (Reid vapor pressure); B. Addition of oxygenates to attain the 2% oxygen content; C. Reduced benzene and other aromatic compounds; D. Reduced olefins (highly unsaturated hydrocarbons); E. Reduced sulfur; and F. Reduced distillation curve (higher percentage of components with boiling points above 200°F and 300°F). It should be noted that alcohols (methanol, ethanol) cannot be used as additives in RFG because they increase the vapor pressure (volatility) of the mixture well above that of pure gasoline. Thus, evaporative emissions will increase in a year-round additive deployment.

The intention behind the introduction of oxygenated and reformulated gasolines is to reduce emissions, while keeping engine performance as close as possible to that of conventional gasoline. However, the emission reductions gains that can be attained with these alternative gasolines is very small compared to those that can be attained with the introduction of natural gas. This issue will be addressed in a later chapter. In the remainder of this chapter, however, natural gas will be examined as an alternative motor fuel.

NATURAL GAS FUEL

Natural gas is a naturally occurring gaseous mixture of hydrocarbons, mostly methane, and non-hydrocarbons and is produced from wells drilled into underground reservoirs of porous rock. In the early days of natural gas production, it was obtained as a by-product from wells drilled for oil production. This has created the misconception that gas always occurs with oil. This is clearly not the case. Today only 25% of the natural gas produced in the US is derived from oil wells. The remainder 75% of the produced natural gas is derived from wells explicitly drilled for natural gas production[17]. Natural gas found with oil is characterized as "associated", while natural gas found on its own is classified as "non-associated". When natural gas is withdrawn from a well it may contain liquid hydrocarbons such as pentane and natural gasoline, readily condensible hydrocarbons such as propane and butane, as well as non-hydrocarbon gases such as carbon dioxide and helium. This natural gas is classified as "wet". The wet natural gas is separated from these components near the site of the well or at a natural gas processing plant. The natural gas is then classified as "dry" and is sent through pipelines to a local distribution company and, ultimately, the consumer. The separated liquid and condensible hydrocarbons are classified as natural plant liquids.

The composition of natural gas at the wellhead varies widely from field to field. Table 2-5 contains the composition of natural gas from selected production locations in the US to show the variability of composition[18]. Natural gas liquids removed form natural gas include propane, butane, pentane and any higher hydrocarbons. Propane and butane are known as liquefied petroleum gas (LPG), whereas pentane and higher hydrocarbons are known as natural gasoline. There is a ready market for all these natural gas liquids, which helps offset the cost of processing. Carbon dioxide and nitrogen are inert gases and are removed to improve the heating value of the remaining gas stream. Helium is present in some natural gas produced in the middle of the continent and Rocky Mountain

TABLE 2-5. Composition of Natural Gas from Various Production Sites in the US and Composition of Marketed Natural Gas

Component	Rio Arriba[1] NM	Stanton[1] KS	Amarillo[1] TX	Marketed[2] US
Methane	96.91	67.56	65.80	94.0
Ethane	1.33	6.23	3.80	3.0
Propane	0.19	3.18	1.70	0.7
Butane	0.05	0.40	0.80	0.5
Pentane/Heavier	0.02	0.40	0.50	N/A[3]
Carbon Dioxide	0.82	0.07	0.00	1.2
Nitrogen	0.68	21.14	25.60	0.6
Helium	0.00	0.00	1.80	0.0
Heating Value BTU/ft^3	1,002	930	818	1,023

1. Percent molecular composition. 2. Percent Volume Composition. 3. Included with butane.

areas. It is regarded as a valuable component and if present in a concentration of 0.3-0.7% or higher is economically recoverable. Hydrogen sulphide, another component of natural gas albeit in minute quantities, must be removed because it is poisonous and very corrosive in the presence of air or water. Pipeline specifications limit the amount of hydrogen sulphide in marketed natural gas to less than 0.36 lb per million scf (5.7 mg/m^3 gas). The hydrogen sulfide removed from natural gas is turned into elemental sulfur and sold as a raw material. Annually, some 1.3 million tons of sulfur (about 1/8 of the US production) is recovered from natural gas. The typical composition of the marketed natural gas in the US is also given in Table 2-5. Natural gas, being an odorless gas, is odorized before distribution to provide a distinctive odor which alerts customers of possible leaks. Commercial odorants such as mercaptans, aliphatic sulfides or cyclic sulfur compounds are added at rates varying from 0.25 to 1.5 lb per million scf (4 to 24 mg/m^3). The energy density of natural gas is too low to be effectively stored in its natural form on board a vehicle. Consequently, natural gas used as a transportation fuel must be either compressed to a very high pressure, typically 3000 psi (200 atm) or higher, or else liquefied and stored in a special cryogenic tank. The former form of natural gas is classified as compressed natural gas (CNG) and the later as liquefied natural gas (LNG). These forms of natural gas as transportation fuel will be examined in greater detail in a subsequent chapter.

A very important characteristic of natural gas as a motor fuel is its very high octane number of about 130. Thus, natural gas can be used in very high compression ratio gasoline engines, thereby improving the combustion efficiency. The ideal compression ratio turns out to be 14:1, if optimization of emissions is taken into account[19]. The resulting efficiency increase at that compression ratio is over 15 percent. The power loss due to the relatively lower stoichiometric energy density of methane, about 10% smaller than that of gasoline, is totally compensated at the higher compression ratio. The two major advantages of methane as a motor fuel are: A. The reduced wear of the engine and B. The reduced engine emissions. Both of these advantages will be examined in a subsequent chapter. With respect to the requirements of natural gas as a motor fuel, it should be noted that if all currently consumed gasoline and diesel fuel were replaced with natural gas, it would require 13 trillion scf natural gas per year. Increased automobile efficiency to be attained through the presently mandated CAFE (Corporate Average Fuel Efficiency) standards as well as future voluntary or mandatory standards will reduce the use of natural gas to about 8 trillion scf per year even after taking into account the long term increase in the vehicular population. While this is a large added consumption for natural gas, it is nevertheless one that can be attained realistically more so than the alternative methanol option. In subsequent chapters, the case will be made that natural gas is the only alternative fuel that has the potential to replace gasoline in a universal fashion with regard to domestic resource availability as well as environmental and economic reasons.

NATURAL GAS AS A GASOLINE REPLACEMENT

The concern of declining crude oil reserves of the early 1970s did not materialize for the world as a whole. The elevated prices of crude oil spurred a large exploratory activity around the world, which has lead to sizeable discoveries of new oil sufficient to last well within the next century. However, exploration within the United States, also at a record pace, did not result in any major new discoveries[20]. In fact, the proved reserves of crude oil in the US have gradually declined to about 26 billion barrels as of 1990, down from 30 billion barrels as late as ten years earlier (1980) which, incidentally, has been the average size of proved reserves since the mid 1950s[21]. The introduction of a multitude of measures to use energy more efficiently in buildings, industry and transportation was proven to be, however, a far more successful operation than the increase in domestic oil exploration.

From 1973 to 1990 the US economy grew by about 50%, while the annual energy use during the same period showed small fluctuations about an average usage of 75.5 quads per year — the energy use in 1973 was 74.3 quads[22]. Thus some twenty years after the first energy crisis in 1973, the US economy was generating 50% more goods and services with an energy use slightly higher than that in 1973. This trend since the mid 1970s has been in variance with the pattern established since the end of the 19th century whereby energy use and the size of the economy were always advancing at a constant ratio to each other.

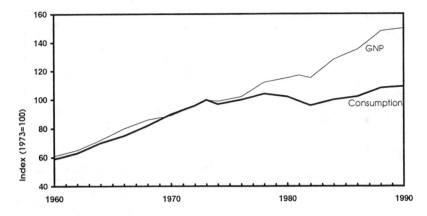

FIGURE 2.1 Growth of GNP and Energy Use in the US from 1960 to 1990 Showing the Impact of Increased Efficiency since 1973 (Source: US DOE).

Figure 2-1 shows the relative increase of the economy and energy use in the US from 1960 to 1990. It has been estimated that if the aforementioned efficiency changes had not occurred since 1973, the US would be importing today twice as much oil, i.e., a staggering 15 to 16 million bbl per day[23].

Transportation was one of the sectors significantly benefitted from the implementation of efficiency. The Corporate Average Fuel Efficiency (CAFE) standards were mandated by the federal government in the mid 1970s and required that the average fuel efficiency of all passenger cars sold by each manufacturer increase annually, on a prescribed fashion, over a period of ten years until it reached the 27 mpg mark. The CAFE standards provided the second and permanently lasting impetus to improve passenger car efficiency. The first impetus was, of course, the very rapid increase in gasoline prices after 1973, which turned the public towards more fuel efficient cars. While gasoline prices today are at the same level as in 1973, if inflation is taken into account, the CAFE standards result in a continued increase in fuel efficiency as older and less efficient cars are replaced year after year with new more efficient ones. Figure 2-2 shows the increase of fuel efficiency from 1973 to 1990. It may be noted that in recent years the average increment in fuel efficiency of the passenger car fleet in the US has been

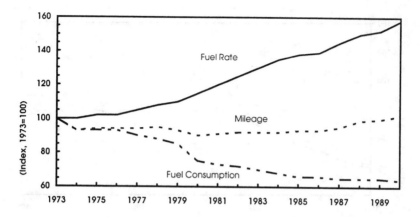

FIGURE 2-2. Passenger Car Fuel Efficiency (Fuel Rate), Fuel Consumption and Mileage in the United States (Source: US DOE)

about 0.5 mpg per year. Given that the average fuel efficiency was 21 mpg in 1991, it will take approximately 12 years for the average fuel efficiency of passenger vehicles to reach the 27 mpg limit. Thus, sometime around the year 2005 the average fuel efficiency of passenger cars in the US will be in the vicinity of 27 mpg. However, this presupposes that no modification of the present standards will occur anytime from now until then. In reality, an increase in fuel efficiency has been advocated for some time now but no decision has been made. It has been proposed that the federally mandated CAFE standards be raised from the present 27 mpg to 40 mpg. Moreover, fuel efficiency standards could be also instituted for light trucks and vans. Auto-manufacturers in the US have opposed so far increase in the CAFE standards as being either detrimental to the future of the US auto industry or otherwise too costly to the consumer. Other authorities hold that a 40 mpg standard is perfectly attainable without any hardship to manufacturers or to consumers. However, in late 1993 the big three US automakers reached an agreement with the president of the United States to attempt to develop on a voluntary basis by the end of this century motor vehicles three times as efficient as those today.

Whatever the case may be, there will be an immediate fuel efficiency windfall by switching fuel from gasoline to natural gas. As it has been already indicated, because of the much higher octane rating of natural gas (130) versus unleaded gasoline (86-92) as well as the need to regain the power loss inherent in switching from a liquid to a gaseous fuel, a compression ratio of 14:1 is more suitable for an internal combustion engine (ICE) fueled by natural gas[19]. By comparison the typical compression ratio for a gasoline fueled ICE is currently under 9:1. The fuel efficiency of the 14:1 compression ratio natural gas fueled ICE increases by 15% compared to the same engine fueled by gasoline. This implies two things: First, the present CAFE standard of 27 mpg based on gasoline jumps to 31 mpg with no change other than switching fuel to natural gas; Second, the proposed 40 mpg CAFE augmentation can be attained by increasing the fuel efficiency of gasoline cars to only 35 mpg and switching fuel to natural gas. This is a tremendous efficiency bonus and a significantly easier goal to attain, thereby lessening the resistance for higher fuel efficiency of the US automakers who have questioned in recent years the wisdom of a 40 mpg gasoline CAFE standard.

The historical data on fuel efficiency of automobiles in the US indicates that since the early 1970s the fuel use by trucks has more than doubled, whereas the use of fuel by passenger cars has remained virtually the same. Thus, passenger cars used 55% of the motor fuels consumed annually and trucks accounted for 44% of the motor fuel consumption in the US, even though passenger cars represented more than 76% of the vehicles in the country. Moreover, trucks are half as efficient as passenger cars. Finally, light trucks are used in larger numbers to transport passengers rather than goods. As a matter of fact, it has been estimated that 45% of the trucks are now used as passenger vehicles up from 27% some 15 years ago. Clearly, there is a need to implement fuel efficiency standards for light trucks. It is reasonable to expect a light truck fuel efficiency in the vicinity of 25 mpg. Once more the use of natural gas as fuel for light trucks with a higher compression ratio can lead to improved fuel efficiency of at least 15% compared to an otherwise identical gasoline powered light truck.

Thus, the replacement of gasoline by natural gas as a motor fuel should and will occur in parallel with increased efficiency in the use of fuel by vehicles deriving their power from an internal combustion engine. The increased efficiency will be the result of higher engine compression ratios to capitalize on the high octane number of natural gas as well as other vehicle improvements independent of the fuel such as reduction in weight, rolling resistance, drag coefficient, transmission losses and auxiliary loads. Under these conditions, the natural gas requirements to power the entire automotive fleet of the US, including passenger cars, light trucks, vans and buses will be under 8 trillion scf per year. This upper limit is arrived under the assumptions that the mandated increased fuel efficiency, present and future ones, will more than off-set the increased number of vehicles on the road resulting in a net 25% reduction in energy use and an additional 15% fuel efficiency will result from the higher compression ICEs running on natural gas. In reality, this upper limit of natural gas consumption in the transportation sector will take at least three and probably four decades, i.e., 2020 or 2030 to reach. By then developments in other technologies such as hybrid propulsion systems will constitute the power plant of choice in automobiles. The ultimate consumption of natural gas as a transportation fuel will be addressed again in subsequent chapters.

Five important issues need to be raised regarding the viability as well as feasibility of the proposed switch of automotive fuel from gasoline and diesel fuel to natural gas:

I.   Domestic Natural Gas Availability to Replace the Present Motor Fuels

II. Fuel Storage Capability On-Board the Vehicle and Vehicle Range

III. Infrastructure Necessary for the Natural Gas Fuel Switch

IV. Environmental Consequences of a Natural Gas Based Transportation

V.   Economics of the Natural Gas Fuel Switch

Each of these issues is examined in great detailed in the following several chapters.

REFERENCES

1. S. P. Parker (ed.), McGraw-Hill Encyclopedia of Energy, 2nd Ed., pp. 518-526, McGraw-Hill Book Company, New York, NY, 1981.

2. Energy Information Administration, Monthly Energy Review – June 1992, pp. 56-66, US Department of Energy, Washington D.C., 1992.

3. S. P. Parker (ed.), <u>McGraw-Hill Encyclopedia of Energy</u>, *loc. cit.*, pp. 291-293.

4. S. P. Parker (ed.), <u>McGraw-Hill Encyclopedia of Energy</u>, *loc. cit.*, pp. 185-186.

5. S. P. Parker (ed.), <u>McGraw-Hill Encyclopedia of Energy</u>, *loc. cit.*, p. 352.

6. Bureau of the Census, <u>Statistical Abstract of the United States 1985 – 105th Edition</u>, US Department of Commerce, Washington, DC, 1985; and Bureau of the Census, <u>Statistical Abstract of the United States 1994 – 114th Edition</u>, US Department of Commerce, Washington, DC, 1994.

7. E. M. Goodger, <u>Alternative Fuels: Chemical Energy Resources</u>, pp. 33-54, John Wiley & Sons, New York, NY 1980.

8. M. J. Riezenman, "Special Report: Electric Vehicles", p. 97, *IEEE Spectrum,* Nov. 1992.

9. R. E. Billings, <u>The Hydrogen World View</u>, pp. 51-102, American Academy of Science, Independence, MO, 1991.

10. C. E. Wyman and N. D. Hinman, "Ethanol: Fundamentals of Production from Renewable Feedstocks and Use as a Transportation Fuel", *App. Biochem. and Biotech.,* v. 24/25, pp. 735-753, 1990.

11. M. A. DeLuchi, Daniel Sperling, R. A. Johnston, "A Comparative Analysis of Future Transportation Fuels", Research Report UCB-ITS-RR-87-13, Institute of Transportation, University of California, Berkeley, CA, 1987.

12. M. Slesser and C. Lewis, <u>Biological Energy Resources,</u> pp. 106-107, John Wiley & Sons, New York, NY, 1979.

13. R.S. Chambers, R.A. Herendeen, J.J. Joyce, P.S. Penner, 'Gasohol: Does It or Doesn't It Produce Positive Net Energy', *Science,* v. 206, pp. 789-795, 1979.

14. D. Pimentel, "Ethanol Fuels: Energy, Security, Economics, and the Environment", *J. Agric. and Env. Ethics,* v. 4, pp. 1-13, 1991.

15. A. L. Waddens, <u>Chemicals from Petroleum</u>, 4th ed., pp. 238-245, Gulf Publishing Company, Houston, TX, 1980.

16. C. J. Winter and J. Nitsch (eds.), Hydrogen as an Energy Carrier, pp.61-62, Spinger-Verlag, Berlin, FRG, 1988.

17. Energy Information Administration, Natural Gas Annual 1991, DOE/EIA-0131(91), p. 242, US Department of Energy, Washington D.C., 1992.

18. Kirk-Othmer (eds.), Encyclopedia of Chemical Technology, 3rd ed., v. 11, pp. 634-638, John Wiley, New York, NY, 1980.

19. R. M. Siewert, P. J. Mitchell and P. A. Mulawa, "Environmental Potential of Natural Gas Fuel for Light-Duty Vehicles: An Engine-Dynamometer Study of Exhaust-Emission-Control Strategies and Fuel Consumption", SAE technical paper 932744 in Advanced Alternative Fuels Technology (SP-995), Society of Automotive Engineers, Warrendale, PA, 1993.

20. Energy Information Administration, Monthly Energy Review – June 1992, loc. cit., pp. 78-79.

21. Energy Information Administration, Energy Information Sheets, pp. 7-8, US Department of Energy, Washington D.C., 1992.

22. Energy Information Administration, Monthly Energy Review – June 1992, loc. cit., p 9.

23. L. Schipper, R. Howarth, and H. Geller, "United States Energy Use from 1973 to 1987: The Impacts of Improved Efficiency", Ann. Rev. Energy, v. 15, pp. 455-504, Annual Reviews, Inc., Palo Alto, CA, 1990.

Chapter 3

Domestic Natural Gas Availability

EARLY HISTORY OF NATURAL GAS PRODUCTION

Natural gas is a mixture of hydrocarbon and non-hydrocarbon gases found in a variety of geological formations beneath the earth's surface, often but not always in association with petroleum. The seepage of natural gas from surface rocks and springs and its combustion properties have been known since the earliest recorded history[1]. There is an abundance of historical and biblical references of flares of natural gas in Egypt, and the Near and Middle East. There is evidence that many of the ancient temples of worship, even before 3000 B.C., were built in the vicinity of known natural gas seepage locations. Flares of natural gas jets escaping from earth fissures and most likely ignited by lightning formed the so-called "eternal fires", which became the focal point of worship at these temples[2]. The Oracle of Delphi and the fire temples of the Caspian Sea, and even the "burning fiery furnace" of the Old Testament may have been natural gas flares. These flares, which burned for centuries, are depicted on ancient coins. The records of travels of Julius Caesar noted that a famous *"fontaine ardente"* or burning spring was located near Grenoble, France[1]. The Chinese were drilling gas wells as early as 1000 B.C. to produce natural gas for space heating, lighting (the first known use of natural gas for light), and for the manufacture of articles of commerce. Gas wells had been also drilled in

53

FIGURE 3-1. Athanasius Kircher described in his travel book on China (1667) the use of burning wells of natural gas for cooking (Bettmann Archive).

Japan beginning in AD 615, although it is not known how the gas was used. It is known that around AD 900 bamboo tubes were used in China to transport natural gas to salt works, where the heat of the burned gas was employed to evaporate water from the brine in order to obtain crystallized salt. Athanasius Kirchner expressed his amazement at the use of burning wells for cooking, as shown in Figure 3-1, in his travel book on China published in 1667.

The early settlers in the United States reported the presence of gas seeps and burning columns in the Ohio Valley and the Appalachians. The first well drilled in the United States, with the expectation to find natural gas, occurred in 1821 near Fredonia, New York. The well was 24 ft deep and gas was transported in log pipes to nearby houses where it was used to light burners. Some four years later, when General

Lafayette during his visit in the United States arrived in Fredonia at 2:00 AM the town was brilliantly illuminated with natural gas in his honor. In 1865 the formation of the Fredonia Gas, Light, and Waterworks Company took place. This was the first natural gas utility in the country. Meanwhile, natural gas was used again to evaporate salt brine starting in 1840 in Buttler County, Pennsylvania.

As the exploration of oil increased in the United States, following the drilling of the first oil well in 1859, so did the discovery of natural gas, even though the latter was invariably wasted by flaring or venting. In 1872 the gas that has been venting from an oil well near Titusville, Pennsylvania, was transported to the town in a 5.5 mi long iron pipeline with a 3.5 inches diameter. This was the first instance of using iron pipe to transport natural gas. The first compressor station was placed in operation in Rexford, Pennsylvania, in 1880. The first long distance pipeline, consisting of wrought-iron screwed together pipe segments with a diameter of 7.9 inches over a distance of 120 mi, was installed between Greenstown, Indiana and Chicago, Illinois soon thereafter. The invention of the Welsbach mantel in 1885 saw the increase of natural gas use for lighting purposes. Nevertheless, industrial sales provided the largest gas markets. As natural gas became more readily available, it was mixed with, and eventually replaced manufactured gas. The natural gas production in the United States, being negligible prior to 1880, averaged 125 billion scf/y in the decade of 1888-1889 and 250 billion scf/y in the decade of 1890-1899[3]. At the dawn of the 20th century, natural gas accounted for 3% of the energy consumption in the country, while oil fared a little better at 4%. By comparison hydropower accounted also for a mere 3%, while fuel wood at 28% and coal at 62% were by far the dominant fuel sources in the United States.

NATURAL GAS PRODUCTION IN THE TWENTIETH CENTURY

The natural gas industry continued to develop locally around major gas producing areas as they were discovered in the Appalachian area, Oklahoma, Kansas, Louisiana, Texas, California, and the Rocky Mountain areas. In 1931 a 1,000 mi long, 2 ft in diameter, high pressure pipeline was constructed form the Texas panhandle to Chicago[1]. This was the first modern, long distance transmission line built to deliver natural gas from the producing states of the south to the large markets located in the north and the east. The development of high strength pipe and of the electric welding process spurred the construction of long distance pipelines. In 1950, less than twenty years later, the length of the natural gas transmission pipelines stood at 113,000 mi. Today, there exist in the United States a network of about 280,000 mi of natural gas transmission pipelines. These transmission pipelines, augmented by an even longer network of distribution pipelines, carry gas to residential, commercial and industrial customers to all states with the exception of Hawaii. The evolution of the natural gas pipeline network in the US is given in Table 3-1 [4][5][6]. The total natural gas pipeline length is broken down in the three main categories consisting of field and gathering, transmission and distribution pipelines.

Natural gas is used primarily as a source of heat in the residential and commercial sectors as well as a source of heat and a feedstock material for a multitude of chemicals in the industrial sector[7][8]. Because of its clean burning quality, the convenience of utilization, low cost, and abundance, natural gas supplies one quarter of the total energy requirements of the United States. The production of natural gas is summarized in Table 3-2 from the turn of the century to the present time[3], [7],[9]. The various terms appearing in Table 3-2 are typical of natural gas production and will be defined here.

Gross withdrawal is gas withdrawn from gas and oil wells. Repressuring gas is the natural gas injected back into oil and gas forma-

TABLE 3-1. Evolution of the Natural Gas Pipeline Network in the United States (miles)

Year	Field & Gathering	Transmission	Distribution	Total
1945	27,000	82,190	201,480	310,670
1950	32,850	113,350	241,570	387,470
1955	45,680	145,970	305,090	496,740
1960	55,850	183,660	391,440	630,950
1965	61,760	211,240	494,520	767,520
1970	66,000	252,000	595,000	913,000
1975	68,000	263,000	649,000	980,000
1980	84,000	266,000	702,000	1,052,000
1985	94,000	271,000	754,000	1,119,000
1990	89,000	276,000	837,000	1,206,000

TABLE 3-2. Historical Data on Annual Natural Gas Production in the United States

Year	Production 10^9 scf/y[1]						
	W/D	R/P	N-HC R	V&F	W P	E L	D P
1900	NA						0.225
1910	NA						0.473
1920	NA						0.872
1930	NA						1.513
1935	2.408	0.000	NA	0.393	2.015	0.041	1.974
1940	3.476	0.145	NA	0.656	2.675	0.058	2.617
1945	5.740	0.900	NA	0.896	3.844	0.177	3.667
1950	8.331	1.247	NA	0.801	6.188	0.182	6.006
1955	10.179		NA	0.774	9.405	0.281	9.124
1960	13.334		NA	0.563	12.771	0.339	12.432
1965			NA		16.606	0.672	15.934
1970	24.067	1.171	NA	0.248	22.648	0.917	21.731
1975	21.104	0.861	NA	0.134	20.109	0.872	19.236
1980	21.870	1.365	0.199	0.125	20.471	0.777	19.403
1985	19.607	1.915	0.326	0.142	17.270	0.838	16.454
1990	21.523	2.489	0.289	0.150	18.594	0.784	17.810

1. W/D: Gross Withdrawals; R/P:Repressuring; N-HC R: Non-Hydrocarbons Removed; V&F:Venting and Flaring; W P: Wet Production; E L: Extraction Loss; D P: Dry Production.

NA = Not Available

tions for pressure maintenance and cycling purposes. The non-hydrocarbon gases removed refer to the carbon dioxide, helium, hydrogen sulfide and nitrogen constituents of natural gas which are separated prior to the marketing of natural gas. Vented gas is the natural gas released into the atmosphere on the site or at reprocessing plants. Likewise flared gas refers to the natural gas burned at the site of production or at reprocessing plants. Wet gas is the marketed natural gas and is the sum of extraction losses and dry gas. Extraction losses refer to the reduction in volume of natural gas resulting from the removal of the natural gas liquids constituents of natural gas (propane, butane, pentane, etc.) at reprocessing plants. Finally, dry gas is the natural gas received through the pipelines by the residential, commercial and industrial customers.

It is interesting to note that in 1964 the wet natural gas production in the United States surpassed the crude oil production in terms of energy content[3]. The dry natural gas production surpassed the crude oil production in the early seventies until 1982 and again after 1988[7].

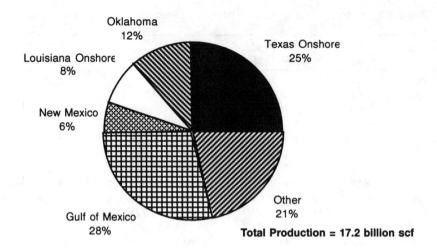

FIGURE 3-2. Natural Gas Production by Area and Relative Contribution in 1991 (Source: US DOE)

Since 1990 the dry production of natural gas in the United States has significantly exceeded the combined production of crude oil and natural gas liquids. Figure 3-2 shows the major natural gas producing areas in the US and the relative contribution of each area in 1991.

CONSUMPTION OF NATURAL GAS

Natural gas is utilized in all four end-use sectors of the energy economy. However, the residential sector has been responsible for the bulk of natural gas customers since the early days of the industry. The residential sector has also been historically the second largest user of natural gas. The commercial sector accounts for the second largest segment of natural gas users and represents the third largest end-user. The industrial sector, with or without electricity utility use, is by far the largest user of natural gas in the country and has been in the that position throughout this century. The transportation sector, which includes use of natural gas to fuel vehicles as well as power the compressors and other machinery of the transmission pipelines, accounts presently for a very small number of customers and a somewhat significant energy end-use. The bulk of customers in the transportation sector are owners of

TABLE 3-3. Natural Gas Customer Distribution by Sector in the United States

Year	Total (x1,000)	R (%)	C (%)	I (%)	T (%)
1935	15,819	93.0	6.5	0.5	
1940	17,600	93.0	6.5	0.5	
1945	19,977	93.0	6.3	0.7	
1950	24,001	92.3	7.2	0.5	
1955	28,479	92.3	7.2	0.5	
1960	33,054	92.0	7.4	0.6	
1965	37,338	92.0	7.5	0.5	
1970	41,482	91.8	7.6	0.6	
1975	44,555	91.9	7.5	0.6	
1980	47,223	92.1	7.4	0.5	
1985	49,971	91.9	7.6	0.5	
1990	54,293	91.8	7.8	0.4	

Notes. R:Residential; C:Commercial; I:Industrial; and T:Transportation. Industrial and Transportation customer representation is combined.

compressed natural gas vehicles and the bulk of energy is consumed in the operation of the pipelines, primarily to drive compressors.

Some data on the distribution of natural gas customers by energy sector are given in Table 3-3[4][5][10]. Notice that the number of transportation sector customers has been traditionally combined with the number of industrial users as the number of the former has been relatively small, i.e., on the order of a few hundred thousand. However, the number of transportation customers is increasing rapidly in recent years as the ownership of compressed natural gas (CNG) vehicles is on the rise. It is expected that ultimately the number of the transportation sector customers will become comparable to that in the residential sector. Likewise the energy use in the transportation sector will reach or even exceed the level of end-use in the industrial sector. The CNG vehicle ownership question and magnitude of end-use will be addressed in a later chapter of this book.

Historical data on the energy use by sector are summarized in Table 3-4[11][12][13]. The net consumption of natural gas given in Table 3-4 refers to the total amount of the fuel used in each of the four energy sectors, i.e., residential, commercial, industrial and transportation. The industrial sector includes also the portion of natural gas used by the util-

TABLE 3-4. Natural Gas Consumption by End-Use Sector in the United States

Year	Total (10^9 scf)	R (%)	C (%)	I (%)	E (%)	T (%)
1930	1,942	15.2	4.2	80.0		0.0
1940	2,660	16.7	5.1	78.2		0.2
1950	6,282	19.1	6.2	60.7	10.0	4.0
1955	9,405	22.6	6.7	54.9	12.3	3.5
1960	12,771	24.3	8.0	51.1	13.5	3.0
1965	15,280	27.7	10.2	42.2	16.4	3.5
1970	21,139	26.0	10.7	39.8	19.9	3.6
1975	19,538	27.1	13.7	38.4	17.4	3.2
1980	19,877	25.2	13.8	38.1	19.5	3.4
1985	17,281	27.1	15.0	36.1	18.7	3.1
1990	18,714	25.2	15.0	40.2	16.0	3.6

Notes. R : Residential; C : Commercial; I : Industrial; E : Electric Utilities and T : Transportation. Industrial and Electric Utility use is combined through 1940.

ities in the generation of electric power. It interesting to note that the relative use of natural gas in the residential sector has stabilized at about 1/4 of the total during the last 40 years. During the same time the natural gas use in the commercial sector has increased by almost a factor of three, accounting presently for almost 1/6 of the total use. Industrial natural gas use has declined over the years, but it still accounts for about 40% of the total use. Electric utilities have been consuming about 1/6 of the total natural gas use. Finally, the transportation sector, which reflects essentially the natural gas use in the transmission of natural gas through the pipeline system accounts for 3 to 4 percent of the total use and has remain unchanged through the years.

It is interesting to compare the average use patterns of natural gas over the years in the different energy sectors. The results of one such comparison are shown in Table 3-5. Note that in the residential and commercial sectors a comparison of scf use per customer is made. In the industrial sector, the production index and the energy index, both referenced with respect to the year 1990, are compared[14] [15]. The industrial production index for a particular year is defined as the ratio of the value of industrial output of that year to the value of the industrial output of the reference year. Obviously, the value of the industrial out-

TABLE 3-5. Natural Gas Use per Customer in the Different Energy End-Use Sectors of the United States for Selected Years

Year	R (scf/y/#)	C (scf/y/#)	I (P Index %)	(E Index %)	E (scf/kWh)
1950	54,163	225,386	24	51	n/a
1960	102,051	417,695	35	87	n/a
1970	144,329	717,455	56	112	10.4
1980	115,169	784,954	77	101	10.3
1990	94,619	662,856	100	100	10.2

Notes. R : Residential; C : Commercial; I : Industrial; and E : Electric Utility; scf/y/# : scf per year per customer. P Index : Production Index , 1990 = 100. E Index : Energy Index, 1990 = 100.

put of a particular year is expressed in dollars of the reference year adjusted through the appropriate consumer price index to 1990 dollars. The industrial energy index for a particular year is defined here as the ratio of the natural gas use in the industrial sector during that year to the natural gas energy use in the reference year. Finally, the electric utilities, as a subset of the industrial sector, are represented by the efficiency of converting natural gas to electricity[16]. The following general conclusions may be drawn regarding the use of natural gas by each of the four energy use sectors.

I. **Residential Sector.** Natural gas use per customer, i.e., household, has declined by almost 35% in the last twenty years due to improvements in the house building envelope (more insulation, reduced infiltration and better windows to reduce the space heating requirements) and increased efficiency of equipment (forced air furnace) and appliances (water heater, cook top, oven, clothes dryer), while the average floor area of houses has been increasing[17].

II. **Commercial Sector.** Natural gas use per customer, i.e., commercial building or business, tripled between 1950 and 1980 and has since declined by about 15% in the last decade because of improvements in the efficiency of equipment as well as some improvement in the envelope of the commercial buildings[17].

III. **Industrial Sector.** The use of natural gas in the industrial sector between 1950 and 1990 has doubled, while at the same time output has quadrupled. In particular, energy use between 1970 and 1990 has decreased by 12%, while industrial output has increased by almost 80% indicating a remarkable improvement (almost a factor of two) in the efficiency with which energy is being used in the industrial sector following the high fuel prices since the 1973 energy crisis[18].

IV. **Electric Utilities.** A very small but steady improvement in the conversion efficiency of natural gas to electricity has been observed over the years. The 1990 average efficiency of this conversion is a little over 32 percent. It should be noted, however, that the efficiency of a 150 MW combined cycle gas turbine/steam turbine system exceeds now 55% (gas turbine exhaust gases generate steam for additional electricity output from a steam turbine) and the efficiency of a 250 kW fuel cell exceeds 50% (with another 30% utilized for low temperature heating such as space and domestic hot water) [19][20]. The continuous implementation of these and other advanced electricity generation technologies have the potential to reduce ultimately the conversion efficiency to as low as 6.5 scf of natural gas per kWh of electricity.

NATURAL GAS RESERVES AND RESOURCES

Natural gas is a non-renewable resource and, because of its value as an energy source, reports of available reserves are of great national interest. The best estimates of the total proven gas reserves in the United States are provided annually by industry associations such as the American Gas Association (AGA) and the American Petroleum Institute (API)[21]. Before the discussion on reserves and resources of natural gas continues, it may be appropriate to define these two terms. Resources of a mineral, fuel or energy source refer to the total estimated amount of that mineral, fuel or energy source, whether or not it has been discovered and whether or not it is currently technologically or economically extractable[22]. Reserves of a mineral, fuel or energy source refer to the total amount of that mineral, fuel or energy source which is known in location, quantity and quality and which is economically recoverable using currently available technologies[22].

There exist three recognized classifications of natural gas which are defined as follows: [22][23]

Nonassociated gas is free gas not in contact with crude oil in the reservoir and free gas in contact with oil where the production of such gas is not significantly affected by the production of crude oil;

Associated gas is free gas in contact with crude oil in the reservoir where the production of such gas is significantly affected by the production of crude oil;

Disolved Gas, or solution gas, is gas in solution with crude oil in the reservoir.

While disolved gas is distinguished from associated gas for estimating more accurately reserves of natural gas, it can be also considered a subset of associated gas form the point of general discussion of reserves and resources. Hence, the more common classification of natural gas consists of nonassociated and associated gas. The current production of natural gas in the United States consists of about 75% *nonassociated* gas and 25% *associated* gas[24].

Another classification of natural gas depends, as it has already been indicated, on its chemical composition and consists of *wet gas* containing condensible hydrocarbons such as propane, butane and pentane, and *dry gas* containing no such condensible hydrocarbons. Moreover, there exist two more terms based on chemical composition, namely, sour gas and sweet gas. The first term indicates the presence of hydrogen sulfide and other sulfur compounds, while the second term indicates gas free of such compounds[25].

In recent years still another distinction has emerged to classify natural gas. Thus, natural gas is also characterized as *conventional gas* or *unconventional gas*. The distinction between conventional and unconventional gas is based on a variety of criteria which are not always the same so that a somewhat fuzzy and shifting boundary is created. Such criteria may include the perceived origin of gas, the technological feasibility of extraction and the economics of production. However, the predominant characteristic of unconventional gas appears to be the way it is found stored in the earth[26]. Obviously unconventional gas belongs to the resources of natural gas rather than the reserves at the present time. Types of unconventional gas include the tight gas formations, shale gas, coal-bed methane, hydropressured and geopressured aquifers, and gas hydrates[26]. These sources of natural gas resources will be examined later in this chapter.

Natural gas, predominantly methane, is believed to have originated in three principal ways: two of the ways, the *thermogenic* and *biogenic* processes, start from organic matter, while a third, the *abiogenic* process, does not need organic matter as the starting point[26]. The thermogenic process refers to the slow decomposition of organic matter in sedimentary rocks due to the earth's heat. This process results in the formation of crude oil and natural gas. The biogenic process refers to the low temperature anaerobic decomposition of organic matter by bacteria resulting in the generation of methane gas such as the well-known "marsh gas". The abiogenic process refers to the possible formation of gas in the deeper parts of the earth during earlier geologic times and the subsequent diffusion of this gas nearer the surface.

Most conventional natural gas is of thermogenic and biogenic origin, while abiogenic gas would be considered unconventional. Natural gas, irrespectively of its origin and prior to becoming useful, has to accumulate in sites where it can be economically exploited. Practically all conventional gas is trapped in porous and permeable sedimentary rocks overlain by a thick impermeable rock or other stratum that can also withstand the considerable pressure at the top of the accumulation.

The systematic estimation of natural gas reserves did not become a normal practice until after the end of World War II, when natural gas emerged as a significant energy source. As in the case of crude oil, the proven reserves of natural gas constitute the best measure of future gas supplies. Unlike crude oil reserves, however, the figure of proven natural gas reserves is not, to a significant extent, a function of the assumptions concerning recovery technology. This is so because 75% to 80% of gas deposits in an accumulation (reservoir) can be taken as economically recoverable versus only 30% for crude oil.

The evolution of proven natural gas reserves in the United States is summarized in Table 3-6 for selected years since 1945[27][28][29]. The proven reserves increased from 1945 to 1970, reached a maximum in 1970 and have declined since then to the same levels as in the late 1940s. On the other hand, the ratio of proved reserves to the with-

TABLE 3-6.   Proved Natural Gas Reserves in the United States since 1945

Year	End of Year Reserves (109 scf)	Ratio of Reserves to Withdrawals (#)
1945	148	31
1950	186	26
1955	224	22
1960	264	20
1965	286	18
1970	291	13
1975	250	12
1980	199	10
1985	193	11
1990	177*	10

Note. Withdrawals refers to the net amount of natural gas removed form the reservoirs during the preceding 12 months.
(*) After the downward revision in 1988 of 24.6 trillion scf from Alaska.

drawals has been stabilized to about 10 since the late 1970s. This is the same ratio that has prevailed for crude oil in this country for more than sixty years. It represents presumably a safe ratio between immediately available supply and prevailing production for natural gas and crude oil. From an economic point of view, there is no need to make available any higher amount of the resource without creating the impression of over-supply which can lead to the drop in price.

The natural gas reserve additions from 1977 to 1991, including dis-coveries and reserve revisions, are shown in Figure 3-3. The annual reserve additions are roughly of the same magnitude as the annual net withdrawals. It should be noted that in 1988 the reserves were revised downwards by 24.6 trillion scf to exclude natural gas from the Alaskan North Slope. This revision was made not because of factors relating to the development of the resource but rather as a result of the fact that these reserves could not be accessible to the lower 48 states via a pipeline for some time to come. It is also instructive to note that 82% of the currently proven reserves of natural gas are of the non-associated type.

The outlook for the long term, i.e., beyond the currently proved reserves, conventional natural gas supply base in the United States, the most thoroughly explored country in the word, has been improving

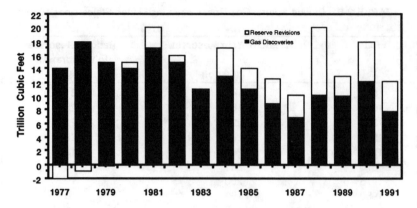

FIGURE 3-3. Natural Gas Reserve Additions in the US from 1977 to 1991
(Source: US DOE)

steadily during the last ten years. The most fundamental change in the natural gas supply outlook has been the recognition of the enormous size of the conventional gas resources. This recognition followed from the discovery of extensive natural gas deposits that are independent of oil. While the trapping and accumulation mechanism for natural gas is similar to that for oil, methane remains stable at temperature and pressure conditions under which crude oil breaks down. Consequently, methane can survive and be recovered, if found, in depths of 30,000 ft or even deeper. The explosive progress in computing capabilities employed in seismological exploration is greatly aiding the delineation of possible gas deposits. New seismic developments support an increase in the estimates of conventional natural gas deposits. This is clearly shown in Figure 3-4 and Figure 3-5. Between 1977 and 1985 the average natural gas reserves added per well were rather constant at 1.5 billion scf, whereas after 1986 the average reserves added per well increased continuously reaching 4 billion scf per well by 1990.

In 1986 the Potential Natural Gas Committee estimated a total of 750 trillion scf for natural gas reserves in the probable, possible and speculative categories in the United States[30][31]. In 1988, the US Department of Energy concluded that the technically recoverable resource base for the contiguous 48 states is 1050 trillion scf[31][32]. At the current rate of consumption, this amount would furnish supplies for

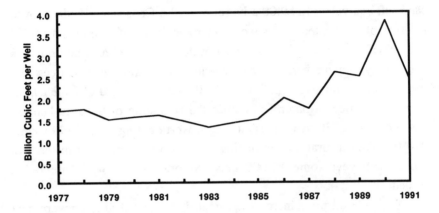

FIGURE 3-4. Average Natural Gas Reserves Added per Well (Producing plus Dry Holes) for Onshore Drilling in the Lower 48 States from 1977 to 1991 (Source: US DOE)

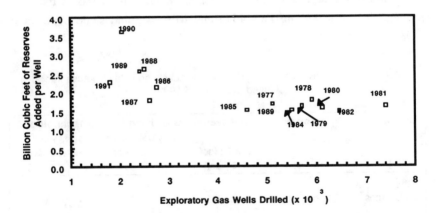

FIGURE 3-5. Average Natural Gas Finding Rate per Well and Well Completions for Onshore Lower 48 States between 1977 and 1991 (Source: US DOE)

more than 50 years. According to the US DOE study more than half of the 1050 trillion scf is judged to be economically recoverable at wellhead prices less than $3.00 per thousand scf. By comparison the natural gas spot market prices between 1986 and 1988 averaged $1.50 per thousand scf, equivalent to $9.00 a barrel of oil[31]. Consequently, the proved reserves of the United States would increase from 170 trillion scf to 770 trillion scf, if natural gas was priced at the same level as crude oil on a per energy content basis. The conventional natural gas resources and reserves are summarized in Table 3-7. It should be noted that the cumulative production of natural gas since the beginning of the 20th century has been about 730 trillion scf. It is also worth noting that in 1990 some 270 thousand natural gas producing wells were in operation in the US, while each year some 10,000 new exploratory gas wells are being drilled[29].

The 1973 oil price increases prompted the United States government and industry to undertake an extensive effort to evaluate unconventional resources. The results of the US study are summarized in Table 3-7[31][32]. Estimates of the resources that are recoverable with current technology are shown also in Table 3-7 at two different cost figures.

Among the large sources of unconventional natural gas is the low-permeability, gas bearing Devonian and Mississippian shale deposits in

TABLE 3-7. Conventional and Unconventional Natural Gas Sources in the United States as of 1990

Source	Resource	Recoverable Gas Using Current Technology at Cost Up To		
		$1.50/Mscf	$3.00/Mscf	$7.50/Mscf
	(10^9 scf)	(10^9 scf)	(10^9 scf)	(10^9 scf)
Conventional				
All Sources[1]	1220 (730)	170 (730)	770	NA[2]
Unconventional				
Eastern Shales	600	0	10	35
Tight Sands	600	0	55	180
Coal Seams	2500	0	10	350
Aquifers	3000-100000	0	0	160
Hydrates	>3400	0	0	>100

1. Numbers in parentheses indicate cumulative production of natural gas to date so that total conventional resource would have been 1950 trillion scf and total conventional proved reserves to date would have been 900 trillion scf, if no production had ever occurred. 2. NA = Not Available; most likely it includes the bulk of the conventional resource.
Note. The cost per thousand scf (Mcsf) is in constant 1988 dollars.

the eastern part of the United States. Artificial fracturing is required to increase the effective porosity of these organic-rich shales and release the tightly held methane. Because these rich shales have thin dimensions, some wells must be drilled horizontally. As it has already been mentioned, techniques for horizontal drilling have evolved rapidly in recent years.

Another large source of unconventional natural gas is the tight sands formations found mostly in the western United States. Both the porosity and the permeability of these formations are low so that hydraulic or explosive fracturing techniques must be employed to recover the gas. Improvements in these fracturing techniques have occurred over the years and research is currently focusing in increasing the length of fractures, confining fractures to the "pay" zone (zone with gas present) and increasing gas flow through the fractures[31].

Coal beds contain very large amounts of methane, which was generated during the transformation of the organic material into coal and was subsequently trapped or absorbed by the coal. This methane gas, once viewed as a hazard to coal mining, has been now recognized as a sizeable source of natural gas[33]. Coal-bed methane can be extracted using closely spaced holes or horizontal drilling. Occasionally, fracturing techniques similar to those employed in tight shale deposits and tight sands can greatly enhance production. Coal bed methane has been the first unconventional natural gas resource to be commercialized in the United States due to favorable tax credits.

The most abundant of the unconventional natural gas resources is the geopressurized aquifers. Such aquifers exist in Oklahoma, in the western states and the Gulf coasts of Texas and Louisiana. Under pressurized conditions, brines at depths of 8,000 to 9,000 ft contain 20 to 40 scf of gas per barrel of brine. An economic technology with which to develop this resource has not been developed. The principal obstacle is the lack of an environmentally satisfactory method to dispose the brine. In addition, the low energy density of the brines may prevent the use of this resource on economical grounds as well.

Methane hydrates constitute another large source of natural gas. These hydrates, otherwise known as clathrates, are icelike compounds of water in which methane and other gases are trapped in a crystalline structure formed by water molecules[34][35]. The composition of the methane hydrate is $CH_4.5_3/_4H_2O$ and consists of a cubic unit of structure containing 46 water molecules with up to eight methane molecules. The methane clathrate resembles ice in physical appearance and has a maximum density of 56.8 lb/ft^3. Thus one cubic foot of methane clathrate contains 171 scf, if all the methane sites are filled, and 156 scf, if only 90% of the methane sites are occupied. Below an 80% methane site occupancy the clathrate is no longer in a stable phase[31][35]. Moreover, the temperature and pressure of a stable methane clathrate is below 86°F and above 411 psi, respectively[26][31][35]. Consequently, methane hydrates tend to occur in Arctic areas at several hundred feet depth onshore and at or near the sea bottom of the oceans.

The practical significance of methane clathrates became apparent in the 1930s, when it was discovered that clathrate formation was a major problem in the pipeline transportation of natural gas under cold conditions. The first confirmed recovery of a natural methane clathrate occurred in 1972 at Prudhoe Bay, Alaska at depths between 1,500 and 2,000 feet. Clathrate samples were also recovered from the Louisiana slope of the Gulf of Mexico at depths ranging from 1,500 to 8,000 feet. Several methods have been proposed for producing gas from clathrates. These include steam injection, hot-water injection and fire flooding, depressurization, and injection of clathrate inhibitors such as methanol and glycols. Even though the recovery techniques of methane from clathrates are in their infancy, the most promising scheme appears to be a combination of depressurization and hot-water injection.

It is important to appreciate the fact that ultimate economic recovery of methane from any source depends on the concentration of methane in that particular source. Table 3-8 presents the typical energy densities encountered in conventional and unconventional natural gas sources[31]. It would appear then that methane from shales and aquifers is a very unlikely proposition. Moreover, methane from coal and tight sands is marginal. This leaves only the gas hydrates as the only potentially viable source of unconventional natural gas, if the appropriate technology is developed.

TABLE 3-8. Energy Density of Various Natural Gas Resources

Natural Gas Resource	Energy Density (scf of CH4/cf of formation)
Conventional Natural Gas	10-20
Coal-Bed Methane	8-12
Western Tight Sands	5-10
Eastern Shales	1- 2
Geopressurized Aquifers	1- 2
Methane Hydrates*	45-50

(*) Assumes a 30% reservoir porosity

SUPPLY OF NATURAL GAS FOR TRANSPORTATION

The amount of natural gas that would be required in the future for transportation needs can be readily estimated. A preliminary calculation is given here, while a more accurate one will be presented in a later chapter. The energy content of the present 7 million bbl/d gasoline and 1 million bbl/d diesel fuel consumption to power passenger cars, trucks and busses can be calculated in a straightforward manner. Assuming an energy content of 5.253 million BTU per barrel for motor gasoline and 5.825 million BTU per barrel for diesel fuel, we obtain for the energy content of gasoline and diesel fuel 13.42 quadrillion BTU/y and 2.13 quadrillion BTU/y, respectively[35]. The energy content of dry natural gas is 1031 BTU/scf[35]. Hence, the equivalent amount of natural gas to the gasoline and diesel fuels used today for vehicular applications will be 13 trillion scf/y and 2 trillion scf/y, respectively. This amount of natural gas is equal to about 3/4 of the present natural gas consumption in the US. Although an increase of the present use of natural gas by 15 trillion scf/y is not impossible, it would be difficult to attain in the foreseeable future by relying exclusively on domestic resources.

However, several developments in parallel with the substitution of the present motor fuels for natural gas will lessen this apparent severity of the supply problem. First, the average efficiency of passenger cars on the road will keep increasing reaching from 20 mpg to 27 mpg under the present standards and eventually 35 mpg under a mandatory or voluntary revision of the CAFE requirements. Proportional increases in fuel efficiency can be also expected in light trucks and vans. Thus, the demand for natural gas fuel will be reduced to 8.6 trillion scf/y. Second, a conversion of all gasoline vehicles to dedicated and optimized natural gas vehicles will increase fuel efficiency by 15%, thereby resulting in a further decrease in the total natural gas demand to 7.5 trillion scf/y. Third, biofuels and electricity may capture a portion of the land transportation fuel market. The market share of biomethane from the anaerobic decomposition of organic wastes could be as high as 10% of the total fuel consumption amounting to a natural gas displacement between 0.5 and 1 trillion scf/y. On the other hand, the population of vehicles in the country is expected to stabilize at about 35% above its present level. Thus, the ultimate natural gas fuel demand may be in the range of 8 to 10 trillion scf/y.

This is a much more reasonable rate of use for natural gas to meet transportation needs and one which can be attained relatively easily by both increasing production beyond the present rate as well as by utilizing the reduction of natural gas in its present uses due to increased efficiency. For example, savings of 1 trillion scf/y are possible in the residential and commercial sectors which currently use 8 trillion scf/y by improving the envelope of buildings to reduce the space heating load and by switching from natural gas to electricity. Moreover, another 1 trillion scf/y can be saved of the 3 trillion scf/y used in electricity generation by switching from natural gas to other fuels such as gasified coal. In addition, an additional 1 trillion scf/y may be saved in the industrial sector, including reduction in gas production and distribution losses. Finally, natural gas liquids, produced with natural gas and other hydrocarbons resulting from the refining of crude oil, which will continue to be used albeit greatly reduced in quantity, may be converted to natural gas at a rate of 2 to 3 trillion scf/y. Thus, a maximum natural gas production of 25 trillion scf/y will be sufficient to meet the land transportation needs of the United States in addition to its present use in the residential, commercial, and industrial sectors as well as in electric power generation.

The conventional resources of the United States, including the proven reserves, are very large indeed. As it has already been indicated, the proven reserves plus the estimated reserve appreciation plus the estimated recoverable undiscovered reserves are on the order of 800 to

1200 trillion scf depending on price. Moreover, the estimated unconventional sources of natural gas in the US, including eastern shales, western tight sands, coal seams, geopressurized aquifers, and methane hydrates are at a minimum on the order 10,000 trillion scf of which 700 to 800 trillion scf are recoverable using current technology at a cost up to $7.5 per thousand scf. Thus, conventional and unconventional recoverable resources of natural gas in the US are adequate for a minimum 60 to 80 years of supply at the rate of 25 trillion scf per year. The historical experience form the production and utilization of crude oil as a transportation fuel shows, however, that this minimum number of years of natural gas supply will stretch out considerably as recoverable resources as well as vehicle efficiency improvements always tend to be underestimated 50 years in advance.

REFERENCES

1. Kirk-Othmer (eds.), Encyclopedia of Chemical Technology, Gas Natural, 3rd ed., v. 11, p. 630, John Wiley, New York, NY, 1980.

2. E. Ayres and C. A. Scarlott, Energy Resources – The Wealth of the World, pp. 10-22, McGraw-Hill Book Co., New York, NY, 1952.

3. G. Jenkins, Oil Economists's Handbook, p. 114, Applied Science Publishers, Ltd., London, UK, 1977.

4. Statistical Abstract of the United States 1963, p. 539, US Department of Commerce, Bureau of the Census, Washington, D.C., 1963.

5. Statistical Abstract of the United States 1970, p. 515, US Department of Commerce, Bureau of the Census, Washington, D.C., 1970.

6. Statistical Abstract of the United States 1992, p. 582, US Department of Commerce, Bureau of the Census, Washington, D.C., 1992.

7. Energy Information Administration, Monthly Energy Review – June 1992, pp. 3-21, US DOE, Washington, DC, 1992.

8. A. L. Waddams, Chemicals from Petroleum, 4th ed., pp. 61-71, Gulf Publishing Company, Houston, TX, 1980.

9. H. H. Landsberg, L. Fischman, and J. L. Fisher, Resources In America's Future, p. 847, published for Resources of the Future, Inc. by the Johns Hopkins Press, Baltimore, MD, 1963.

10. Statistical Abstract of the United States 1963, loc. cit., p. 582.

11. Statistical Abstract of the United States 1963, *loc. cit.*, p. 727.

12. Statistical Abstract of the United States 1992, *loc. cit.*, p. 704.

13. Energy Information Administration, Monthly Energy Review – June 1992, *loc. cit.*, p. 73.

14. Statistical Abstract of the United States 1975, p. 750, US Department of Commerce, Bureau of the Census, Washington, D.C., 1975.

15. Statistical Abstract of the United States 1992, *loc. cit.*, p. 745.

16. Energy Information Administration, Monthly Energy Review – June 1992, *loc. cit.*, p. 73 and p. 91.

17. E. Hirst, R. Marlay, D. Greene and R. Barnes, "Recent Changes in US Energy Consumption: What happened and Why", Ann. Rev. Energy, v. 8, pp. 193-267, Annual Reviews, Inc., Palo Alto, CA, 1983.

18. M. H. Ross and D. Steinmeyer, "Energy for Industry", Energy For Planet Earth : Readings from Scientific American magazine, pp. 35-46, W. H. Freeman and Co., New York, NY, 1991.

19. The three major manufacturers of advanced combined cycle (gas and steam) turbines are General Electric (GE), Siemens and Asea-Brown-Boveri (ABB) with attained field efficiencies of 55%, 55% and 58%, respectively, as of 1994. Phosphoric fuel cells, manufactured by United Technologies and others, provide power and low temperature heat for large commercial building with a combined efficiency of over 80% as of 1994.

20. W. Fulkerson, R. R. Judkins and M. K. Sanghvi, "Energy from Fossil Fuels", Energy For Planet Earth : Readings from Scientific American magazine, pp. 83-94, W. H. Freeman and Co., New York, NY, 1991.

21. See for example the annual publication "Reserves of Crude Oil, Natural Gas Liquids and Natural Gas in the United States and Canada" published jointly each year by the American Gas Association, the American Petroleum Institute, and the Canadian Petroleum Association which contains information on reserves through the end of December of the preceding year.

22. V. D. Hunt, Energy Dictionary, Van Nostrand Reinhold Company, New York, NY, 1979.

23. C. E. Weber, "Estimation of Petroleum Reserves", Ch. 25, p. 12, in Petroleum Exploration Handbook, G. B. Moody (ed), McGraw-Hill Book Company, New York, NY, 1961.

24. Energy Information Administration, Natural Gas Annual 1991, DOE/EIA-0131(91), p. 242, US Department of Energy, Washington, D.C., 1992.

25. Kirk-Othmer (eds.), Encyclopedia of Chemical Technology, Gas Natural, loc. cit., p. 634.

26. M. H. Nederlof, "The Scope for Natural Gas Supplies from Unconventional Sources", pp. 95-117, Ann. Rev. Energy, v. 13, Annual Reviews Inc., Palo Alto, CA, 1988.

27. 9. H. H. Landsberg, L. Fischman, and J. L. Fisher, Resources In America's Future, loc. cit., p. 406.

28. Statistical Abstract of the United States 1975, loc. cit., p. 689.

29. Statistical Abstract of the United States 1992, loc. cit., p. 698.

30. Potential Gas Committee, Potential Supply of Natural Gas in the United States, Colorado School of Mines, Golden, CO, 1987.

31. G. J. MacDonald, "The Future of Methane as an Energy Resource", pp. 53-83, Ann. Rev. Energy, v. 15, Annual Reviews Inc., Palo Alto, CA, 1990.

32. US Department of Energy, "An Assessment of the Natural Gas Resource Base of the United States", Report DOE/W/31109-H1, Washington, D.C., 1988.

33. International Energy Agency, Global Methane and the Coal Industry, IEA/OECD, Organization for Economic Cooperation and Economic Development, Paris, FR, 1994.

34. L. Pauling, The Nature of the Chemical Bond, 3rd ed., pp. 464-473, Cornell University Press, Ithaca, NY, 1960.

35. E. D. Sloan, Jr., J. Happel, M. A. Hnatow (eds.), Natural Gas Hydrates, Annals of the New York Academy of Sciences, v. 715, New York Academy of Sciences, New York, NY, 1994.

36. Energy Information Administration, Monthly Energy Review – June 1992, loc. cit., pp. 138-139.

Chapter 4

Storage of Natural Gas On-Board a Vehicle

FUEL STORAGE REQUIREMENTS

The amount of fuel typically stored on-board a vehicle is dictated by two major parameters. These parameters are the range of the vehicle obtained by the use of the stored fuel and the ease of refueling, particularly with respect to the required time. The present day automotive fuels, gasoline and diesel fuel, have several distinct advantages over other fuels. Both of these fuels have a high heating value (energy per unit mass) as well as a high energy density (energy per unit volume) and both of them are liquid in form under typical ambient temperature and pressure conditions. The high heating value implies a relatively small fuel mass requirement. A high energy density, on the other hand, implies a small storage volume. Finally, the liquid form of the fuel coupled with a high heating value and energy density implies a very rapid refueling capability for most typical applications.

A major drawback of all liquid fuels stems from the necessity to be dispensed at a central facility, i.e., a public refueling station. That is to say, the present motor fuels require that the vehicle owner has to make a special trip to a public refueling station over a period of time typically on the order of a few to several days. The need for centralized dispensing of liquid fuels is necessitated because of practical distribution reasons as well as safety reasons such as high flammability and toxicity.

The present liquid motor fuels, i.e., gasoline and diesel fuel, as well as proposed future liquid fuels consisting in part or totally of methanol or ethanol will also fall in the same category.

It is interesting to note that while the public has accepted the inconvenience of public station refueling, it still values highly the option of being able to refuel at home. This observation has emerged from the marketing studies regarding the promotion of electric vehicles. Home refueling is a sufficiently strong feature to offset in the minds of the public the range limitation of electric cars[1]. As it will be demonstrated in subsequent chapters, natural gas as a gaseous motor vehicle fuel can be readily supplied in a decentralized fashion not only at home but even at the work place. Consequently, natural gas fuel must and will be highly desirable by the public for this feature alone.

The driving patterns of US residents, according to the US Department of Transportation, are summarized in Table 4-1[2]. The average daily driving distance in the US is currently on the order of 41 miles. However, the driving patterns vary from individual to individual and from day to day. It is therefore difficult to infer the daily driving range

TABLE 4-1. Evolution of Driving Patterns and Motoring Trends in the United States

Year Category	1969	1977	1988	1990
Average Miles Traveled per Day	34.0	33.0	32.1	41.4
Average No Persons per Vehicle	—	1.9	1.7	1.5
Average Vehicles Per Household	1.2	1.6	1.7	1.8
Average Annual Miles Traveled				
Per Male Driver	11,352	13,563	13,962	16,632
Per Female Driver	5,411	5,943	6,381	9,543
Average Trip Lengths in Miles				
Work/Business	9.4	9.2	8.6	10.9
Vacation	160.0	95.4	113.0	80.0
School/Church	4.7	6.1	5.5	7.4

Notes. 1. The percentage of time each vehicle type is used when driving is as follows: Passenger Car 80.4%; Truck 13.8%; Van 5.4%; and Other 0.4%.
2. The breakdown of miles driven by purpose of trip is as follows: Work/Business 35.6%; Personal Business 20.9%; Social/Recreational Activities 13%; Shopping 11.9%; Visiting 11.4%; School/Church 4.5%; Vacation/Pleasure Driving 1.4%; and Doctor/Dentist 1.3%.

required for an automobile from the average daily driving distance alone. Consequently, a model must be developed to predict the daily range requirements for an urban vehicle. This prediction may then be used to infer an acceptable vehicle range between refuelings. Such models have been developed in connection with electric vehicle programs where knowledge of daily US driving range requirements is essential to determine the battery size on board the vehicle[3]. A standard Monte Carlo, i.e., probabilistic, simulation process is typically employed to develop a model predicting the daily driving range requirements for an automobile. The input to this model consists of data on average annual mileage as well as data on trip lengths and their frequencies of occurrence. The probabilistic model shows that an automobile in the US with a range of 180 miles can meet all the driving needs of the owner during 98% of the days of the year or at all times other than his or her long vacation trips. Figure 4-1 shows these results of the model for different average annual driving distances. Moreover, the model shows that during 95% of the days in a year (a 95% usefulness index) the daily driving range will be around 80 miles for a vehicle driven a little over 10,000 miles annually, which is the US average. The required daily vehicle range for a 95% usefulness index as a function of the annually

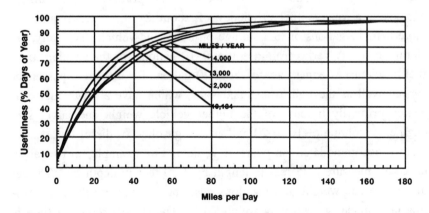

FIGURE 4-1. Model Prediction of Automobile Usefulness Index (Percent of Days in a Year during which Vehicle Range Exceeds its Owners Driving Needs) as a Function of Daily Range and with the Average Annual Mileage as a Parameter.

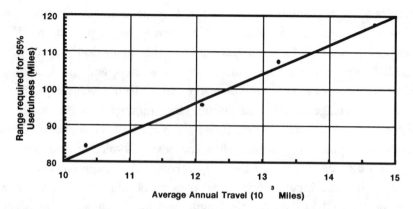

FIGURE 4-2.   Daily Vehicle Range Required for a 95% Usefulness Index as a Function of Average Annual Mileage (Regression Equation: R = 0.0077 A + 2.8278; R : Daily Range Required in miles; A : Average Annual Mileage in miles).

driven miles by the vehicle is shown in Figure 4-2. Incidentally, a 95% usefulness index is considered adequate to cover all driving needs of the vehicle owner other than vacation.

It is apparent from the preceding discussion that a vehicle with a driving range of 320 miles between refuelings will result to a frequency of refueling at a public station of once every four days on the average. This fueling frequency rate is deemed acceptable by the public. Moreover, a vehicle fuel efficiency of about 21 mpg will require no more than 15 gallons of fuel storage on-board the vehicle. Typically, the storage capacity varies from as little as 10 gallons for the smaller, more fuel efficient passenger cars to about 20 gallons for the larger passenger cars as well as the light trucks and vans, which have a lower fuel efficiency primarily because of the higher vehicle weight and larger size engine. A volume of 10 to 20 gallons for gasoline or diesel fuel can be readily accommodated on-board a vehicle. For example, a 15 gallon tank will measure 1.75 feet in length by 1.50 feet in depth by 0.75 feet in height. The weight of 15 gallons gasoline is about 90 lb. The gasoline tank made of steel may weigh 20 lb. The typical refueling time is on the order of 5 to 10 minutes, depending on the size of the tank. The energy content of a 10 gal gasoline tank is approximately 1.15 million BTU and that of a 20 gallon gasoline tank is twice as much.

It is thus apparent that a liquid hydrocarbon constitutes a very effective means to store energy on-board a vehicle powered by a typical internal combustion engine. It should be also noted that the heating value and energy density of the alternative liquid fuel methanol, which is an alcohol, is roughly half that of gasoline so that the fuel volume and weight becomes twice as large for the same vehicle range between refuelings (15 gal and 90 lb of gasoline have the same energy content as 30 gal and 180 lb of methanol). The other alternative liquid fuel ethanol, also an alcohol has a heating value and an energy density about 2/3 that of gasoline, resulting in a 50% increase of fuel volume and weight for the same vehicle range (15 gal and 90 lb of gasoline are equivalent to 22.5 gal and 135 lb of ethanol).

The preceding analysis establishes, therefore, that a 320 mile vehicle range is required so that vehicle refueling at a public central station occurs no more frequently than once every four days, on the average. This average refueling frequency appears to be acceptable by the public. Typical liquid hydrocarbon fuel (gasoline, diesel) tanks are on the order of 10 to 20 gallons and refueling time is on the order of 5 to 10 minutes. Alcohol based fuels will require a 50% (ethanol) to 100% (methanol) increase in tank capacity for the same vehicle range and a proportional increase in refueling time (15 minutes for ethanol, 20 minutes for methanol) — longer refueling times can in part be offset by employing more powerful, i.e., higher flow rate, dispensing pumps. The preceding conclusions are of course supported by everyday experience with the operation of motor vehicles.

Natural gas is a gaseous fuel under ambient conditions of temperature and pressure and as such it has an energy density of about 1/1000 that of gasoline. Obviously, natural gas can not be used in its natural state as fuel on board a motor vehicle. Currently, there exist two commercially available techniques and one experimental technique for storing natural gas on-board a vehicle within the vehicle volume constraints. The two commercially available techniques are: Compressed Natural Gas (CNG); and Liquefied Natural Gas (LNG). The experimental technique is: Adsorbed Natural Gas (ANG). In the remaining sections of this chapter all three of these storage techniques will be examined and evaluated.

COMPRESSED NATURAL GAS

The current storage form of choice for natural gas on-board passenger cars, trucks, vans and buses is high pressure compression. This form of storage known as compressed natural gas (CNG) has an operational pressure between 2,400 and 4,350 psi (more accurately psig, i.e., pressure above the atmospheric pressure). The storage tank is typically cylindrical in shape, is permanently attached to the vehicle, and is refillable. A CNG storage tank for vehicle operation may consist of[4]:

1. All metal (typically steel);

2. Metal liner reinforced with continuous composite filament wrapped over its cylindrical portion (typically steel with fiberglass, E-glass or S-glass composite);

3. Metal liner with continuous composite filament over its cylindrical portion as well as the two domes (typically aluminum with fiberglass composite);

4. Non-metallic liner with a continuous composite filament fully wrapped over the cylindrical and dome portions of it (typically carbon fiber liner with carbon fiber or fiberglass filament).(*)

The walls of a pressurized vessel must be designed to have adequate thickness to withstand the operational pressure during the life of the tank. In reality these tanks are over-designed to withstand a pressure more than two and a half times the operational pressure as a safety factor. This is necessary because a failure of a pressurized tank may lead to an explosion with the possible loss of life and destruction in property. The US Department of Transportation has set, therefore, very stringent safety design criteria and certification processes for such tanks[4]. Given the high pressures that need to be contained, relatively heavy tanks may result unless high tensile strength, lightweight materials are used.

The need for pressurized tanks containing a variety of gases is by no means a new one. From the oxygen tanks for medical and recreation-

---

(*). The natural gas vehicle CNG tanks are characterized as Type NGV2 and are designated as NGV2-x with "x" equal to 1, 2, 3 or 4 depending on the type in direct correspondence with these four types.

al purposes, to acetylene tanks for welding, to nitrogen and helium tanks for scientific and recreational uses, to hydrogen and methane for transportation and other applications, engineers have over the years addressed the design issues and provided the appropriate solutions. For a given volume, a spherical tank comprises the most efficient geometry in terms of weight. However, a cylindrical tank comprises a much more efficient storage configuration in terms of space utilization and has become therefore the preferred shape. In a pressurized cylindrical tank, the circumferential or hoop stress is twice as high as the longitudinal one, requiring twice as thick of a cylinder wall (but not the end caps or domes) than, say, a spherical vessel to contain to same pressure[5]. Doubling of the cylinder wall thickness will almost double the weight of the tank and will significantly increase the cost. Thus, an all metal CNG container does not represent a realistic vehicular tank.

A more economical solution in terms of weight has been developed in the last thirty or so years with the advent of composite materials such as glass fibers, kevlar (aramid) and carbon fibers. The wall thickness of the cylindrical portion of the tank is the same as that of the domes, but it is reinforced with composite fibers wrapped outside the cylindrical surface so as to bring the strength of the tank to the requisite level. Such a design is shown in Figure 4-3. Since composite fibers are very

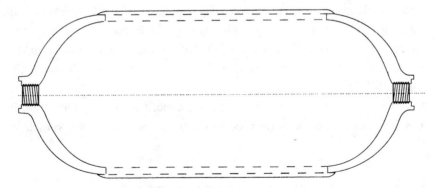

FIGURE 4-3. Composite Reinforced Aluminum CNG Cylinder. Cylinder Body is Manufactured from Corrosion Resistant Aluminum Tube and Hemispherical Head is Spin-Formed with Computer-Aided Manufacturing (CAM) Equipment. Cylinder Body is Reinforced with High Strength Composite Material (Courtesy CNG Cylinder Company, Long Beach, CA).

lightweight and have comparable tensile strength to that of steel, a reduced tank weight results, albeit at somewhat increased cost. Traditionally, steel has been the material of choice for pressurized tanks. A glass fiber, hoop-wrapped steel tank is classified as a composite steel tank[6]. In recent years aluminum has been introduced as a lighter weight alternative. These aluminum tanks are fully-wrapped with glass fibers and are classified as aluminum composite tanks[7].

Since aluminum has about 1/3 the density of steel and 1/2 the tensile strength of steel, an aluminum composite reinforced cylinder will weight 2/3 as much as a steel reinforced cylinder of the same volume and pressure. An all composite material cylinder based on carbon fibers is also possible and has become recently commercially available[8][9]. Given that the density of carbon is about 1/3 that of steel, while the tensile strength of carbon fibers is similar to that of steel, an all carbon composite cylinder will weigh about 1/3 that of a steel composite one and 1/2 that of an aluminum composite one for the same volume and pressure. Table 4-2 summarizes the weights and costs of a typical size cylindrical compressed natural gas tank made of different materials.

The weight penalty associated with the CNG storage tanks diminishes as one moves from steel to all composite materials. Based on the data of Table 4-2, a CNG vehicle would need three of the 13 gallon tanks to equal one 13 gallon gasoline tank in terms of energy content and vehicle range (*). The added weight penalty of a CNG vehicle will be (full CNG tanks vs. full gasoline tank): 228 lb for the steel composite reinforced tank (332 lb vs. 104 lb); 185 lb for the aluminum composite reinforced tanks (289 lb vs. 104 lb); and 39 lb for the all composite tanks (143 lb vs. 104 lb).

It is conceivable, however, that a net benefit in weight may result in CNG vehicles as there is no need to carry so much fuel on a vehicle as

---

(*) In terms of energy content alone the requirement would have been 3.19 13-gal CNG tanks versus a 13-gal gasoline tank. However, the vehicle fuel efficiency of the CNG vehicle could be 15% higher than that of the gasoline one. Thus, in terms of range 2.78 13-gal CNG tanks will be equivalent to one 13-gal gasoline tank. Hence, the average tank volume equivalence ratio of 3 CNG tanks to 1 gasoline tank constitutes a realistic assumption.

TABLE 4-2. Comparative Data of Typical Compressed Natural Gas Cylindrical Tanks for Automotive Application at "77°F and 3,000 psi" Operating Conditions

Material[1]	Steel/Composite	Alum/Composite	All Composite
Dimensions (D x L)	11.3" x 40"	13" x 35"	12" x 36"
Interior Volume	13.2 gal (50.0 l)	13.4 gal (50.8 l)	13.2 gal (50.0 l)
Tank Weight	102 lb	89 lb	39 lb
Fuel capacity	458 scf[2]	462 scf	458 scf[2]
Fuel Weight	8.7 lb	8.8 lb	8.7 lb
Energy Density[1]	4,280 BTU/lb[2]	4,890 BTU/lb	9,873 BTU/lb[2]
Tank Price (1994)	$515	$565	$685

1. The volumetric energy density of any of these tanks is 36,000 BTU/gal compared to 114,000 BTU/gal for gasoline. The weight energy density of a comparable (13 gal) gasoline tank is about 14,500 BTU/lb, including the weight of the steel tank. 2. At 3,600 psi, the steel/composite and the all composite fuel capacity is 14% higher (522 scf) and the energy density becomes 4,880 BTU/lb and 11,255 BTU/lb, respectively.
Note. Respective data from: Pressed Steel Tank Co., Milwaukee, WI; CNG Cylinder Company, Long Beach, CA; and EDO Corporation, College Park, NY.

there is for the gasoline counterpart. The reduction in vehicle fuel capacity is feasible as overnight refueling at home or during business hours at work is possible with natural gas and the typical daily range requirement exceeds 80 miles only 5% of the days in a year. Thus, two rather than three 13-gallon CNG tanks may be used on-board the vehicle. Under this assumption the following weight penalty will result for the different CNG tank materials (full CNG tanks vs. full gasoline tank): 117 lb for the steel composite reinforced tank (221 lb vs. 104 lb ; 89 lb for the aluminum composite reinforced tanks (193 lb vs. 104 lb); and -9 lb (gain) for the all composite tanks (95 lb vs. 104 lb). Consequently, the flexibility of the CNG refueling system allows even for a reduction in the CNG vehicle weight compared to its gasoline counterpart. While composite reinforced steel cylinders have been traditionally used in the past and the lighter composite reinforced aluminum cylinders are being used currently, the even lighter all composite cylinders will become very shortly the CNG tank of choice for natural gas vehicles.

The selection of the tank pressure for CNG has varied between 2,400 psi and 4,350 psi. Higher tank pressures result, obviously, in more fuel being stored within a given volume. Consequently, it makes sense to strive for higher tank pressures. However, increased tank pressures require heavier and more expensive tanks — as well as the heavier and more expensive compressors to refuel these vehicles. Therefore, a trade-off between the magnitude of on-board fuel storage and the storage weight and cost is necessary to determine the ideal CNG storage pressure. It appears that the 3,000 psi CNG pressure is the optimal one[10].

The 3,000 psi optimal choice can be substantiated readily on physical grounds alone by noting the following facts regarding methane. When an ideal gas (totally non interacting molecules in the gas) is compressed, its volume is reduced in direct proportion to the applied pressure so long as the temperature remains constant. This is the ideal gas law in thermodynamics[11]. Thus, theoretically if one started with 1000 scf of natural gas at 14.7 psi (sea level atmospheric pressure) and compressed them to 2,400 psi, 3,000 psi and 3,600 psi, respectively, the resulting end volumes will be 6.13 ft^3, 4.90 ft^3 and 4.08 ft^3. However, all gases deviate from the ideal gas law, particularly as the pressure increases because the resulting higher gas density leads to some molecular interaction. A correction factor, called the compressibility factor, enters the calculation to account for this deviation. A compressibility factor less than one indicates a higher density gas than that predicted by the ideal law, while a compressibility factor higher than one indicates the opposite. The compressibility factor is not only a function of pressure, but of temperature as well.

The compressibility factor of methane up to 10,000 psi and from -94°F to 968°F is shown in Figure 4-4[12]. For methane, the compressibility factors at a 104°F (40°C) constant temperature and 2,400 psi, 3,000 psi and 3,600 psi operational pressures are 0.855, 0.865 and 0.895, respectively. Thus, the actual volume of 1000 scf of natural gas at these three pressures will be: 5.24 ft^3, 4.24 ft^3 and 3.65 ft^3. Hence, a 20% reduction in pressure from 3000 to 2400 psi increases the compressed gas volume by 24%, while a 20% increase in pressure from 3000 to 3600 psi decreases the compressed gas volume by 14%. Consequently, the optimum CNG compression may be around 3000 psi. Finally, it is worth noting from Figure 4-4 that the compressibility factor at 104°F has a minimum of 0.852 at about 2,450 psi and that it changes a little between 2,000 and 3,000 psi. While the preceding analysis does not intend to be all encompassing, it nevertheless shows that increasing

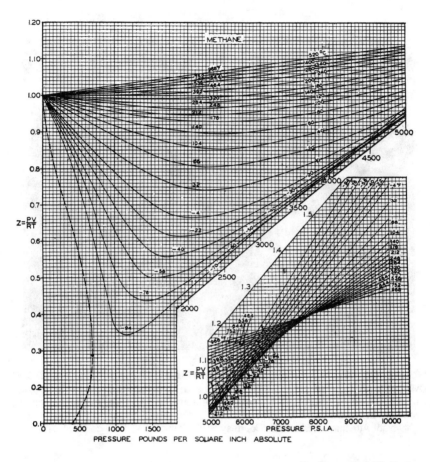

Z = Compressibility Factor

FIGURE 4-4.   Compressibility Factor for Methane to Demonstrate Domain of Optimal CNG Storage Tank Operational Pressure (Mc-Graw Hill Book Company).

the operational CNG tank pressure above 3,600 psi results in rapidly diminishing returns in terms of tank volume reduction.

The compression of natural gas to 3,000-3,600 psi or higher pressures is a well established technology and will be addressed in a subsequent chapter regarding the natural gas distribution.

Natural gas vehicle fuel cylinders have typically a diameter between 10 and 16 inches and a length varying from 35 to 85 inches. Internal volume capacity ranges from 8 gallons (30 liter) to 50 gallons (190 liter) and the corresponding fuel capacity at 3,000 psi varies from a 300

FIGURE 4-5. The 13 gal (50 liter) LiteRiderTM All Composite Reinforced CNG Cylinder for Automotive Use Combines Advanced Aerospace Composite Technology, Computer Aided Design and Analysis, an Automated High Volume Manufacturing Process, an Impermeable Internal Liner, Toughened Exterior Protection and Lightweight Attachment Brackets (Courtesy EDO Corporation, College Point, NY).

scf to 1700 scf of natural gas. Figure 4-5 shows one of the recently developed all carbon fiber composite LiteRider™ CNG cylinders ranging in volume from 12 to 67 gallons. The gas filling/removal opening at the center of one of the end caps of each cylinder is easily discernible. These all composite cylinders have an even large safety factor of 3.3 times the maximum operational pressure of 3,600 psi.

The most commonly employed CNG tank size appears to have a volume of 13 to 15 gallons (50 to 60 liters) and a fuel content of 450 to 550 scf of natural gas at 3000 psi. This fuel content is equivalent to about 5 gallons of gasoline. Consequently, one such CNG tank will provide a range of 100 miles to 150 miles for a vehicle with a respective fuel efficiency of 20 mpg to 30 mpg. Since the availability of home and work refueling with natural gas is feasible, there is no longer the need to store on-board the vehicle fuel providing a driving range in excess of 180 to 200 miles. This CNG refueling feature reduces the weight of the vehicle, improves its fuel efficiency and even more importantly reduces the initial cost of a CNG vehicle.

The safety of CNG containers for vehicles has been exemplary over the years. All such CNG tanks are designed with a minimum service life of 15 years. Stringent quality control requirements must be exercised by the manufacturers. Each vehicular CNG tank is permanently labeled with the following information: "CNG Only", designation NGV2-"x", service pressure, manufacturer's symbol(trademark) and part number, serial number, inspector's symbol (trademark), month and year of manufacture, and date at which the 15 year design life will expire. Each CNG tank is equipped with a pressure relief device to avoid container rupture due to overpressurization in a fire situation. Moreover, each CNG tank before delivery is tested at a pressure 1.5 times its service pressure for 30 seconds or longer depending on the type. Finally, a variety of destructive and non-destructive design qualifications tests are routinely performed on representative CNG tanks of each specific design prior to shipment by the manufacturer[4].

The National Highway Traffic Safety Administration (NHTSA) of the US Department of Transportation (DOT) has established already a federal motor vehicle safety standard for CNG fueled vehicles[12]. This standard enhances the fuel system integrity (tanks plus fuel lines and ancillary components) in frontal, rear or lateral collisions in order to reduce deaths and injuries by fires resulting from fuel leakage during and after crashes involving CNG fueled vehicles. One of the inherent advantages of CNG fuel over all liquid fuels is that in the event of a CNG fuel system leakage the gaseous natural gas disperses very rapidly being lighter than air — a liquid fuel, whether gasoline, diesel fuel or any alcohol, leaking out of a vehicle fuel system must first vaporize before it can disperse in the air during which time the likelihood of fire is very high and so is the potential for serious injury or even death.

Because of the relatively small number of CNG vehicles on the road at the present time, only limited data are available on fire rates. The available data analyzed by NHTSA indicate CNG vehicle fire rates comparable to those of gasoline vehicles (about 2 fire incidents per 100 million vehicle miles travelled). In addition NHTSA reports that there has never been a failure over the road of steel or steel composite CNG tanks during the 25 years that they have been in use. In early 1994, two failures of aluminum composite fully wrapped CNG containers occurred. Both failures, one in Minnesota and the other in California, involved GMC Sierra pick-up trucks — minor injuries to the vehicle operator were reported in one instance and no injuries in the other. Investigation of these two CNG tank failures pinpointed the cause to acid-induced stress corrosion cracking of the fiberglass overwrap on the aluminum tank — in both cases the pick-up trucks were used to transport routinely lead-acid batteries that would occasionally leak sulfuric acid solution onto the CNG tanks. These two incidents have prompted extensive technical evaluations of CNG tank specifications and designs that would further enhance the quality of the CNG storage option — carbon, unlike fiberglass, steel or aluminum does not degrade in the presence of acids and other commonly encountered agents.

Canadian tests have found that aluminum cylinders could withstand 40,000 cycles before fatigue failure and steel cylinders could withstand anywhere between 40,000 and 160,000 cycles. The recently introduced all composite cylinders have a minimum lifespan in excess of 26,000 cycles. At a rate of one cycle per day, i.e., daily filling/emptying, the all composite cylinders will last for more than 70 years, the aluminum/composite cylinders will last for 110 years and the steel/composite ones even longer.

It should be also mentioned that the use of composite materials such as fiberglass or carbon fibers has the added advantage of diminishing the violence of an explosion in the event of a catastrophic failure of the tank. These two composites tend to absorb the expanding gas energy and disintegrate by fracture into very small pieces, unlike metals which absorb less energy in deformation by buckling with the remainder of the gas expansion energy going into the kinetic energy of large pieces[14]. Finally, after ten years in service of more than 50,000 CNG cylinders in Canada, no incident of internal corrosion has ever been found. Thus, concerns of CNG cylinder corrosion due to any minute amounts of moisture and sulfur compounds that may still be left in the natural gas after purification have been proven to be unfounded. Clearly, the CNG storage technology on-board vehicles is already well established and continues to evolve into even better products.

LIQUEFIED NATURAL GAS

The maximum volumetric energy density of natural gas as an automotive fuel can be obtained when it attains a liquid state. This fuel then is classified as liquefied natural gas (LNG). The density of LNG is 3.5 lb/gal. The heating value of LNG is 23,450 BTU/lb (same as for CNG), while the energy density is 89,000 BTU/gal. However, the liquefaction of natural gas requires cryogenic temperatures as Table 4-3 indicates[15][16]. Methane has the lowest boiling temperature of all hydrocarbons. It is interesting to note that ethane, propane and carbon dioxide can be liquefied at room temperature by elevated pressure only. This is not true, however, for methane and nitrogen at any pressure. While the liquefaction process can separate the different constituents of natural gas as each one will condense at its particular boiling temperature, in practice it is less expensive to remove certain components prior to the liquefaction by selective absorption. These components include carbon dioxide as well as water and sulfur compounds. Nitrogen has an even lower boiling point than methane and would therefore never condense. Because of the liquefaction process involved in the production of LNG, the latter can be free of even very small concentrations of impurities such as water, carbon dioxide and hydrogen sulfide, which typically occur in concentrations of 1 ppm, 50 to 150 ppm and 3 ppm or less, respectively, in CNG.

The minimum energy (theoretical) for methane liquefaction is about 390 BTU/lb and the actual energy may vary from 800 to 1200 BTU/lb, depending on the efficiency of the liquefaction plant[17]. Thus, the liquefaction process consumes about 4 to 5 % of the fuel energy content.

The LNG fuel must be stored at -256°F and consequently it requires a cryogenic tank. Heat transfer from the surroundings to the LNG fuel

TABLE 4-3. Approximate Boiling Points (°F) of Major Natural Gas Constituents

Pressure (psi)	14.7	50	100	250	500
Methane	-254	-227	-207	-134	-96
Ethane	-132	-81	-47	+59	—
Propane	-51	+10	+54	—	—
Nitrogen	-321	-297	-281	-234	-207
Carbon Dioxide	-110	-80	-58	+52	—

can take place through all the three modes of heat transfer, i.e., conduction, convection and radiation. The ideal means of limiting heat transfer, therefore, is to surround the cryogenic fluid (LNG) with a vacuum through which neither conduction nor convection can take place. Moreover, radiant heat transfer can be reduced by providing reflecting surfaces to thermal radiation. This is the so-called Dewar vessel whose inexpensive version is familiar to everybody as a "thermos bottle".

Practical LNG tanks for vehicles consist of an inner wall made of 5% nickel stainless steel and an exterior wall made of carbon steel. The space between the two walls, rather than being entirely vacuum, is filled with perlite, a powder insulating material which is prepared by firing certain minerals such as silica, diatomaceous earth, magnesia or asbestos. However, the perlite space is evacuated to 1 mm Hg (Mercury) or less (the atmospheric pressure is 760 mm Hg or 14.7 psi), which is an easy to maintain vacuum. The perlite is the least expensive of cryogenic insulating materials and offers in addition support between the two walls for the containment of mechanical forces. A pressure relief valve lets LNG vapors escape to the atmosphere. Typical evaporation losses from a vehicular LNG tank are small amounting to about 10% over a period of 72 hours. A schematic of a typical vehicular LNG tank with all its controls is shown in Figure 4-6[18]. It is worth noting in Figure 4-6 that an engine coolant heat exchanger is employed to vapor-

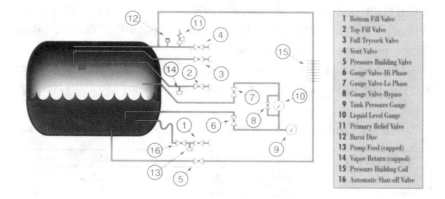

FIGURE 4-6. Typical Horizontal Automotive LNG Fuel Tank with Required Accessories. Stainless Steel Inner and Outer Vessels, Steel and Brass Tubing and Valves, Standby Time 7 Days Minimum (Courtesy MVE, Bloomington, MN).

ize the liquid fuel before it is supplied to the engine. The significant latent heat of vaporization of liquid methane (219 BTU/lb) can thus reduce the size of the traditional engine cooling system.

The volume (gross) of a typical vehicular LNG tank (18 gal or 68 liter) is about 40% larger than the volume of a gasoline tank (13 gal or 50 liter) with the same energy content (1.5 million BTU). Commercially available automotive LNG tanks range in volume from 18 gal (16.2 gal net) to 88 gal (79.2 gal net); have a diameter ranging from 12 inches to 20 inches and a respective length ranging from 50 inches to 96 inches; weigh empty between 100 lb and 350 lb and full 156.7 lb and 627.2 lb, respectively; and all have a working pressure of 70 psi and a maximum allowed pressure of 235 psi. All LNG automotive tanks are designed, constructed and tested according to stringent US Department of Transportation Standards (DOT 4L200). The price of the nominal 18 gallon LNG tank is currently $1875 and can be expected to be somewhat reduced with an increased volume of production.

Refuelling facilities for LNG have to be centralized akin to the present day gasoline and diesel fuel stations. While it is very unlikely that LNG will become the fuel of choice for passenger cars, vans and light trucks, the use of LNG to fuel heavy trucks is very possible [19]. The use of LNG fuel in these instances, not only displaces diesel fuel for a reduced pollution from the exhaust gases, but it also provides the opportunity to refrigerate perishable cargo by first evaporating the fuel through a heat exchanger. At least two major trucking companies, Roadway Express of Akron, OH and Overnite Transportation Co of Richmond, VA are operating some of their trucks on LNG fuel[20]. Depending on the availability of cleaner burning, low-sulfur diesel fuel starting in 1994 and the performance of the trucks running currently on LNG, there could be an increased use of this fuel in limited applications by the end of the century. Another related application of LNG is in the displacement of diesel fuel in locomotives. As of 1994, trials were underway to test the performance of LNG fueled locomotives.

The ideal use of LNG as a fuel, however, is not so much in surface transport as it is in aviation. The higher heating value per unit weight (some 13% more compared to jet fuels), the very low temperature, and the high latent heat of vaporization of LNG offer distinct advantages in air transport[18]. The higher energy density per unit weight of LNG can be utilized to increase either the range of an aircraft or its carrying capacity. The low temperature and high latent heat of vaporization of LNG can be used to cool turbine blade tips and combustor cans, thereby doubling the turbine inlet temperature from the present 1500°F to 3000°F. This temperature increase would lead to a more than triple the power output of the engine at current compression ratios of 10:1. A simultaneous increase in compression ratio to 25:1 will quadrupled the engine power per unit mass of intake air and will increase the efficiency by at least 50%. Moreover, the LNG fuel can circulate in thermally critical parts of the aircraft surface such as the nose, wings and vertical stabilizers to minimize the effect of heat generation due to skin friction, particularly in hypersonic (above Mach 5 speed, i.e., five times the speed of sound) flight.

The alleged Mach 6 reconnaissance aircraft referred to by many as Aurora and built for the US Air Force since the mid 1980s is presumably powered by liquid methane[21]. Moreover, the under development National Aerospace Plane since the late 1980s, albeit at a much lower pace than the Aurora, is also designed to be fueled with liquid methane [21][22]. It is interesting to note that the replacement of the 1.4 million bbl/d of jet fuel currently used in commercial aviation by LNG or liquid methane with the resulting 50% higher fuel efficiency will require some 2.1 trillion scf of natural gas per year including a 10% energy penalty for the required liquefaction energy and evaporative losses.

ADSORBED NATURAL GAS

The desire to use natural gas as automotive fuel at reduced pressures for both safety and compression cost reasons, but without compromising the range of the vehicle, has led to the investigation of the possibility of enhancing on-board storage with the aid of adsorbents. An adsorbent, which is typically a microporous solid, effectively condenses the gas molecules within the pore structure by means of surface-gas interactions. Natural gas stored ideally in an adsorbent material will have a density intermediate between that of the liquid (LNG) and the high pressure gas (3000 psi CNG). Thus, adsorbed natural gas (ANG) will have a very high energy density (per unit volume) without the need

of low temperatures or the need of high pressure tanks. While in principle this is an ideal storage scheme for natural gas as an automotive fuel,
one has to find or develop the right adsorbent material. Figure 4-7a
shows the presently attainable ANG volumetric energy densities and
compares them with CNG volumetric energy densities at different pressures[22].

At the present time activated carbon appears to be the adsorbent
with the greatest potential for storing natural gas at pressures not to

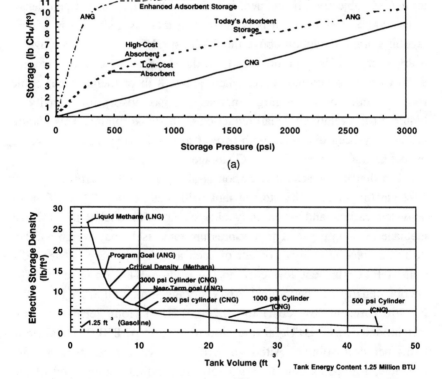

FIGURE 4-7. Comparison of ANG and CNG as Automotive Fuel: (a) Effective
Storage Density vs. Storage Pressure; (b) Effective Storage Density vs. Tank Volume
for a Fixed Energy Content.

exceed 500 psi. The present ANG effective storage density with inexpensive activated carbon adsorbent (less than $4 per lb) is about 4 lb of methane per cubic foot of storage volume. This lower density is equivalent to the energy density of 1500 psi CNG. The near term goal of the ANG effort has been to reach an effective (deliverable) storage of 6 lb of methane per cf corresponding to an equivalent energy density of 2400 psi CNG. Apparently this goal has already been reached, although it will not be known whether the cost goal of activated carbon can be attained until a sizeable production takes place[23].

The long term goal is to reach an effective storage of 12 lb of methane per cubic foot of storage. As Figure 4-7b indicates, the long term ANG objective, if attained, will exceed the equivalent CNG density at 4000 psi. However, it is not clear that there is a significant advantage in storage reduction above the 3000 psi CNG equivalent storage or 8 lb per cf. This is quite obvious from the slope of the effective storage density vs. tank volume curve, where above 8 lb of methane per cubic foot of tank volume a large increase in gas adsorption density is required for a relatively small reduction in the tank volume. This feature has already been discussed with respect to CNG storage. As one would expect, it characterizes also ANG storage.

The density of activated carbon is about 15 to 20 lb/ft^3. A typical 13.2 gal (50 liter) ANG storage tank will thus contain 27 to 36 lb of activated carbon and when fully charged an additional 9 to 21 lb of methane or natural gas. The low pressure tank itself may weigh another 20 to 25 lb. The energy content of such a tank will vary between 0.2 million BTU (present low cost) to 0.6 million BTU (long term). The energy density of the typical ANG storage tank will then be: 3400 BTU/lb (present low cost) to 10,200 BTU/lb (long term) per unit weight; and 15,900 BTU/gal (present low cost) to 37,850 BTU/gal (long term) per unit volume. Although ANG storage cost numbers are not available, it appears that a 13 gal (50 liter) cylinder comprised of the present low cost carbon and containing about 200 scf of natural gas will cost under $250 ($125 container and $125 activated carbon). It remains to be seen whether activated carbon with the requisite higher adsorptivity for methane can be developed at a competitive cost with the compressed natural gas alternative.

WHAT IS THE PREFERRED STORAGE?

It is apparent that several technologies are competing at the present time with regard to the on-board the vehicle storage of natural gas. This is to be expected, however, any time a paradigm shift occurs. In this instance, the paradigm shift refers of course to the substitution of gasoline and diesel by natural gas as the fuel of choice for motor vehicles. In fact, it is rather remarkable that only five different technologies (three CNG, LNG and ANG) are competing for the preferred storage of natural gas on-board vehicles. Table 4-4 summarizes once more the salient characteristics of these five technologies. For comparison, gasoline, ethanol and methanol are also included in the same table.

The comparison of the different natural gas storage technologies amongst themselves and to the conventional storage of liquid fuels is performed on an equal energy basis storage capacity for each fuel system. The basis of comparison is a 12 to 13 gallon gasoline tank, which is typical of most mid-size passenger cars. For the natural gas fuel, the reduced on-board storage is also examined. This reduced on-board storage implies "a vehicle range of about 200 miles by design". As it was mentioned earlier, such an option becomes feasible because of the possibility of home or work refueling with natural gas. Such an option is not

TABLE 4-4. Comparison of Different Fuel Storage Systems On-Board a Vehicle

Fuel Storage System Technology	Volume (gal)	Weight[1] (lb)	Energy (10^3 BTU)	Cost[2] ($)	Range[3] (mi)
Motor Gasoline	12.4	87	1,415	25	332
Ethanol (E100)	18.8	139	1,410	40	331
Methanol (M100)	25.2	186	1,415	50	332
CNG Steel/Comp.[4]	39.6	332	1,420	1545	333
CNG Alum/Comp.[4]	40.3	293	1,435	1695	337
CNG All Composite[4]	39.6	143	1,415	2050	332
LNG[4]	18.0	157	1,435	1875	337
ANG[5]	40.0	200	1,400	?	329

1. Weight includes fuel.
2. Cost of storage only, exclusive of fuel, in 1993 dollars.
3. Assumes a vehicle fuel use of 4260 BTU/mi which is equivalent to a fuel efficiency of 27 mpg.
4. Nearest available commercial size tank(s).
5. Estimated as no commercial systems exist.

possible for gasoline, ethanol and methanol mainly for safety reasons as well as practical distribution problems. The same statement is also true for LNG because of safety reasons and the impractical nature of small scale liquefaction.

The implication of a "200 mile range by design for natural gas vehicles" is that the weight as well as the cost of fuel storage are reduced by about 33 percent. Table 4-5 restates the results of Table 4-4, but with the reduced vehicle range for natural gas. Besides passenger cars, light trucks and vans are also included. Because of the lower fuel efficiency of the latter of 18 to 20 mpg versus 27 mpg for the passenger cars a 30 to 35% more fuel storage is required for the light trucks and vans. Incidentally, the 27 mpg fuel efficiency used as a benchmark in this analysis has been selected because eventually this will be the average fuel efficiency of all passenger cars sold in the country according to the CAFE standards. However, passenger cars with fuel efficiencies of 20 mpg (full size) and 34 mpg (compact size) have also been included for completion.

Given that the fuel efficiency of a natural gas vehicle can be increased by as much as 15% with a higher engine compression ratio, one must take advantage of this feature to reduce the weight and cost of storage as well. This is also reflected in Table 4-5 by supplying the requisite storage so as to maintain the vehicle range at about 200 miles. Finally, Table 4-5 considers only CNG because LNG as well as ethanol and methanol will not be available at home or work and ANG is not yet commercially available. The calculations in Table 4-5 make use of available sizes CNG tanks for the various technologies that result in a vehicle range in the vicinity of the 200 mile design range. This is deemed more appropriate in order to give actual storage costs, rather than try to calculate the size storage required to meet exactly the range requirement.

A fundamental conclusion emerges from the analysis given in Table 4-5. The bigger less efficient vehicles such as full size passenger cars, trucks and vans would require typically three 13-gallon (50 liter) tanks. The medium size passenger cars would require typically two such tanks, and the compact and smaller passenger cars would be able to get by even with one 13-gallon tank. The increase in the compression ratio of

TABLE 4-5. Comparison of Required Compressed Natural Gas Storage On-Board Passenger Cars, Trucks and Vans with a "200 Mile Range by Design" Versus the Respective Standard Gasoline Vehicles

Fuel Storage System	Volume (gal)	Weight[1] (lb)	Energy (10^3 BTU)	Price[2] ($)	Range (mi)
A. Medium Size Passenger Car					
Gasoline 27 mpg					
Motor Gasoline	13.0	92	1,490	35	350
Natural Gas-Regular Compression Engine					
CNG Steel/Comp.[4]	26.4	221	948	1030	190
CNG Alum/Comp.[4]	26.8	196	956	1130	191
CNG All Composite[4]	26.4	96	948	1370	190
Natural Gas-High Compression Engine[3]					
CNG Steel/Comp.[4]	26.4	221	948	1030	218
CNG Alum/Comp.[4]	26.8	196	956	1130	220
CNG All Composite[4]	26.4	96	948	1370	218
B. Full Size Passenger Car, Light Truck, Mini Van					
Gasoline 20 mpg					
Motor Gasoline	17.6	120	2,015	35	350
Natural Gas-Regular Compression Engine					
CNG Steel/Comp.[4]	32.8	285	1,180	1545	205
CNG Alum/Comp.[4]	31.3	220	1,115	1320	194
CNG All Composite[4]	39.6	143	1,415	2055	246
Natural Gas-High Compression Engine[3]					
CNG Steel/Comp.[4]	26.4	221	948	1030	190
CNG Alum/Comp.[4]	26.8	196	956	1130	191
CNG All Composite[4]	26.4	96	948	1350	190
C. Compact Size Passenger Car					
Gasoline 34 mpg					
Motor Gasoline	10.0	71	1,150	20	340
Natural Gas-Regular Compression Engine					
CNG Steel/Comp.[4]	26.4	221	948	1030	239
CNG Alum/Comp.[4]	26.8	196	956	1130	240
CNG All Composite[4]	26.4	96	948	1350	239
Natural Gas-High Compression Engine[3]					
CNG Steel/Comp.[4]	13.2	111	474	515	161
CNG Alum/Comp.[4]	13.4	98	478	565	162
CNG All Composite[4]	13.2	48	474	685	161

1. Weight includes fuel. 2. Present price of storage tank(s) only, exclusive of fuel, in 1993 dollars. Economies of scale, particularly with regard to the all-composite tanks, can easily reduce these costs by a factor of two in the long run. An increase, either voluntary or mandatory, in the CAFE standard to 40 mpg for passenger cars and accordingly for other light-weight vehicles will also reduce the cost of storage to the consumer to about 2/3rds of that shown. 3. Assumes a 14:1 compression ratio and a 15% increase in vehicle fuel efficiency. 4. Nearest available commercial size tank(s).

the engine with the attendant increase in fuel efficiency will help in several instances to reduce on-board storage substantially. From a cost benefit point of view, it is much less expensive to increase the compression ratio of the engine than add more CNG fuel storage to the vehicle.

The underlying premise in all of the preceding discussion is of course the ability to refuel one's car at home or at work instead of or in addition to a public station. As it will be demonstrated in the next and subsequent chapters, this is a very realistic option for natural gas vehicles both technically and economically. The major advantage of natural gas as compared to all other automotive fuels is that it is or can be made available in a decentralized fashion at every home and business. Compressing natural gas to 3,000 psi for CNG or 500 psi for ANG is already a proven technology.

On the other hand, producing LNG in a decentralized fashion, although technically possible, it is prohibitively expensive and may not be desirable, in any case, for safety reasons. The flammability and explosion potential of LNG is not worse than that of gasoline. However, the fact that LNG is a cryogenic liquid and tends to evaporate readily may make it prone to more accidents unless stringent handling procedures are always followed carefully. It is unrealistic to expect every user to be able to adhere to these safety requirements all the time. Moreover, LNG tanks will lose a certain percentage of their content, no matter how well insulated they are. This introduces a significant degree of inefficiency, as much as 10% of the natural gas fuel vented into the air. Thus, LNG is more suited for transportation applications where strict schedules of operation are an integral part of the system. Airlines, railways and long distance trucking companies are thus ideally suited candidates for LNG use from both the safety aspect as well as the minimization of venting (evaporation) losses.

Of the remaining two natural gas fuel storage systems, ANG has not been proven yet to be economical at natural gas densities that will make it desirable for automotive applications. The CNG fuel storage system is thus the only practical one at this time. It is adequate in terms of on-board storage, particularly in view of the flexibility of natural gas delivery in a decentralized fashion. The relatively higher cost of storage can be reduced through proper design of the vehicle range in conjunction with the aforementioned natural gas availability at home and work-place as well as improvements in the vehicle fuel efficiency including engine efficiency by increased compression.

Finally, of the three competing CNG storage technologies, aluminum has some advantage in weight over steel. However, the all composite CNG storage tank is clearly the CNG tank of choice because of the light weight associated with it, which is comparable with the present gasoline system. The weight difference of about 100 lb between aluminum-composite and all-composite tanks represents 3 to 5% of vehicle weight. This extra weight of aluminum-composite tanks will result in an almost 2 to 3% percent reduction in the fuel efficiency of a vehicle (weight is the dominant factor in fuel efficiency in city driving and up to 50 mph freeway driving). Moreover, the all-composite (carbon fiber) pressurized tank represents an added degree of safety in the event of a tank catastrophic failure as it will contain the violence of the exploding gas with minimal injury or damage.

It is clear that the 3,000 to 3,600 psi CNG fuel on-board motor vehicles is the system of choice in terms of natural gas as a transportation fuel. It is also clear that the all composite CNG storage tank is the technology of choice. The optimization of the on-board the vehicle CNG storage, which is possible because of the decentralized availability of natural gas, can lead to a significant reduction in the incremental cost of the natural gas vehicles in addition to not taking-up as much the extra vehicle space for the natural gas fuel tanks.

REFERENCES

1. J. R. Dabels, private communication, Dabels & Associates, Flint, MI, 1993.

2. L. Sharn, "We're Motoring More and More", USA Today, p.5A, October 18, 1991.

3. H. J. Schwartz, "The Computer Simulation of Automobile Use Patterns for Defining Battery Requirements for Electric Cars", NASA Technical Memorandum TM-X-71900, Lewis Research Center, Cleveland, OH, 1976.

4. "American National Standard for Basic Requirements for Compressed Natural Gas Vehicles (NGV) Fuel Containers", ANSI/AGA Report NGV2-1992, prepared by the American Gas Association (AGA) Laboratories, Cleveland, OH on behalf of the Natural Gas Vehicle Coalition (NGVC), Arlington, VA and approved by the American National Standards Institute (ANSI) on August 6, 1992.

5. R. J. Roark and W. C. Young, Formulas for Stress and Strain, 5th ed., pp. 448-451, McGraw-Hill Company, New York, NY, 1975.

6. "NGV Fuel Cylinders-Lightweight Fiber-Reinforced Composite Steel Cylinders for Use in Passenger Cars, Buses, Light Trucks, Vans, Fleet Vehicles and Lift Trucks", Pressed Steel Tank Co., Inc., Milwaukee, WI, 1992.

7. "Composite-Reinforced Aluminum Natural Gas Vehicle Fuel Cylinders-Cylinder Sizes, Weights & Capacities", CNG Cylinder Company, Inc., Long Beach, CA, 1992.

8. H. McCann, "NGV's – Natural Gas Nears Lead In Alternative Fuel Race", WARD'S Auto World, v. 29, no 6, pp. 32-37, June 1993.

9. "LiteRiderTM – Ultra Lightweight NGV Cylinders", EDO Corporation Energy Division, College Point, NY, 1993.

10. J. C. Wilson, S. C. Munchak, M. W. Smith, K. J. Tan, "Alternative-Fuel Vehicles for the Department of the Navy", CRM-92-91, Center for Naval Analyses, Alexandria, VA, 1992.

11. M. W. Zemansky, Heat and Thermodynamics, 3rd ed., Ch. VI: Ideal Gases, pp. 112-138, McGraw-Hill Book Company, Inc., New York, NY, 1951.

12. D. L. Katz, D. Cornell, R. Kobayashi, F. H. Poettmann, J. A. Vary, J. R. Elenbaas, C. H. Weinaug, Handbook of Natural Gas Engineering, McGraw-Hill Book Company, Inc., New York, NY, 1959.

13. US DOT National Highway Traffic Safety Administration , "Federal Motor Vehicle Safety Standards : Fuel System Integrity of Compressed Natural Gas Vehicles", Final Rule, Federal Register, v. 59, no. 79, pp. 19648-19660, April 25, 1994.

14. P. H. Thornton and P. J. Edwards, "Energy Absorption in Composite Tubes", *J. Composite Materials*, v. 16, pp. 521-545, 1982.

15. W.L. Lon, Liquefied Natural Gas, p. 37, John Wiley & Sons, New York, NY, 1974.

16. R. E. Bolz, G. L. Tuve (eds.), CRC Handbook of Tables for Applied Engineering Science, pp. 54-55, 2nd Ed., CRC Press, Boca Raton, FL, 1976.

17. W.L. Lon, *loc. cit.,* p. 46.

18. Minnesota Valley Engineering, Inc., "Let's Clear the Air about LNG : Natural Gas Fuel for the Long Haul", Bloomington, MN, 1993.

19. W.L. Lon, *loc. cit.,* pp. 104-108.

20. P. Richards, "Riding the Methane Train', *Chilton's Automotive Industries*, v. 173, no. 6, p. 198, 1993.

21. S. J. Mraz, "New Eye In The Sky?", *Machine Design*, pp. 22-28, June 25, 1993.

22. D. L. Greene,"Energy Efficiency Improvement Potential of Commercial Aircraft", Ann. Rev. Energy Environ., v. 17, pp. 537-573, Annual Reviews, Inc., Palo Alto, CA, 1992.

23. W. E. BeVier, J. T. Mullhaupt, F. Novato, I. C. Lewis, R. E. Coleman, "Adsorbent-Enhanced Methane Storage for Alternative Fuel Powered Vehicles", SAE Technical Paper Series 891638, Warrendale, PA, 1989.

24. J. Arnold, private communication, Michigan Consolidated Gas Co., Detroit, MI, 1993.

Chapter 5

Infrastructure for Natural Gas Vehicles

THE EVOLUTION OF THE AUTOMOBILE INFRASTRUCTURE

The transformation of America into an automotive culture occurred with extraordinary rapidity after the end of Word War I. In a period of 11 years the automobile registrations in the US zoomed from 8 million vehicles in 1919 to almost 27 million in 1929. Each of these vehicles was driven farther and farther each year — from an average of 4,500 miles per vehicle in 1919 to an average of 7,500 miles in 1929. And each of those cars was powered with gasoline. The automobile was transforming the face of America and in the process the nature of the oil industry as well.

In thousands of towns across the country at the beginning of the decade of the 1920s a single traffic officer at the intersection of the main traffic thoroughfare was sufficient to control traffic. By the end of the same decade the scenery was totally transformed: red and green traffic lights, blinkers, one-way streets, boulevard stops, stringent parking ordinances, continuous flow of traffic along the main arteries on Saturday and Sunday afternoon[1]. The change in the orientation of the oil industry was no less dramatic. Oil demand in the US more than doubled between 1919 and 1929 from a little over 1 million bbl/d to almost 2.6 million bbl/d. The share of oil in the country's energy consumption rose from 10% to 25% in the same period — today, more than 60 years later oil accounts for about 35% of the energy consumption.

The growth of gasoline production in the 1920s was even more spectacular as it witnessed a larger than a fourfold increase. Gasoline and fuel oil accounted together for fully 85% of the total oil consumption in 1929. But while the towns were changing with the invasion of the automobile and the oil industry was adjusting to the new fuel demands, a most momentous development was taking place. The emergence and proliferation of a facility dedicated to the new fuel and the new way of life: the drive-in gasoline station. The number of drive-in gasoline stations had grown from about 12,000 in 1921 to about 143,000 in 1929. The automobile refueling infrastructure had finally come of age.

Before the 1920s most gasoline was sold primarily at garages as well as grocery stores, general stores, hardware stores and other retail establishments. Gasoline was kept in cans or other containers under the counter or out in the back of the store. The product carried no name and the customer could not be sure of the quality of the gasoline, i.e., whether gasoline had been adulterated with cheaper naphtha or kerosene. Moreover, such a distribution system was cumbersome and slow. Some gasoline retailers had experimented with the idea of delivering fuel from home to home. However, this practice never caught on partly because the gasoline wagons delivering the fuel tended to explode frequently. There had to be a better way and it was the drive-in station.

The first drive-in gasoline station was built by the Automobile Gasoline Company in St. Louis, Missouri in 1907. This and subsequent stations were, however, a far cry from the drive-in gasoline station everybody is accustomed to today. A small tin shack housed a couple of barrels of gasoline. Outside, one or two old hot-water tanks were set on high brackets. A garden hose attached to each of these tanks would deliver gasoline to the vehicle tank by gravity. Typically, the facility would be accessible to the main road via an unpaved path. It would take another decade or so before the pumps, metering schemes and dispensing equipment would be developed and become part of the drive-in station, which now consisted of a standard structure with huge signs, restroom facilities, canopies, landscaped grounds, and paved entrances.

These standardized gasoline stations were pioneered by Shell and prolif-
erated at an astonishing rate across the nation.

By the late 1920s, these stations were making money not only from
gasoline sales but also from what were called "TBA" — tires, batteries,
and accessories. A new type of pump, one in which the gasoline was
forced into a glass bowl atop the pump before it flowed through the hose
into the fuel tank of a car, became the standard pump across the nation.
The customer would see the gasoline and would feel reassured of the
quality of the product being purchased. As the gasoline stations spread,
the competition heated up. Gasoline sold at each station had to be adver-
tised with regard to its origin in order to attract customers. The huge
signs atop stations became the symbols of the new age. Texaco's star,
Shell's scallop shell, Sun's radiant diamond, Union's "76", Phillip's "66",
Socony's flying red horse, Gulf's orange disc, Standard of Indiana's red
crown, Sinclair's brontosaurus, Standard of New Jersey's red, white and
blue were all developed as trademarks in order to assure national brand
identification and provide the drivers with a feeling of familiarity, confidence, security and even belonging as they crisscrossed America.

Customers were courted with many amenities and attractions.
Checking and replenishing, if necessary, tire air, radiator water and
engine oil was a gratuity rendered to the public free of charge by the
station attendants. The handing out of free oil company road maps of
the region of each station started out as an advertising idea in 1914
when Gulf was opening its first gasoline station in Pittsburgh,
Pennsylvania. It caught on rapidly with the public and in the 1920s
became an integral part of the service at a gasoline station.

The phenomenal growth of the drive-in gasoline station in the
1920s changed totally the make-up of gasoline retailers in a period of
ten years. In 1920, no more than 100,000 establishments sold gasoline;
fully half of them were grocery stores, general stores and hardware
stores, the other half being garages with a small number of gasoline stations. In 1929 the number of gasoline retail establishments had grown to
300,000. Almost all of them were garages and gasoline stations. The
Great Depression of the 1930s and World War II led to a decline of
automobile registrations as well as automobile production. However,
cars on the road were older and required more maintenance to keep

going. The drive-in gasoline stations would thus expand the types of services offered to include automotive repair for a fee. After World War II, sales and registration of automobiles would increase rapidly and so the need for gasoline drive-in service stations.

By 1972, the number of gasoline service stations had reached its peak of some 226,500 establishments nationwide out of more than 300,000 motor fuel retail outlets[3]. Since then a rapid decline in the number of gasoline service stations has ensued with only 107,000 left as of 1991 and a decline rate of more than 1% per year in recent times. Today, there are about 202,000 gasoline and diesel fuel retail outlets in the United States declining in number annually and with a very different composition mix than two decades ago[4]. Pumper stations, a new type of gasoline retail outlet averaging a 50% higher volume of gasoline sales per station than service stations, and convenience stores are picking up some of the service station lost business. Pumper stations account for almost 55% of the volume of gasoline sold. Convenience and other stores approach a 30 % market penetration, but account for a little over 10% of the volume. The gasoline sales figures for service stations show an economizing trend to increase volume per station as the number of these stations decreases. Finally, pumper stations include the public and private commercial fleet owned refueling facilities.

The reduction in the profit margins of oil companies has led to the elimination of most of the free amenities enjoyed by customers in previous decades. Pumping of gasoline as well as checking air, water and oil cost anywhere between $0.20 to $0.30 per gallon of gasoline or about 20% of the fuel price. Maps are no longer free either. Thus, most customers — 86% in 1992 up from 22% in 1975 — pump their own gasoline. They also visit the station less frequently as the range of cars has increased in recent decades. Finally, several gasoline stations in the cities — built several decades ago when plenty of land was available at a low price — have a prime location, which is sought after for commercial building development. Thus, more and more of such stations are closing down and the land is sold for more profitable developments.

It is evident that the era of the drive-in gasoline station is undergoing a major transition. Although the drive-in station will not disappear totally, it will be replaced and augmented by a more flexible and a more efficient fuel distribution system. This new fuel distribution system will come about as the result of the replacement of gasoline and diesel as motor fuels with natural gas. Hence, the changes with the regard to the automobile infrastructure set in motion some two decades ago, when America became aware for the first time of its heavy dependency on imported oil, are compatible with the introduction of natural gas as the major automotive fuel of the future.

NATURAL GAS FUEL DISTRIBUTION SYSTEM

An extensive network of natural gas pipelines, comprising 280,000 miles, already crisscrosses the nation and connects all States except Alaska, Hawaii and Vermont[5][6]. This is the interstate natural gas pipe line grid which in essence transports natural gas from the producing locations to the consuming areas of the country. As Figure 5-1 shows schematically, natural gas flows primarily from Texas, Louisiana and off-shore the Gulf of Mexico and to a lesser extent form New Mexico and Oklahoma to the northeast, midwest and west.

Two states, Texas and Louisiana, are major interstate natural gas exporters. Two other states, New Mexico and Oklahoma, are intermedi-

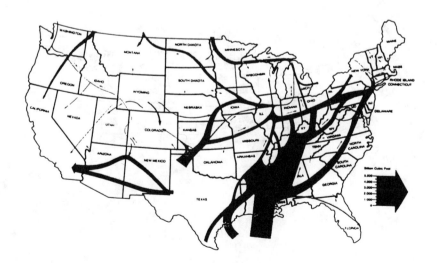

FIGURE 5-1. Principal Interstate Natural Gas Flow Summary (Source: EIA, US DOE).

ate interstate natural gas exporters. Another seven states, Kansas, Colorado, Utah, Montana, North Dakota, West Virginia and Wyoming are smaller natural gas exporters. Alaska has also a huge, but totally undeveloped, potential for exporting natural gas. Figure 5-2 shows the marketed production of natural gas as well as the delivered natural gas

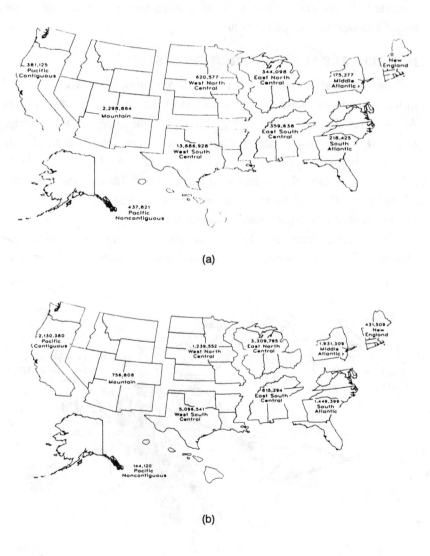

(a)

(b)

FIGURE 5-2. Natural Gas (million scf per year) by Census Division in 1991: (a) Marketed Production; (b) Delivery to Consumers (Source: Energy Information Administration, US DOE).

by census division areas in 1991. It is worth noting that all census division areas produce natural gas with the exception of the New England division, even though only two census division areas produce more than they consume. In fact as of 1991, 31 out of the 50 (or almost 2 out of 3) states in the US produce natural gas[6].

Natural gas extracted from producing wells is transported initially by the field and gathering pipeline system, which had a length of 89,000 miles in 1990, to processing plants, where natural gas liquids are extracted along with non-hydrocarbon gases and other impurities[6]. The processed "dry" natural gas begins then its journey through the interstate pipeline system. Figure 5-3 shows the interstate natural gas movement for all 50 states as of 1991. It is interesting to note the magnitude and complexity of movement from state to state.

The same Figure 5-3 shows also the movement of natural gas across national boundaries. Table 5-1 summarizes the magnitude of imports and exports of natural gas to and from the US[8]. Notice that transport of natural gas from/to Canada and Mexico takes place via pipelines, while the transport of natural gas from Algeria and to Japan takes place in the form of LNG in specially designed LNG tanker ships. Thus natural gas is very different than crude oil in terms of imports and exports. It can be readily imported from, and exported to countries having common land boundaries with the US via pipeline. This limits the possibility of pipeline transport to only Canada and Mexico. On the other hand, trans-

TABLE 5-1. Summary of US Natural Gas Imports and Exports in the Period from 1987 to 1991 (billion scf/y)

Year	1987	1988	1989	1990	1991
Imports					
Canada (pipeline)	993	1276	1339	1448	1710
Algeria (LNG)	0	17	42	84	64
Total	993	1293	1381	1532	1784
Exports					
Canada (pipeline)	3	20	38	17	15
Mexico (pipeline)	2	2	17	16	60
Japan (LNG)	49	52	51	53	54
Total	54	74	106	86	129

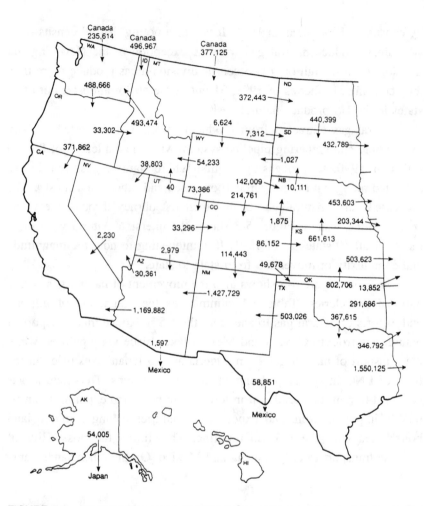

FIGURE 5-3. Interstate Movement of Natural Gas (million scf per day) in the United States in 1991 (Source: EIA, US DOE).

port of natural gas from other continents such as Africa or Asia requires liquefaction and shipping in special LNG tankers. Moreover, special terminal facilities are required to receive LNG. Two such facilities are currently operational in the US, one in Everett, MA and the other in Lake Charles, LA. Consequently, it is unlikely that large quantities of natural gas will be imported to or exported from the US from or to countries other than Canada and Mexico. Incidentally, both of these countries have substantial natural gas resources. Imports from Canada are expect-

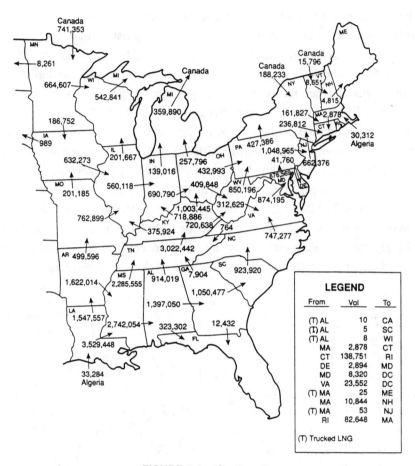

FIGURE 5-3. (Continued)

ed to level at about 2 trillion scf/y within the next few years. Imports to Mexico are the result of new environmental regulations in that country adopted in 1991 and the fact that the infrastructure is lacking to bring gas produced in Mexico to the northern region of it where it is needed.

Returning to the domestic scene, it should be noted that in recent years a significant activity is taking place in expanding the interstate pipeline system. In 1991 alone some 2,000 miles of additional interstate pipeline were placed into use. The boom in interstate pipeline construction is expected to continue over the next 3 to 4 years. The objective of the expanding interstate pipeline grid is to reach new natural gas markets as well as to provide additional capacity to existing markets.

The average total interstate movement of natural gas in the US is about 50 billion scf per day. The daily average interstate movement of natural gas between the six major geographical regions in the country is shown in Figure 5-4 and is summarized in Table 5-2[9]. The total capacity of the interstate pipeline system in the country was 74 billion scf per day in 1990 with an additional 16 billion scf per day planned to be built in the 1990s. Of this planned total some 4.7 billion scf per day capacity was already in place as of March 1992. The maximum interstate demand was 75 billion scf per day in 1990 or little more than the interstate system capacity. However, the fact that the maximum demand slightly exceeds the system capacity is of no concern as natural gas is stored within each region during periods of lesser demand to supple-

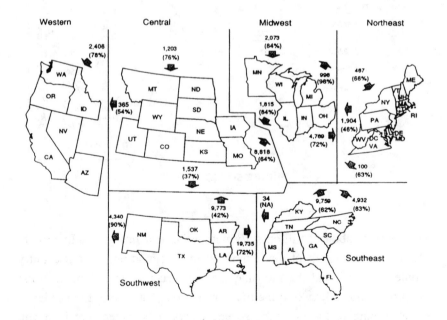

FIGURE 5-4. Interstate Natural Gas Pipeline Capacity (million scf per day) To and From Major Federal Regions and Average Utilization Rates in 1990 (Source: EIA, US DOE).

TABLE 5-2. Regional Summary of Daily Current and Planned Capacity, Maximum Demand and Interstate Movement of Natural Gas in the US as of 1990

Region	Capacity 1990[1] Enter (10^9 scf/d)	Exit	Planned[2] (10^9 scf/d)	Max Demand[3] (10^9 scf/d)	I/S Movement[4] Flow (10^9 scf/d)	Cap. Ut. (%)
Western	7.1	0	4.2	7.6	6.0	84
Southwest	1.6	33.8	2.8	9.0	0.6	72
Central	12.8	10.7	1.7	11.4	6.0	47
Midwest	22.6	7.6	0.7	20.9	14.2	64
Northeast	10.2	2.0	2.6	17.1	7.9	77
Southeast	19.8	14.7	4.1	9.4	14.6	72
Total	74.1	68.8	16.1	75.4	49.3	—

1. Current capacity entering and exiting the region. 2 Planned additional entering capacity. 3. Maximum demand based on firm contracts. 4. Average flow into region in absolute units and as a percent of entering capacity (capacity utilization).

ment the peak demand periods. The average annual utilization factor of the interstate pipeline system is about 66.5% indicating a healthy margin between supply and demand.

The demand of natural gas is characterized by significant seasonal fluctuations. Thus, the high winter daily demand could be twice as large as the low daily summer demand. This is due to the use of natural gas for space heating in the winter. The utilization of the interstate pipeline system is thus optimized in conjunction with the use of regional storage. Withdrawals of natural gas from regional storage are used to augment the natural gas transported by the interstate pipeline system in order to meet the regional demand at any given time. Typically, the storage is depleted during the period of high demand and replenished during the low demand season. Natural gas is stored in impervious underground reservoirs and to a much smaller extend above ground as LNG in large cryogenic tanks. Table 5-3 summarizes the underground natural gas storage capacity in the United States available at the end of 1991[10]. Some 27 states have underground storage in 387 fields totalling 8 trillion scf of capacity. However, the entire capacity is not utilized. In the last few years the working storage level stood at about 3.1 trillion scf, while the amount of base gas necessary as a permanent inventory to maintain adequate reservoir pressure was 3.9 trillion scf[11]. The amount of with-

TABLE 5-3. Underground Natural Gas Storage Capacity in the US as of 1991

State	Capacity (10^{9}scf)	No. Fields (#)	State	Capacity (10^{9}scf)	No. Fields (#)
Arkansas	31	4	Montana	374	5
California	468	10	Nebraska	93	2
Colorado	99	9	New Mexico	95	3
Illinois	950	29	New York	151	22
Indiana	102	23	Ohio	591	22
Iowa	280	9	Oklahoma	363	12
Kansas	301	21	Oregon	10	2
Kentucky	307	25	Pennsylvania	641	49
Louisiana	560	9	Texas	589	26
Maryland	62	1	Utah	115	4
Michigan	995	46	Washington	34	1
Minnesota	7	1	West Virginia	525	39
Mississippi	115	5	Wyoming	106	7
Missouri	30	1	USA Total	7993	387

drawals in 1991 was 2.7 trillion scf and the amount of injections was 2.6 trillion scf during the same year. The total additions and withdrawals of LNG stood at a little over 63 billion scf per year each during 1993.

It is interesting to note that the amount of usable stored natural gas is about 1/6 of the annual usage, while the available storage capacity stands at almost 45% of the current annual usage. By comparison the combined amount of crude oil and petroleum products stored at any given time in the US is on the order of 1 billion bbl or 1/6 of the annual usage. However, this storage represents also the limit of available crude oil and petroleum product storage in the country — the strategic petroleum reserve contains currently an additional 0.6 billion bbl of crude oil [12]. Moreover, natural gas can be stored in underground natural formations, while crude oil and petroleum products are stored in a huge number of above ground tanks which not only need to be replaced as they age, but even more importantly tend to leak contaminating severely the adjacent land and through seepage any groundwater near the surface. The size of underground natural gas storage has increased by more than 30% between 1975, when it was about 6 trillion scf, and the present time. It also appears that the effective (working) underground storage is about 50% of the physical storage size.

It is apparent that the current margin in the utilization factor of the interstate pipeline system, the planned additional interstate capacity and the available regional underground storage of natural gas indicate that the system has the ability to handle easily an increased demand of natural gas from the present actual 18 trillion scf per year (50 billion scf/d x 365 d/y) to a present maximum of 27 trillion scf per year (74 billion scf/d x 365 d/y) to a planned maximum of 33 trillion scf per year (90 billion scf/d x 365 d/y) by the end of this decade.

The interstate pipelines, operated by a multitude of pipeline companies, deliver natural gas "at the city gate", to use a term customarily employed by the natural gas industry, to a variety of customers, typically but not necessarily large ones, such as natural gas utilities, large industrial customers and power generating plants. Natural gas utilities transport natural gas through the distribution pipeline system or network to residential buildings, commercial establishments and industrial facilities within their service territory. The natural gas distribution pipeline system or network in the US is vast and amounted, as of 1990, to 837 million miles of pipelines[7]. The diameter of the distribution pipelines is, of course, much smaller than that of the interstate pipelines. While interstate pipelines have typically a 30-inch diameter, distribution pipelines vary from the 6-inch main pipes all the way down to 1-inch pipes for residential customer distribution.

The extensive distribution pipeline system brings natural gas to the majority of residential, commercial and industrial facilities in the country. The existing availability of natural gas at home or work makes the refueling of natural gas vehicles at such places a very realistic alternative as well as a complementary one and a substitute option to the refueling at a public drive-in natural gas station. The present potential of this particular refueling option will be addressed at some length in the next section, because it is of paramount importance in the penetration of natural gas as a motor vehicle fuel.

NATURAL GAS REFUELING AT HOME AND AT WORK

A unique feature of natural gas among all the other possible alternative automotive fuels is that it is already available at home or at work for a very large segment of the population. The only other fuel with the same feature is of course electricity, but then the vehicle is powered by an electric motor rather than an internal combustion engine. The fact that natural gas has been brought to residential and commercial buildings over the years for space heating, water heating and other similar usages can be and will be a synergistic factor towards the market penetration of natural gas as an automotive fuel. While this synergistic factor should be apparent to most people in the business, it seems that most of them have yet to appreciate fully the magnitude and potential of home and work refueling as a catalyst for the mass introduction of natural gas vehicles.

This catalyst promotes the easier establishment of the necessary infrastructure that must be in place for natural gas vehicles to penetrate the market in large numbers. In the electric vehicle community, for example, the availability of home or work charging is considered as the cornerstone for acceptance of EVs by the public to offset their short range, typically under 100 miles per charge. Home or workplace refueling of an NGV offers, besides convenience, flexibility and cost reduction. The latter consideration is a very critical one with respect to the NGV market penetration, particularly in the early years of the market development. The cost reduction will be discussed in a later chapter. In this section, an analysis of pertinent data will be made to estimate the degree to which natural gas is currently available at home and at work. Moreover, home and work will be treated separately.

Refueling at Home

In 1990 there existed a little over 102 million housing units in the country. Of these units almost 92 million were occupied, the remainder being vacant. The geographical distribution of these housing units as well as the general building type characteristics are summarized in Table 5-4[13]. Although there is some variation from region to region, some 65% of the total housing units are single unit buildings either detached or attached. Another 7% of the housing inventory represent mobile home and trailer units and 13% of the total units are in large (10 or more units per structure) buildings.

The states with the largest housing inventory in descending order and the respective housing growth rate in each of these states between 1980 and 1990 are as follows (m.u. = million units): California 11.2

TABLE 5-4. Selected Characteristics of Housing Units in the US as of 1990

Region	Total Units	1 Unit Det.	1 Unit Att.	2-4 Units	5-9 Units	10+ Units	Mobile Homes	Occup. Units	Vacant Units
Northeast	20.8	10.5	1.7	3.5	1.0	3.5	0.6	18.9	1.9
Midwest	24.5	16.3	0.8	2.4	1.1	2.5	1.4	22.3	2.2
South	36.1	22.5	1.7	2.3	1.7	4.1	3.8	31.8	4.3
West	20.9	12.2	1.2	1.6	1.1	3.2	1.6	18.9	2.0
US	102.3	61.5	5.4	9.8	4.9	13.3	7.4	91.9	10.4

Note. Housing units are grouped in terms of the number of units per building. Numbers represent millions of units.

m.u., 20.5%; New York 7.2 m.u., 5.2%; Texas 7.0 m.u., 26.3%; Florida 6.1 m.u., 39.3%; Pennsylvania 4.9 m.u., 7.4%; Illinois 4.5 m.u., 4.3%; Ohio 4.4 m.u., 6.4%; Michigan 3.8 m.u., 7.2%; New Jersey 3.1 m.u., 10.9%; North Carolina 2.8 m.u., 23.9%; Georgia 2.6 m.u., 30.1%; Virginia 2.5 m.u., 23.5%; Massachusetts 2.5 m.u., 12.0%; Indiana 2.3 m.u., 7.4%; and Missouri 2.2 m.u., 10.4%. Thus, 15 states represent more than two-thirds of the housing units in the country.

The number of households in 1990 stood at 93.3 million, including members of the Armed Forces living off post or with their families on post[14]. The increase in the number of households in the last decade (1981-1990) was 16%, while in the preceding two decades (1971-1980 and 1961-1970) it averaged 27% and 20%, respectively. The average size of the household was 2.63 individuals in 1990, slightly lower than the 2.76 individuals average household size in 1980.

The number of gas utility customers in 1990 was a little over 54 million with almost 50 million residential customers. The bulk of the remainder customers comprised predominantly commercial ones (about 95%) with industrial customers making up the balance[15]. Table 5-5 summarizes the geographical distribution of residential natural gas utility customers as of 1990. The 15 states with the highest number of housing units have also been included. The most striking observation is that the South has about one residential natural gas customer for every three housing units. The Northeast has half as many natural gas customers as housing units. In the Midwest there are almost two natural gas customers for every three housing units. In the West there are three customers for every five housing units. On a state-by-state basis these

TABLE 5-5. Regional Distribution of Gas Utility Industry Customers in 1990

Region State	No of Customers (x10^6) Total	Residential	Region State	No of Customers (x10^6) Total	Residential
Northeast	10.9	10.0	South	13.4	12.2
MA	1.2	1.1	VA	0.7	0.6
NY	4.2	3.9	NC	0.6	0.5
NJ	2.2	2.0	FL	0.5	0.4
PA	2.5	2.3	TX	3.5	3.2
Midwest	16.7	15.2	West	13.2	12.2
OH	3.0	2.8	CA	8.9	8.4
IN	1.5	1.3			
IL	3.5	3.3	US	54.3	49.8
MI	2.8	2.7			
MO	1.3	1.2			

numbers vary considerably. In New Jersey, for example, the ratio of natural gas customers to housing units is to 2:3 versus 1:2 for the region (Northeast). In California, as another example, the same ratio is 3:4 versus 3:5 for the region (West).

The numbers in Table 5-5 can serve as a lower (minimum) bound of what percentage of housing units have access to natural gas today within the various regions of the country. Thus, it is apparent that in 1990 there were some 50 million residential customers served by a natural gas utility out of a possible 92 million customers — one for each occupied housing unit. Consequently, it would appear that a minimum of 54% of the housing units in the country have currently direct access to natural gas. In reality, however, a larger percentage of households has access to natural gas. In non-owner occupied multifamily units there is typically one meter, i.e., one customer, for the entire building. In these instances, the cost of electric and gas utilities is incorporated in the monthly rent. Thus, it is likely that some 5 million residential customers (i.e., multifamily building residential meters) out of the 50 million total represent in reality 25 million households. Consequently, a more realistic number of households having access to natural gas is a little over 76% of the total number of occupied households in the country.

Similar conclusions may be reached by examining the fuel characteristics of heating equipment and appliances of the occupied houses in

TABLE 5-6. Evolution of Heating Equipment and Appliance Fuel Characteristics For Occupied Housing Units in the US from 1950 to 1990.

Year	1950 (10^6)	(%)	1960 (10^6)	(%)	1970 (10^6)	(%)	1980 (10^6)	(%)	1990 (10^6)	(%)
Occupied Units	42.8	100	53.0	100	63.4	100	80.4	100	91.9	100
Heating Fuel										
Utility Gas	11.4	27	22.9	43	35.0	55	42.7	53	46.9	51
LPG	0.8	2	2.7	5	3.8	6	4.5	6	5.3	6
Cooking Fuel										
Gas*	25.5	60	33.8	64	36.6	58	38.0	47	N/A	—
Water Heating										
Gas	N/A	—	N/A	—	N/A	—	N/A	—	42.8	47

(*) Includes utility gas and LPG.

the country. Table 5-6 shows the contribution of natural gas (utility) and LPG (tank, bottle) fuels to space heating, cooking and water heating in housing units[16]. Other fuels used for the same purpose but not shown in Table 5-6 include electricity, fuel oil and kerosene, wood, coal or no fuel. Space heating represents the most widespread use of natural gas at 51% of the total number of occupied housing units as of 1990. The penetration of natural gas for space heating in housing units is a good indicator of the lower limit availability of natural gas at home.

However, it is reasonable to assume that there may be instances where natural gas may be used, for example, for cooking or water heating, but not for space heating and vice versa. It is indeed common in multi-family units to use natural gas for water heating only or for space heating only while the rest of the end uses (space heating/cooking or water heating/ cooking, respectively) are supplied by electricity. Thus, an upper limit of the number of housing units having access to natural gas can be deduced based on appliance data by assuming that about two-thirds or 66% of all units have both natural gas space heating and water heating.

It is reasonable then to estimate that some 72% (mean of 76% and 66%) of households or 67 million of occupied housing units have access

TABLE 5-7. Selected Characteristics of New Single Family Houses in the US

Year	1970	1980	1985	1990
Total Houses (1000)	793	957	1,072	966
Average Floor Area (ft^2)	1,500	1,740	1,785	2,080
Gas Heating Fuel (%)	62	41	49	59
Parking Facilities				
Garage (%)	58	69	70	82
Carport (%)	17	7	5	2
None (%)	25	24	25	16

to natural gas. It is also worth pointing out that the users of LPG represent exclusively mobile homes, trailers and similar facilities.

One would expect that one-unit (single family) houses will have a higher natural gas penetration than the average of the housing stock. This is borne out of data for the new one-unit houses built in the last twenty years[17]. Table 5-7 summarizes some of the pertinent characteristics for new single family housing. Typically some 60% of new single unit houses have direct access to natural gas. It is instructive to note that the uncertainty in the availability of natural gas in the late 1970s resulted in a significant drop in the number of new houses having natural gas. Since then, however, natural gas as a residential space heating fuel has rebounded to its previous degree of penetration. This is due to the gradually regained confidence of the public regarding the abundance of natural gas during the 1980s. This confidence has continued to improve in the 1990s, thereby increasing further the penetration of natural gas in the residential market.

It should be also noted that some 82% of all the new single-family houses have a garage that can be used for the installation of a natural gas compressor for home vehicle refueling. Finally, it is instructive to note that not all households in the United States own an automobile. The pertinent information on a regional basis is given in Table 5-8[18]. The data show that more than 10% of households in the country do not own any motor vehicles. Moreover, the percentage of households with no vehicles is the highest in the Northeast at 20%, and the lowest in the Midwest and the West with less than 10% in each region. Finally, the

TABLE 5-8. Regional Household Motor Vehicle Ownership in the US as of 1990

Region	Total US	North-East	Mid-West	South	West
Households (x10^6)	91.9	18.9	22.3	31.8	18.9
Households w. MV (x10^6)	81.3	15.2	20.4	28.3	17.3
Households w. MV (%)	88.5	80.4	91.5	90.0	91.5
Motor Vehicles (x10^6)	151.5	27.3	38.8	52.0	33.4
Motor Vehicles (%)	100.0	18.0	25.6	34.3	22.0
MV per H/H (#)	1.65	1.45	1.74	1.64	1.77
MV per H/H w. MV (#)	1.86	1.79	1.90	1.84	1.93

Notes. H/H : Household; MV : Motor Vehicle.

number of vehicles per household is the highest in the West and the lowest in the Northeast. In all likelihood, households with no motor vehicles are located in urban areas and comprise multi-family housing units. In addition, the number of vehicles owned by households in multi-family housing units is most likely below the average.

The conclusion to be deduced from the preceding data is that at least 2 out of 3 and as many as 4 out of 5 motor vehicles owned by individuals must be associated with housing units which have access to utility natural gas. Thus, some 100 to 120 million vehicles out of the 151.5 million passenger cars, light trucks and vans owned by individuals could be refueled today with natural gas at home, if a residential (slow fill) compressor was installed in the garage or carport of each house or housing unit.

Refueling at Work

The number of non-residential customers of the natural gas utilities stood at 4.5 million as of 1993 according to the data in Table 5-5. Of these 4.5 million non-residential customers, 4.3 million were commercial customers and the remainder 0.2 million were industrial customers [15]. These commercial customers represent a variety of businesses associated invariably with commercial buildings which serve as the locations of business transactions. In 1989, there were some 4.5 million commercial buildings in the US with a total floor space of 63.1 billion square feet[19]. The distribution of commercial buildings in the US on the basis of geographical location and building principal activity are summarized in Table 5-9 and Table 5-10, respectively. Both the number of buildings as well as the corresponding floor space per region are included. The total number of workers employed by region is also included.

Of the 80 million workers employed in all the commercial buildings in the country in 1989, the number of government personnel was 17.3 million. The number of government owned buildings was 577 thousand with a floorspace area of 14.3 billion square feet (The numbers in Table

TABLE 5-9. Selected Characteristics of Commercial Buildings in the US on a Regional Basis as of 1989.

Region	Total US	North-East	Mid-West	South	West
No Bldgs (x 10^3)	4,528	783	1,046	1,847	851
Floor (x 10^9 ft^2)	62.2	13.6	16.0	22.0	11.6
No. Workers (x 10^6)	80.0	17.6	19.2	27.4	15.8

TABLE 5-10. Selected Characteristics of Commercial Buildings in the US on a Principal Activity Basis as of 1989.

Principal Activity	No Buildings (1,000)	Floor Space (billion sq.ft.)
Assembly	615	6.8
Education	284	8.1
Food Sales	102	7.9
Food Services	241	1.2
Health Care	80	2.1
Lodging	140	3.5
Mercantile/Services	1,278	12.4
Office	679	11.8
Public Order and Safety	50	0.6
Warehouse	618	9.2
Parking Garage	42	1.0
Other	62	1.5
Vacant	333	4.2

TABLE 5-11. Fuel Type Usage in Commercial Buildings in the US as of 1989

Fuel Type	Elect-ricity	Natural Gas	Fuel Oil	Pro-pane	District Heat	Other
No Bldgs (10^3)	4,297	2,439	586	348	105	155
Floor (10^9 ft^2)	61.6	41.6	12.7	4.7	6.9	3.6

Note. Fuels used alone or in combination.

5-9 include both non-government and government buildings). The distribution of different fuel usage in the commercial buildings is given in Table 5-11[19]. It is interesting to note that while 54% of commercial buildings have direct access to utility natural gas, the floorspace of these buildings represents 66% of the total commercial building floor area in the country. The distribution of the work force size per number of commercial buildings, total floorspace and the average building floorspace are given in Table 5-12[19]. The total number of workers within each category are also included.

TABLE 5-12. Work Force Size in Commercial Buildings in the US as of 1989

Work Force Size	<5	5-9	10-19	20-49	50-99	100-249	>250
No. Bldgs (x 10^3)	2,280	906	507	381	132	79	32
Total Floor (x 10^9 ft^2)	13.3	7.9	6.5	9.7	7.4	6.8	9.8
Mean Bldg (x 10^3 ft^2)	5.8	8.8	12.7	25.4	56.1	85.9	308.0
No. Workers (x10^6)	5.7	6.3	7.4	13.1	9.8	13.8	23.9

It can be assumed conservatively that 90% of these workers use daily a private automobile to and from work, rather than public transportation. Moreover, the average vehicle occupancy could vary from 1.5 to 1.2 persons per vehicle. It can be then estimated that some 48 million to 60 million privately owned vehicles are driven daily to the workplace. On the other hand, the commercial building fuel usage indicates that two out of three workers are in a building which has direct access to utility natural gas. This number is deduced from the data in Table 5-

11 on the basis of the ratio of commercial building floor area with natural gas fuel (41.6 billion ft^2) to the total commercial building floor
area. Floorspace rather than number of buildings is the correct measure
on which to base the number of workers in a commercial building.
Thus, it can be concluded that anywhere between 32 and 40 million passenger cars, light trucks and vans are driven daily to a workplace which
has direct access to natural gas. If appropriate slow fill refueling facilities for NGV were to become available at the workplace, then as many
as 40 million privately owned vehicles could be refueled at work with
natural gas on a regular basis.

The manufacturing or industrial sector of the economy employed
18.9 million workers in 1990[20]. The number of establishments stood at
369 thousand, of which 126 thousand employed 20 or more persons.
Thus, some 3.7 million workers were associated with the smaller, under
20 employees, manufacturing facilities, while 15.2 million were
employed in the larger 126 thousand establishments. The number of
industrial natural gas utility customers was 214 thousand in 1990. It is
very reasonable to assume that all the larger manufacturing establishments in the country will have direct access to natural gas. The same
may be true with about 50% of the smaller facilities as well. Thus, a
minimum of 17 million industry workers may be employed in manufacturing facilities with direct natural gas access. Using the same criteria as
for the commercial building employees (90% private auto transportation,
1.2 to 1.5 vehicle occupancy), it can be estimated that between 10 and
13 million passenger cars, light trucks and vans are driven by their owners daily to industrial facilities with natural gas refueling potential.

The estimated numbers of privately owned vehicles that could be
refueled at home or at work with natural gas on the basis of the natural
gas distribution system presently in place in residential and commercial
buildings as well as industrial facilities are summarized in Table 5-13.

Vehicles owned by private corporations and vehicles owned by
local, state governments as well as the federal government have not
been considered so far. These vehicles, which numbered 37.5 million in
1990, can be also refueled at commercial buildings and industrial establishments. The same or higher potential exists for refueling at these sites
as for privately owned vehicles — 66% of vehicles at commercial sites

TABLE 5-13. Potential for Home and Workplace Refueling of Privately Owned Natural Gas Vehicles in the US on the Basis of the Natural Gas Distribution System in Place as of 1990

Refueling Location	Number of Vehicles[1] (10^6)	Penetration[2] (%)
Residential Building	100-125	66-80
Commercial Building	32-40	65
Industrial Establishment	10-13	90

1. Total number of privately owned vehicles was 151.5 million in 1991.
2. Penetration is the ratio of the vehicles with access to natural gas refueling to the total number of vehicles in the category.
Note. There is a double count in the number of vehicles as on several occasions vehicles will have access to both home and work refueling.

and 90% of vehicles at industrial sites — with the present natural gas distribution system. Thus, the potential exists for refueling at the business site anywhere between 25 and 34 million of corporate owned vehicles. Incidentally, the federal government owns or leases some 0.6 million vehicles and the state governments across the country own 2.3 million vehicles. The remainder of the fleet vehicles are owned by local governments, public utilities and private corporations.

NGV REFUELING STATION TECHNOLOGY

A fundamental difference in the refueling of natural gas vehicles in the future versus gasoline vehicles at the present time will be the ability to refuel NGVs both at home and at work. The technology is already mature, but nevertheless it continues to develop. This unique feature of natural gas as a transportation fuel will result in the virtual elimination of the drive-in stations in urban and sub-urban areas. Large drive-in stations will of course be in existence along freeways and other major roads away from the urban environment.

The CNG fuel infrastructure is almost in place with one last element missing from the system. The missing element is the means by which natural gas from the distribution system is introduced into the storage tanks on-board the vehicle. Representative systems for both residential refueling and commercial/industrial refueling will be presented here.

A residential or individual refueling system can typically accommodate one, two or even three vehicles depending on the daily driving distance per vehicle. The residential refueling station consists essentially of
an electrically driven compressor that compresses natural gas from the
low pressure line residential natural gas to a final pressure of 3,000 psi
in the vehicle fuel tank. The refueling device can be placed outdoors as
shown in Figure 5-6 and requires connection to a natural gas line and a

(a)

FIGURE 5-6. Residential (a) and Small Commercial (b) On-Site Natural Gas Slow
Refueling System (Courtesy: Fuelmaker Corporation, Salt Lake City, UT).

220 V single phase electric power supply[21]. It has a length of 21 inches, a width of 20 inches, a height of 39 inches and weighs 145 lb. The nominal power use is 1.3 kW at a natural gas flow rate of 1.8 scf per minute (inlet gas pressure 1/4 psig).

A retractable refueling hose of several feet in length, which is equipped with a special nozzle, can be plugged in the vehicle. Fueling begins by pressing the "start" button and can be terminated by pressing

(b)

FIGURE 5-6. (Continued)

the "stop" button on the control panel of the appliance. Some of the safety features of this appliance include: an automatic shutdown when the vehicle tank is full; the gas pressure remaining in the fill hose is automatically reduced at the end of the fill cycle; if a vehicle is driven away before the hose is unplugged, the hose will disconnect from the refueling device and the system will shut down immediately; and if the hose is severed, the system shuts off instantly. Although not necessary in a residential application, a meter can be installed before the inlet to each refueling appliance to measure natural gas use. The typical 13.2 gal (50 l) CNG tank will be filled from empty in about 4 hours and 15 minutes.

The residential fueling system can fill one vehicle at a time or two vehicles simultaneously as each appliance has two dispensing hoses. One or more of these refueling systems can be used in commercial and other facilities where several vehicles may be available to be refueled. The switch over from several such small CNG units to one or more high flow rate, fast refueling units is a function of the number of vehicles that need to be refueled each day. This switch-over number of vehicles appears to be on the order of about 100 and definitely no less than fifty[22]. Scheduled maintenance of the residential refueling system occurs every 2000 hours of operation to replace worn out parts. Otherwise, the life of the appliance is indefinite, although for practical reasons it is assumed to be 15 years.

A higher flow rate and a faster refueling natural gas system consists essentially of a bigger compressor as well as proportional compressed natural gas storage capability. The latter is required because the natural gas distribution line flow rate is not sufficient to fill the on-board the vehicle tanks in a period as short as 5 to 10 minutes with a compressor of reasonable size. A medium size single or dual compressor configuration with the requisite storage as shown in Figure 5-7 constitutes a typical arrangement for a faster rate CNG refueling system appropriate, for example, for a fleet operation of up to 30 vehicles[23]. Each compressor consists of three stages and is of the wobble plate type with encapsulated oil as coolant and as lubricant. A 10 hp (7.4 kW) electric motor is required to drive each compressor. The electric line requirement is a 415 V three-phase 60 Hz power source. The storage consists of US DOT approved standard steel cylinders allowing a 3600 psi maximum opera-

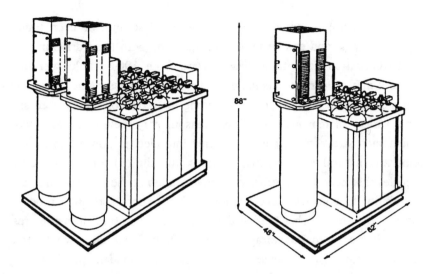

FIGURE 5-7. Medium Size CNG Refueling System Consisting of a Single or Dual Compressor, Storage and Dispenser. Maximum Capacity of 25 scf/min for One Fast or Up to Four Slow Fills, Unmetered Flow, Appropriate For Up to 30 Vehicles for Fleet Operators or Similar Refueling Activities (Source: Rix Industries, Oakland, CA)

tional pressure. For the single compressor 12 cylinders are used with a 5,520 scf capacity, while for the dual compressor 20 cylinders are used with a 9,200 scf capacity. The refueling rate of this system, depending on the pressure of the available natural gas distribution line, varies between 8.5 scf/min and 12.5 scf/min for the single compressor and twice as much for the dual compressor (inlet pressure 1/4 psig to 10 psig). The volume of natural gas that can be dispensed at 3,000 psi is 2,676 scf for the single and 5,757 scf for the dual compressor system. The single compressor system weighs 3,600 lb and the dual one 5,900 lb. Safety and operation features include weather protected key lock switch, automatic high/low-stop pressure switch, discharge check valve, priority fill panel and compressor top-off, adjustable discharge pressure, regulator with high and low pressure gauges, 10-ft fill hose with isolating valve, fill vent valve and dispensing nozzle. Additional features not shown in Figure 5-7, include a one-hose or a four-hose fill post, a dual natural gas dryer assembly and a slow fill pressure regulator. The typical life expectancy of such a system is 15 years with the requisite regular maintenance.

Larger compressors delivering up to 1000 scf/min or even higher flow rates exist and can be used in conjunction with large drive-in public CNG station accommodating upward from 100 vehicles per day. While it may be early to decide on a specific compressor size, it appears that a 50 scf/min compressor is becoming the most commonly used size for a variety of reasons[22][24]. These reasons may include the ease with which such size compressor can be tied into electric power supply systems and natural gas distribution lines, the limited number of CNG vehicles that need to be refueled at any location at the present time, and the ability to combine several of this size compressors in a modular fashion to meet a higher fueling demand. Thus, the 50 scf/min compressor with the requisite storage of about 20,000 scf and two to four metered natural gas dispensers may become the standard public refueling CNG unit in urban and suburban areas.

Larger size compressors may eventually be installed at major drive-in CNG stations along the nation's highways where several hundred or even thousands of vehicles may be refueled daily. Figure 5-8 shows schematically the major components of a large CNG refueling facility [25]. The major added features to a large CNG refueling station include priority and sequencing systems as well as the ability to meter the use

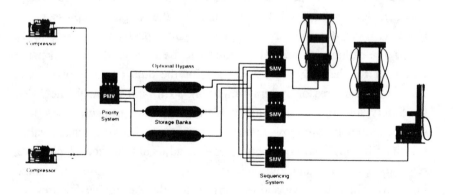

FIGURE 5-8. Schematic of Major Components in a Large CNG Refueling Facility Showing Compressors, Priority System (Priority Manifold Valve), Storage Tanks, Sequencing Systems (Sequential Manifold Valve) and Two-Hose (Passenger Car, Light Truck, Van) and One-Hose (Bus, Heavier Truck) Dispensers (Courtesy: Marcum Fuel Systems, Inc., Denver, CO).

of natural gas per customer and an associated billing scheme. The priority system decides, depending on the instantaneous natural gas fueling demand, to switch from storage to direct refueling. The sequencing system, one for each dispenser, selects a dispenser's gas supply and directs the flow of high pressure gas from gas storage tanks to the appropriate dispenser. The purpose of these sub-systems is to optimize the availability of high pressure gas to the dispensers of the facility.

Each dispenser may have up to two delivery hoses for passenger cars, vans and light trucks or only one delivery hose for heavier trucks and buses where very high flow rates are necessary because of the much larger on-board storage of these vehicles. Figure 5-9 shows these two types of dispensers and summarizes also their main characteristics. The metering of natural gas through the dispenser is accomplished by a means of a very accurate mass flow control device. This device consists of a "sonic nozzle" equipped with pressure and temperature sensors that can instantaneously correct for any fluctuations in these two parameters to account properly for the natural gas mass passing through the dispenser. An instant card reader mounted on the front panel of the dispenser in the electronics section, as shown in Figure 5-10, has a cumulative transaction memory and a full networking communications and billing capability through a dial-up modem. Thus, a reliable 24-hour service is possible without the need of an attendant.

Figure 5-11 shows a passenger car at a public drive-in station and a bus at a bus depot both being refueled with CNG. There is no apparent difference between gasoline refueling and CNG refueling in either case.

If ANG storage were to be successfully developed to the point where it would become the fueling technology of choice, instead of CNG, the same basic refueling equipment will be used for either the on-site residential, medium commercial or large public drive-in stations. The only difference would be the modifications required to the components, if any, to compress natural gas to only 500 psi rather than 3000 or 3600 psi pressure.

The fueling of vehicles with LNG, on the other hand, requires a totally different type of infrastructure development than CNG. The liquid physical state of LNG makes its distribution characteristics somewhat similar to the distribution characteristics of gasoline and diesel

No. Hoses: 2

Op. Press.: 5000 psi

Flow Rate: 400 scfm per hose

Fill Press.: 2400 psi- to 3600 psi

Accuracy: 99+%

Size: 38 in w/84 in h/ 18 in d

Weight: 350 lb

(a)

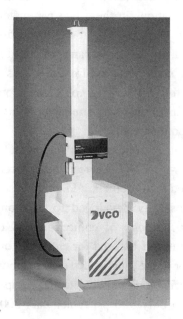

(b)

No. Hoses: 1

Op. Press.: 5000 psi

Flow Rate: 5,000 scfm

Fill Press.: 3000 psi- to 3600 psi

Accuracy: 99+%

Size: 30 in w/100 in h/ 42 in d

Weight: 375 lb

FIGURE 5-9. Representative CNG Dispensers: (a) For Passenger Cars, Light Trucks and Vans; and (b) For Buses and Heavier Trucks (Courtesy: Marcum Fuel Systems, Inc., Denver, CO).

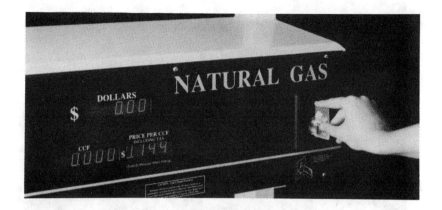

FIGURE 5-10. Insert Card Reader for Passenger Car, Light Trucks and Vans CNG Dispensers which Includes Cumulative Transaction Memory and Billing Capabilities through a Dial-up Modem for a 24-hour Unattended Operation (Source: Marcum Fuel Systems, Inc., Denver, CO).

fuel. Figure 5-12 depicts the major elements of the LNG infrastructure as a vehicular fuel[26]. There are five major elements as follows: Liquefaction; Transportation; Regional Storage; Distribution to Local Storage; and Vehicle Dispensing.

Liquefaction takes place at facilities located in the vicinity of readily available large quantities of natural gas such as interstate pipelines or even large production fields. The LNG is then stored in large storage facilities of up to 200 million gallons in capacity. The liquid is kept at atmospheric pressure and transferred through insulated pipes to delivery vehicles for transportation. Transportation of LNG from the liquefaction plants is made in cryogenic tank trailers or cryogenic rail cars. Tank trailers hold 12,000 gal of LNG, while rail trailers can transport 30,000 gal. The LNG is kept at low pressure under 25 psi during transportation and is unloaded by pump at regional storage facilities.

Regional storage consists of large vertical or horizontal cryogenic vessels of up to 85,000 gal capacity and low pressure. Distribution to local storage facilities, which comprise essentially the vehicle fueling facilities, is performed with tank trucks of 500 to 7,500 gal capacity. Local storage is done in cryogenic storage tanks that are designed to capture and reliquefy the LNG vapor by increased pressure. This feature

(a)

(b)

FIGURE 5-11. Typical CNG Refueling Facilities: (a) Public Passenger Car, Light Truck and Van Drive-In Station; (b) Municipal Bus Refueling at Bus Depot (Courtesy: Marcum Fuel Systems, Inc., Denver, CO).

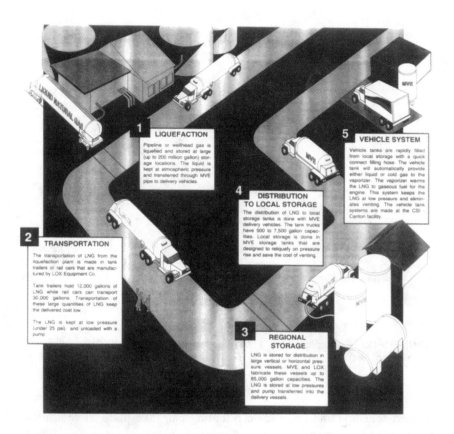

FIGURE 5-12. Major Elements of an LNG Automotive Fuel Infrastructure (Courtesy: MVE Cryogenics, Inc., Bloomington, MN).

reduces the venting losses. Dispensing of LNG to vehicles equipped with cryogenic storage tanks is carried out by pumping through a quick connect filling hose as shown conceptually in Figure 5-13. It should be pointed out that the technology for all five elements of the LNG infrastructure is well developed, but only the liquefaction element is significantly in place at the present time in 27 states[10].

Given the relative complexity of the LNG infrastructure and the cryogenic nature of the LNG fuel, it is unlikely that LNG will ever replace gasoline in a large scale. However, LNG may serve as a transportation fuel in applications where vehicles operate within a well

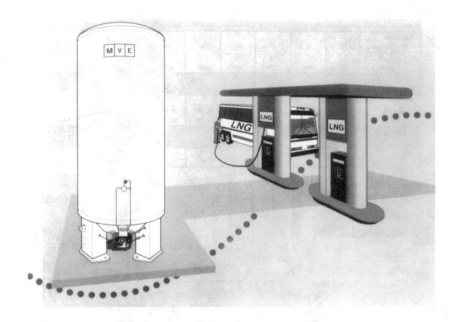

FIGURE 5-13. Conceptual LNG Filling Station (Courtesy: MVE Cryogenics, Inc., Bloomington, MN).

defined schedule and large scale refueling can take place in centralized locations. Under such conditions LNG refueling can be greatly simplified and evaporative losses greatly diminished. Thus, LNG may be a suitable fuel for sizeable heavy truck private fleets, buses in large municipal fleets, and even railway locomotives.

It should be also noted that the use of LNG as an aviation fuel could be implemented relatively easier compared to a vehicular LNG distribution system. An aviation LNG infrastructure would terminate at the regional storage (airport) element and require no more than a 1/5th as large liquefaction, transportation and regional storage size facilities as an a motor vehicle LNG infrastructure.

NGV FUELING CONNECTORS AND FUEL METERING UNITS

The discussion in this chapter can not be completed without discussing two important technical issues, one regarding the nature of the natural gas vehicle fueling connection devices and the other concerning the proper natural gas fuel metering unit.

Fueling Connection Device. Essentially a natural gas vehicle connection device comprises a nozzle (dispensing side) and a receptacle (vehicle). One of the major concern areas is the compatibility of vehicle fueling connection devices. In the early days of this new industry, it is natural to encounter more than one type of fueling connection devices such that one manufacturer's nozzle may not connect to another's receptacle. The vehicle user must carry adapters in order to fuel the vehicle which is hardly a practical procedure. Currently, three CNG connection devices, identified as Hansen, Sherex and Stäubli, have established themselves in North America. Public preference will decide ultimately which of these devices (nozzle and receptacle) is going to become the universal one for all vehicles and refueling facilities.

Another area of concern is that connection devices may have been adapted from other applications and are not specifically designed for use with either compressed or liquefied natural gas vehicles. The need for a CNG fueling connecting device standard became apparent a few years ago as the number of vehicles running on that fuel was expanding rapidly. The first edition of such a standard was approved by both the American National Standards Institute (USA) and the Interprovincial Gas Advisory Council (Canada) in February of 1994[27]. The aforementioned two current as well as any future CNG connecting devices (nozzle and receptacle) must comply with this standard for safety and performance reasons.

Three main parameters affect user safety and system compatibility: A. Service Pressure; B. Disconnect Venting; and C. Design Life. According to the aforementioned standard three service pressures may be operated in North America: 2,600 psi, 3,000 psi and 3,600 psi. Nozzles transferring high pressure gas must be fully and safely depressurized prior to being disconnected from the receptacle. The standard recognizes three nozzle types (Type 1, 2 and 3), each with a specific depressurization mechanism. The Type 1 Nozzle is primarily intended for use at public fill stations, the Type 2 Nozzle is intended mainly for fleet vehicle applications, and the Type 3 Nozzle is intended primarily for residential and fleet applications. The design life is a function of the frequency of use. The standard requires that all receptacles meet or exceed 10,000 connect/disconnect cycles. Moreover, the nozzles are classified as Class A or Class B with a 100,000 cycle life and a 20,000 cycle life, respectively. Finally, the standard mandates design specifications with respect to the type of mating materials, geometry and tolerances, which must be utilized in the certification of a submitted nozzle and receptacle. As with any new product, usage will suggest improvements in the design of the CNG connecting devices which will then be reflected in future editions of the present standard.

Fuel Metering Unit. Natural gas sold in the different parts of the country does not have the exact same composition. This is the result of the even greater variability of the natural gas produced from underground reservoirs as it has already being discussed. Processing of the wet natural gas makes the resulting dry natural gas much more consistent in composition, but some differences remain. Thus, the producing and processing natural gas companies sell natural gas to the pipeline companies on the basis of energy content rather than volume. Moreover, the local distribution companies sell natural gas to their customers on the basis of energy content as well, even though they measure volume of gas sold (typically cubic feet). The monthly bill of the customer is adjusted by a factor, slightly larger or slightly smaller than one, to reflect the average energy content of the gas delivered to the customer in comparison to the energy content of a standard natural gas composition with a given price specified by the state's Public Utility Commission (PUC).

Natural gas sold as a vehicular fuel at home or at work must likewise reflect the energy content rather than volume for the final determination of cost to the consumer. This can be readily accomplished by adjusting the metered volume with the aforementioned energy factor, whether the same meter is employed as for the rest of the uses (i.e., space heating, water heating, etc.) or a separate meter is used for vehicle fuel consumption only. However, natural gas sold as a vehicular fuel at a public station through a third party is not under the control of the PUC. In that instance the state's Weights and Measures office has the jurisdiction to ensure that a customer purchases at each station within the state fuel measured in a well defined unit, whether this unit is based on volume, mass or energy. The problem then is one of determining the appropriate unit for natural gas fuel. As far as a natural gas vehicle is concerned and for that matter the operator of the vehicle, the important measure of natural gas fuel is its energy content or the number of BTUs delivered from the dispenser to the tank.

Traditionally, the National Institute of Standards and Technology (NIST), formerly known as the National Bureau of Standards, issues handbooks annually that provide recommendations to state Weights and Measures (W&M) offices with regard to legal and technical aspects of measuring products sold to the consumers. States can either adopt these recommendations as written or modify them or reject them. Changes and additions are made at the annual National Conference on Weights and Measures by majority vote.

The initial proposal by NIST was to recommend to all state W&M offices the use of mass as a measure of natural gas fuel expressed in units of pounds or kilograms. A mass measure would have required the employment of very expensive metering equipment at each CNG dispenser requiring mass meters with automatic density compensation to correct for specific gravity. Moreover, this type of metering does not ensure delivery of a constant amount of energy.

A more practical and a truly energy representative metering system has to be based on the "Wobbe Number or Index" of the fuel[28]. This number, which is defined as the ratio of the fuel lower heating value to the square root of the fuel specific gravity, is proportional to the energy delivered at a given pressure. For this reason, all gas utilities monitor very closely the Wobbe Index of the gas delivered to the customers and try to maintain it constant, if possible, by blending gases together. In fact, the Wobbe Index is the most tightly controlled natural gas index. Thus, if the Wobbe Number of natural gas stays constant, the energy delivered will depend on monitoring the square root of the gas specific gravity. The latter quantity is inversely proportional to the volume flow rate of the fuel. Low-cost meters are already available that can measure just that. Consequently, measuring the energy content of dispensed natural gas is not only feasible, but it is also relatively inexpensive.

In July 1994, the NIST finally approved the "Gallon Gasoline Equivalent or "gge" unit for natural gas. This is an energy unit equal to 114,000 BTU, which is the average energy content of one gallon gasoline fuel used by the EPA to determine vehicle emissions and fuel economy. A gge comprises 110.6 scf or 5.9 lb of natural gas of the average composition. The gge unit can be also used to measure other alternative fuels, including methanol, ethanol and propane. The advantages of natural gas measured and sold in gge units are several. A direct cost comparison can be made with gasoline and diesel fuel. A fuel-economy determination in miles per gge is possible and a fuel efficiency comparison to other fuels can be established. The consumer can be assured that the fuel quality will translate into miles traveled. The new unit of measure offers recognition to NGVs. Finally, the gge units paves the way for the adoption of the "lge" unit or "Liter Gasoline Equivalent" in those parts of the world where the liter is the unit of selling gasoline so that NGVs receive recognition throughout the world.

REFERENCES

1. D. Yergin, The Prize – The Epic Quest for Oil, Money and Power, Ch. 11, pp. 208-211, Simon & Schuster, New York, NY, 1991.

2. J. J. Flink, The Automobile Age, Ch. 8, pp. 129-157, The MIT Press, Cambridge, MA, 1992.

3. Statistical Abstract of the United States 1975, 95th Ed., p. 574, Bureau of the Census, US Department of Commerce, Washington, D.C., 1975.

4. Alternatives to Traditional Transportation Fuels, DOE/EIA-0585/O, Energy Information Administration, US DOE, Washington, DC, 1994.

5. Natural Gas Annual 1991, DOE/EIA-013(91), p. 21, Energy Information Administration, US DOE, Washington, D.C., 1992.

6. Statistical Abstract of the United States 1992, 112th Ed., p. 582, Bureau of the Census, US Department of Commerce, Washington, D.C., 1992.

7. Natural Gas Annual 1991, loc. cit., p. 16.

8. Natural Gas Annual 1991, *loc. cit.,* p. 35.

9. Capacity and Service on the Interstate Natural Gas Pipeline System 1990 – Regional profiles and Analyses, DOE/EIA-0556, Energy Information Administration, US DOE, Washington, D.C., 1992.

10. Natural Gas Annual 1991, *loc. cit.,* pp. 39-40.

11. Monthly Energy Review 1992, DOE/EIA-0035(92/06), p. 74, Energy Information Administration, US DOE, Washington, D.C., 1992.

12. Monthly Energy Review 1992, *loc. cit.,* p. 45 and p. 130.

13. Statistical Abstract of the United States 1992, 112th Ed., *loc. cit.,* p. 566.

14. Statistical Abstract of the United States 1992, 112th Ed., *loc. cit.,* p. 46.

15. Statistical Abstract of the United States 1992, 112th Ed., *loc. cit.,* p. 582.

16. Statistical Abstract of the United States 1992, 112th Ed., *loc. cit.,* p. 722.

17. Statistical Abstract of the United States 1992, 112th Ed., *loc. cit.,* p. 711.

18. Statistical Abstract of the United States 1992, 112th Ed., *loc. cit.,* p. 614.

19. Statistical Abstract of the United States 1992, 112th Ed., *loc. cit.,* pp. 726-727.

20. Statistical Abstract of the United States 1992, 112th Ed., *loc. cit.,* pp. 732-733.

21. "Convenient On-Site Natural Gas Refueling", Fuel Maker Corporation, Salt Lake City, UT, 1993.

22. E. Hutzinson-Buhler, City of Long Beach (Calif.) Gas Company, private communication, 1993.

23. "Single and Dual Compressor-Gas Packaged Filling Centers", Rix Industries, Oakland, CA, 1993.

24. M. Marelli, Southern California Gas Company, private communication, 1993.

25. "CNG Dispensing, Metering and Control Equipment for Natural Gas Vehicle Fueling Stations", DVCO Fuel Systems, Inc., Longmont, CO, 1993.

26. "Let's Clear The Air About LNG – Natural Gas Fuel For The Long Haul", Minnesota Valley Engineering LNG Group, Bloomington, MN, 1993.

27. "American National Standard/Canadian Gas Association Standard for Compressed Natural Gas Vehicle (NGV) Fueling Connection Devices", ANSI/AGA NGV1-1994 and CGA NGV1-M94, American Gas Association, Cleveland, OH and Canadian Gas Association, Toronto, ON, 1994.

28. Kirk-Othmer, Encyclopedia of Chemical Technology, "Interchangeability and Substitution of Gaseous Fuels", v. 4, pp. 302-304, A Wiley-Interscience Publication, John Wiley & Sons, New York, NY, 1982.

Chapter 6

Environmental Implications of Natural Gas As Automotive Fuel

THE NATURE OF AUTOMOTIVE POLLUTION

The replacement of the horse drawn carriage by the automobile in the early twentieth-century America had many advantages. Speed of travelling and distance covered were the obvious ones. But there was another advantage which was particularly true in large and medium size cities. This very little known and rarely publicized advantage was the improvement of the urban environment. In New York City alone at the turn of the century, horses deposited on the streets every day 2.5 million pounds of solid and 60 thousand gallons of liquid excrements[1]. These excrements in the form of dry dust irritated nasal passages and lungs. Flies that bred on the ever present heaps of the excrements carried more than thirty communicable diseases. In addition, traffic was often clogged by the carcasses of overworked horses that would collapse during summer heat waves or would be destroyed after stumbling on slippery pavements and breaking their legs in the winter. About 15 thousand dead horses were removed from the streets of New York City every year. A 1908 estimate taking all factors into account concluded that the cost of not banning horses in New York City was approximately $100 million a year.

New York City might have been the worst example of the horse transportation culture because of its high concentration of population, but every major city was experiencing similar conditions. Fortunately, most Americans still lived in rural areas or farms and were not affected by these conditions. However, the population was moving away from the country side and into the cities. The 1920 United States census would show for the first time in the history of this country that the majority of the population lived in towns with 2,500 people or more. It is inconceivable to imagine the majority of the people living in urban areas in 1920 under the same conditions as those prevailing in New York City at the turn of the century. As a matter of fact, the replacement of the horse by the automobile with its higher mobility and improved environmental quality was making possible this shift in the demographics of the population. Yet, the automobile was not entirely free of environmental consequences.

The combustion of any fuel gives rise to small amounts of noxious compounds. As long as the number of the vehicles on the road was small, the air pollutants released in the exhaust gases would disperse into the atmosphere and disappear through the natural assimilation process of the environment. Some 50 years later, however, the concentration of vehicles in some of the major metropolitan areas of the country would be such that air pollutants were manifesting themselves even in a visible fashion. Southern California and in particular the Los Angeles basin with its limited natural air circulation because of the surrounding mountains would become the premier example of automotive air pollution.

Air pollutants are classified by their physical state into particulate pollutants (minute fragments of matter in solid or liquid form) or as gaseous pollutants[2]. If a pollutant is emitted directly into the atmosphere, it is classified as a primary pollutant. If a pollutant is formed as a result of some reaction in the atmosphere following the release of a reactive compound, the resultant pollutant is classified as a secondary pollutant. Most secondary pollutants result form photochemical reactions that utilize energy from the sun. On occasion a pollutant released into the atmosphere may be a primary pollutant in its emitted form and may then undergo a reaction and become a secondary pollutant of another form.

TABLE 6-1. Historical Data on Air Pollutant Emissions in the United States.

Year	Emissions[1]					
	PM	SOx	NOx	NMOG	CO	Pb
1940	23.1	17.6	6.9	15.2	82.6	NA
1950	24.9	19.8	9.4	18.1	87.6	NA
1960	21.6	19.7	13.0	21.0	89.7	NA
1970	18.5	28.3	18.5	25.0	101.4	204
1980	8.5	23.4	20.9	21.1	79.6	71
1990	7.5	21.2	19.6	18.7	60.1	7

1. All emissions in million metric tons per year except lead in thousand metric tons per year. PM : Particulate Matter; SOx : Sulfur Oxides; NOx : Nitrogen Oxides; NMOG : Non Methane Organic Gases; CO : Carbon Monoxide; Pb : Lead.

The four principal sources of air pollution, on a weight basis, are: transportation, fuel combustion from stationary sources (e.g., power plants), industrial processes (e.g., steel mills, crude oil refineries, smelters, producers of chemicals, paper, textiles and rubber products), and solid-waste disposal (e.g., incinerators, sanitary landfills). The historical evolution of air pollutant emissions in the US is given in Table 6-1[3]. Transportation, as shown in Figure 6-1 and Table 6-2, accounts for over 40% of all air pollutants by weight and includes ships, airplanes,

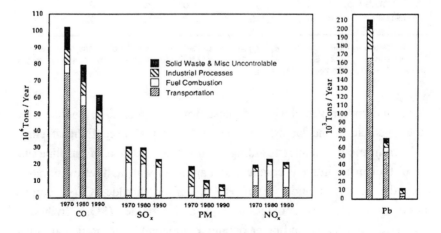

FIGURE 6-1. Comparison of Transportation and All Other Sources of Air Pollution in the US on a Weight Basis in 1990 (Source: US EPA).

TABLE 6-2. Air Pollution Emissions by Pollutant and Source in the US
from 1970 to 1990.

Year/ Source	Air Pollutant[1]					
	CO	SOx	NMOG	PM	NOx	Pb
1970 Total	101.4	28.4	25.0	18.5	18.5	204
Transportation	74.4	0.6	10.3	1.2	8.0	163
Automobiles	65.3	0.3	9.1	0.9	6.3	156
Fuel Combustion	4.5	21.3	0.6	4.6	9.1	10
Elec. Utilities	0.2	15.8	—	2.3	4.4	—
Industrial Proc.	8.9	6.4	8.9	10.5	0.7	24
Solid Waste Disp.	6.4	—	1.8	1.1	0.4	7
Misc. Uncontr.	7.2	0.1	3.3	1.1	0.3	—
1980 Total	79.6	23.4	21.1	8.5	20.9	71
Transportation	56.1	0.9	7.5	1.3	9.8	59
Automobiles	48.7	0.4	6.2	1.1	7.9	56
Fuel Combustion	7.4	18.7	0.9	2.4	10.1	4
Elec. Utilities	0.3	15.5	—	0.8	6.4	—
Industrial Proc.	6.3	3.8	9.2	3.3	0.7	4
Solid Waste Disp.	2.2	—	0.6	0.4	0.1	2
Misc. Uncontr.	7.2	0.1	3.3	1.1	0.3	—
1990 Total	60.1	21.2	18.7	7.5	19.6	7
Transportation	74.4	0.6	10.3	1.2	8.0	163
Automobiles	65.3	0.3	9.1	0.9	6.3	156
Fuel Combustion	4.5	21.3	0.6	4.6	10.1	10
Elec. Utilities	0.2	15.8	—	2.3	4.4	—
Industrial Proc.	8.9	6.4	8.9	10.5	0.7	24
Solid Waste Disp.	6.4	—	1.8	1.1	0.4	7
Misc. Uncontr.	7.2	0.1	3.3	1.1	0.3	—

1. All emissions in million metric tons per year except lead in thousand metric tons per year. PM :
Particulate Matter; SOx : Sulfur Oxides; NOx : Nitrogen Oxides; NMOG : Non Methane Organic
Gases; CO : Carbon Monoxide; Pb : Lead.

trains and motor vehicles[3]. Of these four transportation sources, the
motor vehicle is the largest contributor to air pollution. Exhaust emissions from motor vehicles resulting from the combustion of gasoline and
diesel fuel in an internal combustion engine as well as fuel evaporation
from the vehicle include water (H_2O), carbon dioxide (CO_2), carbon
monoxide (CO), nitrous oxides (NO_x), sulfur oxides (SO_x), hydrocarbons (HC), aldehydes and other organic compounds, and particulate matter (PM). The four major primary air pollutants from a motor vehicle are
CO, HC, NO_x and PM — particulate matter is predominantly emitted

form diesel fuel burning vehicles. Carbon dioxide (CO_2), even though it is emitted in much higher concentrations than all the other emissions combined, is not viewed as a pollutant per se because it has different environmental implications than the other emissions.

Hydrocarbon emissions result from the inefficient combustion of the fuel as well as from fuel evaporation either from the fuel tank or the engine crankcase. Thus the use of alcohols such as methanol and ethanol as fuels will result in the emission of these compounds into the atmosphere as pollutants. Natural gas of course consists of hydrocarbon gases. However, natural gas as a fuel eliminates the evaporative emissions, because it is stored under pressure in leak tight tanks.

Particulates of most concern are carbon from the incomplete combustion of the fuel and lead from tetra-ethyl lead in gasoline as octane booster. Other lesser particulates include the three fuel additives boron, manganese and nickel, barium which is used as a smoke suppressor, phosphorus which is added as a corrosion inhibitor, and cadmium which occurs in the tetra-ethyl lead.

Secondary pollutants formed after the primary pollutants reach the atmosphere include nitrogen dioxide (NO), ozone (O_3), peroxyacyl nitrates (PAN) and aldehydes.

The first heavy use of coal as a fuel in England during the 16th century resulted in the observation of smog, which was understood to be a mixture of smoke and moisture. This is the classical smog and most often occurs in the winter months[4]. It has a reducing effect because it takes oxygen from the materials with which it interacts. This is due to the oxidation of sulfur dioxide (SO_2) to sulfur trioxide (SO_3) and the reaction of the latter with moisture (H_2O) to form sulfuric acid (H_2SO_4). Coal and to a smaller extent crude oil and its products such as diesel oil contain sulfur which is oxidized to sulfur dioxide upon combustion.

A more recent type of smog is the so called photochemical smog. The oxidizing effects associated with photochemical smog come from some of the secondary air pollutants. Ozone is one such pollutant which is formed with the aid of sunlight acting on nitrogen dioxide (NO_2), which originates in motor vehicle exhaust. Nitrogen dioxide dissociates readily into nitrogen monoxide (NO) and atomic oxygen (O). The oxygen atom joins an oxygen molecule (O_2) to form ozone. The brown color of the photochemical smog observed primarily in the summer when solar radiation reaches its strongest intensity is due to the light absorption properties of nitrogen monoxide.

The atomic oxygen from the dissociation of nitrogen dioxide may also oxidize hydrocarbons to form a reactive compound of the form HCO, which in turn reacts with more oxygen atoms to from a very reactive species HCO_3, which in chemistry is called a radical. This radical can react with more oxygen to form ozone or with nitrogen dioxide to form peroxyacyl nitrates (PAN).

It should be noted that the lighter hydrocarbons are more stable and therefore more difficult to oxidize. In particular, methane cannot be oxidized to yield radicals under the conditions prevailing on the surface of the earth (temperature and solar intensity). Methane is thus classified as a non-reactive hydrocarbon. Consequently, the hydrocarbon emissions from motor vehicles are separated into reactive (RHC) and non-reactive (NRHC) ones. The reactivity of HCs will be addressed in more detail in a later section. In general all the organic gas emissions including reactive hydrocarbons are classified as non-methane organic gases (NMOG).

Thus, the operation of present day motor vehicles results in the generation of several air pollutants in varying degrees. These pollutants include: vapors of the fuel itself; carbon monoxide; nitrogen oxides; a variety of hydrocarbons and organic compounds; a variety of particulates; sulfur oxides; and a host of secondary reactive chemicals such as ozone and PAN generated from a solar radiation assisted interaction of nitrogen oxides and reactive hydrocarbons with oxygen in the atmosphere. The generation of all these pollutants by motor vehicles is the result of the employment of the internal combustion engine in conjunction with gasoline and diesel as fuels. However, the use of alternative fuels with an internal combustion engine can significantly modify the nature as well as the emitted quantity of these air pollutants. As it will be presented in a later section, natural gas of all alternative fuels has the capacity to reduce dramatically the air pollutants from the operation of automobiles in a practical, i.e., economically feasible fashion.

Total elimination of air pollution from automobiles is impossible to attain as the production of any fuel at the present time, from crude oil to electricity, results in the generation of some type of pollution. The elimination of pollution from the vehicle itself can be only attained with the replacement of the internal combustion engine with a different power plant and this will be discussed in a subsequent chapter. However, the wisdom of such a motor vehicle will be also examined in a later chapter in view of the capacity of the natural environment to assimilate pollutants released below a threshold level.

THE EFFECTS OF AUTOMOTIVE POLLUTION

The variety of pollutants generated by the operation of the present day motor vehicles have different implications for the environment. Most affect the health of humans, animals and plants. Others may have long term consequences on the climate and implicitly, therefore, the well being of mankind. A summary of the health and long term climatic effects of automotive air emissions will be given here on a pollutant by pollutant basis.

The characteristic feature of automotive pollution is its wide spreading such that the whole population is affected along with the urban, suburban and rural environment. On the other hand, the duration of exposure may vary within wide limits depending on the traffic density as well as weather conditions at any given location and time. Furthermore, it is important to know how certain pollutants can accumulate in the body of a living organism or the inanimate environment in the absence of the long periods, free of exposure, that are required by the organism or the inanimate environment to eliminate them through natural processes. All this must be kept in mind when attempting to evaluate the effects of motor vehicle pollution on health and the environment.

The health effects of air pollutants generated by automobiles can be both short term as well as long term. Short term health effects imply a high enough exposure that may result in serious injury and death if the pollutant happens to be toxic. The short term health effects are therefore well understood, but rarely encountered in a large population with regard to the operation of motor vehicles. Table 6-3 summarizes the threshold limit values of selected emissions, typically encountered in motor vehicle operation[5]. The threshold limit value is the accepted limit of concentration for repeated human exposure. The long term health effects are those

TABLE 6-3. Concentration in Air Threshold Limit Value and Principal Effect of Inhalation Above Threshold Limit Value for Selected Air Emissions Encountered in the Operation of Automobiles

Emission (Pr. Effect of Inh.)[1]	Threshold Value (ppm)	(mg/m^3)	Emission (Pr. Effect of Inh.)	Threshold Value (ppm)	(mg/m^3)
Acetaldehyde (I)	200	360	Methanol (T)	200	260
Benzene (T)	25	80	Naphtha (N)	500	2000
Cadmium (T)	-	0.2	Nickel (T,C)	-	1
Carbon Dioxide (T)	5000	9000	Nitrogen Dioxide (T)	5	9
Carbon Monoxide (T)	50	55	Octane (N)	500	2350
Ethanol (N)	1000	-	Ozone (T)	0.1	0.2
Formaldehyde (T)	5	6	Propane (N)	1000	1800
Lead (T)	-	0.2	Sulfur Dioxide (I)	5	13
Methane (O)	None	None	Tetraethyllead (T)	-	0.075

1. Refers to effect of inhalation of emission. Symbols: C = Carcinogenic; I = Irritant; N = Narcosis; O = No Effect; and T= Toxic.
Notes. Acetaldehyde and formaldehyde are emitted primarily in the combustion of ethanol and methanol fuels, respectively. Benzene is an unleaded gasoline additive to increase the fuel octane number and is emitted in the exhaust gases or escapes by evaporation either from the tank or during refueling. Tetraethyllead is the leaded gasoline additive to increase the octane number.

due to a chronic low level — below the threshold of Table 6.3 — exposure to the pollutants that may adversely affect health in a cumulative fashion over a period of several years. These long term health effects are much more difficult to quantify and cannot be dealt with on an individual cause and effect basis. They are rather of a statistical nature akin to the effects, for example, of cigarette smoking. For example, a recently concluded epidemiological study indicates a 30% difference in death rate from heart disease, respiratory diseases and lung cancer between the most and least polluted cities in the US[67]. When one considers that the population being exposed to automobile air pollutants includes people of all ages, states of health, occupation, and so on, and that these differences affect an individual's response to a pollutant, it seems likely that there is no threshold below which damage does not occur. Thus air pollutants, in a fashion similar to that assumed for ionizing (nuclear) radiation, could be causing damage at any exposure level and this damage would be roughly proportional to the exposure. Nevertheless, the federal government in a much criticized approach to air pollution has set thresh-

TABLE 6-4. National Ambient Air Quality Standards in the US as Prescribed by the 1970 Clean Air Act

Pollutant	Averaging Time	Primary Standard Level	Secondary Standard Level
Carbon Monoxide	8 hr[1]	10 mg/m^3 (9 ppm)	10 mg/m^3 (9 ppm)
	1 hr[1]	40 mg/m^3 (35 ppm)	40 mg/m^3 (35 ppm)
Nitrogen Dioxide	Annual (Arith. Mean)	0.100 mg/m^3 (0.05 ppm)	0.100 mg/m^3 (0.05 ppm)
	1 hr[1]	0.240 mg/m^3 (0.12 ppm)	0.240 mg/m^3 (0.12 ppm)
Hydrocarbons (Non-Methane)[2]	3 hr (6 to 9 am)	0.160 mg/m^3 (0.24 ppm)	0.160 mg/m^3 (0.24 ppm)
Ozone	1 hr[1]	0.240 mg/m^3 (0.12 ppm)	0.240 mg/m^3 (0.12 ppm)
Sulfur Oxides	Annual (Arith. Mean)	0.080 mg/m^3 (0.03 ppm)	-
	24 hr[1]	0.365 mg/m^3 (0.14 ppm)	-
	3 hr[1]	-	1.300 mg/m3 (0.50 ppm)
Particulates	Annual (Geom. Mean)	0.075 mg/m^3	0.060 mg/m^3
	24 hr1	0.260 mg/m^3	0.150 mg/m^3
Lead	3 months	0.0015 mg/m^3	0.0015 mg/m^3

1. Not to be exceeded more than once a year. 2. A non-health related standard used as a guide for ozone control.

old standards for a variety of air pollutants, as shown in Table 6-4, through the 1970 Clean Air Act Amendments[6]. These threshold standards with their subsequent revisions represent the current air quality yardstick under the name of the National Ambient Air Quality Standards. They cover carbon monoxide, nitrogen dioxide, non-methane hydrocarbons, ozone, particulates and lead.

Carbon Monoxide. Carbon monoxide is the pollutant whose effects on the human organism are the most well understood. It has a 250 times

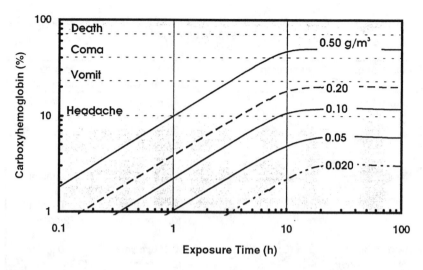

FIGURE 6-2.   Concentration of Carboxyhaemoglobin in the Blood of Humans as a Function of Exposure Time and Different CO Ambient Air Concentrations. The Slope of the Curves is a Function of the Level of Human Activity.

greater affinity for haemoglobin than oxygen. Thus, carbon monoxide replaces oxygen in haemoglobin thereby inhibiting the normal respiratory function of it, which is the transport of oxygen from the air to the body tissues. The level of carbon monoxide concentration in the blood in terms of the proportion of carboxyhaemoglobin (HbCO) depends on the concentration of carbon monoxide in the air, the duration of exposure and the pulmonary ventilation. Curves have been developed showing the HbCO concentration in the blood as a function of these parameters. Some of these curves are reproduced in Figure 6-2. Increased pulmonary ventilation, which is the result of an increased metabolic rate due to a more intense activity, results in a much faster uptake of CO and a reduction in the time it takes for the HbCO concentration to reach its plateau for any given ambient CO concentration. The concentration of HbCO in the blood of smokers and non-smokers exposed to the same CO concentrations has been monitored over a period of several days. The measurements revealed a more than three times higher HbCO concentration in the blood of the smokers (a CO ambient concentration of 25 ppm resulted in a maximum HbCO concentration of 2% for the non-smokers and 7% for the smokers)[7].

Although average urban CO concentrations are typically low, concentrations as high as 54 ppm have been measured during a traffic jam in a Los Angeles freeway, 100 ppm in Detroit traffic, and 59 ppm in a parking garage[5]. It can be assumed that a daily CO average exposure of 30 ppm may apply to an individual travelling by car in an urban area and one of up to 80 ppm may apply to a pedestrian standing at a heavily travelled intersection[7]. The consequences of hypoxia (reduction in the transport of oxygen to the tissues) can be classified into three categories as follows depending on the CO concentration[7][8][9]:

I. High concentrations above 50 ppm persisting for several hours result in functional but non-specific disorders such as headaches and nausea; concentrations of 100 ppm for 9 hours or 900 ppm for 1 hour produce discomfort; concentrations of 100 ppm for 15 hours or more produce a severe distress; and a concentration of 4,000 ppm becomes lethal in less than one hour.

II. Lower concentrations on the order normally experienced in urban areas with congested traffic over a long period of type may result in hypoxia attacks to individuals already suffering from ischemic arteriopathy. Such attacks can occur in the coronary arteries (heart) and cerebral arteries (brain). A critical level of 2.5% HbCO in the blood has been established by the World Health Organization (WHO) for this type of attack corresponding to a chronic exposure to CO of about 13 ppm.

III. Low chronic concentrations accelerate the formation of atheroma plaques resulting in premature aging of the arteries, but it has not been possible to determine a limiting concentration for this effect.

New research suggests that exposure to low levels of carbon monoxide and a diet deficient in protein may result in a reduced pregnancy rate[10]. While additional studies will be necessary to establish conclusively this result, it appears plausible that carbon monoxide may account in part for the rising infertility rate in the US and other developed countries.

There is a limited amount of data regarding the effect of carbon monoxide on plants. Reports indicate the increase of peroxydase activity (enzyme forming hydrogen peroxide) and ethylene (gas involved in fruit ripening and induction of flowering) synthesis by trees in the vicinity of freeways[11]. A premature loss of plant foliage has been also observed.

Nitrogen Oxides. Nitrogen (NO_x) oxides refer to a mixture of two compounds: nitrogen monoxide (NO) and nitrogen dioxide (NO_2). The concentration of nitrogen oxides in urban environments may rise to about 1 ppm during peak traffic hours[8]. Nitrogen monoxide is a colorless gas, but nitrogen dioxide absorbs sunlight strongly at short wavelengths (blue and green) thereby producing the characteristic brown color of photochemical smog that Los Angeles has made famous. The photochemical smog, which derives from the exhaust of the modern automobile, is responsible for the generation of ozone as well as PANs. These gaseous products of the photochemical smog happen to be biologically even more active than the nitrogen oxides. Nevertheless, nitrogen oxides, ozone and PANs are all strong irritant agents of the pulmonary alveoli (air cells) resulting in an inflammatory reaction. A certain adaptation of the lungs has been observed in the case of short exposures. These irritant agents favor the onset of pulmonary infections and the induction of respiratory allergies. Epidemiological studies have shown that for persons of good health the average concentration of NO_2 should not exceed 0.05 ppm over any 24 hour period. For more sensitive individuals, particularly those suffering from lung ailments such as asthma, chronic bronchitis and emphysema, this NO_2 concentration is too high. However, there are no data to establish a more suitable value. While nitrogen oxides have the potential to be phytotoxic, they do not appear to cause any plant damage because of their low concentration unless they are associated with other pollutants such as ozone and sulfur dioxide[11].

Hydrocarbons. Hydrocarbons are emitted by vehicles either as a result of fuel evaporation or because of incomplete combustion. With the exception of methane, which is non-reactive, they form the other major primary constituent of photochemical smog besides nitrogen dioxide leading to the formation of the secondary pollutants ozone and PANs. Reactive hydrocarbons, and in particular benzene and its homologue compounds along with other aromatic polycyclic hydrocarbons emitted from motor vehicles, are known to be carcinogenic. However, the cause-and-effect relationship between the reactive hydrocarbons (non-methane) in air pollution and cancer rates is almost impossible to prove because of the long latent period of cancer. The suspicion of a carcinogenic potential alone plus the ability to generate secondary pollutants constitute strong enough reasons to control non-methane hydrocarbon pollutants and by extension all non-methane organic gases.

Besides causing respiratory distress, the secondary pollutants (ozone and PANs) are also eye irritants. Ozone reduces the ability to perform physical exercise and can make breathing difficult in some people at concentrations as low as 0.01 ppm, which is very common in urban areas. On the other hand, PANs cause most of the eye irritations even at concentrations as low as 0.7 ppm. Plants appear to be even more sensitive than humans to ozone and PANs. Levels of PAN as small as 0.01 to 0.05 ppm can produce damage to a plant within an hour. Leafy vegetables are the most sensitive, but even trees can get damaged. Ozone is almost as bad for vegetation. Chronic exposure of plants to these secondary pollutants can cause an irreversible damage, adversely affect growth, and decrease the plant resistance to climatic stresses as well as diseases[11]. It is needless to point out that damage to crops and forests can have significant economic implications.

Particulate Matter. A large number of extremely fine particles are emitted by the automobiles. These particles are mainly found in the exhaust gases, but they can also originate in other parts of the vehicle such as tires and brakes. Approximately 70% of the emitted particles have a size range of 0.2 to 0.6 microns with an average diameter of 0.3 microns. These particles consist of both inorganic and organic compounds. The quantity of solid material produced in the exhaust is on the order of a few milligrams per gram of gasoline burned in the engine[12].

The majority of the organic fine particles are emitted from diesel engines and consist of carbon clusters formed during combustion. The carbon nucleus of these particles is surrounded with adsorbed hydrocarbons. Because of their small diameter, these particles can escape readily any exhaust trap mechanisms and what is even worse, they can penetrate deep into the lungs reaching the alveoli. Some 80% of the inhaled fine particles are lodged into the lungs for long periods of time.

Incidentally, typical dust particles on the air have a much larger diameter, 2 microns or larger, and can therefore be readily trapped in the upper respiratory passage and be subsequently rejected. The diesel fuel exhaust particles have been proven to have mutagenic effects in the laboratory. However, epidemiological studies have only recently been able to quantify their effect to the population exposed to them[67]. Fine particle pollution, which manifests itself as white haze in the air, appears to be responsible for about 60,000 deaths a year or 3% of all US mortality. Thus, fine particulate air pollution has more serious health consequences than previously thought. This observation may lead to a revision of the particulate matter standard by EPA as early as 1997.

The inorganic particles emitted from motor vehicles may include typically a number of metals such as chromium, manganese, vanadium, iron, aluminum, cadmium, nickel and lead. These metals come either from fuel additives or from the regular wear of automotive components. With the exception of lead, it is very difficult to quantify the automotive contribution of such heavy metals in the overall air pollution. Many of these metals have been recognized as toxic by industrial medicine. For example, cadmium, nickel and chromium are carcinogens and manganese is toxic to the nervous system. It is unlikely, however, that any of these heavy metals, other than lead, emitted from automobiles will have any detectable effect on humans.

Lead. Lead found in the human body is attributed primarily (60%) to gasoline additives and to a secondary degree to other sources such as water supply systems, paints, canned food, to mention a few of the most common secondary sources. The lead contribution in the human body from gasoline increases to 80% of the total in areas of heavy motor traffic[7]. Lead, at the observed levels of exposure, is acting on the porphyrin of the red blood cells whose increase in number is an indication of a restriction in the synthesis of haemoglobin. Such an effect can be detected for lead concentrations in the blood of as low as 15 micrograms per deciliter — a concentration of 35 micrograms per deciliter is considered normal. This effect, although detectable, cannot be regarded as a pathological one in the absence of anemia.

The most important effect of lead, as far as public health is concerned, is in the brain development of children in terms of intelligence

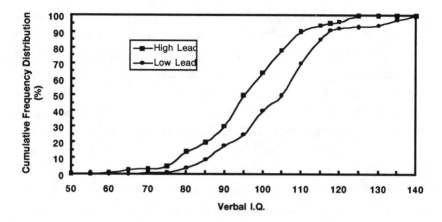

FIGURE 6-3. Cumulative Frequency Distribution of Verbal IQ Scores in Children with High and Low Lead Levels (Source: New England J. Med., 306:367, 1982).

and behavior. Figure 6-3 shows the impact on the IQ scores of children with high and low lead concentration in their bodies[13]. It appears that a 10 point reduction in the IQ at the 50 percentile level is observed between children with high and low lead levels.

More recently, it has been found that exposure of children to lead results also in the loss of hearing. These effects are apparently reversible if the lead level is reduced to normal during childhood, but become permanent in later life. The deposition of lead is directly correlated to the traffic density. Thus, the lead content in the air and on vegetation near busy streets and freeways may range from 500 ppm to 2,500 ppm[11]. However, the lead concentration drops off by about an order of magnitude within a distance of about 75 ft on either side of the road. Commercial crops whose leaves are consumed by humans (lettuce, spinach, cabbage, beans and other vegetables) show a significant increase in surface coated lead, if they are grown near freeways. These crops are unsuitable for human consumption, even if 50% of the lead deposits are removed by acid washing. On the other hand, protected edible plants like seeds, tubers (potatoes), bulbs (onions), roots (radishes, carrots),growing near freeways show no increase in lead content, suggesting that lead salts are immobile in the soil and cannot be taken up by the plant roots.

Aldehydes. Aldehydes constitute, strictly speaking, part of the non-methane organic gases emitted by automobiles and are intimately associated with alcohol fuels as primary pollutants. Aldehydes can also be secondary (photochemical smog) air pollutants. They irritate the upper respiratory tract and eyes in concentrations as low as 0.1 ppm. Such concentrations can occur in the exhaust of internal combustion engines burning hydrocarbon fuels without any catalytic converters. Formaldehyde, in particular, is classified as a mutagenic substance and consequently its limiting concentration must be set accordingly very low. Formaldehyde, which is generated in relatively high rates in methanol burning internal combustion engines, presents the most concern to public health specialists and clean air regulators with regard to alcohol fuels. Proponents of methanol as a motor vehicle fuel have argued that the emission of formaldehyde can be reduced to very low levels with appropriate catalysts. However, the validity of this claim has yet to be demonstrated beyond doubt. Acetaldehyde, generated primarily by the combustion of ethanol, is not toxic as it can be metabolized by the human body. Consequently, it has a threshold value more than fifty times higher than formaldehyde.

Alcohols. Ethanol and methanol are the two alcohols of interest in automotive emissions. Both constitute part of the non-methane organic gases emitted by automobiles utilizing them as fuel. Ethanol, when inhaled in the small concentrations in the atmosphere that could arise from the use of gasohol or even E100 (neat ethanol) fuels, does not appear to constitute a public health risk. Methanol, on the other hand, is a very toxic substance that can enter into the human body via the lungs by inhalation of vapors in the air or via the skin by absorption. Ingestion of a few milliliters of methanol can be fatal. Methanol is oxidized in the human body into formaldehyde and then into formic acid. Both of these metabolic products are the actual toxic substances. Methanol tends to accumulate in the body and the maximum acceptable concentration of continuous exposure in the absence of non-exposure periods necessary for the elimination of its metabolic products is 3 ppm[7]. Low rates of exposure to methanol can cause irritation and damage to the optical nerve, while chronic exposure to methanol can lead to permanent decrease in visual acuity.

Acid Rain. The reaction of NO_x and SO_x in the atmosphere with water results in the formation of acids that are contained in aerosols. These aerosols have a very short residence time in the troposphere ranging from two days to one week. They are washed out by rain. In recent decades, it has been noticed that rain has become more acidic giving rise to the term "acid rain". The increased acidity of the rain has resulted in the gradual increase in the acidity of lakes and streams with subsequent damage to fish and aquatic life. Lakes and other bodies of fresh water in the northeastern United States and northern Florida as well as in eastern Canada, southern Norway and Sweden, Taiwan and Japan have shown elevated levels of acidity and several of these are now barren of fish.

It is also suspected that acid rain harms crops and forests. Forest decline observed in southern Germany since the mid 1980s has been attributed to acid rain, although the mechanism is not well understood. The most plausible explanation appears to be the stress hypothesis, according to which the pollutants in the air reduce in essence the ability of the trees to withstand extreme climatic conditions and the continuous attack by disease. Finally, acid rain has a severe damaging effect on materials, including metal corrosion, stone and concrete erosion, paint discoloration and fabric deterioration. It has been estimated that in 1970 air pollution damage on materials alone was $2.2 billion annually ($7.5 billion in 1990 dollars)[14].

Acid rain is not the result of the automobile use alone. Power generation and industry combined generate more air pollutants leading to the formation of acid rain than transportation. It is interesting to note that the average contribution of acidity in the rain east of the Mississippi is due two-thirds to SO_x and one-third to NO_x[15]. The contribution of SO_x and NO_x in the acidity of precipitation West of the Mississippi is about equal, while in Southern California SO_x contributed one-third and NO_x two-thirds of the acidity in the rain. The changing significance of SO_x and NO_x from east to west of the US reflects the predominant source of acid rain emissions: coal power plants, heavy industry in the east and automobiles in the west.

The evolution in the concentration of air pollutants in the US since 1975 is summarized in Table 6-5[3][16]. It is worth noting that a significant reduction in the concentration of air pollutants has occurred across

TABLE 6-5. Evolution of the Average National Ambient Air Pollutant Concentrations in the US from 1975 to 1990

Pollutant	Unit	Mon. Stat.[1]	EPA St.[2]	1975	1980	1985	1990
CO	ppm	248	9.0	11.68	8.68	6.99	5.89
Ozone	ppm	288	0.12	0.154	0.143	0.123	0.114
SOx	ppm	374	0.03	0.015	0.011	0.009	0.008
PM	mg/m^3	1,750	75.0	60.0	61.6	47.7	47.3
NOx	ppm	116 0	.053	0.026	0.027	0.024	0.022
Pb	mg/m^3	139	1.5	0.88	0.69	0.26	0.07

1. Number of monitoring stations as of 1990.
2. Federal air quality standard per Table 6-4.

the board in one and a half decades even though the economy of the country has more than doubled and the automobile fleet has increased by almost 50% during the same period. This reduction has been the result of pollution control measures for both stationary and mobile sources mandated by the Federal Government since 1970. The pollution control measures pertaining to motor vehicles will be addressed in the next two sections.

AUTOMOTIVE AIR POLLUTION LEGISLATIVE CONTROL

The dramatic nature of air pollution may be best appreciated through the impact of certain disasters that occurred in the first half of this century. In all these cases the occurrence of a temperature inversion layer above an area generating heavily air pollutants sealed-in the air below and caused serious illness, discomfort and excess death[2]. In December 1930, a thick, stagnant fog enveloped a heavily industrialized area of the Meuse Valley in Belgium resulting in the death of sixty-three persons and the illness of 6,000 persons from throat irritations, hoarseness, coughing, and breathlessness. In October 1948, a similar fog blanketed Donora, PA, where over a period of 4 days twenty persons died and 6,000 became ill with coughs, sore throats, headaches, burning eyes, and nausea. In December 1952, London, UK experienced an extremely dense fog for 4 days which has since become known as the "Killer Smog of 1952". In a seven day period following the inception of this fog, as shown clearly in Figure 6-4, some 1,600 deaths above the norm were reported and cardiorespiratory illnesses increased sharply.

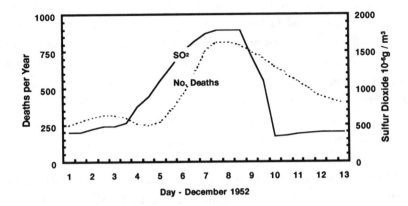

FIGURE 6-4. Pollutant (SO_2) Concentration and Deaths during the London 1952 Air Pollution Episode (Source: E.T. Wilkins, Journal of the Royal San. Inst., 74 (1), 1954).

Several milder air pollution episodes were also recorded in large American cities such as New York City, Nashville and New Orleans. In all these instances power generation and industrial activities, rather than mobile sources, were the main source of pollution. Fortunately, the impact of transportation based air pollution was discovered in connection with material and plant damage rather than human health failure.

The first evidence of the existence of photochemical smog was discovered in Los Angeles in the early 1950s, when it was found that the observed deterioration of the rubber of automobile tires was due to the elevated presence of ozone at ground level. The origin of this ozone was then traced to NO_x and hydrocarbons as has been discussed in the previous section. A little earlier, in the late 1940s, it was observed that flowers and citrus trees were suffering damage that could not be explained by known causes. However, the impact of the automobile to the air pollution had become visible in Los Angeles as early as 1940 when the brown haze of NO_x began to materialize.

The first legislation to control auto emissions was passed in 1947, when California prescribed the first crankcase emissions control[2]. By 1963 all US auto manufacturers voluntarily installed a blow-by control device to eliminate crankcase emissions (oil vapors, CO and HC) on all vehicles. However, crankcase emissions accounted for only a small fraction of automotive pollution. The tailpipe exhaust and evaporation of fuel from the carburetor and fuel tank had yet to be tackled. The first federal air pollution control act passed in 1955 and provided limited guidance to the states regarding air pollution problems. In 1963, the Clean Air Act was passed, followed by the Air Quality Act of 1967 (Public Law 90-148). These acts authorized extended research into the nature and extent of the nation's air pollution problem and established, among others, the right of the federal government to set national exhaust emission standards. A national air-sampling network was also initiated.

The Clean Air Act Amendment of 1970 (Public Law 91-604) established automobile exhaust standards for the 1973-1974 models and beyond as indicated in Table 6-6, extended the network of air pollution monitoring stations to a large number, and established criteria for compliance and enforcement of such standards by the Environmental Protection Agency (EPA). Needless to mention that the Clean Air Act covered mobile as well as stationary air pollution sources. Subsequent amendments to the Clean Air Act through 1990 have consistently reduced the amount of exhaust pollutants allowed by automobiles as shown in Table 6-6[17][18][19].

However, the EPA has also been under pressure since 1970 to relax the automobile emission standards. Twice in the 1970s (1973 and 1977) and twice in the 1980s (1980 and 1984) the federal standards were either adjusted or delayed. In parallel, California has also instituted different auto exhaust standards since the mid 1970s, which are also included in Table 6-6. The California standards required reduced NOx emissions but in return allowed higher CO emissions[17][18].

The Clean Air Act Amendment of 1990 requires the following schedule of implementation: 40% in 1994 model year, 80% in 1995 model year and 100% in 1996 and beyond. The latest California standards established in 1988 are identical to the 1990 federal standards but will go into effect one year earlier (1993 model year).

The Clean Air Act Amendment of 1990 established also requirements for the so called clean fuel vehicles. These clean fuel vehicle standards are stricter than those for gasoline or diesel fuel vehicles. However, the 1990 Clean Air Act Amendment does not specify any particular fuels. Rather, any fuel, including reformulated gasoline, that can

TABLE 6-6. Evolution of Motor Vehicle Exhaust Emission Standards in the United States and California in Grams of Pollutant per Mile Driven (g/mi)

Year	CO	NMHC[1]	NOx	PM[2]	HCHO[3]
Passenger Cars and Light Trucks (gasoline or diesel fuel)					
1960[4]	84.4	24.8	4.1	—	—
1970	34.0	4.1	6.0[4]	None	None
1975	15.0	1.5	3.1	None	None
1980	7.0	0.41	2.1	None	None
1982	7.0	0.41	1.0	0.6	None
1985 (Calif.)	7.0	0.41	0.7	0.4	None
1987	3.4	0.41	1.0	0.2	None
1989 (Calif.)	7.0	0.41	0.7	0.08	None
1994[5]	3.4	0.25	0.4	0.08	None
1993 (Calif.)	3.4	0.25	0.4	0.08	None
Passenger Cars and Light Trucks (clean fuels)[6]					
1996 50k-mile	3.4	0.125	0.4	0.08	0.015
100k-mile	4.2	0.156	0.6	0.08	0.018
2001 150k-mile	3.4	0.075	0.2	0.08	0.015
100k-mile	4.2	0.090	0.3	0.08	0.018

1. Non methane hydrocarbons extended to non methane organic gases (NMOG) after 1996. 2. Particulate matter applying only to diesel fueled vehicles. 3. Formaldehyde. 4. Pre- and Un-controlled vehicle emissions. 5. This is a 1996 standard, which requires 40% compliance of the 1994 model year cars and 80% of the 1995 model year cars. 6. Light trucks with a 6,000 lb gross vehicle weight rating. The 1994 Chrysler production minivan operating on CNG has attained the following average emissions: CO 0.3 g/mi, NMOG 0.005 g/mi and NOx 0.04 g/mi.

meet these standards will be classified as a clean fuel. Moreover, the clean fuel vehicle standards, to be implemented in two phases in 1996 (Phase I) and 2001 (Phase II), are required to be met at 50 thousand and 100 thousand miles as shown in Table 6-6. This is a significant improvement over the gasoline and diesel fuel standards for passenger cars and light trucks that must be met only at the time of the vehicle initial sale by the manufacturer.

In California, a pilot test program will be established by EPA to demonstrate the effectiveness of clean-fuel vehicles in controlling air pollution. This program is applicable only to passenger cars and light trucks. Clean fuel vehicles will be produced and sold in a number that meets or exceeds 150,000 vehicles in model years 1996 through 1998 and 300,000 vehicles in model years 1999 and thereafter. Vehicles under this program will be required to meet the same Phase I (1996) and Phase II (2201) emission standards.

Potential clean fuels include at the present time alcohols, such as methanol or ethanol, in blends of 85% or more alcohol with gasoline or any other fuel, reformulated gasoline and diesel fuel, natural gas, liquefied petroleum gas, hydrogen and electricity.

There are additional regulatory measures in areas heavily polluted with CO and ozone. All carbon monoxide non-attainment areas with concentrations above 9.5 ppm must sell only oxygenated fuels during the high CO season (winter). Starting in 1992, the minimum oxygen content of the automotive fuel is 2.7% by weight. Reformulated gasoline is to be phased in the nine cities with the highest ozone levels starting in 1995. Reformulated gasoline fuel specifications require increased oxygen content as well as reductions in benzene, aromatic hydrocarbons and heavy metals. Moreover, reformulated gasoline fuels must meet restrictions on emissions of non-methane organic gases as well as formaldehyde.

The Clean Air Act Amendment of 1990 set additional requirements. A cold start standard for passenger cars and light trucks will be phased in during the model year 1994 according to which CO emissions should not exceed 10 g/mi when the vehicle is operated at $20^\circ F$ ambient temperature. EPA is directed to promulgate standards for on-board fuel vapor recovery during refueling with an efficiency of 95% to be implemented four years after the establishment of the standard. Moreover, EPA will promulgate regulations covering evaporative emissions of hydrocarbons from all gasoline vehicles taking place during operation and over two or more days of vehicle non use under summertime weather conditions. Finally, the EPA must promulgate regulations taking effect in the 1994 model year for manufacturers to install diagnostic systems on all new passenger cars and light trucks. These diagnostic systems must be capable to: accurately monitor the vehicle emission system for deterioration or malfunction; alert the vehicle owner of need for repair; and store and retrieve appropriate fault codes.

The state of California adopted in 1989 clean vehicle standards that are expected to become the backbone of the state's clean air efforts into the 21st century[20]. These standards redefine "clean" vehicles and phase

TABLE 6-7. California Clean Vehicle Emissions Standard (g/mi), Year of Implementation and Clean Vehicle Representation as Percent of New Vehicle Market

Vehicle Category	Emission Standard			New Vehicle Market Penetration[1]					
	NMOG	CO	NOx	2%	10%	15%	20%	25%	75%
TLEV	0.125	3.4	0.4		94		96		
LEV	0.075	3.4	0.2					97	03
ULEV	0.040	1.7	0.2	97		03			
ZEV	0.0	0.0	0.0	98	03				

1. Numbers indicate the last two digits of the year of implementation from 1994 to 2003.

in the use of cleaner burning and non-traditional fuels to power them. These standards, which are shown in Table 6-7, include the nation's first mandatory production of zero emission vehicles to use electricity as a fuel under present technology. The other clean vehicle categories and the schedule of their implementation is as follows: transition low emission vehicles (TLEV) 10 to 20 percent of new vehicle production between model years 1994 and 1996; low emission vehicles (LEV) 25 to 75 percent of new vehicles between model years 1997 and 2003; ultra low emission vehicles (ULEV) 2 to 15 percent of new vehicle production between model years 1997 and 2003; and zero emission vehicles (ZEV) 2 to 10 percent of new vehicles between model years 1998 and 2003[19]. Incidentally, the size of the California new vehicle market is currently about two million vehicles annually. The California Air Resources Board has proposed fuel/vehicle systems capable of attaining these low emission standards.

The first diesel exhaust particulate standards for passenger cars and light trucks were established by the EPA in 1980 and went into effect in 1982[21]. The state of California decided to adopt its own diesel particulate standards starting in 1985 but with a more aggressive schedule of reduction in emissions. In 1981, the EPA also established diesel particulate emissions for heavy trucks and buses. However, a four year delay by a new Administration at EPA for re-evaluation ensued and the standards became law only in 1986. The implementation did not begin until the 1988 model year as shown in Table 6-8. The schedule of particulate emission reduction for buses was accelerated by 3 years after the 1991

TABLE 6-8. Diesel Heavy Truck and Bus Particulate Emission Standards in the United States in Grams per Brake-Horsepower-Hour (Grams per kWh)

Year	Particulate Emission	
	Heavy Truck	Urban Bus
Pre-1988[1]	1.00 g/bhph (1.34 g/kWh)	1.00 g/bhph (1.34 g/kWh)
1988	0.60 g/bhph (0.80 g/kWh)	0.60 g/bhph (0.80 g/kWh)
1991	0.25 g/bhph (0.34 g/kWh)	0.10 g/bhph (0.13 g/kWh)
1994	0.10 g/bhph (0.13 g/kWh)	0.05 g/bhph (0.065 g/kWh)[2]
1998	0.10 g/bhph (0.13 g/kWh)	0.05 g/bhph (0.065 g/kWh)

1. Estimated emission as no standard existed. 2. May be relaxed to 0.07 g/bhph if technology is not available to meet the proposed level.

model year, because of the special need of pollution control in urban areas. These heavy truck and bus standards are required to be met over the full life of the vehicle or engine, rather than over 50 thousand miles or even 100 thousand miles as is the case for passenger cars and light trucks. It should be also noted that the Clean Air Act Amendment of 1990 prescribes the following emissions for heavy-duty engine trucks and buses in the 1991-1998 period: a 15.5 g/bhph CO emission; a 1.3 g/bhph HC emission; and a NOx emission of 5.0 g/bhph through 1994 becoming 4.0 g/bhph in 1998.

The state of California has also imposed diesel fuel specifications that go into effect in 1993[20]. According to these specifications the sulfur content of diesel fuel is to be reduced from the precontrol value of 0.3% to 0.05% after controls. Likewise the content of aromatic hydrocarbons in diesel fuel is to be reduced from an average precontrol level of 31% to 10% starting in 1993 — small refiners are allowed to reduce aromatic hydrocarbons to 20% only[20]. These diesel fuel standards have been also adopted by the EPA and will go into effect across the nation in 1996.

The average concentration of air pollutants across the country appears to be well below the limits for hourly and daily exposure set forth by the 1970 Clean Air Act. Unfortunately, this is not true on a regional basis where the levels of CO and ozone exceed the standards several days in each year. Some 100 metropolitan areas failed to meet

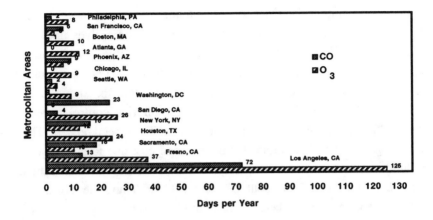

FIGURE 6-5. Average Number of Days Exceeding the Federal Ozone and Carbon Monoxide Standards in the Most Polluted Regions of the US During the Two Year 1989-1990 Period.

the ozone standard for at least one day in 1989-1990 and 50 metropolitan areas failed to meet likewise the carbon monoxide standard in the same period[3]. California in particular shows the largest number of nonattainment regions. Figure 6-5 presents the average number of days over the federal ozone and carbon monoxide standards for the top violating regions in the two year period of 1989 and 1990[3][20].

Southern California, where some 15 million people live and over 10 million vehicles exist, fails to meet the ozone standard one out of three days each year and the carbon monoxide standard one out of six days each year. The chronic health consequences of this exposure to air pollution have been established beyond doubt at this point[20]. One study found that the lung capacity of school children, who have lived all their lives in Southern California, is diminished by an average of 25% compared to children of the same socioeconomical background living elsewhere in the country. Another study evaluated the lungs of a large number of young adults, aged 14 to 25 years old, victims of traffic accidents and homicide. Nearly all were lifelong residents of Southern California and were not likely to have been affected by a lifetime of smoking or exposure to occupational hazards that would have lead to lung disorders. Varying degrees of chronic lung inflammation was found in 75% of the subjects studied and nearly all had chronic bronchitis.

All these findings underscore the potential of air pollution to create life-long health problems, which do not manifest themselves until later in one's life. It is very difficult, but nevertheless feasible, to estimate the health and other (vegetation, materials, property values) costs associated with air pollution in the country. Studies indicate that the annual avoided cost, i.e., the benefit, from air and water pollution control measures in the US amounts to 1% and 1.2% of the GNP, respectively[22]. These percentages of the GNP values for the avoided cost due to air and water pollution control are corroborated by studies in Germany which actually show a damage equal to about 2% of the GNP. Thus, the avoided air pollution cost in the US because of control measures may on the order of $60 billion annually, while the incurred damage may be as high as $120 billion annually at the present time. In addition, more than 80% of the 1% of the GNP avoided cost for air pollution control refers to health effect benefits.

What is far better known, however, than the avoided annual air pollution cost is the annual cost of air pollution abatement invested by individuals, businesses and the government towards this goal. In 1989, some $91.5 billion were spent for air, water and solid waste control[3]. Air pollution control accounted for $32.7 billion of the total, while water and solid waste pollution control accounted for $36 billion and $23.2 billion, respectively. Of the $32.7 billion spent for air pollution control, mobile sources accounted for 56.7% ($18.5 billion) and stationary sources for the remainder. The mobile source air pollution control cost consists essentially of expenditures to reduce emissions in passenger cars, trucks and other land vehicles.

It appears then that the benefit to cost ratio in air pollution control in the US is on the order of two, i.e., the benefit (avoided cost) is twice as much as the cost of abatement. Conversely, the air pollution abatement investment represents, even though sizeable by itself, only 50% of the magnitude of the avoided health, property and other damage costs due to reduced air pollution. Moreover, an additional annual investment of $30 to $50 billion may be required to totally eliminate the health damage due to the remaining air pollution. If one half of this damage is due to mobile sources, then an additional ultimate investment of $1,250 per vehicle and vehicle infrastructure would be necessary ($25 billion annually — in 1990 dollars — divided by 20 million new vehicles sold each year after 2020 when the number of vehicles in the US will reach a constant level independent of the population).

AUTOMOTIVE AIR POLLUTION TECHNOLOGICAL CONTROL

The passage of the 1963 Clean Air Act and its subsequent Amendments made the automobile manufacturers responsible for the development of technologies to meet the imposed emission standards. The only technology available to meet the progressively more stringent emission standards has been the automobile catalytic converter. Catalytic converters are needed to meet emission standards of all passenger cars. Moreover, catalysts are being used in recent years to meet emission limits of light trucks and vans. Catalytic converters have been in use in the US since the 1974 model year. Up to that point in time the less stringent emission standards were met by simply changing engine calibration including a leaner air/fuel ratio and a retardation of the spark. It was felt by the automotive manufacturers that any further engine calibration would have resulted in an unacceptable fuel consumption and driveability. Thus, the introduction of catalysts not only improved the vehicle performance but it also arrested and reversed the decline of fuel efficiency which has occurred in the previous six years (1968-1974).

Initially catalytic converters were used to control carbon dioxide and reactive hydrocarbons. The nitrogen oxide emission standard could be met through 1980 by using exhaust gas recirculation back into the engine that resulted in the formation of less nitrogen oxide. The catalysts used were oxidation catalysts containing the noble metals platinum and palladium[17]. A typical catalyst used by General Motors contained 0.05 oz t (1.55 grams) of noble metals with a 5/2 ratio between platinum and palladium. A development that paved the way for the feasibility of the catalytic converter was the removal of lead from gasoline. This was necessary in order to prevent the contamination of the catalyst that would render it ineffective.

Two basic catalyst structures have been used, distinguished by the configuration of the catalyst support. The two support systems are alumina pellets and alumina coated ceramic monoliths. The pellets are approximately 1/8th-inch in diameter and are comprised of thermally stable transitional alumina (Al_2O_3). The monoliths consist of a ceramic material such as cordierite ($2Mg, 2Al_2O_3, 5SiO_2$).

The catalytic converter consists of an inlet plenum, a narrow louvered catalyst bed, and an exhaust plenum. Exhaust gases flow in at the top of the converter through a decreasing inlet plenum, pass through the catalyst, and exist through an increasing outlet plenum. This design ensures flow uniformity, low flow restriction, and minimal catalyst movement. The converter exterior shell and internal parts are typically made of stainless steel for a low cost, corrosion resistant and high temperature durability product. The sizes of pellet-type catalysts employed, for example, by General Motors in 1975 were 160 cu-in (2.6 liter) and 260 cu-in (4.3 liter).

The introduction of such a catalyst in 1975 was met with some concern and criticism regarding the potential of the high catalyst surface temperature to cause fire. Subsequently, these concerns were proven to be unfounded. Another concern, also found unsubstantiated, was the potential of the catalytic oxidation of sulfur dioxide to sulfuric acid emitted in the exhaust.

The more stringent NO_x emission standard after 1980 necessitated the introduction of the so called "three-way-catalyst" since 1981. Exhaust gas recirculation was no longer adequate to control nitrogen oxides. A new catalyst and a new emission approach had to be developed, which could simultaneously remove carbon monoxide, reactive hydrocarbons and nitrogen oxides. The hydrocarbons and carbon monoxide are oxidized to CO_2 and H_2O, while nitrogen oxide is reduced to nitrogen according to the reactions:

$$HC + O_2 \longrightarrow CO_2 + H_2O$$
$$CO + O_2 \longrightarrow CO2 + H_2O$$
$$NO + CO \text{ and } H_2 \longrightarrow N_2 + CO_2 \text{ and } H_2O$$

The noble metal rhodium combined with platinum has the property to catalyze all three reactions, if the catalytic converter is operated at an air/fuel ratio close to the stoichiometric composition (for gasoline 14.6 : 1 mass of air to mass of fuel to convert all the fuel to water and carbon dioxide)[17][23]. A schematic diagram illustrating the principle of operation of a three-way catalyst is shown in Figure 6-6. An air mass to fuel

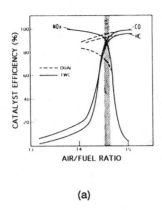

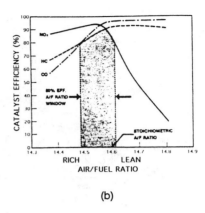

(a)

(b)

FIGURE 6-6. (a) Efficiency Comparison of Dual and Three-Way Automotive Catalysts vs. Air/Fuel Ratio; (b) Detail of the Three-Way Catalyst "Window".

mass ratio equal to the stoichiometric one is characterized as an equivalence ratio of one. Values of the equivalence ratio less than one represent rich fuel mixtures (excess fuel) and values larger than one reflect lean fuel mixtures (excess air).

Complete conversion of the reducing species (HC, CO) is favored under conditions of excess air, while the conversion of the oxidizing species (NO) is favored under excess fuel conditions. It is only around the region of stoichiometry, actually somewhat to the fuel rich side, where there exists a "window" for efficient, simultaneous removal of all three species. The task of the modern engine electronic control system is to maintain the air/fuel ratio as tightly as possible within this window over all possible variations in driving conditions. The catalytic converter system, on the other hand, must be designed with as wide a window as possible without compromising the catalyst activity. The present embodiment of a three-way catalyst consists of either pellets (thermally stable alumina) or a monolithic ceramic material (cordierite) as a support and 0.03 to 0.1 oz t (0.9 to 3.1 g) of platinum, 0.005 to 0.017 oz t (0.2 to 0.5 g) of rhodium and 0 to 0.1 oz t (0 to 3.1 g) of palladium as the active materials. In addition to these three noble metals, three way catalysts contain the base metal cerium and possible other metal additives such as lanthanum, nickel and iron to improve the conversion perfor-

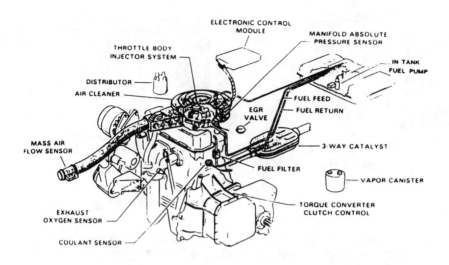

FIGURE 6-7. Closed-Loop Emission Control System on a Three-Way Catalyst Equipped Vehicle (Source: General Motors Corporation).

mance during rapid air/fuel ratio changes and to stabilize the alumina support against thermal degradation.

In order to provide the proper air/fuel ratio required for the three-way catalyst a closed loop electronic control system has been developed comprised of an engine exhaust oxygen sensor and on-board microprocessor to provide the necessary control capability. A diagram of the control system component is shown in Figure 6-7. The microprocessor receives signals from the oxygen sensor and a number of other sensors and generates output signals to control engine air-fuel, spark timing, transmission converter clutch, and a variety of other engine and drive-train functions. The operating temperature of the catalytic converter, warmed up by the engine exhaust gases, is typically 600 to 900°F and is required for the reactions to take place at the highest efficiency. No reactions or reduced catalytic efficiency occur in a cold catalyst, encountered typically up to several minutes after a vehicle cold start. Currently, two types of catalytic converters are used to meet the passenger car and light truck emission standards in the US: three-way converters and dual-bed converters. Both contain a three-way catalyst, but in the dual-bed converter the three-way catalyst is followed by an air-injection/oxidation catalyst.

In the US the exhaust catalytic converters must be able to maintain high conversion efficiency for 50,000 miles or five years. The federal regulations require that exhaust emissions not exceed the standards within this compliance period. Because catalysts become deactivated over time, the automotive manufacturers build into the design measures to offset this loss of reactivity. These measures include: initial vehicle emissions below the standards; selection of materials which are more durable in the exhaust environment; and prevention of the accessibility to modify the vehicle operation that could alter emissions.

The major mechanisms of catalyst deterioration are thermal damage due to exposure to very high temperatures, poisoning by contaminants in the exhaust, and mechanical damage of the catalyst support. Exposure of catalysts to high temperature oxidizing conditions damages the CO conversion, whereas catalyst poisoning damages the HC oxidation capability. Oxidizing conditions (lean air-fuel mix) have been observed to damage three way catalysts at lower temperatures more so than reducing conditions (rich air-fuel mix). Vehicle conditions that can produce high catalyst temperatures are, for example, repeated misfire resulting in the oxidation of large amounts of fuel over the catalyst as well as driving at very high speeds. Excessive temperature can also damage the catalyst by sintering the noble metal as well the catalyst support. Typical catalyst poisons are lead and phosphorus both of which are found in gasoline. Unleaded gasoline has a maximum allowed lead content of 0.05 g/gal and a typical lead content of 0.003 g/gal. Lead is not believed to be a major catalyst poison at the 0.003 g/gal level. On the other hand, use of leaded gasoline (lead content 1.2 g/gal) damages irreversibly a three way catalyst, particularly its HC and NO_x conversion capability. It is worth mentioning that a 1984 survey contacted by the EPA found a 14% fuel switching of the vehicles tested from unleaded to leaded gasoline. The same survey showed that 21% of the tested vehicles had a component in the vehicle emission control system tampered with or missing. Regular vehicle inspection as well as the phasing out of leaded gasoline are expected to reduce the incidence of such occurrences in the future. Phosphorus is a potential poison of automotive catalysts, but its levels in gasoline are very low (0.2 g/l) to have any effect. However, the engine oils contain phosphorous in high concentrations (1.2 g/l), which is the source of contamination of the catalysts. Sulfur dioxide from the combustion of sulfur contained in the fuel does not affect the noble metal catalysts as strongly as it affects the base-metal catalysts. Other catalyst poisoning agents are organo-silicon compounds and manganese fuel additives.

The supply of noble metals and particularly the supply of rhodium is of concern to automotive manufacturers. The natural occurrence of platinum and rhodium in the crust of the earth is in the ratio of about 17:1, while the respective ratio of these two metals varies between 10:1 (US) and 5:1 (Europe) in three-way catalysts. This implies that a disproportionately higher percentage of rhodium is used in automobiles. In 1985, for example, 31% of western world platinum demand (total annual demand 2.81 million oz) and 54% of the western demand of rhodium (total annual demand 0.25 million oz) were used in automobile catalysts[24]. Consequently, the recovery of platinum, palladium and since 1990 rhodium from spent automobile catalysts has become a source of these noble metals.

THE AUTOMOBILE AND CLIMATIC CHANGE

The gaseous and particulate emissions of motor vehicles discussed so far affect the quality of the environment, particularly the health of humans, on a local basis and very near the surface of the earth where they are generated. Unfortunately, other automobile gaseous emissions appear to have the potential for a global environmental impact by affecting the climate of the earth. The two very much discussed such effects are the global warming and the ozone depletion. However, motor vehicles are not the sole cause of such effects. In this section, the present and future contribution of automobiles to climatic change will be assessed. In particular, the merits of natural gas as a motor fuel will be examined vis-a-vis gasoline and other alternative fuels.

Global Warming. Global warming, better known as the greenhouse effect, may be the result of the increasing concentration of certain gases in the atmosphere which cause the retention of infra-red radiation. Thus, the temperature of the surface of the Earth as well as the that of the lower atmosphere tend to increase. Water vapor, because of it abundance, is by far the most important greenhouse gas. Water vapor is added to, and removed from the atmosphere in a natural equilibrium cycle driven by solar radiation through the processes of evaporation and precipitation. Carbon dioxide, the second most important greenhouse gas, is added to the atmosphere both by natural as well as anthropogenic processes. Natural processes include volcanic eruptions and the continuous formation and decay of biomass. The burning of fossil fuels and the accelerated destruction of biomass (rainforests) are the major anthropogenic processes in the net release of excess carbon dioxide into the atmosphere. Other greenhouse gases include the chlorofluorocarbons (CFCs) and related gases (HFCs and HCFCs), methane (CH_4) and nitrous oxide (N_2O).

Table 6-9 summarizes the common greenhouse gases, their origins, rate of buildup in the atmosphere and contribution to global warming as of the early 1990s[25]. It is worth noting that the concentration of CO_2

TABLE 6-9. The Common Greenhouse Gases, Origins, Rates of Buildup in the Atmosphere and Contribution to Global Warming in the Early 1990s

Gas[1]	Principal Source	Rate of Increase/ Concentration[2]	Contribution to Global Warming
CO_2	Fossil fuel burning (77%) Deforestation (23%)	0.5% per year/ 353 ppm	55%
CFCs	Refrigerants, Foams, Solvents	4% per year/ 280 ppt CFC-11 488 ppt CFC-12	24%
CH_4	Rice Paddies, Enteric Fermentation, Gas Leakage	0.9% per year/ 1.72 ppm	15%
N_2O	Fertilizer Use, Biomass Burning	0.8% per year/ 310 ppb	6%

1. Tropospheric ozone generated as a secondary air pollutant may have a significant but as yet unquantified greenhouse effect contribution.
2. Concentration units: ppm = part per million, ppb = parts per billion, and ppt = parts per trillion.

in the atmosphere at the dawn of the industrial revolution era (circa 1860) has been estimated at about 270 ppm. By 1958, when the monitoring station of Mauna Loa in Hawaii began operation, the CO_2 concentration had increased to 316 ppm. The next three decades witnessed a more than 11% cumulative CO_2 concentration increase leading to a present value of 353 ppm. If the current rate of CO_2 increase is sustained, a doubling of the pre-industrial revolution concentration will be reached by the year 2030.

The contribution to global warming in Table 6-9 is based on the increase in the concentration of the greenhouse gases since the beginning of the industrial revolution. Thus, the CO_2 concentration has increased by about 80 ppm and accounts for about 55% of the global warming. All the other greenhouse gases combined have an effective CO_2 concentration increase of about 65 ppm, even though the actual mass quantities of these gases released into the atmosphere are smaller by an order of magnitude or more compared to carbon dioxide. This is due to the significantly higher effectiveness of methane, the CFCs and nitrous oxide to absorb infra-red radiation compared to carbon dioxide as Table 6-10 indicates [25][26][27][28]. The instantaneous as well as the residence or life time average global warming potential of these gases relative to carbon dioxide are given in Table 6-10. It is important to appreciate the significance of the residence time as the factor determining the ultimate global warming potential of a particular gas. This fact is frequently ignored, particularly in the case of methane where it has the greatest impact. In addition, the residence time of methane in the atmosphere is not known precisely and numbers as low as 8 years and as high as 14 years have been quoted in the literature [25][26].

Nitrous oxide results from the microbiological interactions of bacteria with nitrogen compounds in soils, including fertilizers. In the last four decades global nitrogen fertilizer consumption has increased by more than an order of magnitude approaching 80 million tons per year. According to one recent estimate, an average of 36 to 50% of the fertilizer escapes in the atmosphere as gaseous nitrogen (ammonia (NH_3), nitrogen (N_2) and nitrous oxide) [29]. Contrary to claims in several books on global warming, nitrous oxide does not appear to be created in the combustion of fossil fuels [30]. However, the decomposition of ammoni-

TABLE 6-10. Residence (Life) Time and Global Warming Potential Relative to Carbon Dioxide of Various Greenhouse Gases

Gas	Residence	Global Warming Potential			
	Time (yr)	Instantaneous		Life Time Average	
		Molar	Weight	Molar	Weight
CO_2	230	1	1	1	1
CH_4	10	27	75	2.6	7
N_2O	160	200	200	180	180
CFC-11	60	12,000	1,080	4,000	1,300
CFC-12	120	15,800	1,568	10,000	3,700
HCFC-22	15	—	—	810	410

um nitrate, a fertilizer, under heating releases also nitrous oxide. Thus, biomass burning has the potential of releasing N_2O as well.

The atmosphere contains currently 2,750 billion tons of carbon dioxide. In the beginning of the industrial revolution this figure stood at 2,100 billion tons[25][31]. This increase has been the result of fossil fuel burning and more recently of deforestation. Presently, the annual release of carbon dioxide in the atmosphere is 18.5 billion tons from fossil fuel burning and 7.5 billion tons due to deforestation. The terrestrial biota — all life on land — absorbs around 375 billion tons of carbon dioxide annually from the atmosphere for photosynthesis. Respiration from the biota releases 183 billion tons of carbon dioxide back into the atmosphere. Another 183 billion tons are released from the bacterial decomposition of dead plant matter. This implies that some 8 billion tons of CO_2 are retained in the terrestrial biota each year presumably derived from the excess 26 billion tons of carbon dioxide released from fossil fuel burning and deforestation.

In the oceanic domain, carbon dioxide is also drawn from and returned to the atmosphere as a result of biological and chemical processes. Carbon dioxide is taken into solution as bicarbonate ion and by single cell plants (phytoplankton) for photosynthesis. A total of 337 billion tons of CO_2 are drawn annually from the atmosphere by this mechanism. From the surface waters some 330 billion tons of CO_2 are returned to the atmosphere by diffusion from the seawater and as a result of plankton respiration. The net result is that 7 billion tons of

CO_2 are sequestered annually by the oceans also derived from the excess 26 billion tons of carbon dioxide released from fossil fuel burning and deforestation

Consequently, the net increase of carbon dioxide in the atmosphere amounts to 11 billion tons annually, i.e., 26 billion tons from fossil fuels and deforestation minus 15 billion tons retained by the terrestrial biota and sequestered by the oceans. Incidentally, the amount of CO_2 in the oceans is on the order of 150,000 billion tons and that in carbonate sedimentary rocks on the surface of the earth is on the order of 2,000,000 billion tons[31]. Thus, it would appear that the 11 billion tons of net CO_2 release into the atmosphere is relatively insignificant. On the other hand, the total atmospheric CO_2 is cycled through the biosphere in a rather short time on the order of 10 years or less. Unfortunately, it is not known how stable the carbon cycle system is with respect to small perturbations. It is conceivable that a chaotic behavior might ensue at some point that could have catastrophic implications for the environment[32]. Consequently, the concern over the rising CO_2 concentration in the atmosphere is not unfounded.

The more immediate implication is, of course, the potential for a rising global temperature anywhere from 2 to 4°C which could have adverse effects on food production, availability of water, coastal flooding and on disease vectors. The US is the largest contributor to atmospheric CO_2 with an annual contribution of 4.5 billion tons or 24% of the world total. About one-third of this CO_2 is due to automobile emissions. The substitution of gasoline with other fuels has the potential to increase as well as decrease this amount. Table 6-11 summarizes the CO_2 from the combustion of a variety of fuels containing the same amount of energy[33]. For comparison purposes electricity has also been included with an average CO_2 emission of 1.41 lb per kWh for the country[33]. It is well known that of all the fossil fuels natural gas is the least offensive to the environment. In fact, the combustion of natural gas relative to all other fossil fuels results not only in the reduction of CO_2 released to the atmosphere, but it also contributes significantly smaller amounts of CO, NO_x, and reactive hydrocarbons.

The numbers in Table 6-11 ignore the fact that energy is expended for the production and distribution of all fuels resulting in additional

TABLE 6-11. Carbon Dioxide Emission from the Direct Combustion of Various Fuels

Fuel	CO_2 Emission Rate (lb/10^6 BTU)	Ratio Relative to Methane
Methane	114.8	1.00
Natural Gas[1]	116.0	1.01
Propane	139.2	1.21
Gasoline	160.8	1.40
Diesel Oil	167.5	1.46
Methanol	137.8	1.20
Ethanol	147.1	1.28
Electricity[2]	135.0	1.17

1. Assumed mass composition: Methane 92.2%, Ethane 4.9%, Propane 1.7%, Butane 0.9%, Pentane 0.3%. 2. Average US electricity generation rate 10,600 BTU/kWh.

carbon dioxide emissions. For example, methanol may be produced from natural gas at a 70% efficiency or from coal at an even lower conversion efficiency. Distribution of natural gas by pipeline may expend 5% of the energy transported, while electricity distribution through power lines results in about 10% energy losses. Crude oil refining into gasoline consumes some 10% of the crude oil content. Table 6-12 summarizes the total annual CO_2 emissions, including production and distribution inefficiencies as well as conversion of other greenhouse gases to equivalent CO_2 mass, for the present automobile fleet in the US under a variety of fuel scenarios[35][36][65]. In Table 6-11 no allowance has been made for the 15% fuel efficiency improvement for natural gas fueled vehicles as explained earlier[37]. Likewise, no allowance has been made for a 3% to 5% fuel efficiency improvement for alcohol fuel powered vehicles[36].

The potential reduction of carbon dioxide emission rates due to alternative fuels (natural gas and alcohols) as well as the more efficient combustion process of the latter versus gasoline/diesel is included in Table 6-12 for a variety of feedstock materials. The use of natural gas in lieu of gasoline or diesel fuel results in an almost 30% reduction in the atmospheric emission of carbon dioxide, even after the greenhouse potential of escaping methane to the atmosphere in the exhaust gases is

TABLE 6-12. Total Greenhouse Gas Emissions Expressed in Equivalent Carbon Dioxide Mass for Different Automotive Transportation Fuel Scenarios

Fuel/Feedstock	Total CO_2 Emissions (10^9 ton/y)		Ratio Relative to Present Fuel[1]	
Gasoline and Diesel/Crude Oil	1.469^2	1.469^3	1.00^2	1.00^3
CNG/Natural Gas	1.189	1.034	0.81	0.70
Methanol/Natural Gas	1.422	1.354	0.97	0.92
Methanol/Coal	2.903	2.765	1.98	1.89
Ethanol/Corn[4]	1.336	1.272	0.91	0.87

1. Present refers to the 1992 motor gasoline and diesel fuel use in the US.
2. The vehicle fuel efficiency is assumed to be the same as for the gasoline or diesel fueled vehicle.
3. The vehicle fuel efficiency is assumed to increase by 15% for natural gas and 5% for the alcohols compared to that of an identical gasoline/diesel fuel powered vehicle as a result of higher compression ratio engines optimized for the particular fuel.
4. The fossil fuel energy input for the cultivation of corn (fuel, fertilizers, irrigation, etc.) is roughly equal to the output energy in corn. Moreover, it is impossible to grow the requisite amount of corn because of land limitations.

considered. The amount of methane in the exhaust gases can be assumed to be the average 0.125 g/mi on the basis of tests — 2.8 liter, V-6 engine, 24.6 mpg vehicle fuel efficiency[37]. Thus, the use of natural gas as a transportation fuel has the potential to reduce CO_2 emissions in the US by almost 450 million tons annually or about 10% of the present total CO_2 release from this country.

The amount of methane released annually into the atmosphere is not known precisely. The best estimate is 505 million tons with a range varying from 400 to 600 million tons per year[38][39]. The concentration of methane in the atmosphere had remained constant at 0.6 ppm throughout the historical times until about three hundred years ago. It had risen to 0.8 ppm at the beginning of the industrial revolution and has more than doubled since then to the 1.7 ppm concentration of today. Table 6-13 gives the major global sources of methane and the corresponding average emission estimates[38][39]. It contains also best estimates of the corresponding emission values of methane for the United States[26][40][41][42][43]. It is important to point out that the use of natural gas as a universal automotive fuel in the US will result in an added methane release in the atmosphere of 0.250 million tons/yr (190 million vehicles x 10,500 mi/yr/vehicle x 0.125 g/mi = 249,375 tons/yr). This is a very small amount compared to the methane release from other sources.

TABLE 6-13. Sources of Methane with the Estimated Average Value of the Global and the US Contribution in Million Tons per Year as of 1990

Source	Estimated Annual Contribution	
	Global	USA
Landfills	50	3^1
Coal Mining	30	3^2
Oil and Natural Gas Systems	45	6^3
Ruminants/Livestock	90	10^4
Animal Wastes/Wastewater	35	2^5
Rice Cultivation	115	2^6
Biomass Burning	30	< 1
Natural Wetlands	100	1^7
Oceans/Insects	30	< 1

1. Currently, 100 of the total 6,000 active and 30,000 closed landfills in the US are tapped for methane production of about 15 billion scf/yr or 0.3 million tons/yr. Since gas production in sealed landfills drops off, it is assumed that current production is about 10% of the total which may be escaping to the air.
2. It is assumed that US coal mining, accounting for about 20% of the world production, may be releasing methane on a prorated basis of the global value. However, production of coalbed methane in the US stands at 350 billion scf/yr.
3. The vented natural gas annually is less than 100 billion scf and the natural gas lost during transmission is assumed to be another 200 billion scf.
4. Cattle generate methane at a rate of 14 scf/head/day and the total head count is about 100 million.
5. Prorated from the global value on the basis of the population of the US vs. the world (less than 5%) and discounting the collection of methane in wastewater treatment plants in the US.
6. Prorated from the global value on the basis of 7 million tons rice production in the US which is less than 2% of the world total rice production.
7. Prorated from the global value on the basis of US wetlands area (less than 1% of the world total).

Methane in the atmosphere is destroyed at a rate of 420 million tons per year by reactions with OH- (hydroxyl radicals) and 30 million tons by reactions with Cl- (chlorine) and O- (oxygen) atoms in the stratosphere and by soil uptake[39]. This leaves a net release of 45 million tons per year of methane in the atmosphere. It is interesting to note that ^{14}C (radioactive carbon-14) studies have shown that about 20% of the net methane released annually in the atmosphere is from fossil fuels (coal, oil, natural gas, methane hydrates, other unknown sources of old methane) and the remainder 80% are of biologic origin[39].

Ozone Depletion. Chlorofluorocarbons were invented in 1930 and significant production did not begin until after World War II. Currently, some 40% of the consumption of CFCs in the US is devoted to air-conditioning and refrigeration. Mobile air-conditioning, comprised of CFC-12, amounts to 54.1 thousand tons per year or 13% of the total annual consumption of CFCs in the country[25]. Table 6-14 shows the breakdown of CFC-12 use as of 1990. Because the A/C compressors of automobiles are not hermetically sealed due to the fact that they are mechanically driven by the vehicle engine (unlike the compressors of stationary A/C units as well as refrigerators that are electrically driven), CFC-12 tends to leak more readily to the atmosphere. The vibrations and the harsher in general environment inherent in a mobile application tend also to compound the leakage problem through deteriorating hoses, seals and fittings. Moreover, the typical automotive-shop practice has been to vent the CFC in the atmosphere during any repairs. Thus, it is reasonable to assume that the 54 thousand tons CFC-12 used annually in vehicles will end up within a period of about ten years into the atmosphere with an equivalent greenhouse potential of 200 million tons of carbon dioxide per year. Incidentally, the total production of CFCs in the US was on the order of 400 thousand tons per year in 1990.

Besides being very potent greenhouse gases, CFCs have been also suspected to be a serious cause of stratospheric ozone depletion, which protects the earth's biota from the sun's ultraviolet (UV) radiation. Chlorofluorocarbons are very stable gases and can therefore migrate to the top of the stratosphere over a period of several years without break-

TABLE 6-14. Estimated US Consumption of CFC-12 for Mobile
Air-Conditioning as of 1990

End Use	CFC-12 Consumption Absolute Use (1,000 tons/yr)	Relative Distribution (% Total)
Initial Charge of A/C Units		
US Made	14.7	27.2
Imported	2.8	5.2
After Market	1.0	1.8
Recharge of A/C Units		
After Leakage	13.5	25.0
After Service Venting	18.2	33.6
After Accident	3.9	7.2

ing down. There, however, the highly energetic UV radiation succeeds in breaking down the CFC molecules, which as a result release chlorine atoms. The chlorine atom acts as a catalyst for ozone decomposition. In addition to CFCs, nitrogen oxide can also act as a catalyst to destroy ozone in the stratosphere. Nitrogen oxide (NO) can be found in the stratosphere either from the exhaust of supersonic aircraft flying in the lower stratosphere or else from the decomposition of nitrous oxide (N_2O) into nitrogen and nitrogen oxide by UV radiation. As it has been discussed already, nitrous oxide is generated at the surface of the earth mainly by the decomposition of fertilizers and then migrates to the stratosphere over a period of time as it is also a stable molecule.

Since the early 1970s there has been an animated debate about the effect of human activities on the ozone layer. At various times atmospheric chemistry experts have identified several culprits such as the exhaust of high flying aircraft (cancellation of the commercial supersonic aircraft development in the US in the mid 1970s), CFCs as aerosol propellants (elimination of CFCs from aerosol canisters in the early 1980s in the US and more recently in Europe), the increased use of fertilizers, and CFCs as industrial cleaning fluids and refrigerants. In recent years the debate has focussed on the role of CFCs and their destruction of ozone over Antarctica. Continuous measurements of ozone levels showed a dramatic decline each October during the 1980s. Moreover, the October values of total ozone over part of Antarctica declined by over 50% between 1979 and 1987. While CFCs have the ability to destroy ozone in the stratosphere, it was found that the current CFC build-up could explain at most a 1% global reduction of ozone according to standard chemical theory[44]. New theories, centered on the peculiar conditions that developed in the antarctic winter vortex, have been developed to account for the observed decrease of ozone. It appears that the intense cold produces clouds of ice crystals which accelerate the depletion of ozone through a complex process of surface chemistry[44].

As a result of these developments, the US has agreed as a signatory of the 1987 Montreal Protocol to accelerate the phase-out of CFCs, including CFC-12. The production of CFC-12 in the US will cease at the end of 1995. A new mobile A/C refrigerant, HFC-134a (hydrofluorocarbon) has already begun to substitute CFC-12 in new motor vehicles and will take over completely after 1996. Moreover, CFC-12 is no longer allowed to be vented and will be recycled after 1996 until the inventory is totally depleted. The HFC-134a has zero ozone depletion potential as it contains no chlorine. Moreover, its greenhouse potential is about 1/10th that of CFC-12 which it replaces — HFC-134a is very similar to HCFC-22 in global warming potential[45]. It is worth noting that in 1991, a NASA study concluded that since 1978 a 5% ozone layer depletion has occurred across much of the Northern Hemisphere above a latitude of 30-35 degrees, including most of the United States, Europe and Asia[46]. This reduced ozone layer appears in the winter and extends well into the spring months, resulting in a possible doubling of the incidence of skin cancer rate over the next 50 years and causing as many as 200 thousand extra deaths in the United States alone.

NATURAL GAS AND AUTOMOTIVE AIR POLLUTION

The automobile air pollution reduction measures put in effect during the last twenty years have, in principle at least, induced the automotive manufacturers to produce vehicles with a significantly lesser quantity of offensive emissions to the environment. It is very likely that the emissions of HC, CO, NO_x and PM per vehicle have been reduced by an order of magnitude between the late 1960s and today. However, the number of vehicles during the same period has doubled. Moreover, it takes several years for the newer vehicles to replace the existing fleet. If, for example, the average life of a passenger car or light truck is 10 years, the entire fleet may be renewed every 20 years. Finally, the high concentration of automobiles in metropolitan areas results in localized pockets of pollution that can not be alleviated even with these dramatic reductions in emissions since the early 1970s. It is becoming exceedingly more difficult to reduce further automobile emissions beyond the 1994 standards. On the other hand, a substantial reduction in emissions per vehicle is required in order to attain good quality area everywhere across the country.

Thus, the focus of automotive emission reductions must be shifted form a better control of the engine and the improvement of the catalytic converters to an all together different fuel or fuels that can accomplish the task. Only three automotive fuels have the potential to reduce vehicular emissions by an order of magnitude or more from those of the 1994 federal standard. These fuels are: *natural gas, electricity* and *hydrogen*. However, electricity and hydrogen suffer currently from major technological limitations that make them unlikely candidates for large scale motor vehicle fuel application in the next twenty years. Only natural gas can serve as the immediate replacement of gasoline and diesel fuel for automotive applications. The issues of future technological development will be addressed in a later chapter. The potential reduction of automobile emissions from the use of alternative fuels will be examined in this section.

Numerous tests of alternative fuel vehicles with respect to emissions have been performed in the last ten years and the results have been summarized in a variety of publications[35][36]. The alternative fuels include methanol, natural gas, hydrogen and electricity. Information on ethanol and propane or LPG emissions appear to be very limited. The major drawback of most of these data is the lack of consistency in testing. There exist a tremendous variability in the type of vehicles tested, age of vehicles, the types of emission controls or lack thereof, and the type of emission measurements performed. Moreover, none of these vehicle engines were optimized as specific alternative fuel engines. Consequently, all these data are not easy to interpret and do not lend themselves to a conclusive answer.

In general, the CNG vehicles displayed a very dramatic and consistent degree of CO emission reduction of more than an order of magnitude. Non-methane HC emissions were consistently also reduced by minimum of 60% to over 90% in several instances. However, the NOx emission stayed the same or was reduced by as much as an order of magnitude in few instances, while it increased in others. Another fuel also tested extensively, albeit in a similarly non-reproducible manner has been methanol. Tests on a variety of methanol powered vehicles showed a small, up to 30%, reduction or zero reduction or even an increase in CO. The same result was true for NO_x emissions. On the other hand, hydrocarbon emissions were reduced by as much as 50%, but more typically by half as much. In addition, formaldehyde emissions increased by about 100%, on the average.

In order to have a meaningful comparison of the air emissions for different fuels one must use the same vehicle or at least engine size with these fuels and optimize the engine for the particular fuel. Such studies fortunately do exist, but they are small in number and have been obtained in the last few years. Thus, the focus of the emissions of alternative fuels to be presented here will be based on these results. Needless to mention that all of these studies are very extensive in coverage and thorough in execution. Consequently, the small number of these studies does not diminish their value. The California Air Resources Board has been testing and comparing alternative fuels to gasoline as part of the implementation of new air quality standards for the state. Figure 6-8 shows a 1989 emission comparison including gasoline, methanol, LPG and CNG as fuels[47]. These vehicle emission numbers are also summarized in the same figure. The emission numbers in Figure 6-8 are in quantitative agreement with the preceding summary of earlier results. However, no specifics are given with respect to the type and age of the catalytic converter, the size of the engine, the compression of the engine and any other system optimization, and the air/fuel ratio. Nevertheless, it is apparent that methanol and LPG offer a 20 to 25% reduction in air pollutants, while CNG offers an almost 80% reduction in pollutant emissions compared to gasoline. Between methanol and LPG, the former has about 30% lower CO emissions and the latter offers almost a factor of two reduction in smog forming emissions (ROG and NO_x). It is important to note that the fuel/air ratio as well as the catalyst configuration can be adjusted in a CNG fueled vehicle such that more CO and less NMOG and NO_x are generated.

Starting in the model year 1993 and continuing in the 1994 and 1995 model years GM, Ford and Chrysler have marketed dedicated CNG vehicles. The emissions of these vehicles are by now well documented and are summarized in Table 6-15[48][49][50][51][52][53]. These vehicles included the GMG Sierra truck (5.7 L V-8 engine running on CNG only), the Ford Crown Victoria (4.6 L V-8 engine running on CNG only), the Dodge Ram van (5.2 L V-8 engine running on CNG only) and the Chrysler Caravan/Voyager Minivan (3.3 L V-6 engine running on CNG only). It is worth noting that the engines of these vehicles had the same compression ratio as their gasoline counterparts, i.e., 9:1, with the exception of the Crown Victoria at 11:1. Hence they were not opti-

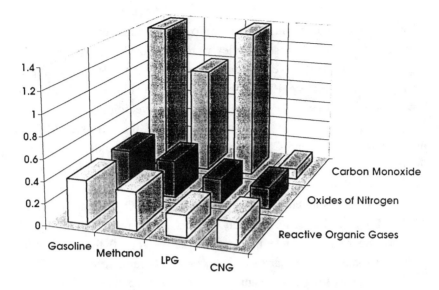

	Gas.	Meth.	LPG	GNG
CO	1.4	1.0	1.4	0.1
NMOG	0.4	0.35	0.2	0.2
NO_x	0.4	0.35	0.23	0.2
Total	2.2	1.7	1.8	0.5

FIGURE 6-8. Comparison of Average Emissions g/mi of Vehicles Powered by Alternative Fuels in 1989 (Source: California Air Resources Board).

TABLE 6-15. Air Emissions of CNG Alternative Fuel Vehicles Available in 1993, 1994 and 1995 According to Federal Certification Test Procedures (FTP)

Vehicle	Engine	NO_x	NMOG	CO
1993 GMC Sierra Truck	5.7 L	0.20 g/mi	0.14 g/mi	1.40 g/mi
1993 Dodge Ram Van	5.2 L	0.02 g/mi	0.02 g/mi	1.04 g/mi
1994 Ford Crown Victoria	4.6 L	0.09 g/mi	0.02 g/mi	0.64 g/mi
1995 Dodge Ram Van[1]	5.2 L	0.08 g/mi	0.02 g/mi	1.30 g/mi
1995 Chrysler Mini Van[2]	3.3 L	0.04 g/mi	0.005 g/mi	0.30 g/mi

1. Certified by CARB in 1994 as meeting the 1997 LEV California standard.
2. Certified by CARB in 1994 as meeting the 1997 ULEV California standard.

mized for the higher compression ratio appropriate for higher octane fuels. However, all of these vehicles were optimized with respect to the requisite air/fuel ratio to reduce emissions below the 1993 California air quality standard for the 1992, 1993 model year vehicles and the 1998 low emission standards for the 1995 model year vehicles.

A comparison of the relative emissions of the Chrysler Minivan fueled with gasoline and CNG as well as the ULEV standard is given in Figure 6-9[50]. The 1994 (1995 model year) CNG fueled minivan emissions are relative to the 1993 California/1994 US gasoline standard and the 1998 ULEV standard: NO_x 10% and 20%; CO 9% and 18%; and NMOG 2% and 12.5%, respectively. Moreover, the three way catalyst in the gasoline fueled vehicle may remain active for 50 thousand miles, while the same or a similar catalyst in the CNG fueled vehicle will last at least twice as long since natural gas does not contain any poisonous materials such as lead and other metals or phosphorous. In the case of

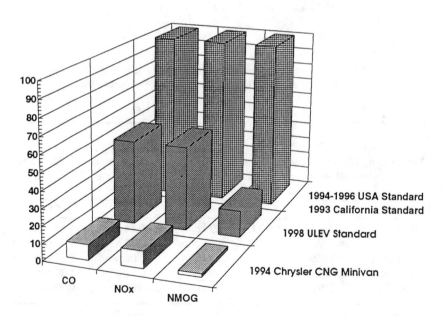

FIGURE 6-9. Comparison of FTP Emissions of the 1995 CNG Chrysler Mini Van Relative to the 1993 California (and 1994 Federal) Low Emission Standard and the 1998 California ULEV standard.

methanol/gasoline fuel blends, the life of the three way catalyst may be extended minimally, if any at all.

It is also interesting to point out that the 1993 Dodge Ram van was the first vehicle to meet the 1998 ULEV standards in California after 4,000 miles of operation[52]. The 1995 Dodge Ram van has been certified by CARB as an LEV meeting the 1998 standard[53]. The 1995 Chrysler Mini van has been certified as a ULEV meeting the 1998 standard[53]. Both of these certifications, the first ones for any automobile manufacturer, are over the life of the vehicle which is assumed to be 100 thousand miles. It is interesting to note that no other alternative fuel, besides CNG, has been certified yet as either LEV or ULEV. No automotive manufacturer has been able to establish yet the LEV and even more so the ULEV emission levels with any of the other competing alternative fuels methanol, ethanol, propane and reformulated gasoline. This fact alone is indicative of the potential of natural gas as automotive fuel to reduce emissions versus all the other aforementioned candidate fuels.

An extensive study was performed by GM to determine the range of exhaust of pollutants from the 2.8 L engine, which is the typical one in most midsize GM passenger cars, for gasoline (base case) and CNG (base case and higher compression ratios)[37][54]. Moreover, this engine has been also used in the methanol/gasoline VFVs for which emission data are also available and therefore a direct comparison between emissions form alternative fuels can be made. The base case engine compression ratio is 8.9:1 and the higher compression ratios are 11.5:1 and 14:1 (for CNG only). A variety of catalysts were considered including platinum/palladium bead bed (Pt/Pd BB), platinum/palladium monolith (Pt/Pd M), palladium bead bed (Pd BB) and production three way platinum/palladium/rhodium bead bed (Pt/Pd/Rh BB) and "aged" production three way platinum/palladium/rhodium monolith (Pt/Pd/Rh M-A). The engine was evaluated for a range of engine speeds and loads representative of those experienced by the 2.8 L engine with a 3 speed transmission powering a Chevrolet Corsica on the federal test procedure (FTP) emissions schedule.

The GM study revealed that at the base compression ratio, i.e., same as for the gasoline fuel, the most effective emission control strategy for the CNG fuel was to operate the engine slightly rich of the stoichiometric ratio with the use of a platinum/palladium (non-rhodium) three way catalyst. This ideal slightly rich stoichiometric ratio is between 1.000 and 1.002, depending on whether the Pt/Pd three way catalyst is a bead-bed or a monolith, respectively. An increased fuel efficiency of about 4% was observed with CNG fuel over gasoline fuel at this slightly rich stoichiometric ratio for CNG — incidentally, the optimal level of gasoline fuel emissions are also obtained at the stoichiometric ratio. A lean fuel/air mixture gave an improved fuel efficiency of about 12% higher compared to the gasoline fuel at stoichiometric ratio. However, the resulting HC and NO_x emissions were unacceptably high. Table 6-16 summarizes the results of the base case study for gasoline and CNG fuels at different stoichiometric ratios and with two catalyst types. It is interesting to note that the use of CNG fuel very near or at stoichiometric ratio gives extremely low NMOG and NO_x emissions and significantly reduced CO emissions.

Lean engine operation with the CNG fuel resulted in very low CO emissions but highly elevated ones for NMOG and NO_x. The emission of CH_4 has increased substantially for the lean air/fuel mixture. Increased fuel efficiency is also favored by the lean ratio. Moreover, the bead-bed catalyst affords a slim efficiency increase versus the monolith catalyst, because of the smaller back pressure drop of the exhaust gases encountered in the former one. Finally, all the other catalysts that were examined showed a much lesser efficiency in oxidizing NMHC gases than the two types of platinum and palladium. Actual vehicle tests on a dual fuel (gasoline/CNG) Chevrolet Celebrity with a 2.8-liter engine gave a good agreement between vehicle emission data and the aforementioned results of the FTP cycle dynamometer study.

In order to explore the effect of increased compression ratio on emission control and fuel economy for natural gas fuel, the same study of the 2.8-Liter engine was carried out at 11.5:1 and 14:1 compression ratios[37]. The 2.8-Liter 60° V-6 aluminum-head engine was modified by changing pistons and gasket thicknesses. A production port fuel injection (PFI) system was used for the gasoline fuel. For the natural gas fuel, the gaseous fuel was initially mixed with the air through a continuous single-point injection by employing a throttle body fuel injection

TABLE 6-16. Comparison of Measured Emissions of a 2.8-Liter Engine at a 8.9:1 Compression Ratio Operated with Gasoline and CNG over the City (FTP) and Highway Simulated Driving Conditions

Catalyst Fuel	Pt/Pd Bead-Bed		Pt/Pd Monolith		
	Gasoline	CNG	CNG	CNG	CNG
Equivalence Ratio[1]	0.988	1.000	0.757	1.002	0.775
Fuel Economy					
City mpg	21.5	22.5	24.4	22.2	23.7
Highway mpg	29.8	30.6	33.0	30.3	31.8
55/45 mpg	24.6	25.6	27.7	25.3	26.8
FTP Emissions					
NMOG g/mi					
Engine Out	3.010	0.168	0.221	0.181	0.224
Tailpipe Out	0.191	0.011	0.081	0.004	0.097
CO g/mi					
Engine Out	18.5	9.94	1.28	7.61	1.20
Tailpipe Out	0.528	0.179	0.006	0.090	0.024
NO_x g/mi					
Engine Out	2.58	2.17	0.477	1.75	0.485
Tailpipe Out	0.114	0.050	0.449	0.010	0.480
Greenhouse Gases (55/45 Tailpipe)					
CO_2 g/mi	351	257	234	260	241
CH_4 g/mi	0	0.113	1.45	0.013	1.76

1. Equivalence ratio near 1 is stoichiometric, lower than 1 is lean.

(TBFI) engine system. A prototype gaseous port fuel injector (GPFI) was developed later-on and was employed with the same emission results as the TBFI well pre-mixed air-fuel charge. The increase in compression ratio resulted in increased HC engine-out emissions and decreased exhaust temperature, thereby making the emission control more challenging. The previously developed emission control strategy employing near stoichiometric operation and Pt/Pd catalysts resulted in an excellent control of HC, CO and NO_x emissions.

The results of these studies are presented in Table 6-17. The fuel efficiency of the high compression CNG engine increased by 15% compared to the base case compression ratio gasoline powered engine. Moreover, the estimated 7% power loss for the CNG fuel at the base compression ratio versus the gasoline fuel was essentially regained at the increased compression ratio. It was determined through testing that combustion, emissions and performance of the engine with CNG versus pure CH_4 are similar, but generally better.

The Pt/Pd catalyst used in the measurements given in Table 6-17 was of the bead-bed configuration and was "aged", i.e., it had an 80 hour

TABLE 6-17. Comparison of Measured Emissions of a 2.8-Liter Engine at a 11.5:1 and 14:1 Compression Ratio Operated with CNG over the City (FTP) and Highway Simulated Driving Conditions Using an "Aged" Pt/Pd Bead-Bed Catalyst

Compression Ratio	11.5:1		14.0:1	
	Stoic.	Lean	Stoic.	Lean
Equivalence Ratio	1.007	0.763	1.011	0.746
Fuel Economy				
City mpg	23.6	25.6	24.4	26.0
Highway mpg	29.8	30.6	33.5	34.5
55/45 mpg	26.7	28.9	27.8	29.3
FTP Emissions				
NMOG g/mi				
Engine Out	0.456	0.665	0.469	0.935
Tailpipe Out	0.026	0.134	0.038	0.221
CO g/mi				
Engine Out	7.31	1.41	9.65	2.38
Tailpipe Out	0.177	0.018	0.119	0.038
NO_x g/mi				
Engine Out	2.00	0.966	1.91	0.683
Tailpipe Out	0.074	0.918	0.194	0.642
Greenhouse Gases (55/45 Tailpipe)				
CO_2 g/mi	246	225	235	213
CH_4 g/mi	0.29	2.15	0.50	4.00

of operation prior to these measurements. The purpose of using an aged catalyst was to obtain results representative of the emissions after a long term operation of a CNG fueled vehicle — "fresh" catalysts are extremely more efficient, but their efficiency diminishes rapidly in the first several hours of operation and remains fairly constant thereafter.

Restoration of the efficiency of the Pt/Pd catalyst to the "fresh" level may be obtained by heating the catalyst so that it stays above a minimum temperature throughout the operation of the vehicle — this includes also preheating the catalyst during a cold start. The improvement in emission control by a warmed-up catalyst are given in Table 6-18 at the 14:1 compression ratio and the two types of Pt/Pd catalyst configuration. It is evident that a warmed-up Pt/Pd catalyst offers exceptional emissions control. The bead-bed configuration performs better in terms of fuel efficiency and also offers a slightly better emissions control.

It is interesting to note that the high compression CNG engine can readily meet the California ULEV emission standards with or without warmed-up catalysts, particularly with respect to NMOG and NO_x emissions that are the most difficult to attain with a gasoline fuel. Moreover, the required catalyst is also simplified as it no longer requires rhodium as a third noble metal constituent. Incidentally, the platinum and palladium loading of the Pt/Pd bead-bead catalysts used in the GM experiments were as follows: 0.072 oz t (2.3 g) of platinum and 0.029 oz t (0.9g) of palladium on ceria (CeO_2) modified alumina (Al_2O_3) support[55].

As it has been mentioned already the CNG fuel injection into the engine cylinders was initially performed by employing a continuous single point injection and body throttle injection. There has been a perception by some in the technical community that a gaseous PFI is a difficult and risky venture and that significant problems with fuel maldistribution or undesirable fuel-air stratification may occur. Prototype GPFIs developed, for example, by the AC Rochester Division of GM and tested in CNG engines totally dispelled these concerns. In fact, GPFIs do not present some of the difficulties encountered in the development of gaseous TBFIs, which include objectionable noise, physical

TABLE 6-18. Comparison of Measured Emissions of a 2.8-Liter Engine at a 14.0:1 Compression Ratio Operated with CNG over the City (FTP) and Highway Simulated Driving Conditions Using a Warmed-Up (Fresh Equivalent) Pt/Pd Catalyst

Catalyst Configuration	Pt/Pd Bead-Bed	Pt/Pd Monolith
Equivalence Ratio	1.007	1.008
Fuel Economy		
City mpg	25.2	25.6
Highway mpg	33.1	30.2
55/45 mpg	28.3	27.5
FTP Emissions		
NMOG g/mi		
Engine Out	0.536	0.543
Tailpipe Out	0.010	0.013
CO g/mi		
Engine Out	11.7	8.75
Tailpipe Out	0.217	0.139
NO_x g/mi		
Engine Out	2.40	2.44
Tailpipe Out	0.011	0.017
Greenhouse Gases (55/45 Tailpipe)		
CO_2 g/mi	246	256
CH_4 g/mi	0.125	0.063

blockage of engine air-flow that reduces maximum power up to 5% and fuel maldistribution.

The preceding results indicate that a stoichiometric CNG engine at high compression ratio and a Pt/Pd catalyst can readily achieve ULEV emission standards and increased fuel efficiency. A lean burning CNG engine, on the other hand, has the potential for an even higher fuel efficiency, i.e., a 20% increase at the 14:1 compression ratio compared to the base gasoline engine, but it requires more elaborate catalysts to control NMOG emissions. Moreover, it presents greater engineering challenges and higher costs, because it requires the development of extensive hardware and control systems along with numerous engine modifications to ensure that the power output is not diminished versus a gasoline engine of the same displacement. Thus, a lean stoichiometric CNG engine constitutes a potentially long term prospect.

The emissions of LPG fuel were also compared to those of gasoline on a Buick LeSabre with a 3.8 L V-8 engine[56]. The compression ratio of the engine was not modified and the near stoichiometric air-fuel engine operation was maintained. The standard three-way catalyst was also unmodified. Previous experience with LPG has shown that its use requires the same type of catalyst as gasoline. Moreover, the higher octane rating of LPG fuel compared to gasoline may eventually result in a 10.5:1 increased engine compression ratio. The measured emissions and fuel efficiency for LPG versus gasoline are given in Table 6-19. A closed-loop Impco Model 125 carburetor system was used for the LPG fueled LeSabre. The major advantages of LPG as a fuel over gasoline are: the reduction in CO_2 greenhouse gas; the reduced reactivity of the HC emissions as they consist of 50% or more propane, which is less reactive than gasoline HC emissions; and the sealed, pressurized fuel system that could control evaporative and running loss emissions very effectively. Moreover, emissions are improved at cold ambient conditions. A Canadian study on the 1989 Chevrolet Blazer model with a 5.7-L engine pointed out this advantage of the LPG fuel[56][57]. At 70°F ambient temperature the gasoline and the LPG fueled vehicles showed no consistent difference in emissions. However, for an ambient starting temperature of 46°F, the HC, CO and NO_x emissions were 0.67, 10.90

TABLE 6-19. Emissions and Fuel Economy of a 1990 Buick Le Sabre with a 3.8-Liter Engine Operating on Gasoline and LPG and Using a Gasoline Three-Way Catalyst

Fuel	NMHC (g/mi)	CO (g/mi)	NO_x (g/mi)	CO_2 (g/mi)	Fuel Economy[1] (mpg)
FTP Cycle					
Gasoline	0.14	2.65	0.65	446	19.8
LPG	0.19	2.56	0.34	389	19.7
Highway					
LPG	0.02	1.06	0.24	215	26.2

1. Miles per gallon of gasoline equivalent for LPG fuel.

and 1.10 g/mi for gasoline and 0.30, 4.67, and 0.36 g/mi for LPG, respectively.

Exhaust and evaporative emissions for methanol-gasoline blends have been investigated quite extensively by the Auto/Oil Air Quality Improvement Research Program[58]. This is a cooperative research program initiated by the three domestic automobile manufacturers and fourteen petroleum companies with a principal objective the development of data on the potential improvements of vehicle emissions and air quality through the use of alternative fuels and reformulated gasolines. As part of this research effort 19 prototype flexible/variable fuel vehicles (FFV/VFV) were tested. These 19 vehicles represented seven FFV/VFV technology types and were supplied by GM (8 vehicles/2 models), Ford (7 vehicles/3 models) and Chrysler (4 vehicles/2 models). The vehicles had 9,000 to 33,000 miles on their odometers and therefore their catalysts were "aged". Three different fuels were tested at least twice for each vehicle in accordance with the FTP cycle. The results of the emission measurements are summarized in Table 6-20[58]. The three fuels were M0 (100% gasoline), M10 (90% gasoline, 10% methanol) and M85 (15% gasoline, 85% methanol). The M85 fuel represents the most likely methanol blend as an alternative fuel. The M10 represents a splash blend between M0 and M85 that could occur by a random refueling of an FFV/VFV with M0 or M85.

The Reid vapor pressure of M0 was 8.7 psi and that of M85 was also raised to the same value by adding butane. By contrast the vapor pressure of the M10 was 12 psi and was left unaltered. Thus, M10 results in excessive evaporative and running losses of HC, NMOG and methanol compared to the M0 and M85 fuels. The fuel efficiency for the three fuels was also measured. The use of the M85 fuel showed an average 3% fuel efficiency increase compared to the M0 (base case) gasoline fuel. Finally, formaldehyde emissions increase by more than 400% between gasoline (M0) and the standard methanol fuel blend (M85). Incidentally, in Table 6-20 the NMHC is given separately and is also included in the NMOG.

The 1990 Clean Air Act Amendment requires that in addition to alternative fuels reformulated gasoline will be required in several non-attainment areas. Phase 1 of this program begins in 1995 and Phase 2,

TABLE 6-20. Average Emissions Data for Prototype Flexible Fuel Vehicles and Variable Fuel Vehicles Operating on Gasoline and Methanol/Gasoline Blends over the FTP Simulated Driving Conditions

Parameter	Fuel		
	MO	M10	M85
FTP Emissions			
NMHC (g/mi)	0.24	0.23	0.14
NMOG (g/mi)	0.24	0.24	0.28
CO (g/mi)	2.81	2.59	1.93
NOx (g/mi)	0.40	0.40	0.49
Methanol (g/mi)	0.00	0.01	0.20
Benzene (mg/mi)	15.0	12.0	2.4
Formaldehyde (mg/mi)	2.8	2.6	15.0
Fuel Efficiency (mpg)	20.4	20.3	21.1
Diurnal, Hot Soak Evaporation and Running Loss			
HC (g/test)	1.73	2.27	1.46
NMOG (g/test)	1.69	2.85	2.34
Methanol (g/test)	0.00	0.90	1.02
Benzene (mg/test)	37.6	37.1	32.0

which requires even more emissions reductions, would go into effect in the year 2000. California regulations require more extensive reformulation of gasoline compared to the federal regulations. Phase I went into effect in 1992 and requires increased oxygenation of gasoline in the winter times by using additives such as ethanol, MTBE and ETBE (methyl- and ethyl-tert-butyl ether). These oxygenated additives reduce the CO emissions, but they also increase the NO_x emissions, hence they are limited only in the winter months when photochemical smog is not as pronounced. Phase 2 will go into effect in 1996. Table 6-21 summarizes the properties of reformulated gasolines. Among other changes, the Reid vapor pressure is reduced from a present value of more than 9 psi, the current benzene content of over 2% by volume is also reduced and so is the content of olefins from a present value of 13% by volume. At the present time testing is under way to determine the emissions resulting from the use of reformulated gasolines. However, the results of these extensive tests will not be announced until they are completed[51].

TABLE 6-21. Properties of Future Reformulated Gasolines per EPA and CARB

Property	1990 US Avg.	1997 US Est.	1996 Calif. Est.
Reid Vapor Pressure (psi)[1]	8.7	8.1	7.0 max
Driveability Index[2]	1180	1170	1100 max
Benzene (% volume)	1.5	1.0 max	1.0 max
Oxygen (% mass)	0	2.0 min	1.8 - 2.2
Aromatics (% volume)	32	32	25 max
Olefins (% volume)	9	9	6 max
Sulfur (ppm)	339	339	40 max
Deposit Control Additive	Maybe	Yes	Yes
Lead	No	No	No

1. Summer value. 2. This index relates the warm-up performance of vehicles to fuel volatility and is the sum of the three distillation temperatures (^0F) at which 10%, 50% and 90% of the fuel has boiled-off in a standard test.

Since the introduction of MTBE, a methanol derivative, as the oxygenated agent of choice in several areas of the country in the winter of 1992, complaints have arisen among the public that its vapors, which have a characteristic odor, inhaled during gasoline pumping have resulted in severe headaches and nausea[59]. The EPA maintains that MTBE should not have caused such effects, but nevertheless is investigating the complaints.

An important consideration of the organic gases emitted in the combustion of different fuels is their reactivity or potential to produce ozone. That is to say, 1 g of organic gases at the tailpipe of a gasoline powered engine versus a methanol powered one versus a CNG powered engine are not equivalent because of different composition. It is thus important to consider not only the mass of emitted organic gases, but also their composition. To this end, the reactivity must be defined of the different organic gases that appear at the exhaust of an internal combustion engine operated with gasoline, methanol-gasoline blends, LPG and natural gas. Recently, W.P.L. Carter using detailed kinetic modeling to calculate ozone formation during air pollution scenarios defined a reactivity factor for each volatile organic compound(VOC)[60]. This reactivity factor is an incremental reactivity of an individual volatile organic compound calculated by the increase in the ozone formed when the

TABLE 6-22. Maximum Carter Reactivity Factor of Common Volatile Organic Gases Emitted from ICEs Fueled with Gasoline, M85, LPG and Natural Gas

VOC	Carter RF $mg\ O_3/mg\ VOC$	VOC	Carter RF $mg\ O_3/mg\ VOC$
Methane	0.01	Ethane	0.15
Ethene	5.30	Ethyne	0.37
Propylene	6.60	Propane	0.33
Butane	0.64	2-M-Propane	0.85
1,3-Butadiene	7.70	Benzene(s)	0.28 - 7.40
Toluene	1.90	Cyclohexane	1.36
Pentane	0.64	Formaldehyde	6.20
Methanol	0.45	Acetaldehyde	3.80
Acrolein	4.60	Acetone	0.39

VOC was added to the base set of atmospheric conditions divided by the amount of VOC added. Table 6-22 summarizes the maximum values of the "Carter Reactivity Factor" for the major organic compounds generated from the combustion of gasoline, methanol, LPG and natural gas.

On the basis of the typical constituents of the organic gas emissions for a particular fuel, a reactivity adjustment factor (RAF) can be calculated for that particular fuel. The RAF is defined as the ratio of the sum of the reactivities of the particular fuel to the sum of the reactivities for gasoline. For example, the California Air resources Board has determined that the RAF for M85 is 0.41, although the data from Table 6-22 and Table 6-23 indicate an M85 reactivity closer to 0.85[51]. The reactivity of CNG at about 0.2 or even lower is the least of any alternative fuels. Thus, in Table 6-15 the equivalent NMOG emission of the 1995 Chrysler Minivan is 0.005 g/mi x 0.2 = 0.001 g/mi. It is worth noting that the reactivity of methane is more than an order of magnitude smaller than any of the other VOCs. Thus, methane is considered a non-reactive organic gas with respect to the formation of ozone and photochemical smog. Methanol is 45 times more reactive than methane, and formaldehyde is 620 times more reactive than methane.

The major organic gases and their rates of emission from gasoline, M85, LPG and natural gas are given in Table 6-23[37][57][59]. It should be noted that the list of emitted VOCs for natural gas is all inclusive under the conditions given in the table notes. All the other fuels produce a

TABLE 6-23. Major Reactive Volatile Organic Gases Emission Rates in mg/mi for Gasoline, Methanol/Gasoline Blend (M85), Liquefied Petroleum Gas and Natural Gas Fuels in an Internal Combustion Engine Equipped with Proper Catalytic Converters over the FTP Driving Conditions

Volatile Organic Gas (Non-methane)	Fuel			
	Gas	M85	LPG	CNG
Benzene	16.5	3.5	0.6	0.1
1,3 Butadiene	1.2	0.1	0.0	0.0
Formaldehyde	2.8	15.0	0.9	0.2
Acetaldehyde	0.8	0.2	0.8	<0.1
Acetone			0.2	<0.1
Ethane			11.5	19.6
Ethene	0.0	0.0	0.0	5.3
Propane			130.9	1.5
Methanol	0.0	200.0	0.0	0.0
Butyne			0.0	0.2
Octane	136.9	0.1	0.0	
Cyclohexane				0.1
Propylene	0.0	0.0	2.8	0.0
Ethylene	0.0	0.0	9.1	0.0

Notes. 1. The FTP fuel efficiency for the four fuels is as follows: gasoline 20.4 mpg; M85 21.1; LPG 19.7 mpg; and CNG 24.5 mpg. 2. The CNG fuel assumes a 14.0:1 engine compression ratio, a Pd/Pt aged catalyst, and a positive crankcase ventilation. 3. The methane emissions are : Gasoline 22.8 mg/mi; M 85 11 mg/mi; LPG 43.3 mg/mi and CNG 715 mg/mi. 4. The benzene values include evaporative losses.

very large number of additional VOCs not listed in Table 6-23. All of the these additional VOCs are generated at very small rates, but some of them are very reactive. Because methane, the main constituent of natural gas, is the simplest hydrocarbon, its combustion produces a relatively small number of VOCs, most of which are ultimately oxidized by the catalytic converter. It turns out that about 95% of the organic gas emissions of a CNG fueled ICE at a high compression ratio is methane and of the remainder 2.6% is ethane, the next most inert VOC after methane[37]. Although the significance of the nature of the HC emissions from a health point of view cannot be readily quantified, it should be apparent to everyone that the utilization of natural gas fuel is far superior to any other fuel in that regard. Figure 6-10 compares the emissions of the most reactive organic gases generated from gasoline, the M85 methanol/gasoline blend and natural gas fuels.

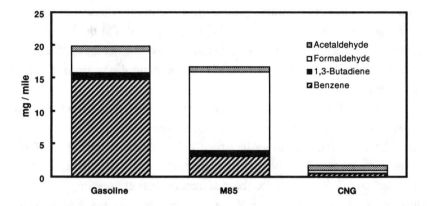

FIGURE 6-10.   Comparison of the Rate of Emission of the Most Reactive Organic Gases in the Exhaust of ICEs Fueled with Gasoline, M85 and Natural Gas for the FTP Driving Conditions (Assumed Fuel Efficiency: Gasoline 20.4 mpg; M85 21.1 mpg, CNG 23.5 mpg).

What can be quantified, on the other hand, is the potential of ozone formation for the different fuels. This is accomplished with the aid of the aforementioned Carter reactivity factors and applies only to the organic gas content of the total emissions. The reactivity of CO for ozone formation is slightly higher than that of methane. Natural gas fueled vehicles produce the least amount of CO and NO_x. Thus by ignoring both CO and NO_x in the ozone formation calculations for the different fuels, the balance is slanted against natural gas and in favor of all the other fuels. On the other hand, natural gas vehicles produce a relatively large amount of methane in the exhaust which even though non-reactive could have some small ozone formation contribution. Thus, two types of calculations can be performed. In the first calculation, only non-methane organic gases (NMOG) are considered. In the second calculation all or total organic gases (TOG) are included.

Two calculated parameters are of interest in comparing different fuels. The first parameter is the potential ozone production rate of the emission and is expressed in mg O_3/mi. The second one is the incremental reactivity of the emission and is expressed in mg O_3/mg emission. For all the fuels, except natural gas, whether the methane in the exhaust is included or not makes very little difference in the potential ozone production. For natural gas the ozone formation potential increases if the TOG rather than the NMOG is considered. On the other hand, inclusion of methane in the incremental reactivity calculation decreases its value for all fuels and particularly so for natural gas since methane has such a small reactivity.

A calculation of these two parameters has been carried out by GM, among others, for a variety of production vehicles fueled by gasoline, M85, LPG, and CNG. In order to afford a direct comparison of the ozone forming potential of the different fuels, this calculation has been modified so as to account for the differences in fuel consumption of the different vehicles. The results of this analysis are summarized in Table 6-24 and are plotted in Figure 6-11. It is apparent from these calculations that natural gas is superior to any other automotive fuel by a large margin with respect to ozone formation, air pollution in general and by inference damage to human health, vegetation and material property.

Methanol, on the other hand, displays a wide variability in terms of ozone formation potential depending on the nature of the catalyst used. The lower prediction in Table 6-24 for ozone formation by methanol is within the limits predicted by other models[61]. However, a heated catalyst is a necessity for methanol, if any improvement of smog formation over that of gasoline is possible[62]. A heated catalyst with natural gas as a fuel will, of course, virtually eliminate the VOC generated ozone potential — the corresponding values in Table 6-24 will be reduced by

TABLE 6-24. Potential Ozone Production Rates in mg O_3/mi and Incremental Reactivities in mg O3/mg emission for Gasoline, Methanol, LPG and Natural Gas as Automotive Fuels Calculated for the FTP Driving Conditions

Fuel	Em. Rate (mg/mi)		Pot. O_3 Prod. Rate		Incr. Reactivity	
	NMOG	TOG	NMOG	TOG	NMOG	TOG
Gasoline	196	218	180	180	1.78	1.59
M85[1]	50/250	61/261	131/263	131/263	1.00	0.81
LPG	157	200	102	102	0.51	0.43
CNG	38	712	10	15	0.08	<0.01

1. Lower NMOG, attained with an electrically heated catalyst, does not include evaporative and running loss emissions that could easily double the NMOG emission rate.

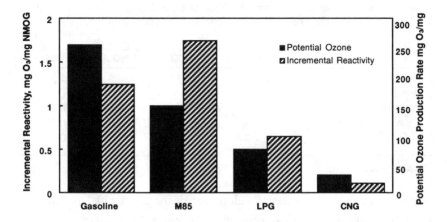

FIGURE 6-11. Comparison of Potential Ozone Production Rates and Incremental Reactivities for Gasoline, Methanol, LPG and Natural Gas as Automotive Fuels Calculated for the FTP Driving Conditions.

at least a factor of four. This VOC reduction coupled with the much lower NOx emissions from a natural gas fueled engine compared to methanol, indicates that the problem of smog formation will totally disappear with natural gas becoming a universal automotive fuel.

The replacement of diesel fuel with methanol, propane and natural gas in diesel engines is another area where alternative fuels can make a big difference in terms of clean air despite the introduction of clean diesel fuel. The Orange County Transit Authority (OCTA) in Southern California has been evaluating since 1992 six Cummins L10 diesel engines installed in buses and running on methanol, propane, and natural gas. A comparison of the emissions of these diesel engines running on low sulfur diesel fuel as well as methanol and natural gas is shown in Table 6-25[63][64]. The methanol fuel contains 3% Avocet, a proprietary cetane improver made by ICI. The purpose of the cetane additive is to improve the ignitability of the fuel in the compression-ignition engine, thereby avoiding the use of glow plugs. The methanol powered Cummins L10 heavy-duty diesel engine has been plagued with problems of excessive formaldehyde emissions and engine stalling. Cummins

TABLE 6-25. Comparison of Emissions from the Cummins L10 Diesel Engine Using Low Sulfur Diesel Fuel, Methanol and Natural Gas in g/mi

Fuel	NMOG	CO	NO_x	PM
Low Sulfur Diesel	2.2	13.5	32.5	1.25
Methanol + 3% Avocet				
w/o oxidation catalyst	NA	10.8	16.0	0.70
w/ oxidation catalyst	NA	0.5	15.0	0.40
CNG	0.2	3.1	14.2	0.25

NA: Not Available

engineers abandoned further development of the methanol L10 and concentrated instead in the development of the natural gas L10 engine.

Early in 1993, Cummins became the first engine manufacturer to introduce a natural-gas powered production model, the L10-240G, as an alternative to heavy duty diesel engines (typically employed in Class 7&8 vehicles with a gross weight in excess of 26,000 lb). This engine has been certified already by the California Air Resources Board as a low emission engine. It beats current emission standards by over 50% and already exceeds those set for the end of the century. Cummins has over 115 engines running in customer fleets now. Most of them are used in city buses, although there is a refuse fleet in New York City using five engines. More recently, another heavy duty CNG engine, the Detroit Diesel Corporation DDC Series 50G, has been also certified by CARB as a low emission engine as well. Other heavy duty diesel engine manufacturers such as Caterpillar (Caterpillar 3306 G engine) have developed CNG fueled heavy duty engines that are currently undergoing testing in order to be certified as low emission. Finally, Cummins (Cummins B series), Detroit Diesel (DDC Series 30G)/Navistar (T444 engine), Hercules (Hercules 5.8L engine and Hercules 3.5L engine) and Tecogen (Tecogen 7000 engine) have also developed medium duty CNG engines that will undergo testing for low emission certification by CARB in 1995. These medium duty CNG engines will be replacing heavy duty gasoline engines or medium size diesel engines typically employed in medium weight vehicles (Class 3-5, 10,000-19,500 lb; and Class 6, 19,501-26,000 lb).

NATURAL GAS AND AUTOMOBILE FUEL CYCLE EMISSIONS

In comparing the air pollution characteristics of different automotive fuels, one is inclined to consider only the emissions from the tailpipe of the vehicle. In this approach then, electricity as an automotive fuel is assumed to be non-polluting as an electric vehicle has zero vehicle emissions. However, electricity is generated in power plans utilizing a variety of fossil fuels such as coal, oil, natural gas, nuclear energy and renewable resources such as hydropower, wind power and geothermal energy. Thus, one must also include in the calculation the air pollution generated during the fuel cycle. The fuel cycle consists of all the activities from extraction, conversion, transportation and up to the delivery of the fuel to the vehicle fuel storage system be it a gasoline tank, a CNG high pressure cylinder or a bank of batteries.

While the processes involved in each fuel cycle are well known and understood, the calculation of air emissions is rather involved as one has to account for very many processes. Fortunately, a comprehensive study on automobile fuel cycle emissions has just become available[65]. The salient results of this study, which considered gasoline, reformulated gasoline (RFG), natural gas, liquefied petroleum gas (LPG), electricity, ethanol and methanol, are presented later on here. The major interest in the automobile fuel cycle is of course the comparison between natural gas and electricity as vehicular fuels. Everybody will agree that an electric vehicle utilizing utility power is not in reality a zero emission vehicle, notwithstanding the claims to the contrary of electric utilities and other interested parties.

The air emissions resulting from the fuel cycle of the seven fuels considered in the aforementioned study are summarized in Table 6-26. Because of the more stringent air quality standards in general as well as the high contribution of renewable electric power generation in California, the emissions are given both for the US on the average and California. A small reduction in these emissions will take place in the years to come under existing legislation. Thus, the anticipated future values of automotive fuel cycle emissions are not repeated here. The various assumptions entering the calculation of the data in Table 6-27 have been stated in the notes at the end of that table. The major reduction in the

Table 6-26. Automotive Fuel Cycle Emissions in g/mi for Seven Fuels in the US and California at the Present Time

Fuel	NMOG	NO_x	CO	SO_x	PM	CO_2[1]
United States[2]						
Gasoline	0.254	0.226	0.080	0.044	0.013	84.8
RFG	0.252	0.239	0.083	0.044	0.013	93.8
LPG	0.120	0.366	0.099	0.008	0.006	17.2
CNG[4]	0.083	0.053	0.061	0.299	0.006	78.1
Electricity	0.056	1.192	0.060	2.669	0.041	339.1
E85	0.194	0.642	0.257	0.546	0.037	361.0
M85	0.174	0.575	0.149	0.012	0.009	154.2
California[2,3]						
Gasoline	0.254	0.226	0.080	0.044	0.013	84.8
RFG	0.252	0.239	0.083	0.044	0.013	93.8
LPG	0.080	0.147	0.062	0.008	0.005	17.2
CNG[4]	0.079	0.053	0.020	0.004	0.002	53.6
Electricity	0.043	0.210	0.128	0.033	0.017	113.8
E85	0.088	0.155	0.065	0.009	0.005	361.0
M85	0.109	0.193	0.081	0.012	0.006	154.2

1. Emissions included methane and other greenhouse gas effects. 2. The vehicle efficiency assumed is that of the Chrysler minivan at 22 mpg in its ICE version and 0.48 kWh/mi for the electric version. 3. The California case reflects only the in-state portion of fuel cycle emissions. 4. Includes emissions from the operation of an electrically driven compressor delivering the fuel at 3,600 psi.

fuel cycle emissions will occur as the vehicle efficiency increases. Thus, a 40 mpg vehicle fuel efficiency will almost half the fuel cycle emissions. Such fuel increase is a very realistic prospect for CNG vehicles as will be discussed in a later section. On the other hand, an electric vehicle with twice the present efficiency, i.e., 0.25 mi/kWh may be more difficult to attain in the foreseeable future because of the weight of present day batteries. Thus, reductions in the fuel cycle for electricity will be more difficult to materialize in the next 10 to 20 years.

The emissions in Table 6-26 do not include evaporative emissions from the refueling and during operation of the vehicle. These are estimated to be on the order of 0.194 g/mi for gasoline, reformulated gasoline, methanol and ethanol fuels. No refueling evaporative emissions take place with natural gas and LPG as both of these fuels are stored under pressure and are delivered to the vehicle tank via leakproof fittings.

TABLE 6-27. Full Fuel Cycle Emissions (Fuel Cycle plus Vehicle Emissions) for the 1995 Chrysler Mini Van Operating on Gasoline, CNG, M85 and Electricity in the United States as of the mid 1990s

Fuel Type[1]	Emission (g/mi)					
	NMOG	NO_x	CO	SO_x	PM	CO_2
Gasoline	0.698	0.626	3.462	0.044	0.013	468
CNG	0.088	0.093	0.420	0.004	0.002	371
M85	0.553	0.593	3.481	0.012	0.006	539
Electricity	0.056	1.192[2]	0.060	2.699[2]	0.041	339[2]

1. The vehicle efficiency is assumed to be 22 mpg in its ICE version and 0.48 kWh/mi for the electric version. 2. The California emissions are for NO_x 0.210 g/mi, for SO_x 0.033 g/mi and for CO_2 134 g/mi as California imports most of its fossil fuel generated electricity from other states and uses renewable resources.

A comparison of the full fuel cycle emissions for the Chrysler mini-van on four different fuels can be now performed on the basis of the preceding results. Table 6-27 summarizes the obtained emissions for the US as a whole. These results show what levels of emissions are feasible at the present time anywhere in the country — compare also the NO_x, SO_x and CO_2 emissions for California.

Several observations can be made regarding electricity as an alternative automotive fuel by comparing the results in Table 6-27. The conclusions of this comparison may be summed as follows.

- CO_2 Electricity is better than all carbon fuels with the exception of natural gas, where the difference is rather small (unless most of the electricity in the country becomes nuclear and/or renewable).

- CO Electricity has a clear advantage by more than an order of magnitude over all carbon containing fuels except for natural gas where the advantage is a factor of seven.

- NMOG The advantage of electricity is better than an order of magnitude over all fuels except natural gas where the advantage is only a factor of two.

- NO_x Natural gas has an advantage over electricity by a factor larger than ten and a factor of six over other carbon fuels.

- SO_X Natural gas has an advantage over electricity by more than two orders of magnitude and a factor varying between three to more than ten for all other carbon fuels (55% of electricity in the US is generated by coal which contains sulfur).

- PM   The advantage of natural gas over electricity is more than an order of magnitude.

Thus, electricity has an advantage over natural gas in two emission categories, i.e., carbon monoxide and non-reactive organic gases. Natural gas has an advantage over electricity in the other three emission categories, i.e., nitrous oxides, sulfur oxides and particulates. Electricity and natural gas are about even in one category, i.e., carbon dioxide.

Moreover, electric vehicles may create another source of pollution resulting from the increased use of batteries some of which contain highly toxic metals such as lead and cadmium. Thus, it is not obvious that a zero-emission-vehicle powered by utility electricity is better for the environment than an ultra-low-emission- vehicle powered with natural gas. A calculation has been performed by the author on lead emissions form the use of recycled lead-acid batteries. The simple calculation indicates that if all the vehicles in the country were electric, and were using lead-acid batteries with a 20 thousand mile life, and if a 99% lead recycling was feasible during the manufacturing of new batteries from the recycled ones, then as much lead will be emitted to the air as it was emitted when all gasoline was leaded. A 99.9% lead recycling will still put an order of magnitude more lead into the environment than present day unleaded gasoline does. Incidentally, natural gas will reduce the amount of lead in the air by more than a factor of ten from that emitted by present day unleaded gasoline.

This chapter on the environmental effects of natural gas *vis-a-vis* other automotive fuels cannot be completed without mentioning in passing that the five pollutants emitted by motor vehicles (CO, NO_X, NMOG, SO_X and PM) have been compared only in terms of absolute emission levels. The implication is that all five are equivalent, although it is recognized that some are more harmful than others by setting different maximum ambient levels. However, these maximum ambient levels for each one of them set forth in Table 6-4 point to a severity factor different than one. For example, if carbon monoxide is assigned a severity factor of one as the least harmful of the five pollutants then the following severity factors may be assigned to the remaining four pollutants: NMOG 62.5; NO_X 100; SO_X 125; PM 133.3. The introduction of severity factors to combine pollutants from motor vehicles has not received any particular attention in the US, although it has been used in European studies[66]. It should be pointed out that if such pollutant weighting or severity factors were to be utilized in comparing the emissions from CNG versus gasoline, electric or other vehicles, the CNG fueled vehicles will show an even greater pollutant advantage over all other vehicles fueled by the competing alternative fuels, as well as the present fuels.

REFERENCES

1. J. J. Flink, The Automobile Age, p. 136, The MIT Press, Cambridge, MA, 1990.

2. D. E. Painter, Air Pollution Technology, ch. 2 , ch. 3 and ch. 11, Reston Publishing Company, Reston, VA, 1974.

3. Statistical Abstract Of The United States 1992, 112th Edition, pp. 213-217, Bureau of the Census, US Department of Commerce, Washington, D.C., 1992.

4. J. M. Fowler, Energy and the Environment, 2nd ed., pp. 157-174, McGraw-Hill Book Company, New York, NY, 1984.

5. R. E. Bolz and G. L. Tuve (eds.), CRC Handbook of Tables for Applied Engineering Science, 2nd ed., Chemical Hazard Information, pp.766-770, CRC Press Inc., Boca Raton, FL, 1979.

6. J. M. Fowler, Energy and the Environment, loc. cit., p. 637.

7. M. Chiron, "Effects of Motor Vehicle Pollutants on Health", pp. 1-10, , Catalysis and Automotive Pollution Control, A. Crucq and A. Frennet (eds.), Elsevier Science Publishers B.V., Amsterdam, The Netherlands, 1987.

8. R. E. Bolz and G. L. Tuve (eds.), CRC Handbook of Tables for Applied Engineering Science, loc. cit., p. 733.

9. R. Joumard, M. Chiron, R. Vidon, "La Fixation du Monoxyde de Carbone sur l' Hemoglobine et ses Effets sur l' Homme", Institute de Recherche des Transports, Paris, France, 1983.

10. J. Singh and L. M. Cheatum, "Polluted Air, Low Protein = Infertility", *Science News*, v. 144, p. 30, 1993.

11. R. Impens, "Automotive Traffic: Risks for the Environment", pp. 11-29, Catalysis and Automotive Pollution Control, A. Crucq and A. Frennet (eds.), Elsevier Science Publishers B.V., Amsterdam, The Netherlands, 1987.

12. A.H.Rose, "Automotive Exhaust Emissions" in Air Pollution, A.C. Stern (ed.), v. II, pp.40-80, Acedemic Press, New York, NY, 1962.

13. H. L. Needleman, L. A. Leviton, D. Bellinger, "Lead Associated Intellectual Deficit", *New England J. Med.*, pp. 306-367, 1982.

14. J. F. Yocum and J. B. Upham, "The Effects of Air Pollution" in Air Pollution, A.C. Stern (ed.), 3rd ed. v. II, pp. 65-116, Acedemic Press, New York, NY, 1977.

15. R. R. Gould, "Energy and Acid Rain", v. 9, pp. 529-559, Ann. Rev. Energy, Annual Reviews, Inc., Palo Alto, CA, 1984.

16. Statistical Abstract Of The United States 1985, 105th Edition, p. 200, Bureau of the Census, US Department of Commerce, Washington, D.C., 1992.

17. K.C. Taylor, "Automobile Catalytic Converters", pp. 97-116, Catalysis and Automotive Pollution Control, A. Crucq and A. Frennet (eds.), Elsevier Science Publishers B.V., Amsterdam, The Netherlands, 1987.

18. R.W. Mellde, I.M. Maasing, T. B. Johansson, "Advanced Automobile Engines For Fuel Economy, Low Emissions, And Multifuel Capability", v. 14, pp. 425-444, Ann. Rev. Energy, Annual Reviews, Inc., Palo Alto, CA, 1989.

19. Clean Air Act of 1992, Report 102-1018, Washington, D.C., October 5, 1990.

20. "California Air Quality : A Status Report", pp. 21-28, State of California Air Resources Board, Sacramento, CA, 1991.

21. D. W. Pearce, J. J. Warford, World Without End, published for the World Bank, Washington, DC by Oxford University Press, New York, NY, 1993.

22. M. P. Walsh, "Control Of Diesel Particulate Emissions", pp.51-67, Catalysis and Automotive Pollution Control, A. Crucq and A. Frennet (eds.), Elsevier Science Publishers B.V., Amsterdam, The Netherlands, 1987.

23. H. S. Gandhi and M. Shelef, "The Role of Research in the Development of New Generation Automotive Catalysts, pp. 199-214, Catalysis and Automotive Pollution Control, A. Crucq and A. Frennet (eds.), Elsevier Science Publishers B.V., Amsterdam, The Netherlands, 1987.

24. B.J. Cooper, W.D.J. Evans and B. Harrison, "Aspects of Automotive Catalyst Preparation, Performance and Durability", pp. 117-141, Catalysis and Automotive Pollution Control, A. Crucq and A. Frennet (eds.), Elsevier Science Publishers B.V., Amsterdam, The Netherlands, 1987.

25. J. Leggett (ed.), Global Warming:The Greenpeace Report, Oxford University Press, New York, NY, 1990.

26. J. Falk and A. Brownlow, The Greenhouse Challenge, Penguin Books Australia, Victoria, AU, 1989.

27. D. A. Lashof and D. R. Ahuja, "Relative Contributions of Greenhouse Gas Emissions to Global Warming", Nature, v. 344, pp. 529-531, 1990.

28. A. L. Hammond, E. Rodenburg and W. Moomaw, "Accountability in the Greenhouse", Nature, v. 347, pp. 705-706, 1990.

29. R. E. Turner, "Fertilizer and Climate Change", Nature, v. 349, pp.469-471, 1991.

30. R. M. Harrison, S. J. de Mora, S. Rapsomanakis, W.R. Johnston, Introductory Chemistry for the Environmental Sciences, Cambridge University Press, Cambridge, UK, 1991.

31. R. S. Kandel, Earth and Cosmos, Pergamon Press, Oxford, UK, 1980.

32. N. Hall (ed.), Exploring Chaos, W. W. Norton & Company, New York, NY, 1993.

33. G. J. MacDonald, "The Future of Methane as Energy Resource", v. 15, pp. 53-83, Annual Reviews of Energy, Palo Alto, CA 1990.

34. SAE, Electric and Hybrid Vehicle Technology, SP-915, p. 39, Society of Automotive Engineers, Warendale , PA, 1992.

35. M. A. DeLuchi, R. A. Johnston, and D. Sperling, "Methanol vs. Natural Gas Vehicles: A Comparison of Resource Supply, Performance, Emissions, Fuel Storage, Safety, Costs, and Transitions", SAE Technical Paper Series No. 881656, International Fuels and Lubricants Meeting and Exposition, Portland, OR, 1988.

36. M. A. DeLuchi, D. Sperling, and R. A. Johnston, "A Comparative Analysis of Future Transportation Fuels", Institute of Transportation Studies, University of California, Berkeley, CA 1987.

37. R. M. Siewert, P. J. Mitchell and P. A. Mulawa, "Environmental Potential of Natural Gas Fuel for Light Duty Vehicles: An Engine-Dynamometer Study of Exhaust-Emission-Control strategies and Fuel Consumption", SAE Technical Paper Series No. 932744, Fuels and Lubricants Meeting and Exposition, Philadelphia, PA, 1993.

38. K. B. Hogan, J. S. Hoffman and A. M. Thompson, "Methane on the Greenhouse Agenda", Nature, v. 354, pp. 181-182, 1991.

39. P. J. Crutzen, "Methane's Sinks and Sources", Nature, v. 350, pp. 380-381, 1991.

40. M. Valenti, "Tapping Landfills for Energy", Mech. Eng., pp. 44-47, January 1992.

41. EIA, Natural Gas Annual 1991, DOE/EIA-0131(91), US Department of Energy, Washington, DC, 1992.

42. EIA, Monthly Energy Review-June 1992, DOE/EIA-0035(92/06), US Department of Energy, Washington, DC, 1992.

43. G. Lean, D. Hinrichsen and A. Markham, Atlas of the Environment, Prentice Hall Press, New York, NY, 1990.

44. W. J. Burroughs, Watching the World's Weather, pp. 172-175, Cambridge University Press, Cambridge, UK, 1991.

45. S. Masien and R. Demke, "Current and Future Refrigerants for Chillers", pp. 62-63, ASHRAE Journal, v. 35, no. 5, May 1993.

46. R. Pool, "Ozone Loss Worse Than Expected", *Nature,* v. 350, p. 451, 1991.

47. SCE, *Research Newsletter,* v. 30, no. 1, p. 2, Southern California Edison Co., Rosemead, CA, 1991.

48. *NGV Today,* Premiere Issue, January 1993, The Gas Company, Los Angeles, CA 1993.

49. M. Marelli, private communication, The Gas Company, Los Angeles, CA, July 1993.

50. Natural Gas Vehicles Information Packet, "Emissions Comparisons of Vehicle Fuels", The Gas Company, Los Angeles, CA, 1994.

51. Technology Advancement Office 1992 Progress Report, Vol. II, Project and Technology Status, pp. 13-17, South Coast Air Quality Management District, Diamond Bar, CA, 1992.

52. R. O. Geiss, W. M. Burkmyre, J. W. Lanigan, "The Technical Highlights of the Dodge Compressed Natural Gas Ram Van/Wagon", SAE Technical Paper Series No. 921551, Natural Gas: Fuels and Fueling, SP-927, Society of Automotive Engineers, Warrendale, PA, 1992.

53. "Chrysler Corporation's Compressed Natural Gas Vans and Wagons", Chrysler Corporation Fleet Operations, Southfield, MI, 1994.

54. S. H. Cadle, P. A. Mulawa, D. L. Hilden and R. Halsall, "Exhaust Emissions From Dual-Fuel Vehicles Using Compressed Natural Gas and Gasoline", Air & Waste Management Association, 90-96.8, 83rd Annual Meeting & Exhibition, Pittsburgh, PA, 1990.

55. R. M. Siewert and P. J. Mitchell, "Method for Reducing Methane Exhaust Emissions from natural Gas Engines", US Patent No. 5,131,224, July 21, 1992.

56. D. L. Hilden, P. A. Mulawa and S. H. Cadle, "Liquefied Petroleum Gas as an Automotive Fuel: Exhaust Emissions and Their Atmospheric Reactivity", Report FL-775/EV-382, General Motors Research Laboratories, Warren, MI 1991.

57. C. Dempsey, "Propane Fueled Engines and the Impact of Decreasing Temperature on Exhaust Emissions – A Year Round Advantage", Proc. 1990 Winsdor Workshop on Alternative Fuels, Windsor, ON, 1990.

58. R. A. Gosse, J. D. Benson, V. R. Burns, A. M. Hochhauser, W. J. Koehl, L. J. Painter, R. M. Reuter, B. H. Rippon, and J. A. Rutherford, "Methanol/Gasoline Blends and Emissions", *Automotive Engineering*, v. 100, no.4, pp.19-21, 1992.

59. J. Raloff, "New Probes of Gas Additive's Toxicity", Science News, v. 143, p. 182, 1993.

60. W. P. L. Carter, "Development of Ozone Reactivity Scales for Volatile Organic Compounds", Final Report to EPA Contract CR-814396-01-0, Chem. Proc. and Char. Division, Research Triangle Park, NC, 1990.

61. A. G. Russell, D. St. Pierre, J. B. Milford, "Ozone Control and Methanol Fuel Use", *Science,* v. 247, pp. 201-204, 1990.

62. B. Cooper, "The Future of Catalytic Systems", *Automotive Engineering*, v. 100, no. 4, pp. 9-12, 1992.

63. Technology Advancement Office 1992 Progress Report, Vol. II, Project and Technology Status, loc. cit., pp. 34-45.

64. *NGV Today*, Spring Issue, April 1993, The Gas Company, Los Angeles, CA 1993.

65. K. G. Darrow, "Light Duty Vehicle Full Fuel Cycle Emissions Analysis", report GRI-93/0472, prepared by Energy International, Inc., Bellevue, WA for Gas Research Institute, Chicago, IL, 1994.

66. O. Hohmeyer, Social Costs of Energy Consumption, Springer-Verlag, Berlin, FRG, 1988.

67. C. Suplee, "Dirty Air Can Shorten Your Life, Study Says: Death Rate is Higher in Worst Cities", p. A1, *The Washington Post,* March 10, 1995.

Chapter 7

Economics of the Natural Gas Fueled Automotive Transportation System

THE COMPONENTS OF THE END-USE PRICE
OF THE NEW SYSTEM

The end-use price to the consumer of a natural gas based automotive transportation system includes the costs of the many new and different elements that will comprise the change from the present system. There are several elements associated with the fuel switch of passenger cars, trucks and vans from motor gasoline and diesel fuel to natural gas fuel. The costs of these elements can be grouped into two main categories: First, natural gas vehicle incremental costs pertaining to the modification of the engine (i.e., higher compression ratio, gas fuel injection system, etc.), fuel delivery system (i.e., gaseous fuel port injection, etc.) and fuel storage (CNG or LNG tanks); second, natural gas fuel costs consisting of dispensing equipment costs to the customer/public (i.e., public natural gas station, home compressor, etc.) and of the natural gas cost (i.e., production, transportation and distribution). There exists already a large body of information regarding the magnitude of these costs. Consequently, these costs with their evolution in time are well understood and will be discussed in subsequent sections. Since natural gas is the central element in the fuel switch, it makes sense to begin the economic analysis by considering first the natural gas fuel pricing make up.

The price of natural gas fuel delivered to the consumer be it residential, commercial or industrial is the sum of associated costs and profits. The costs of natural gas can be classified into three general categories: I. Commodity costs; II. Transportation costs; and III. Distribution costs[1]. These three categories reflect the major steps or transactions involved. The three transactions with the respective participating entities are as follows: I. The exploration, development drilling and extraction from the reservoir by a producer; II. Gathering, processing and long distance transportation by pipeline operators; and III. Distribution to consumers by utilities and other local distribution companies. In the case of natural gas fuel, there is a fourth transaction involved, namely the dispensing of gas to a vehicle as CNG either at a public station or at a business place or at home.

Thus, the price that the consumer has to pay for natural gas to fill a vehicle will consist of the sum of four components as follows: I. The wellhead price; II. The transportation tariff; III. The local distribution company (LDC) mark-up; and IV. The dispensing mark-up. Table 7-1 summarizes the various components of the customer price associated with the use of natural gas as a transportation fuel. As it has already been mentioned, the actual cost of a natural gas automotive transportation system will also include the incremental cost of the vehicle specified by the automotive or original equipment manufacturer (OEM). Each of the four price components of natural gas as a motor fuel will be examined in the following sections.

NATURAL GAS WELLHEAD PRICE

Natural gas producers have shown tremendous improvements in productivity in the last ten years. Some of these improvements are the result of new exploration and production technologies[1]. New seismic techniques have helped identify gas resources with greater precision, while advances in drill-bit design have improved drilling rates, thus

TABLE 7-1. Summary of the End-Use Price Components of a Natural Gas Fueled
Automotive Transportation System

Price Component	Description
Natural Gas Motor Fuel	
Wellhead Price	Price paid to the producer of natural gas, which reflects the commodity cost.
Transportation Tariff	Price paid to pipeline company by LDC for transportation and storage of natural gas from producing area to local receipt point.
Local Distribution Markup	Amount charged by distribution company to deliver gas to public station or home.
Dispensing Markup	Amount charged by CNG or LNG station to the public or cost of CNG dispensing equipment for home refueling.
CNG/LNG Vehicle	
OEM CNG/LNG Vehicle Price	Incremental price of a CNG or LNG vehicle over a comparable gasoline/diesel fuel one.

reducing drilling time. The introduction of "real-time" bit location, for instance, has opened up whole new areas of directional drilling.

Meanwhile, engineering advances now enable producers to explore and produce in areas previously considered infeasible. The development of relatively inexpensive but powerful computer work stations has also enabled the natural gas producers to collect, process, and interpret large amounts of seismic data in a 3-D format. The 3-D seismic techniques have revolutionized the search for natural gas by mapping the geologic structures with great accuracy[2]. The collected data are processed and reprocessed so that gas deposits can be "seen" trapped in sands as "bright spots" in computer generated images. This technology has been applied successfully in the exploration of the Gulf of Mexico for natural gas even by small or independent producers[3]. Advances in drill bit design have also contributed to increased productivity. A new drill bit tracking technique, referred as measurement while drilling (MWD), allows the driller to keep accurate tracking in real time of the location of the bit while drilling. This has made it possible to drill horizontal and other directionally drilled wells with greater effectiveness. Horizontal and directional wells allow a greater area of the reservoir to be tapped by a single well than would be only possible using several conventional vertical wells. The result has been a very large increase in gas recovery per well. For example, older wells recompleted using horizontal drilling techniques have shown increases in production of up to 4,000 percent. Horizontal drilling has gain rapid acceptance among all producers, both large and small[4]. Some of the other technologies, however, such as advances in offshore platform design for deep water natural gas production, can be utilized only by the major producers (major oil companies) who have access to sufficient capital[5].

Besides new technology other factors have helped producers to improve productivity and reduce the finding costs of natural gas. Drilling efficiency, measured by the number of wells drilled per active rig, increased from an average of 30 during the period 1981-1985 to an average of 35 during the period from 1986 to 1990. This increase in efficiency has been the result of intense competition between drilling contractors to maintain market share following the decline in drilling after 1981. Another factor resulting in increased productivity is the so called degree of basin maturity, whereby producers move to less explored geologic areas rather than continue drilling in mature basins. Since producers find the largest fields in a basin first, the finding rate in a region declines as the resource base is depleted or the basin matures. The less explored geologic regions for natural gas in the US are generally offshore areas or deeper onshore areas.

All the preceding factors have had a significant impact on the cost of natural gas production. For example, the cost of drilling a gas well onshore in the contiguous 48 States decreased from about $1.1 million in 1982 (1991 dollars) to $0.4 million in 1991[1]. Moreover, the gas finding rate in the lower 48 States was 3.8 billion scf per exploratory well in 1990. This rate was two and one-half times the gas finding rate in 1981. Finally, the proved natural gas reserve revisions in the US averaged 4,293 billion scf per year from 1984 to 1991 up from 474 billion scf per year for the period from 1978 to 1983.

It should be noted, however, that data from the early 1970s suggest that the gas finding rate is lower today than what it was twenty years

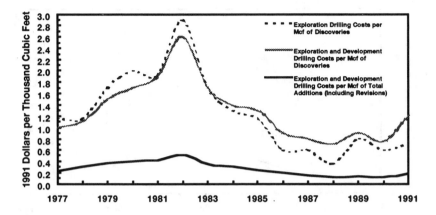

FIGURE 7-1.   Natural Gas Finding Costs for Onshore Wells in the Lower 48 States from 1977 to 1991 in 1991 Constant Dollars per Thousand Cubic Feet (Mcf) (Source: EIA, US DOE).

ago. This result may indicate resource depletion. It may also reflect the fact that wellhead prices were artificially low twenty years ago so that only the very best, i.e., the largest, natural gas prospects were developed. As Figure 7-1 shows, nevertheless, the cost of finding natural gas has declined by about 300% since 1982 in constant dollars and it stood at about $1 per 1000 scf in 1991 ($1.14 per 1000 scf for new discoveries and $0.67 per 1000 scf for reserve additions, including the cost of dry wells). It is interesting to note that gas finding costs have increased somewhat in recent years because of the increased emphasis on drilling for unconventional gas (tight sands and coal seam wells).

The natural gas producing industry, unlike the crude oil production industry, remains relatively unconcentrated as of 1991. The top four producers account for 17% of the production and 20% of the reserves. The top 10, 20, 40 and 300 producers account respectively for 31%, 42%, 51% and 58% of the production and 38%, 49%, 58% and 65% of the reserves. It turns out that since 1985 independent producers have increased their share of the market both in production (7%) and reserves (15%).

Annual average wellhead prices have declined in real terms every year since 1983 as Figure 7-2 shows. The average wellhead price was $1.64 per 1000 scf in 1991. The deregulation of the natural gas industry,

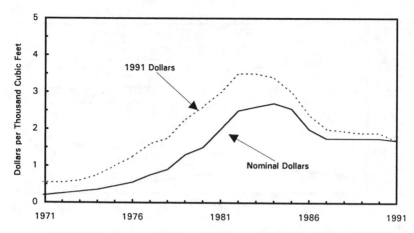

FIGURE 7-2. Wellhead Natural Gas Prices from 1970 to 1991 in Nominal and 1991
Constant Dollars (Source: EIA, US DOE).

which allows the producers to sell their gas directly to the end users,
has increased the wellhead price volatility since 1987. However, new
financial instruments such as the gas futures market have become available in recent years in order to reduce the exposure of producers and
consumers alike to price volatility. It is projected that the wellhead price
of natural gas will rise to $2.04 (1991 dollars) per 1000 scf in 1995 and
$2.56 per 1000 scf in 2000[6].

NATURAL GAS INTERSTATE PIPELINE TRANSMISSION TARIFFS

Regulatory and legislative changes during the past ten years have
also led to a more efficient transmission segment of the natural gas
industry. The open access to interstate pipelines, which began in the
mid-1980s, was further advanced in 1992, when the Federal Energy
Regulatory Commission (FERC) issued Order 636[7]. This order
addresses a broad range of issues relating to the interstate transportation
of natural gas and the services provided by pipeline companies.

Since the early 1980s, regulatory initiatives have considerably encouraged market competition. Natural gas transportation programs were initiated to alleviate oversupply problems by allowing pipeline companies to
release excess supply and transport it for other purchases. These initial

short-term responses to market conditions have evolved into a complete restructuring of the interstate pipeline industry to allow more participation in the purchase and transportation of natural gas. As of January 1, 1993, all controls on wellhead prices of natural gas were removed, thereby ending forty years of price controls on interstate supplies.

The provisions of FERC Order 636 allow for the more efficient use of the interstate natural gas transmission system by fundamentally changing the way pipeline companies conduct business. First, interstate pipelines are required to "unbundle" or separate their sales and transportation services. Thus, a pipeline company is prevented from giving preference to its own gas sales over those of other suppliers. This feature increases competition among gas producers and diminishes the market power of pipeline companies. Second, interstate pipeline companies must provide open access transportation services that are equal in quality whether the gas is purchased directly from the pipeline company or from another user. Competition in the industry should increase as all gas merchants are afforded equal transportation opportunities and services. Third, the use and further development of major natural gas market centers is encouraged where many buyers and sellers can make or take gas deliveries.

These market centers must be located in the vicinity of large pipeline system interconnections. Moreover, these market centers must have two additional characteristics to function properly: I. Many buyers and sellers must have access to, and participate in the market activities at the market center; and II. There must be a market center management, ideally formed by one or more pipeline companies, that could be capable to match buyers and sellers physically by using electronic information and control systems to arrange transactions. Some market centers have developed naturally near major production areas or near major consumption areas with storage fields or pipeline interconnections as shown in Figure 7-3. More market centers are expected to be developed in the future near locations where several pipeline systems interconnect in the vicinity of large production or storage field areas.

Natural gas market centers will benefit consumers by: reducing transaction costs; forcing pipeline companies to compete; increasing the purchasing and selling opportunities for all buyers and sellers; increasing reliability to core customers; allowing the aggregation of supplies by

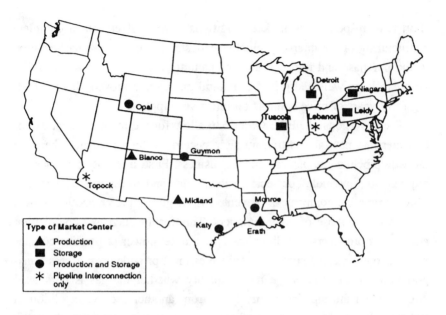

Market Center	No. Pipeline Companies	Pipeline Intercon'n	Production Area	Storage Area
Blanco, NM	3		X	
Detroit, MI	6	X		X
Erath, LA	28		X	
Guymon, OK	16	X	X	X
Katy, TX	23	X	X	
Lebanon, OH	6	X		
Leidy, PA	6	X		X
Midland/Waha, TX	15		X	
Monroe, LA	14	X	X	X
Niagara, NY	6	X		X
Opal, WY	12	X		
Topock, AZ	5	X		
Tuscola, IL	5	X		X

FIGURE 7-3.   Market Centers for Natural Gas in the United States as of 1991 (Source: Federal Energy Regulatory Commission).

many companies instead of the pipeline companies only; and promoting the exchange of pricing information. Potential disadvantages such as increased complexity and loss of control of gas supplies by an individual pipeline company are not deemed to be serious enough to offset the expected advantages of competition and increased efficiency.

A fourth and highly controversial provision of the FERC Order 636 is the requirement that pipeline companies switch from the modified fixed-variable (MFV) rate design to the straight fixed-variable (SFV) rate design[1]. In the MFV rate design all variable costs and the fixed costs associated with the pipeline company return on equity and associated income taxes are included in the commodity charge (amount of gas purchased), while all other fixed costs are recovered in the two part demand charge consisting of a peak day demand charge (monthly charge to reserve "on-demand" delivery based on the reserved capacity for the peak day) and an annual demand charge (annual charge to take "on-demand" delivery based on annual gas volume purchased). In the SFV rate design all fixed costs are allocated to the one part demand charge consisting of the peak demand charge (renamed reservation fee) only and all variable costs are allocated to the commodity charge (renamed usage charge).

The policy rational in introducing the MFV rate design in 1983 consisted of maximizing pipeline throughput and enabling natural gas to compete more effectively with alternative fuels such as oil. The policy rational in 1992 to develop the SFV rate design consisted of fostering competition at the wellhead, facilitating the creation of national markets for gas, promoting non-distortionary price signals (no longer newer pipeline facilities are at a disadvantage over older depreciated ones), and optimizing capacity use (costs of firm peak-day service are borne by those who use it).

It is worth pointing out that the provisions of the SVF rate design promote indirectly the use of natural gas as a transportation fuel for a number of cost reducing reasons. They allow competition at the wellhead, level the playing field among all producers, do not penalize the construction of new interstate pipelines that may be necessary to meet increased throughput for transportation use and promote the use of off-peak natural gas for vehicle refueling at home and business.

An analytical study was performed to estimate how different design rates affect the firm transportation service tariff paid by different types of pipeline customers (local distribution companies, marketeers, other pipeline companies, electric utilities and industrial customers)[1]. The study used a composite pipeline company developed from six interstate pipeline companies serving the East Coast and covered six States. As part of this study, an extensive load factor sensitivity analysis was conducted for representative customers in three of the six States. Some of the results are reproduced in Figure 7-4. It is interesting to note that the SFV rate design shows the largest variation between low and high load factors. Moreover, the SVF rate design results in lower interstate transportation tariffs for load factors of 75% or higher. Finally, it is important to note that the interstate pipeline transportation tariff is on the order of $1 per 1,000 scf of natural gas.

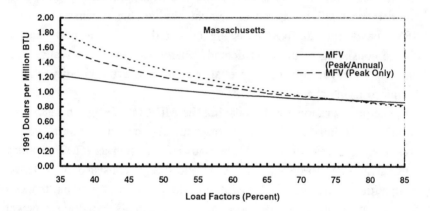

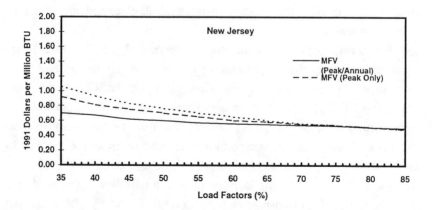

FIGURE 7-4. Estimated Natural Gas Tariffs for Firm Transportation Service by a Composite Pipeline Company as a Function of Load Factor for Two East Coast States (Source: Energy Information Administration, US DOE).

NATURAL GAS LOCAL DISTRIBUTION COMPANY MARKUP

Natural gas end users include residential and commercial customers as well as industrial firms and electric utilities. These customer groups have very different energy requirements and thus quite different service needs. Residential and commercial customers have high seasonal requirements, mainly consuming gas in the winter months, and for health and safety reasons need a highly reliable supply. As a result, residential and commercial customers require on-demand service, known as "firm" service. In contrast, many industrial and electric utility customers receive natural gas through a lower priority service known as "interruptible service". During periods of peak demand service to these customers can be interrupted in order to deliver natural gas to the firm service customers. Since a large number of industrial and utility customers have fuel switching capability, they are unwilling to pay for firm service. Thus, they can purchase natural gas form an LDC or pipeline company at a lower price than residential and commercial customers and at a reduced security to the supply as well. Increasingly, however, the industrial and utility sectors are adding cogeneration and combined-cycle plants that rely heavily on natural gas and require more supply security than has been traditionally accorded these customers.

Residential and commercial customers rely almost completely on LDCs or pipeline companies acting as LDCs for their supply and service and have no practical alternative means to purchase natural gas. In contrast, large industrial customers and electric utilities have substantial knowledge of the market as well as the ability to contract directly for gas supplies from producers, or brokers or pipeline companies. These large volume natural gas users can then contract with a pipeline company or an LDC for transport and delivery of the required gas.

Since 1984 the industrial sector has been increasingly receiving delivery of natural gas under this option, called off-system sales. The industrial sector off-system sales have increased from 25% in 1984 to 67% in 1991, reflecting unmistakably the ability of large industrial customers to negotiate gas contracts with suppliers offering the lowest price. Of the remaining 33% of on-system industrial customers, the supply was divided evenly between LDCs and intrastate or interstate pipeline companies. Undoubtedly, the off-system industrial customers are able to negotiate natural prices well below those realized by the on-system industrial customers.

The natural gas as a transportation fuel belongs to the residential and commercial end users for several reasons. First, the location of refueling can be available either at home, at the work place or at a public station. Second, the reliability of fuel availability must be very high. Third, the ability to switch to other fuels, i.e., gasoline, although it is theoretically possible, it may not be practical (vehicle runs only on natural gas) or convenient. The only major difference in residential and commercial customer requirements for natural gas between its present utility (space conditioning, water heating, etc.) and its use as an automotive fuel will be the usage pattern.

The natural gas requirement as an automotive fuel is year-round rather than seasonal. This change may have implications in terms of the LDC price mark-up because residential natural gas vehicle refueling, which is slow by nature, will be done most likely at night. Depending on the amount of natural gas used during off-peak hours for refueling versus the amount of natural gas used for space heating and other uses during on-peak hours, the LDC may be able to reduce the firm service transportation charge it has to pay to the pipeline companies.

In essence home vehicle refueling has the potential to even out the severity of daily peaking. For example, the average household in the US uses annually about 95 million BTU (MMBTU) of natural gas for space heating, water heating, cooking and clothes drying, of which 65% is for space heating[8]. An automobile with a 21 mpg fuel efficiency, the current national average, will require a little less than 60 MMBTU annually, if it were fueled with natural gas. Thus, the natural gas used for space heating in the average household is comparable in volume to the annual natural gas fuel requirement of the average passenger vehicle today. If two vehicles were to be fueled at home, then the usage of natural gas for vehicle refueling can, on the average, virtually eliminate the daily peaking due to space heating demand.

Vehicle fueling with natural gas at home has obviously the potential to reduce the end-use price paid by the residential customers. The same can be true for commercial customers, other than public natural gas sta-

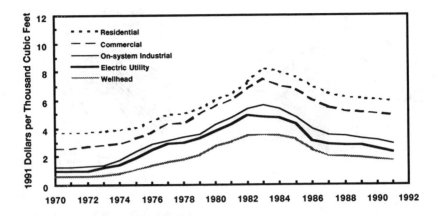

FIGURE 7-5.   Natural Gas End-Use and Wellhead Prices from 1970 to 1991 (Source: Energy Information Administration, US DOE).

tions, who may opt to install natural gas fueling facilities for their fleet vehicles and possibly their employees or even customers, depending on the nature of the business. Thus, vehicle fueling with natural gas at home or at work can accelerate the on-going reduction of the end-user price of natural gas to residential and commercial customers. This end-user price reduction, which began in 1984 as Figure 7-5 shows, has been, of course, the result of wellhead and other price reductions as discussed in the previous sections. It is interesting to note that between 1984 and 1991, the wellhead price of natural gas was reduced by 50%, while the citygate price was reduced by 43%[1]. In the same time period, the end-user price of residential, commercial, on-system industrial and electric utility customers was reduced by 26%, 33%, 50% and 54%, respectively.

For the residential and commercial customers the LDC mark-up is roughly 50% of the end-use price. This high mark-up is directly related to the high quality of service required by these customers, as it has already been explained. Moreover, the pipeline company transportation tariff and the LDC mark-up components account for two-thirds or more of the end-user price for either residential or commercial customers. Thus, the wellhead price component of the end-user price is one-third or less of the total price. The breakdown by components of the end-user

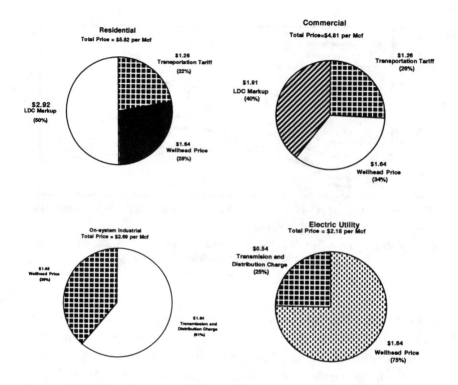

FIGURE 7-6. Components of Natural Gas Prices by End-User Sector as of 1991 in $/1,000 scf and Percent Contribution (Source: Energy Information Administration, US DOE).

price in the residential, commercial, on-system industrial and electric utility sectors are given in Figure 7-6 for the year 1991. It is interesting to note that for the industrial and electric utility sectors, the wellhead price of natural gas is the largest component of the end-user price accounting for 60% to 75% of the total. In addition, the transmission and distribution charges are combined into one number, because most industrial and electric utility customers bypass the LDC and obtain natural gas directly from the interstate pipeline system.

Obviously, the residential and commercial end-user price is much less dependent on the wellhead price than the end-user price of the industrial and electric utility customers. As a matter of fact, the contribution of the wellhead price on the end-user price of the residential and commercial customers has been diminishing since 1984, when the use of open access transportation services began and the natural gas spot market was developed. For example, the wellhead price accounted for 43% of the total residential customer end-user price in 1984, but only 28% in 1991. The commercial sector experienced a similar drop in percentage points of the wellhead component contribution to the overall end-user price during the 1984 to 1991 period. By contrast, the relative contribution in the end-user price of the wellhead component has remained roughly unchanged in the industrial and electric utility sector during the same period. On the other hand, both the industrial and electric utilities customers have seen significant reductions in the cost of transportation and distribution since 1984.

Regression analysis was used to determine how quickly the wellhead price changes are incorporated into the end-user price[1]. The results of the analysis suggest that wellhead price changes are fully reflected in end-user prices within three months. As expected, changes in the wellhead price have a dampened effect on residential and commercial customer prices. The analysis indicates that a 10% decrease, for example, in the wellhead price would result in a 3% or less decrease in the residential and commercial prices within three months. Incidentally, the partial decontrol of wellhead prices began with the Natural Gas Policy Act of 1978 and full decontrol went into effect on January 1, 1993 as provided by the Natural Gas Wellhead Decontrol Act of 1989.

Because the LDC mark-up plays such a significant part in determining the end-user prices in the residential and commercial sectors, it is useful to examine the way an LDC calculates rates for different classes of customers. Each State has its own Public Utility Commission (PUC) which regulates all LDCs in that State. While the ratemaking provisions as specified by the PUC of each State may vary from one State to another, some general rate making principles apply in all 50 States. The State PUC determines which LDC expenses can be passed through to the customers and establishes the LDC allowed rate of return. Based on these measures, the LDC determines rates for different customer classes given the allocation of expense and return allowed for each customer class.

An actual example of the end-price differential between a residential customer and an on-system industrial customer from a representative

TABLE 7-2. Actual Example of Residential and On-System Industrial Rate Calculations for the Local Distribution Service of Natural Gas from a Typical LDC in the South United States*

Allocation of Expenses by a Local Distribution Company	Residential Customer	Industrial Customer
Investment in Plant and Equipment	$2,000	$400,000
Annual Cost of Service		
Depreciation @ 3.3%	$ 66	$ 13,200
Return @ 11% Levelized Investment	$ 154	$ 30,800
Income Taxes @ 4% of Lev. Invest.	$ 56	$ 11,200
General Taxes @ 1% of Lev. Invest.	$ 20	$ 4,000
Operation and Maintenance Expense	$ 60	$ 3,000
Total Cost of Service	$ 356	$ 62,200
Annual Gas Purchases (10^3 scf)	80	256,000
Rate Required to Earn Cost of Capital in $ per10^3 scf		
Margin Rate (Cost Service/Gas Purchase)	4.45	0.24
Gas Cost at Wellhead	1.50	1.50
Pipeline Transportation and Fuel Service	0.30	0.30
Pipeline Demand Charge on MFV Basis	0.95	0.27
Total Rate Required	$7.20/$10^3$scf	$2.31/$10^3$scf

(*) Adapted from Ref.1. Note. Levelized Investment = 70% x Investment.

LDC in the South is reproduced in Table 7-2[1]. In this example, the LDC rate structure with respect to depreciation, return on investment, income taxes and general taxes is the same for both customers on a percentage basis of the respective investment on plant and equipment. The operation and maintenance expenses are 4 times as high for the residential customer than the industrial one as a percentage of the respective investment on plant and equipment (3% versus 0.75%). In addition the gas cost at the wellhead as well as pipeline transportation cost and fuel charges are the same for both customers on a per volume of natural gas basis. On the other hand, the pipeline demand charge is two and one-half times higher for the residential customer on a per volume basis. Finally, the plant and equipment investment is 200 higher for the average industrial customer, who, however, uses 3,200 as much natural gas as the average residential customer annually. Thus, there is 16 to 1 advantage of the industrial customer over the residential one in terms of volume on natural gas purchased for every dollar of plant and equipment investment on the part of the LDC.

This last factor and to a lesser degree the operation and maintenance expenses and the pipeline demand charges, rather than the rate structure itself, result in a $7.20/1,000 scf end-price for the residential customer versus a $2.31/1,000 scf end-price for the industrial customer or a larger than a 3 to 1 end-price ratio of the former customer to the latter one.

Adoption of the SFV rather than the MFV rate design under FERC Order 636 may reduce the pipeline total cost by a as much as factor of two for residential and commercial customers — which in this example translates to about $0.60 per 1,000 scf. It is, however, apparent that a significant decrease of the LDC markup can only occur if the annual natural gas use were to double or triple per residential customer by using natural gas as transportation fuel but without increasing proportionally the investment on plant and equipment. This point will be examined in detail in the following section. Finally, Figure 7-7 and Figure 7-8 give the average price of natural gas delivered to residential and commercial customers, respectively, in the US in 1991.

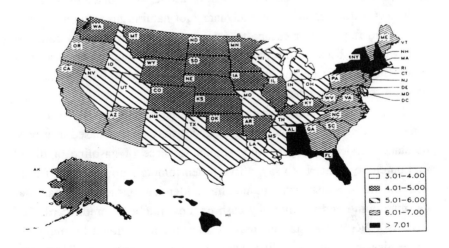

FIGURE 7-7. Average Price of Natural Gas in Dollars per Thousand Cubic Feet Delivered to US Residential Customers in 1991 (Source: EIA US DOE).

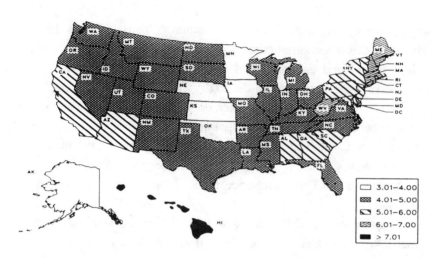

FIGURE 7-8. Average Price of Natural Gas in Dollars per Thousand Cubic Feet Delivered to US Commercial Customers in 1991 (Source: EIA US DOE).

NATURAL GAS MOTOR FUEL DISPENSING MARKUP

As it has been mentioned already on several occasions, natural gas may be accessible as a motor vehicle fuel under two different circumstances: A. Fast refueling at a public station or at a business location; and B. Slow refueling at home as well as at the work place or business. A distinct difference and major advantage of natural gas refueling is that there is no fuel spill or escape to the atmosphere, which is so common with gasoline, because the pressurized natural gas fuel requires a leakproof fitting between the nozzle of the dispenser and the receptacle valve of the vehicle tank.

In the first refueling instance, compressed natural gas (CNG) or in some instances liquefied natural gas (LNG) may be purchased at a public station under conditions very similar to these of gasoline or diesel fuel purchases. That is to say, a five to ten minute stop for a fast fill-up with the aid of a dispensing pump almost identical to the all too familiar gasoline pump and payment by cash or most likely by credit card. The CNG or LNG public stations may be owned and operated by major oil companies, natural gas utilities, and independent operators. These stations will be open to the general public in a very similar fashion to today's gasoline public stations. Private business, utilities, fleet operators, school districts and local, state and federal government agencies may also own a combination of fast and slow fill stations located on their premises exclusively for the needs of their respective fleets. In the slow refueling instance, which is limited to CNG only, residential supplied natural gas is compressed to the requisite pressure. The compression device is envisioned to become another standard household appliance as part of every new home construction. In the meantime, the household CNG compressor can be retrofitted in an existing home. The rate of refueling with CNG at home will typically take place during the night. Depending on the natural gas rate structure, a separate meter may be used to separate the consumption of natural gas for fueling from that for other household uses. The economics of these two options for natural gas refueling will be examined next. In addition, the slow refueling option can be also available at the site of small size businesses where the employees can refuel during the day-time while at work. Similarly, slow fill stations could be found in shopping centers and other major commercial centers for public use as well as on the premises of private fleets for private use.

The number of commercial natural gas vehicle (NGV) fueling stations has been increasing in recent years at a rate of almost 50% annually[9]. By the end of 1990 there were a little over 300 such stations nationwide. The number of NGV fueling stations had approached 500 by the end of 1991 and stood at about 700 by the end of 1992. The NGV fueling stations approached 1000 by the end of 1993 and had exceeded 1250 by the end of 1994. The plan is to open on the average 200 new CNG stations each year through the 1990s. A driver may refuel with natural gas in 43 States and the District of Columbia. Colorado leads the way with about 9% of the total number of stations, Ohio is second with 7% and California is third with 6% of the total. Natural gas utilities operate the majority of these stations. The owners and operators of non-utility stations range from school districts to private business that have NGVs in their fleets and to major oil companies such as Amoco, Chevron, Phillips 66, Shell, Texaco and Unocal. An example of the spreading of natural gas fueling stations is given in Figure 7-9 which shows the availability of NGV fueling in Southern California as of the

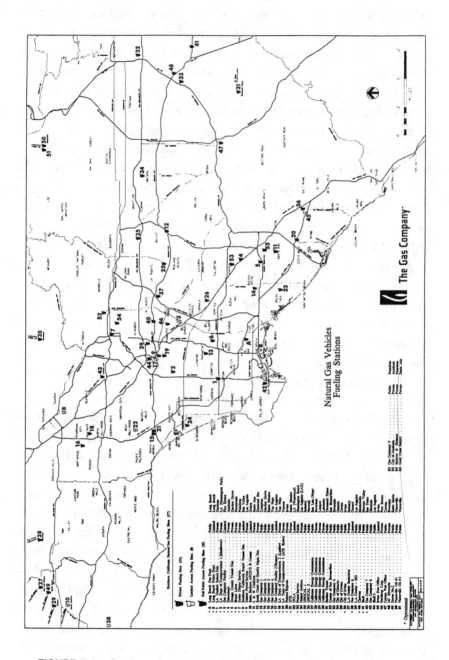

FIGURE 7-9. Southern California Natural Gas Fueling Sites Operational and Planned by the 4th Quarter 1994 (Courtesy: The Gas Company, Los Angeles, CA).

3rd quarter of 1994. Out of a total of 55 natural gas stations, 22 are private, i.e., limited to the owner's NGVs, 26 are fully public and 7 offer limited public access, i.e., require a prior arrangement, which is usually a 24-hour notice.

An important question during the early phases of the development of the infrastructure of public natural gas fueling stations is the optimal size of such a facility. The size of the public natural gas refueling facility is currently specified by the amount of natural gas that the station can dispense at any given time and is measured in cubic feet of natural gas per minute (cfm). Thus, the size may range from a low of about 10 cfm to several hundred cfm to over one thousand cfm. The optimal size of the facility is determined on the basis of the associated costs and expected revenues. The optimization consideration is crucial in the early days of infrastructure development when the available capital is limited and the number of NGVs is also small. That is to say, the objective is to provide access to as many vehicles as possible over a wider area by building several small stations rather than a few large ones.

The major cost in a public natural gas refueling station is the cost of the compressor. Typically, the compressor cost is about $1,000 per 1 cfm of capacity in the 150 cfm capacity range. Smaller compressors may have up to 20% higher cost per cfm and larger ones up to 20% lower cost. In addition to the compressor, the station has to have high pressure storage tanks, possibly natural gas drying equipment, dispensers and an automatic credit card billing system. There is a large variability in costs associated with public natural gas stations at the present time. This is to be expected in the early days of the evolution of a new system such as the vehicular natural gas infrastructure, where the system design has not mature yet. Nevertheless Table 7-3 summarizes the total costs associated with different capacities of public natural gas stations as they can be best ascertained from a variety of sources[10],[11],[12]. With regard to the optimal sizing of a public natural gas facility it appears that it should be on the order of 150 cfm and possibly smaller rather than larger. While the economies of scale favor larger stations in terms of cost, the current low density of NGVs favors the smaller stations in terms of revenue. Technology as well as system design maturity will reduce further the cost of the natural gas public station. However, compressor technology

TABLE 7-3. Estimated Total Cost of Public Natural Gas Stations
as a Function of Station Size in 1993 dollars

Station Size	50 CFM	100 CFM	150 CFM
Station Total Cost	$150 K	$250 K	$350 K
Total Cost Per CFM	$3.0 K	$2.5 K	$2.3 K

Note. A 50 cfm natural gas station will dispense in a 12 hour period of operation the equivalent of 300 gallons of gasoline.

and high pressure storage are already mature. Dispenser technology, automatic credit card billing and system design, on the other hand, can further mature. Thus, the cost reduction of the public natural gas station system may be reduced by no more than 20% of the present cost given in Table 7-3 for each station size.

The contribution of the cost of the public gas station to the price of the natural gas as a transportation fuel can be readily estimated. The life expectancy of the equipment of the station is estimated to be 15 years. Moreover, a 10% discount rate is assumed. The annual cost of the facility, i.e., mortgage payment, will be $32,895 for the 100 cfm size station*. In addition, the cost of operation and maintenance of the station is assumed to be equal to 5% of the cost of the facility or $12,500 annually — the assumed automatic debit credit card system eliminates the need of an attendant. The volume of natural gas that can be sold by a 100 cfm station operating 12 hours daily for 365 days every year is 26.28 million scf. This 50% annual utilization factor of the station capacity results in a surcharge of $1.25 per 1000 scf of natural gas due to capital costs and $0.48 per 1,000 scf due to operation and maintenance costs. Thus, the total surcharge of natural gas as a transportation fuel at a public refueling station will be $1.73 per 1,000 scf ($0.19 per gallon equivalent). If this surcharge is added to the average commercial natural gas price of $4.81 per 1,000 scf, it will give a final price of vehicular natural gas of about $6.54 per 1,000 scf ($0.73 per gallon equivalent).

(*). For an initial investment I, a station life expectancy t, and a rate of return on the investment r (discount rate), the annual cost of the facility K is : $K = I /[(1/(1+r)t)]$. If I = $250,000, t = 15 years and r = 0.1, one obtains K = $250,000/7.6 yr = $32,895/yr.

In reality, however, the commercial customer owning a public natural gas station is a relatively large customer from the LDCs point of view. Consequently, the actual price of natural gas from the LDC to the commercial customer/owner of the natural gas refueling station will be less than the average national commercial price of $4.81 per 1,000 scf. This latter price may be closer to the on-system industrial price as the calculation in Table 7-2 would indicate. Thus, a lower bound of the average price of natural gas as a transportation fuel will be the on-system industrial price ($2.69/1,000 scf) plus the cost of the public station capital and operation ($1.73/1,000 scf) which result to a price of $4.42 per 1,000 scf ($0.50 per gallon equivalent). Obviously, the utilization factor of the refueling station can affect the capital cost portion of the vehicular natural gas price significantly.

As it turns out, the average price of vehicular natural gas is currently about the same as or in most instances slightly less than the average commercial natural gas price in any given area. Table 7-4 gives the price of natural gas as an automotive fuel sold at public refueling stations in selected States during 1991. The price of commercial natural gas as well as the city gate price are also included for comparison. It is interesting to note the significant variation in vehicular natural gas prices among the different States. The basic reason of this variation is the relatively small sample available at this time. Local, state and other regulatory differences may also account for the price variability. Finally, the degree of utilization and the ownership of different public stations have also a significant impact on the final price of natural gas as an automotive fuel. The direct purchasing of natural gas from transmission pipeline companies may explain the below city gate prices of vehicular natural gas in Michigan and Ohio. Nevertheless, the average price differential of the 17 States in Table 7-4 with a higher vehicular natural gas price than the city gate price is $1.65 per 1,000 scf, which is very close to the estimated $1.73 per 1,000 scf mark-up because of the public natural gas refueling station costs. The average vehicular natural gas price of the 19 States in Table 7-4 is $4.20 per 1,000 scf, while the average commercial natural gas price of the same States is $4.78 per 1,000 scf. This average vehicular natural gas price of 19 States is $0.22 per1,000 scf less than the estimated above national average of $4.42 per

TABLE 7-4. Average Price of Natural Gas as Vehicle Fuel Sold at Public Refueling Stations in Selected States of the US During 1991 and Comparison to the City Gate and Commercial Prices

State	Price ($/1000 scf)			
	Vehicular	City Gate	Pr. Diff.	Commercial
Arizona	3.82	2.45	1.37	5.07
California	5.77	2.80	2.97	5.50
Colorado	3.44	2.85	0.59	4.04
Florida	4.73	2.51	2.22	4.92
Illinois	3.41	2.91	0.50	4.56
Indiana	4.71	3.05	1.66	4.61
Louisiana	3.56	2.56	1.00	4.90
Massachusetts	3.90	3.37	0.53	6.17
Michigan	2.15	3.08	-0.93	4.70
Nevada	3.72	2.33	1.39	4.34
New York	4.68	2.49	2.19	5.47
North Carolina	4.65	2.69	2.16	4.53
Ohio	2.97	3.05	-0.08	4.76
Oklahoma	3.83	2.04	1.79	3.91
Pennsylvania	5.26	3.27	1.99	6.00
Tennessee	4.11	2.73	1.38	4.76
Texas	5.49	2.88	2.61	4.01
Utah	5.52	3.89	1.63	4.50
Washington	4.06	1.91	2.15	4.06

Notes. The price differential is between vehicular and city gate natural gas prices. The selected States are the ones with the highest use of vehicular natural gas in the country.

1,000 scf — the average commercial natural gas price of these 19 States is also lower by $0.03/1,000 scf than the national average.

Incidentally, the predicted higher vehicular natural gas price of $6.54 per 1,000 scf sold at public refueling stations still corresponds to a price of $0.73 per gallon of gasoline equivalent fuel. By comparison, the national average price of unleaded regular gasoline in 1991 was $1.14 per gallon and that of premium gasoline was $1.32 per gallon[12]. Thus, natural gas as transportation fuel sold at public refueling stations has a 50% to almost 100% cost advantage over gasoline.

The alternative option for natural gas vehicles is home refueling. Among all alternative fuels, including gasoline and diesel fuel, natural gas is the only automotive fuel with this characteristic — electricity could be also considered as having the same characteristic, although the vehicle requires a totally different and significantly more expensive propulsion system. The present cost of a home natural fueling system consisting of an appropriate compressor and dispensing hose, all in one unit, is on the order of $3,000. This system needs maintenance every 2,000 hours of operation which costs about $200. The long term cost of the compressor system is projected to be reduced to about $1,500 per unit on the basis of experience gained in the production of this new technology. The maintenance cost is not expected to change. Several questions arise with the possibility of home fueling of automobiles. These questions may be grouped in two categories: first, ownership and acquisition of the compressor system or appliance ; and second, impact of home fueling of vehicles on the price of residential natural gas.

The acquisition and ownership of the home compressor system can occur in a number of different ways. The local gas utility may install the device and maintain ownership of it in perpetuity or over a period of time after which the equipment is owned by the homeowner. The compressor system is then part of the utility investment in plant and equipment to deliver natural gas in an identical fashion to the distribution gas line and gas meter. In a different scenario, the compressor system becomes a mandatory piece of equipment for all new construction and its cost is integrated in the cost of the building. In both of these instances the utility maintains the appliance at no cost to the homeowner — in reality the cost of maintenance is folded in the gas rate. A third possibility is for the home owner to purchase the compressor system and for the utility to provide separately metered and priced natural gas. As a variance, a third party or company owns and maintains the compressor which includes a separate gas meter. The homeowner pays for the gas consumed at a rate that includes the cost of the equipment. Other ways of compressor acquisition and ownership are possible. However, the first two scenarios appear to be the least complex to implement, may produce the maximum benefit to the homeowner/natural gas vehicle(s) owner and the utilities, and promote the switching of the present transportation fuels to natural gas.

The price of natural gas delivered to a residential customer will have to be modified, i.e., reduced, because the use of natural gas at home has the potential to more than double. For example, the annual use of natural gas in the average household can increase from 100 MMBTU to 220 MMBTU with two cars fueled at home. Table 7-5 summarizes the results of the analysis for three cases: no home refueling capability; home refueling with compressor owned by the home owner and amortized as part of the home mortgage; and home refueling with compressor owned by the utility.

Certain general conclusions arise form the numerical example of Table 7-5. First, the modification of price of natural gas sold to the resi-

TABLE 7-5. Example of Modifications of the Residential Rate From a Typical LDC for Three Different Scenarios of Household Ownership of Natural Gas Vehicle Fueling Equipment

Allocation of Expenses by a Local Distribution Company	Residential Customer		
	Case I	Case II	Case III
Investment in Plant and Equipment	$2,000	$2,000	$5,000
Annual Cost of Service			
Depreciation @ 3.3%	$ 66	$ 66	$ 206
Return @ 11% Levelized Investment	$ 154	$ 154	$ 385
Income Taxes @ 4% of Lev. Invest.	$ 56	$ 56	$ 140
General Taxes @ 1% of Investment	$ 20	$ 20	$ 50
Operation and Maintenance Expense	$ 60	$ 160	$ 160
Total Cost of Service	$ 356	$ 456	$ 841
Annual Gas Purchases (10^3 scf)	100	220	220
Rate Required to Earn Cost of Capital in $ per10^3 scf			
Margin Rate	3.56	2.07	3.82
Gas Cost at Wellhead	1.50	1.50	1.50
Pipeline Transport. and Fuel Service	0.30	0.30	0.30
Pipeline Demand Charge on SFV Basis	0.95	0.80	0.80
Total Rate Required in $ per10^3 scf	6.31	4.67	6.42
or $ per gallon equiv.	0.71	0.52	0.72

Case I: No home fueling; Case II : Home fueling with equipment as part of the building; Case III : Home fueling with equipment owned by natural gas utility.
Notes: A $1,500 compressor system would result in Case III in a total cost of service of $678, a margin rate of $3.08 per 1,000 scf and a total rate required of $5.68 per 1,000 scf. The compressor has to be refurbished after a use of 240 thousand scf (2000 hr x 120 scf/hr) or once every two years at a cost of $200 which translates to $100/yr.

dential customer because of home fueling is a very strong function of the non-automotive portion of natural gas use at home as well as the cost of the home compressor and the cost of its maintenance. The present compressor price of $3,000 and a local natural gas utility ownership of it produce a minimal increase in natural gas price from the prevailing residential rates. This implies that the $3,000 cost of the compressor can be entirely offset by the reduced margin rate due to the more than doubling of the use of natural gas. Reduction of the cost of the compressor to half its present price and utility ownership of it, results in a 10 to 15% reduction in the price of residential natural gas.

Ownership of the compressor by the household lowers the residential natural gas price by about 25 to 30% of its present price. Obviously, in this case the mortgage payment will be higher as it includes the cost of the compressor. Let us assume a 30 year loan with a 10% interest rate and a borrower with income in the 30% bracket, i.e., an after tax interest rate of 7 percent. The monthly net increment in the mortgage payment will be $20.15 for a $3,000 compressor and $10.07 for a $1,500 compressor[13]. Thus, the net increment in the mortgage payment will be between $121 and $242 annually. At the same time the price of the non-automotive portion of the household natural gas use has decreased by $1.64/1,000 scf for a total decrease of the natural gas bill by $164 annually — this implies a break even price for the compressor appliance of about $2,000. Clearly, the decrease in the cost of the household (non-automotive) portion of natural gas use at home can offset the increase in the mortgage payment. The convenience of fueling at home, whose monetary value is unknown but in all likelihood exceeds $6.5 per month, added to the reduction in the residential natural gas bill more than offset the net increase in mortgage payment (a worker making $10 per hour and taking 15 minutes off from his or her work to fuel a natural gas vehicle at a public station has theoretically lost $25 of wages).

Natural gas home vehicle fueling with the compressor being part of the standard building equipment rather than owned by the utility appears to be advantageous because it can bring the present residential gas price closer to the levels of the current commercial gas price with no additional cost incurred to the homeowner. Moreover, the home owner will have access to automotive fuel at a lower price than that charged by a public refueling station — in exchange of slower or overnight refueling. The average price of residential natural gas for selected states in 1991 is given in Table 7-6. It is interesting to observe that if residential natural gas is used also as automotive fuel, even without any change to the present rate, would be significantly less expensive than gasoline.

THE INCREMENTAL COST OF A NATURAL GAS VEHICLE

The use of natural gas as fuel in a vehicle with an internal combustion engine necessitates certain modifications from, as well as specific additions to, its gasoline counterpart. Figure 7-10 shows pictorially all the differences between a natural gas vehicle and a gasoline vehicle. Although the vehicle in Figure 7-10 is a passenger car, the same differences hold true between natural gas and gasoline vans and light trucks. These differences are outlined below:

- Increased Engine Compression Ratio/ Hardening of Cylinder Heads.
- Natural Gas Fuel Injection System.
- Low Pressure Natural Gas Regulator.
- Engine Coolant Lines for Heating of Pressure Regulator.
- Intermediate Fuel Line to Engine.
- Compressed Natural Gas Tanks in Trunk and/or Underbody.
- Fueling Point CNG Valve.
- Solenoid Valves, One For Each Tank.
- Solenoid Operated High-Pressure System CNG Fuel Valve.
- High Pressure CNG Fuel Regulator.
- Stone and Heat Underbody Tank Shield.
- Mini-Spare Tire Relocated in Underbody

The nature of most of the above elements of a compressed natural gas vehicle is self-explanatory. A brief description of the less apparent of these elements follows.

The increased engine compression ratio is desirable in order to take advantage of the high octane number of natural gas and produce a higher fuel efficiency. Higher compression ratios necessitate the thermal hardening of the piston heads for engine durability, because of the ensuing elevated temperatures.

TABLE 7-6. Average Price of Residential Natural Gas in Selected States of the US as of 1991

State	Price ($/10³ scf)	State	Price ($/10³ scf)
Arizona	6.99	Nevada	5.61
California	6.27	New York	7.35
Colorado	4.59	North Carolina	6.24
Florida	8.98	Ohio	5.28
Illinois	4.95	Oklahoma	4.72
Indiana	5.46	Pennsylvania	6.76
Iowa	4.81	Rhode Island	7.63
Louisiana	5.77	Tennessee	5.19
Massachusetts	8.11	Texas	5.71
Michigan	5.07	Utah	5.44
Montana	4.52	Washington	4.68

Note. Multiply $/10³/scf by 0.115 in order to convert this natural gas price into $/gal gasoline equivalent.

1992 Natural Gas Crown Victoria

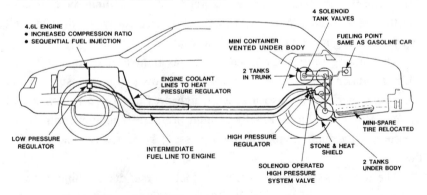

FIGURE 7-10. Pictorial Representation of the Differences in a Natural Gas Fueled Vehicle, the 1992 Crown Victoria Passenger Car, from its Gasoline Counterpart (Source: Ford Motor Company).

A new fuel injection scheme must be employed with gaseous fuels which behave differently than liquid fuel vapors. The high pressure natural gas is converted by expansion to a low pressure fuel prior to being injected into the engine. This expansion results in the cooling of the natural gas (Joule-Thomson effect), possibly below the freezing temperature of water, so that any moisture in the fuel could freeze inside the regulator and fuel lines and eventually block the gas flow[14]. In order to eliminate the accumulation of ice inside the low regulator and adjacent fuel lines, engine coolant is circulating through a heat exchanger around the low pressure regulator.

The volume of the compressed natural gas tanks is larger than the gasoline tank they replace. Some of these tanks may fit in the underbody and the remainder will have to be placed in the trunk of the vehicle, thereby reducing the available volume for storage from a comparable gasoline vehicle. In order to regain some of the trunk space, the spare tire which is normally placed inside the trunk, is reduced in size (mini-tire) and relocated in the underbody behind the rear bumper. Eventually, the spare tire will be totally eliminated as new tire designs coming now into production allow driving the vehicle up to 250 miles with a flat tire. A shield is placed appropriately in the underbody to protect the tanks located there from road debris ejected by the tires as well as from the engine and exhaust system heat.

The fueling port is modified to be gas tight as the content of the tanks is under pressure. Each tank has its own high pressure valve. Moreover, there exists also a system high pressure valve to control all the tanks in the vehicle. Finally, a high pressure regulator controls the pressure of the fuel leaving the high pressure system valve and entering the fuel line.

The incremental cost of a CNG vehicle versus its gasoline counterpart displays a significant variability depending on the source of the information. An early estimate by the US Department of Energy gave an incremental cost of $750 per vehicle[15]. A later estimate by Battelle placed the same cost at $1,950 per vehicle[16]. In 1992 the US Government acquired a large number of GNG vehicles through the General Services Administration (GSA) which is responsible for all such purchases[17]. The CNG vehicles included 600 GMC Sierra 3/4 -

ton pickup trucks with an incremental cost of $3,975 and 25 Chrysler Ram vans with an incremental cost of $7,400. However, the incremental cost of the commercially available 1995 Chrysler CNG Ram van as well as the 1995 Chrysler CNG minivan are slightly under $3,800 at the present time.

The major source of incremental cost is due to the CNG tanks and their high pressure valves. A typical 50 l (13 gal) tank is priced at about $500 if it is steel-fiberglass wound, at $600 if it is aluminum-fiberglass wound and at $700 if it is all composite. The price of a twice as large tank may be 15% less on a per tank volume basis. The cost of the high pressure valve is typically on the order of $100 per tank. Thus, use of three tanks will cost about $1,800 per vehicle.

The typical cost for the system of the high-pressure system valve, high-pressure regulator, low-pressure regulator, engine coolant heat exchanger to low-pressure regulator and the engine fuel injection system is on the order of $1,500. Thus, the total incremental costs due to added or modified components for, say, the GMC Sierra will be $3,300 per vehicle. An additional mark-up of $700 per vehicle is not unrealistic to cover labor costs, marketing, handling, etc., of the limited production vehicle.

Thus, it is reasonable to expect an average $4,000 incremental cost between CNG and gasoline vehicles at the present time. Incidentally, the very high incremental cost of the Chrysler Ram van in 1992 must have been to a very large degree the result of the very limited production (about 50 Ram vans sold in 1992 versus 2,200 GM Sierra trucks). The long term incremental cost for a "large number" of CNG production vehicles may be reduced to below $2,000 per vehicle to reflect the cost of additional components as engineering, assembly, marketing, and other costs will be the same as those of gasoline production vehicles. The magnitude of the "large number" of CNG production vehicles per manufacturer cannot be precisely defined, but it is definitely on the order of 100,000 vehicles per year or more.

Present costs of after market conversion of gasoline vehicles to CNG also vary as a function of the size of the vehicle engine and on-board storage. However, the average cost to the consumer, including components and labor, are on the order of $5,000 per vehicle for a vehicle engine of 4.5 L to 5.5 L and a vehicle range of 150 to 200 miles[18].

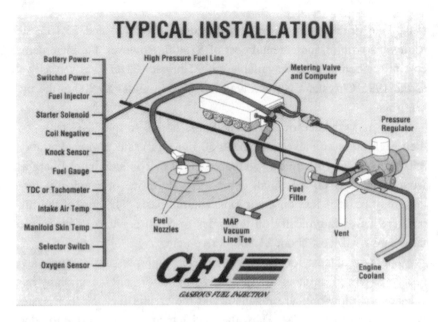

Engine Conversion Parts : Not Shown Fuel Tanks, Valves and High Pressure Regulator

FIGURE 7-11. Natural Gas Conversion Kit of a Gasoline Vehicle
(Source : Stewart and Stevenson).

A cost of $3,500 is a more likely conversion figure for smaller passenger vehicles. There are several conversion kit manufacturers in the US at the present time[19]. A typical conversion kit installation is shown in Figure 7-11. The engine compression ratio is not increased in a gasoline vehicle conversion to CNG primarily because of engine design durability considerations.

Conversion kits exist also for diesel fueled vehicles. In this instance, however, a number of options are available. These options include: a dual fuel system; rebuilding the existing engine to run on natural gas; and replacing the diesel engine with a factory built comparable engine running on CNG. The dual-fuel system, occasionally referred to by the terms pilot ignition or fumigation, means a diesel engine partially fueled by natural gas while it retains the diesel fuel. This is the least expensive conversion, but it produces no emission benefits compared to a modern diesel engine, and the displacement of diesel fuel by natural gas fuel may not be significant. The rebuilding of the diesel engine to run on natural gas only represents an intermediate expense between dual-fuel and engine replacement. In this instance, of course, the compression ratio of the diesel engine has to be reduced, the cylinder heads have to be modified to accept gaseous spark-plugs and a turbocharger has to be added to regain full engine power and torque. Such a conversion kit of a diesel engine to natural gas costs upwards of $7,000 depending on the size of the engine. Because of reduced engine pressure and the non-corrosive nature of the fuel the engine life is extended significantly. Emissions are reduced typically up to 1/3 of the initial diesel engine. Finally, the diesel engine replacement with a factory built CNG engine is the most expensive option, typically twice as expensive as the engine rebuilt option, but it offers the least fuel consumption and the most reduction in emissions.

The typical natural gas conversion kits carry a 50,000 mile warranty, which is transferable form one vehicle to another. All CNG tanks have, on the other hand, a certified life expectancy of 15 years and can be used in most instances in more than one vehicle.

Conversion to LNG is a very similar process with a few extra components added (see Figure 4-6) to allow for the evaporation of the liquid fuel as well as the capture and recirculation of the boiled off fuel. The cost of an LNG fueled vehicle will be probably higher than the cost of a CNG fueled vehicle because of the more expensive cryogenic tanks, even through a smaller volume capacity is required, and the added liquid to gas and gas boil-off recapture components.

THE COST OF OPERATING A NATURAL GAS VEHICLE

There are several advantages of using natural gas as a fuel compared to gasoline with regard to engine maintenance. These advantages are the result of reduced ware on the engine components due to the gaseous nature as well as simple composition of natural gas compared to gasoline. These advantages translate into: I. Less frequent change in engine oil; II. Less frequent replacement of spark plugs; and III. Reduction in carbon deposits in the engine cylinders, which theoretically increases the engine life. Unfortunately, there exist limited data to quantify the economic benefit of these advantages at the present time. The US Postal Service will have within the next several years the largest fleet of natural gas vehicles in the country and the expectation is that the operation of this fleet will provide substantiated data on the economic benefits of the aforementioned advantages[20]. Incidentally, the question is not whether these advantages are real, but rather what is the magnitude of the resulting economic benefit. Based on discussions with several individuals operating natural gas vehicle fleets across the country, the following tentative quantification of economic advantages emerges.

The replacement of engine oil can be halved in frequency from, say, once every 3,000 miles or whatever the recommended distance is to twice as many miles. Assuming a $30 cost per oil change, the net benefit is $0.005 per mile for the natural gas vehicle versus the gasoline one. Tune ups, including spark plug and other minor component changes, normally occur once every three years or about 33,000 miles and typically cost $150 for the average gasoline vehicle. Natural gas vehicles may triple the extent between tune-ups up to 100,000 miles. This results in an average net benefit of $0.003 per mile for the natural gas vehicle.

The reduced wear of the engine is by far the most difficult economic advantage to quantify. Modest estimates place the increase in the life expectancy of a natural gas fueled engine to about 25% over its nominal life expectancy with gasoline fuel. In order to quantify the economic benefit of this advantage, one can proceed in two ways.

First, this projected increase in life expectancy, which could amount from 25,000 to 50,000 extra miles driven on the factory engine, avoids the cost of an engine overhaul during the life of the vehicle. This cost will be typically on the order of $2,000 to $2,500 depending on engine size (number of cylinders).

Alternatively, the increased life expectancy of the vehicle may result in the postponement of buying a new vehicle near the end of the life of the first one, which is on the average 7 or 8 years. Naturally, the obsolescence of a vehicle after 7 or 8 years may accelerate its replacement even if its engine is mechanically sound. Nevertheless the postponement of purchasing a new vehicle by even one year will save the owner the corresponding payments of a new vehicle, which at an average of $200 per month, in current dollars, will amount to $2,400 total. The assumption here is that the escalation in price of new vehicles will be the same as the increase in the consumer price index.

Thus, the annual savings of a natural gas vehicle over its gasoline counterpart due to increased vehicle engine longevity or postponement in the purchase of a new vehicle are on the order of $300 in current dollars. It is assumed that the natural gas vehicle will have an eight year life versus seven years for its gasoline counterpart.

Finally, the CNG storage tanks have a fifteen year life so that they can be refurbished and used for the life of a second vehicle at the end of the life of the first vehicle. Thus, the salvage value of each CNG tank in current dollars will be at least $250 per tank or $750 per vehicle with three tanks.

The costs and benefits of operating a natural gas vehicle are summarized in Table 7-7. It is interesting to note that federal, state and local financial incentives are available already to promote the use of alternative fuel including natural gas. The Energy Policy Act of 1992 allows deductions for both vehicles and refueling facilities[21]. The tax deduction for any clean-fuel (natural gas, liquefied petroleum gas, hydrogen, electricity and any other fuel at least 85% of which is methanol, ethanol, any other alcohol or ether) qualifying vehicle (at least four wheels for use on public streets, roads and highways) applies to the incremental cost of the vehicle up to $2,000 for vehicles under 10,000 lb gross vehicle weight, $5,000 for vehicles in the 10,000 to 26,000 lb category and $50,000 for vehicles over 26,000 lb or buses with a seating capacity of at least 20 adults (not including the driver). For electric vehicles only, the deduction is 10% of the cost of the vehicle , but not to exceed $4,000 per vehicle. The tax deduction for clean-fuel refueling facilities is not to exceed $100,000 per facility (not including a building and its structural components).

As an example (see Table 7-7) consider an incremental cost of $4,000 for a natural gas vehicle and a $2,000 cost for a residential compressor for home refueling. An annual refueling appliance maintenance fee of $50 is assumed for a two-vehicle household. Moreover, a homeowner tax bracket of 30% is assumed. Of the $4,000 vehicle incremental cost, only $2,000 may be deducted which results in a marginal tax

TABLE 7-7. Value of Incremental Annual Costs and Benefits Associated with the Ownership and Operation of Natural Gas, Methanol and Reformulated Gasoline Vehicles Versus a Base Gasoline Vehicle Each Driven 11,000 per Year and Having a Fuel Efficiency of 27 MPG

Cost(-)/Benefit(+)	Natural Gas	Methanol/M-85	Reform. Gasoline
New Vehicle Price	-$500	-$ 79	0
Maintenance	+$ 88	-$110	0
Life Extension	+$300	0	0
Salvage Value	+$107	0	0
Fuel	+$204	-$509	-$305
Home Fueling (net)	-$145	N/A	N/A
Total Cost/Benefit	+$ 59	-$698	-$305
Federal Tax Credits Through 2001			
Vehicle	+$ 75	+$ 24	0
Rebates (if available)			
Local Gas Utility	+$250	N/A	N/A
State	+$215	+$215	+$215

Notes. This is a zero discount rate calculation. Life expectancy of natural gas vehicles 8 years, all others 7 years. Gasoline price $1.25/gal, natural gas fuel price $0.75/gal equivalent ($6.52 per 10^3 scf), M-85 price $1.25/gal or $2.50/gal gasoline equivalent and reformulated gasoline price $2.00/gal. Home fueling net cost includes potential reduction in natural gas pricing for gas consumed in non-automotive uses.

reduction of $600. This tax reduction translates into $75 per year throughout the 8 year life of the natural gas vehicle. For the refueling facility, considered an integral part of the housing unit, the marginal tax reduction is $600, which translates into $40 per year throughout an assumed 15 year life for the compressor.

The federal vehicle tax deduction stays in effect until December 31, 2001 after which time it will be phased out gradually by the year 2005. Starting in 2002 a 25% reduction of the aforementioned deduction will go into effect, in 2003 the reduction is increased to 50% and in 2004 the reduction is further increased to 75% and there will be no longer a deduction in the year 2005.

States and local utilities may offer additional tax deductions or rebates above and beyond those prescribed by the Federal Government.

The State of California, for example, offers a $1,500 tax credit for every clean fuel vehicle, but the annual budget available to pay for these rebates can cover only a very small number of vehicles (about 1,000). Natural gas utilities offer considerably more substantial incentives. The Gas Company, for example, which is the natural gas utility in Southern California offers rebates to the owners of natural gas vehicles, which begin at $1,750 for vehicles with gross weight under 10,000 lb, increase to $2,500 for vehicles between 10,001 and 19,500 lb, increase further to $4,500 for vehicles in the 19,501 to 26,000 lb range and finally peak at $7,500 for vehicles over 26,000 lb — in all instances the rebate cannot exceed 50% of the incremental or conversion cost of the vehicle.

A comparison of the costs associated with other clean fuels is also included in Table 7-7. The incremental cost of a methanol vehicle is assumed to be $550 per vehicle[17]. This was the incremental cost of 2,000 M-85 Plymouth Acclaim contracted by the US Government through GSA in 1992. Methanol is a relatively corrosive fluid to a variety of components and in particular those made of plastic or rubber materials. It is thus estimated that the maintenance of methanol fueled vehicles will increase by about $0.01 per mile[17]. Moreover, the price of M85 is the same as premium gasoline, but M85 has a little more than half the energy content of gasoline per gallon[22]. Thus, the commercial M85 price is about $2.50 per gallon of gasoline equivalent in variance to the $1.70 price quoted informally by the California Energy Commission, an apparently staunch methanol proponent agency[17]. The discrepancy in price is in part due to the underestimated cost of public methanol dispensing facilities. For example, the California Energy Commission and the US Department of Energy have estimated the cost of a single tank and dispensing equipment facility between $45,000 and $50,000[15][23]. A recent cost estimate for installing a methanol facility at the Naval Weapons Station Concord, California placed the cost at about $80,000[17]. This facility consists of a single 15,000 gal tank, a two-hose dispenser, a leak detection device, cathodic protection and a fuel restraint concrete pad.

Reformulated gasoline is the third alternative fuel considered in Table 7-7. In this case, the only difference in cost between a vehicle fueled with reformulated gasoline and one fueled with gasoline is the cost of the fuel itself. The cost of reformulated gasoline (Phase II) is estimated to be on the order of $2 per gallon. For example, one type of reformulated gasoline is comprised of E85, which will be the least expensive one. Ethanol is priced currently at $1.40 per gallon, including a 13% transportation cost and dealer profit markup[24]. Since ethanol has 2/3 the energy content of gasoline on a per volume basis, the E85 price will be $2.00 per gallon gasoline equivalent ($1.40 x 0.85 / (0.66) + $ 1.20 x 0.15 = $2.09). Any other type of oxygenated or reformulated gasoline which contains ethanol or ethers such as MTBE or ETBE is bound to be also more expensive than conventional gasoline by about 15% because of the higher cost of all these components. The retail price of the different motor fuels as of early 1995 is compared in Figure 7-12 on an energy equivalence basis.

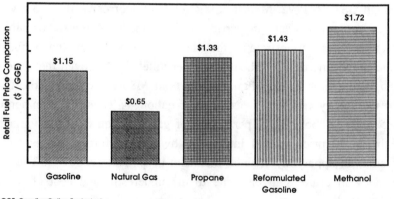

GGE=Gasoline Gallon Equivalent
1 GGE=1 gal Gasoline=1.3 gal Propane=2 gc 'ethanol=110 scf Natural Gas

FIGURE 7-12. Comparison of Lower Retail Price, as of Early 1995, for Gasoline and Four Alternative Fuels on an Energy Basis. A Price Range of $0.30/GGE for Each Alternative Fuel Reflects the Variability Encountered Across the Country. Gasoline Includes Oxygenated Gasoline as well. Reformulated Gasoline Refers to Phase 1. Methanol Represents the M85 Blend. All Fuels with the Exception of Natural Gas Are Sold by The Gallon (Volume Unit) rather Than Gasoline Gallon Equivalent (Energy Unit). Hence the Actual Energy Content of the Liquid Fuels and in Particular of the Gasolines is Unknown. Thus, the Retail Price per Gal Has Been Converted to the Comparison Retail Price per GGE Based on the Assumption that 1 Gal Gasoline or Reformulated Gasoline Equals 1 GGE (114,000 BTU) and that 1 GGE of LPG Equals 1.3 Gal LPG and 2 Gal M85 (1 GGE Natural Gas Equals 110 SCF Natural Gas).

It is also important to note parenthetically that liquid fuels such as oxygenated and reformulated gasolines are sold by volume (gal) rather than energy content (BTU). This is very misleading to the consumer, however, because all of these fuels may contain as much as 10% less energy per unit volume than the typical unleaded gasoline. Thus, the consumer not only pays a higher price for these fuels at the pump but is also required to purchase 10% more fuel for the same driving distance. This translates into a $0.15 per gal hidden increase in price of the oxygenated and reformulated gasolines. Moreover, most consumers are bound to miss the 10% or so reduction in the fuel efficiency of their vehicles by using these gasolines unless they keep good records. Early indications following the January 1, 1995 introduction of reformulated gasoline in nine metropolitan areas (Los Angeles, CA; San Diego, CA; New York, NY; Chicago, IL; Baltimore, MD; Houston, TX; Philadelphia, PA; Milwaukee, WI; and Hartford, CT) tend to confirm these predictions. Motorists say that the new gasoline impedes car performance, cuts gas mileage and makes people sick[25].

An alternative way to calculate the cost effectiveness of switching gasoline vehicles into natural gas vehicles is the pay back period of the investment. To be cost effective the conversion has to have a payback period less than the life of the vehicle. Obviously, the shorter the payback period is for a fuel the more cost effective the particular fuel becomes. An important element in pay back calculations, as in any economic analysis, is the selection of the appropriate value of the discount rate[26]. A variety of arguments have been advanced over the years as to the proper value of the discount rate, particularly as it applies to economic decisions related to the environment. A value of 10% appears to be in the middle of the proposed range. In general, a low discount rate will favor the switch from gasoline to natural gas as the results in Table 7-7 indicate, while a high discount rate favors no change from the present state of affairs. Table 7-8 summarizes the calculations for natural gas and methanol. It is apparent that under the previous assumptions natural gas switching is a very viable alternative. The same cannot be said, however, for methanol or any other fuel.

The pay back period for natural gas fuel switching is on the order of two years. This short payback period is possible if a State tax credit as

TABLE 7-8. Present and Long Term Payback Calculations for Natural Gas and Methanol Fuel Switch for a Vehicle Driven 11,000 Miles Annually and Having a 27 MPG Fuel Efficiency

Cost (-) / Benefit (+)	Present Value (Long Term Value) For	
	Natural Gas/CNG	Methanol/M85
Incremental Capital Cost	-$5,540 (-$2,770)	-$ 727
Maintenance	+$ 538	-$ 489
Life Extension	+$1,588	0
Salvage Value	+$ 542	0
Fuel	+$1,148	-$2,727
Home Fueling Mortgage	-$1,184 (-$592)	N/A
Federal Vehicle Tax Deduction	+$ 600 ($0)	+$ 165
Federal Refueling Tax Deduction	+$1,000 ($0)	N/A
State Tax Credit	+$1,500 ($0)	+$1,500
Local Utility Rebate	+$1,750 ($0)	0
Total Cost/Benefit	+$1,942 (+$454)	-$2,278
Payback Period	2.0 -2.5 Yrs	Infinite

Notes. An escalation rate of 5% is assumed for the cost of maintenance, price of fuel, future new vehicle value, and future CNG tank value. The period of calculation is 7 years for the NGV and 6 for the M85 vehicle. The tax bracket is assumed to be 30% for home fueling equipment cost mortgage deduction as well as the federal clean-fuel tax deductions. All other assumptions are the same as those in Table 7-7. Long term value shown if different from present value.

well as a utility rebate on the order of $1,500 each are simultaneously available. Moreover, the availability of either a State tax credit or a utility rebate of about $1,500 is required to make the natural gas fuel switching economically viable, but with a longer payback period approaching the life of the vehicle. The assumed fuel price of $0.75 per gallon equivalent ($6.52 per 1,000 scf for home refueling) is on the conservative side as it is higher than even the average residential natural gas price in the country. Table 7-8 includes also the long term costs and benefits for natural gas fuel switching. It is once more apparent that in the absence of federal state and local tax deductions, credits and rebates and if the aforementioned long term cost reductions in the incremental costs of natural gas vehicles and refueling equipment is materialized, natural gas as automotive fuel is also the only viable alternative fuel to gasoline.

All the preceding calculations have not addressed the economic value of environmental benefits due to the use of alternative fuels and in particular natural gas. As it has already been discussed, natural gas has the highest potential among alternative fuels along with electricity and hydrogen, the latter two generated from specific sources only, for a cleaner environment and a reduction in the greenhouse effect. Currently, no provisions exist in the US to account for these benefits. The notion of imposing a carbon tax proportionally to the carbon dioxide produced by any fuel has been discussed in recent years, but no firm action has been taken. The same taxation notion can also apply to the pollutants emitted in air. Suggested taxes are: $100 per ton of carbon in carbon dioxide; $150 per ton of sulfur oxides; and $100 per ton of nitrous oxides[27]. This tax will penalize all carbon containing fuels or fuels generated from such fuels, including electricity. Natural gas will be penalized the least, however, thereby increasing its relative cost advantage over the other fuels, particularly gasoline and methanol, by a $100 to $200 per vehicle annually.

Sweden has been the first country to impose the so called "green taxes" on the carbon and sulfur contents of fuels since 1991, which result in a carbon dioxide tax rate of about $40 per ton for all fuels and a sulfur content tax rate of $10 per lb for coal and fuel oil[26][28]. This green tax amounts to $0.36 per gallon of gasoline and alcohols, $2.43 per 1,000 scf of natural gas and $0.06 per kWh of coal generated electricity. The natural gas carbon tax corresponds to $0.28 per gallon gasoline equivalent and could result in a $32 per year lower tax than gasoline, if natural gas were used as automotive fuel for a 27 mpg vehicle driven 11,000 miles annually. Thus, environmental taxes on transportation fuels and energy, if ever instituted in the US, would further improve the cost advantage of natural gas over its automotive fuel competitors.

REFERENCES

1. Energy Information Administration, <u>Natural Gas 1992: Issues and Trends</u>, DOE/EIA-0560(92), US DOE, Washington, DC, 1993.

2. Energy Information Administration, "Three-Dimensional Seismology – A new Perspective", *Natural Gas Monthly*, December 1992, DOE/EIA-0130(92/12), US DOE, Washington, DC,1992.

3. S. C. Hurdley, J. R. Murphy, S. S. Mastoris, "3D CAEX Help Independent Add Reserves Inexpensively in Ship Shoal Area of Gulf", *Oil and Gas Journal*, p. 65, January 18, 1993.

4. G. Moritis, "Drilling Technology", *Oil and Gas Journal*, p. 54, February 26, 1990.

5. EXXON Corporation, "Discovery of Giant Mobile Bay Field off the Coast of Alabama with Estimated Reserves of One Trillion Cubic Feet ", 1991 Annual Report.

6. Energy Information Administration, <u>Annual Energy Outlook 1993</u>, DOE/EIA-0383(93), US DOE, Washington, DC, 1993.

7. Federal Energy Regulatory Commission, Order No. 636, 57 *Federal Register* 13267, 1992; Order No. 636-A, 57 *Federal Register* 36128, 1992; Order No. 636-B, 57 *Federal Register* 42408, 1992.

8. R. H. Williams, G. S. Dutt, H. S. Geller, "Future Energy Savings in US Housing", <u>Ann. Rev. Energy</u>, v. 8, pp. 269-332, Annual Reviews, Inc., Palo Alto, CA, 1983.

9. Energy Information Administration, <u>Natural Gas Annual 1991</u>, DOE/EIA-0131(91), US DOE, Washington, DC, 1992.

10. E. Hutzinson-Buhler, private communication, City of Long Beach, CA, 1993.

11. M. Marelli, private communication, The Gas Company, Los Angeles, CA, 1993.

12. Energy Information Administration, <u>Monthly Energy Review June 1992</u>, p. 108, DOE/EIA-0035(92/06), US DOE, Washington, DC, 1992.

13. E. P. DeGarmo and J. R. Canada, <u>Engineering Economy</u>, 5th ed., Macmillan Publishing Co., Inc., New York, NY, 1973.

14. T. Baumeister, E. A. Avallone, T. Baumeister III, Mark's Standard Handbook for Mechanical Engineers, 8th ed., p. 4-51, McGraw-Hill, New York, NY, 1978.

15. US Department of Energy, Assessment of Costs and Benefits of Flexible and Alternative Fuel Use in the US Transportation Sector – Technical Report IV: Vehicle and Fuel Distribution Requirements, DOE/PE-0095P, Washington, DC, 1990.

16. Battelle Laboratories, "Effects of Alternative Fuels on the US Trucking Industry", Final Report to the ATA Foundation, Columbus, OH, 1990.

17. J. C. Wilson, S. C. Munchak, K. J. Tan, "Alternative-Fuel Vehicles for the Department of the Navy", CRM 92-91, Center for Naval Analyses, Alexandria, VA, 1992.

18. C. Mylam, private communication, Valley Power Products, City of Industry, CA, 1993.

19. The Natural Gas Vehicle Coalition," NGVC Member Business Guide - March 1993 Edition", Arlington, VA, 1993.

20. H. Dinh, private communication, US Postal Service, Engineering, Research and Development, Merrifield, VA, 1993.

21. House of Representatives US Congress, Energy Policy Act of 1992, Report 102-1018, pp. 251-256, US Government Printing Office, Washington, DC, 1992.

22. L. Brooke, "Fuels' Parade", Chilton's Automotive Industries, v. 172, No. 3, pp. 27-33, March 1992.

23. California Energy Commission, Cost and Availability of Low Emission Motor Vehicles and Fuels, Vol. I and II, Report AB 234, Sacramento, CA, 1989.

24. N. Hohmann and C. M. Rendleman, "Emerging Technologies in Ethanol Production", Agriculture Information Bulletin Number 663, US Department of Agriculture, Washington, DC, 1993.

25. K. V. Johnson and R. Tyson, "Motorists Rebel over 'Clean' Gas", p. A1; and R. Tyson and K. V. Johnson, "Some Places Have Had their Fill of 'Clean' Gas", p. 3A; USA Today, February 20, 1995.

26. D. W. Pearce, J. J. Warford, <u>World Without End</u>, pub. for The World Bank by Oxford University Press, New York, NY, 1993.

27. L. R. Brown, C. Flavin, S. Postel, <u>Saving the Planet</u>, p. 145, W. W. Norton & Co., New York, NY, 1991.

28. P. Bohm, "Environment and Taxation: The Case of Sweden", in <u>Environment and Taxation: The Cases of the Netherlands, Sweden and the United States of America</u>, Organization for Economic Co-operation and Development, Paris, FR, 1993.

Chapter 8

Natural Gas Vehicle Market Penetration

THE TIMETABLE OF TECHNOLOGICAL CHANGES

The substitution of gasoline and diesel fuel by natural gas as the transportation fuel of choice represents a technological change from the currently prevailing state of affairs. It is a technological change because it requires engine modifications, different fuel storage systems, and a different fuel delivery infrastructure. Fortunately, all these are incremental changes from the conditions of today. The major technological change, however, is of a conceptual nature as the transportation sector moves away form liquid fuels and gradually espouses gaseous fuels. Any technological change takes significant amount of time to diffuse into the market and become mainstream technology. Natural gas as a transportation fuel and the technological changes that it entails are no exception. Thus, it behooves us to examine first the previous experience regarding the timetable involved in the diffusion of a new technology into the market place. This generic examination will provide sufficient insight as to the expected timetable for natural gas to become the pre-eminent fuel in the transportation sector of the United States.

The dynamics of technology change are largely not appreciated by many people, including policymakers and government officials. The popular argument of the 1970s "If we can put a man on the moon, why can't we solve the energy crisis?" with its simplicity and intuitive appeal is indicative of the danger of misunderstanding technology and the potential consequences of this misunderstanding[1]. In today's environment, the emphasis on clean air with the attendant requirements for the selection of appropriate alternative fuels and vehicle types under the rubric of alternative transportation strategies can lead to technological blunders that can waste much needed resources and delay the implementation of more realistic, but less glamorous solutions. In the next several paragraphs, the process of commercial change will be briefly described and the concept of technological life cycle will be discussed. Both of these notions can be very useful in planning.

Technological change comprises a far more complex process than it is often perceived to be. It is inexorably tied with economics because it represents the processes by which better technologies are introduced into economic activity[2]. Consequently, technological feasibility devoid of economic feasibility is meaningless. One important point to be brought out is the limited effectiveness of government intervention in the dynamics of technological change. However, government has the ability to level the playing field through proper legislation that compensates for earlier market distortions. Successful commercialization of a new technology within a market economy occurs when it becomes available at a cost that allows the private sector to realize an acceptable return on the total capital required to produce and market it. This market is not a perfect one, but rather a real market as it exists with lack of perfect information, government interference, and a multitude of externalities[3]. The consumer passes the ultimate judgement on the value of the technology. Public choices and values determine the commercial success of any technology. Technology described by the terms "best" or "most cost effective" is judged as such in the context of the marketplace, rather than in an abstract or theoretical manner. The challenge is to select from among a variety of criteria, systems, conceptual frameworks and analytical tools, the most appropriate ones possible. The question then arises "How does a technology reach the point of commercialization or the point of public acceptance?".

The successful commercialization of any product, be it a jet engine or an electric vehicle battery, goes through five discrete stages as follows[1]:

A   Invention

B   Development

C   Commercial Introduction

D   Commercial Diffusion

E   Established Stage

Invention entails the generation of an idea for a product and a conceptual way to produce it. Economics is irrelevant at this stage. The development stage involves the optimization of the design of the product until a working model is constructed. The purpose here is to eliminate technological uncertainties and improve operational efficiencies in order to determine expected costs and producibility of the product. A full scale model is not required at this stage, unless a smaller model is not scalable with respect to technological uncertainties. The development stage provides also information as to the expected cost of the product at the established stage. While at the end of this stage variance from the established cost will be high, the expected value of the cost has been determined. If the costs are too high to offer hope for adequate profit, then the technology is not viable commercially. In this instance, the product is dropped or else is put on hold in the hope of a new factor arising in the future that may reduce costs. The development stage is not intended to reduce costs, but rather to determine them.

The third stage, commercial introduction, deals with market or regulatory uncertainties and at the same time it narrows further the range of cost variance. In this stage, full scale production facilities become operational. Market uncertainties such as marketing programs, distribution channels, maintenance support organization, market segmentation and differentiation, character of the technology and the industry are all studied in depth. Regulatory and legislative uncertainties are also explored. Only after all the cost, market, and regulatory uncertainties have been addressed, does the fourth stage, commercial diffusion, begins. Widespread production in a growing number of facilities takes place, the product is disseminated widely into the marketplace, and other competitors with a similar product enter the market. Costs decrease because of product and process innovation. Finally, the established stage is reached, where the product or technology reaches its maturity along with production processes, and marketing strategies.

The five stage process to commercialize technology has parallels to the growth and development of biological systems. This has been established by observing that the market penetration of successful products over time can be described, similarly to the growth of a biological population in its habitat, by the so called logistic or S-shaped curve(*)[4][5][6]. An example of the logistic curve referring to the growth of natural gas pipelines in the US is shown in Figure 8-1[7]. It is necessary to point out that a logistic curve tends to a maximum value, which in biological systems is characterized as the carrying capacity of a habitat to sustain the particular organism or species — this will be the point of stable equilibrium where there is zero growth, i.e., the number of births equals the number of deaths. The second important characteristic of the logistic curve is the length of the maturity time, which is defined as the time period between the 10% and 90% habitat penetration by the particular species. In the case of technology or product development, the notion of the species habitat is replaced with the concept of the market and the resulting maximum market capacity for the particular product as well as the life cycle of the particular product. In the example of the length of the US natural gas pipelines (gathering, transportation and distribution) the maximum market capacity is on the order of 1,350,000 miles and the life cycle period is about 55 years. Incidentally, the present (1990) length of the natural gas pipelines in the US is 1,206,000 miles or about 89% of the ultimate market limit.

One may be tempted to argue that the natural gas pipeline market capacity and life cycle have been dictated by the past and present natural gas use for residential and commercial buildings, industrial compa-

---

(*) The simplest S-shaped curve for any variable N (organism, product, technology, etc.) is described by the logistic equation $dN/dt = r N (N_0-N)$, where N_0 is the carrying capacity or market limit (100% saturation value) for N, t is the time, and r is a constant reflecting the rate at which the limit is reached. The constant r is characteristic of N, but independent of N_0 and represents a measure of the dynamics of N penetrating the habitat or market. Thus, the value of r determines the maturity time or life cycle of N, which is defined as the time difference between the occurrence of the 10% and 90% saturation values. It can be readily deduced that if f represents the fractional habitat or market share of N at time t , where f is defined by the equation $f = N/N_0$ then $f/(1-f) = exp(rt-c)$ or $log\{f/(1-f)\} = rt-c$ expresses the dominance of N in the habitat or market place at any time. The constant c signifies a time delay t_0 effect on N, where $t_0 = c/r$, to take account of the time required for an organism to reach maturity (age of being able to reproduce) or for a technology or product to undergo the invention and development stages.

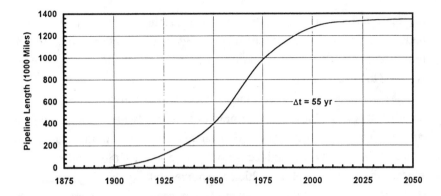

FIGURE 8-1. Growth of Natural Gas Pipe Lines in the US Represented by a Logistic Curve — Saturation Length 1.35 Million Miles; Maturity or Life-Cycle Time 55 Years; and Occurrence of 50% Saturation in 1962.

nies and utility power generation. The inclusion of transportation as another market use for natural gas can conceivably modify the natural gas market capacity and life cycle. However, this is not likely to happen on the basis of a large body of evidence. This is an important issue that will be addressed in great detail in a later section.

Suffice it to say here that technological change is frequently "path dependent"[2]. Path dependency can only be understood as a part of a historical process. A certain technology or market structure can continue to dominate well beyond its socially optimal length of time. Once a technological decision has been made, it is very difficult and costly to be reversed at a later time. Decisions taken in the past with respect to automotive fuel types and emission controls will dictate the future course of action in conjunction with new technologies and environmental requirements.

In this regard, the internal combustion engine is not a technology whose time has come and gone. However, gasoline and diesel fuel as motor fuels represent technologies whose utility has been declining — they are no longer socially optimal. On the other hand, throwing out the "baby with the bath water", i.e., replacing the internal combustion engine with an electric motor and gasoline with electricity is not a socially optimal solution either. The maximum utility may be obtained by retaining the internal combustion engine and replacing the current fuels with natural gas fuel. There is sufficient evidence to indicate that this is indeed the path that the transportation sector will be moving to, if there is going to be a change.

More than twenty years ago it was demonstrated that the replacement of an old technology by a new one proceeds also along a logistic curve[6]. That is to say, the market shares of both winning and losing technologies follow the logistic growth curve — in biology terms as one species dies out (gasoline vehicles) another one (natural gas vehicles) takes up the freed habitat (transportation sector). An example of the logistic substitution of the two different technologies in the air transportation market, piston engine and jet engine, are given in Figure 8-2, where both the evolution in the performance versus time as well as the market saturation versus time for the two aircraft engines are shown[2][6][8]. It is interesting to note that the time to reach maturity, i.e., the life cycle for each technology has been about 30 years. The lag of substituting one technology with the other has also been, coincidentally, 30 years — the time lag is defined as the time period between the 50% saturation point of each of the two logistic curves. This is probably one of the shortest time lags between technology substitution.

In general, there will be more than two competing technologies at any given time. Each of these technologies is then at a different stage of its logistic substitution within the market. Each competing technology undergoes three distinct substitution phases: growth, saturation, and decline. A classic example of this logistic substitution mechanism is the replacement of wood by coal in the second half of the nineteenth century, of coal by oil in the first half of the twentieth century and the on-going replacement of oil by natural gas as the primary energy source of the United States. This is shown in Figure 8-3, where the fractional market share is shown for all four technologies over a two-hundred year period[7].

In the early part of the 19th century fuel wood saturated the energy market. Coal reached the 1% market penetration in 1817. By about 1880, when oil reached the 1% penetration, wood and coal accounted for about 50% each of the energy market. Coal reached its maximum penetration of almost 75% around 1915, at which time oil and fuel wood occupied each 10% of the market and natural gas had a 3% mar-

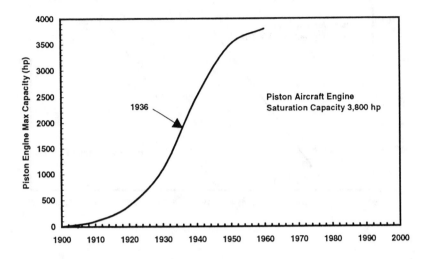

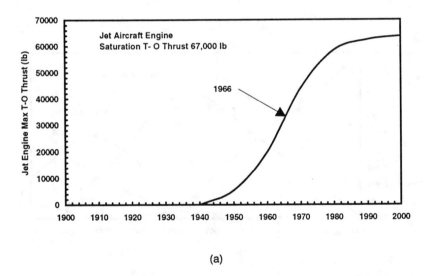

(a)

FIGURE 8-2. Logistic Replacement of Aircraft Engines Described by: (a) Performance (Maximum Horsepower (hp) for Piston Engines and Take-Off Thrust (lb) for Jet Engines); and (b) Fractional Market Saturation. The Substitution Lag Between These Two Technologies is Clearly Shown.

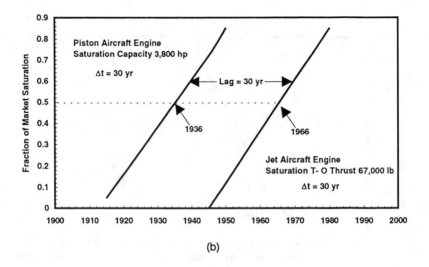

(b)

FIGURE 8-2. (Continued)

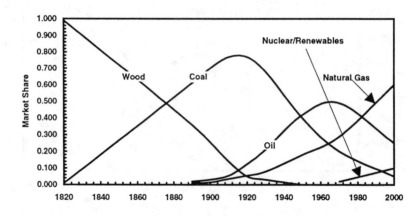

FIGURE 8-3. The Measured and Predicted Logistic Substitution of Primary Energy Resources in the United States Over a Two-Hundred Year Time Period.

ket share. Oil reached its maximum penetration of almost 50% by 1970 and has been declining in market share ever since. It is predicted that natural gas, which is now approaching a 25% penetration, will exceed oil as the primary US energy source around the year 2000. Natural gas has a relatively low slope of market entry (growth rate) indicating that it may reach a 70% or even higher penetration by the year 2030, unless another competing technology materializes.

A very important aspect of the life cycle concept deals with the competition between technologies. Every competitor technology undergoes three distinct substitution phases which comprise the "life-cycle" of the technology. One can define the qualitative stages of the "life-cycle" of any technology as follows: the embryonic, growth, and maturity stages. Figure 8-4 compares the relationship between the three

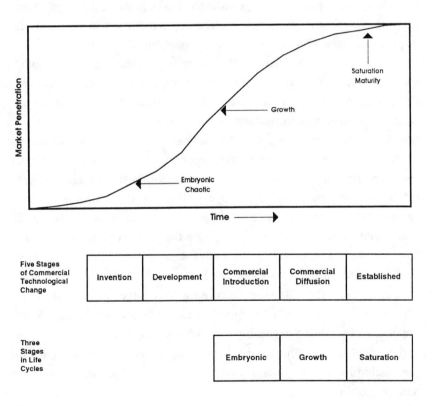

FIGURE 8-4. Comparison of Five Stage and Three Stage Theories of the Dynamics of Technological Change.

technology life cycle stages and the five stages of commercial technological changes mentioned earlier[1].

While there is a correspondence between the two models, each illu-
minates a different issue. In the embryonic stage, the new product or technology is characterized by a large number of new ideas and a large
number of entrants competing for the same niche or market. Those ideas
and entrants that survive move into the growth stage. The number of
entrants is further reduced and economies of scale and experience make it
extremely difficult for others to enter the competition. Thus, barriers are
raised. The stage of maturity is reached when the market gets saturated,
the price elasticity of demand approaches unity and product innovation is
becoming very slow. Moreover, the industry is dominated by a small
number of firms producing the particular product or technology. Whatever
the driving force from one stage to another of a given technology (market
growth, evolutionary advances in technology, reduction in cost and price
of product), the logistic growth curve is followed with regularity.

It is important to point out that there is, in nature, a certain optimal
speed or rate in the growth and maturity of any biological organism in
its habitat, which is very uniquely characteristic of that organism as it
competes against other organisms within the same habitat. This observation indicates a great degree of robustness in the logistic substitution
phases. Likewise, each technology appears to have its own uniquely
characteristic rate of penetration or substitution in the market. Thus, the
acceleration of one or more life cycle stages or the fusing of stages in
haste to move a product or technology forward can produce catastrophic
results and essentially delay or eliminate the product from the market as
other competing technologies take advantage of the situation. Moreover,
the time to reach maturity (90% penetration) for almost all technologies
is always more than 20 years according to a large number of studies.
The minimum of the "life-cycle" period constitutes indeed a very
important observation regarding the time scales of the dynamic evolution of new technologies to be kept in mind as natural gas and other
fuel technologies are positioning themselves in the market place to
replace gasoline.

LIFE CYCLE OF NATURAL GAS AS A TRANSPORTATION FUEL

There is little doubt, if any, that natural gas as a transportation fuel representing a technological change will follow logistic growth evolutionary patterns and display a characteristic life cycle before it reaches maturity. The question becomes then whether one can establish the length of this particular life cycle. In order to attempt to provide an answer, it is instructive to understand some of the issues involved. First, there must be in place a technology that can provide the requisite engine, fuel storage and emission control changes from the gasoline and diesel powered vehicles to natural gas ones. Second, there must be also in place a technology for the requisite refueling infrastructure. In previous chapters the state-of-the-art regarding both the vehicle and the refueling technologies has been examined in detail.

It is apparent that both natural gas vehicle technology and natural gas refueling infrastructure technology are well beyond the invention stage and in most instances are also beyond the development stage of their commercial technological change. Thus, it is fair to state that natural gas as a transportation fuel is at the very early stage of commercial introduction. The Clean Air Act Amendment of 1990, the Energy Policy Act of 1992 and the 1997 mandatory introduction of ULEVs in California and possibly other States may be used to signify for practical purposes the beginning time of commercial introduction of natural gas as a transportation fuel in the United States. Hence, it is also fair to observe that natural gas as a transportation fuel is no more than a few years into the embryonic stage of its life cycle. It is important to appreciate that the invention and development stages for natural gas powered vehicles have been in continuous evolution in the US in the last ten or fifteen years, albeit by a small number of individuals and companies.

Having established the probable onset of commercial introduction of natural gas as a transportation fuel around the mid 1990s and no later than the year 2000, one can now attempt to determine the length of the life cycle of this technological change. A first source of information may come from the lessons of past history. As it has been presented in an earlier chapter, the automobile has had an impressive expansion of its numbers in the United States since the turn of the century, when there

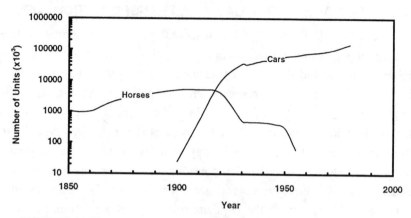

FIGURE 8-5. Number of Road Horses and Automobiles in the United States.

were only several thousand on the road. Figure 8-5 shows this increase and compares it with the corresponding number of horses employed in transportation[9]. It is interesting to note that the automobile substitution curve shows two distinct periods in time. The first period began in 1900 and ended in 1930, while the second period continues today. This implies that the growth of the automobile did nor follow one, but rather two logistic curves. The explanation for this occurrence is that these two trends indicate two distinct phases in the dissemination of motor vehicles in the United States.

The first period of growth represented the substitution of motor vehicles for horse-drawn road vehicles, obviously in urban areas where the latter were predominantly found. At the end of this phase the horse-drawn vehicle became practically extinct, because the motor vehicle offered an advantage of speed thereby increasing the radius of business and leisure transport. It is important to note that during this phase the automobile was using the same infrastructure as the horse-drawn vehicle, namely urban roads, but with the added feature of the gradual introduction of the public gas station.

In the second phase, the automobile emerged as a competitor of longer distance transport or intercity transport which until then was the exclusive purview of the railways. However, this expansion required the development of new infrastructure, namely the surfaced new urban roads, rural roads and eventually highways with the attendant services[10]. Hence, the growth was much slower.

Figure 8-6 gives the logistic growth curves for the substitution of motor vehicles for horses and the substitution of surfaced roads for unsurfaced ones[9]. The life cycle of the first phase was only 12 years, while the life cycle of the second is 73 years. It is important to note the overlapping between the two phases as obviously surfaced roads began to increase simultaneously as automobiles were replacing horses. The mileage of surfaced roads in the US parallels very well the growth of automobiles as is shown also in Figure 8-6. It is interesting to note, however, that the life cycle of the length in miles of surfaced roads is 50 years and that of all road vehicles is 100 years. It is important to note that the mileage of surfaced roads has already reached saturation. Hence, the increases in the number of vehicles come from a slowly expanded utility and the increased population.

Another important observation deduced by comparing Figure 8-5 and Figure 8-6(a) is that the decline of the numbers in road horses began around 1910, when the motor vehicles represented only a 12% penetration of the road horse market (not the ultimate automobile market). A potential implication of this observation in the substitution of natural gas for gasoline is that it may require the presence of some 25 to 30 million natural gas vehicles on the road before the number of gasoline vehicles begins to decline. The other observation is that while the life cycle of the automobile substitution for the horse drawn vehicles was 12 years, the actual length of time was about 30 years. That is to say, it took the automobile about 10 years to reach a 10% penetration, 12 more years to move to a 90% penetration and another 8 years to exceed a 99% penetration.

These numbers represent very relevant information regarding the substitution of natural gas for gasoline, because of the similar circumstances then and now. The bulk of the infrastructure now as at the turn of the century was in place, namely the existence of roads. In fact the situation today is even more favorable as there is very little additional road surfacing required compared to then. On the other hand, the surfacing of urban roads then may have been viewed as an additional benefit of the

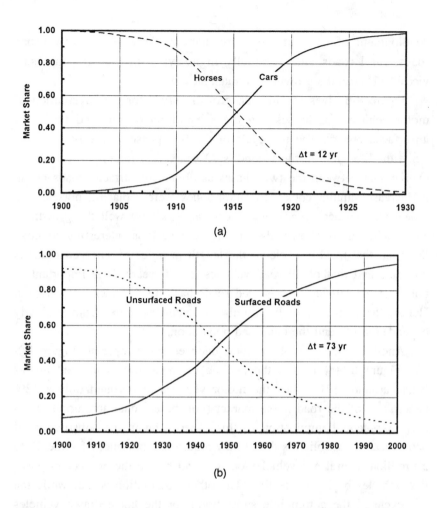

FIGURE 8-6. Logistic Growth of the Motor Vehicle and Infrastructure in the United Sates: (a) Substitution of Vehicles for Horses; (b) Substitution of Surfaced Roads for Unsurfaced Roads; and (c) Mileage of Surfaced Roads and Number of All Road Vehicles.

automobile compared to the road horse. Today this benefit no longer exists as one moves form gasoline to natural gas. But there is a different benefit now associated with natural gas. This benefit is reduced pollution in terms of local air quality as well as from the elimination of fuel spills and escape of vapors while refueling. As more and more natural gas vehicles become part of the landscape, the public begins to recognize this

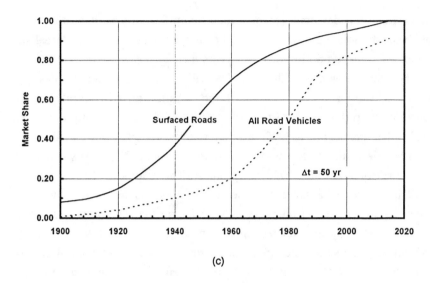

(c)

FIGURE 8-6. (Continued)

benefit and the growth of the natural gas vehicles on the road rises expo-
nentially. This initial period may take 10 years to evolve. Moreover, the
refueling facility situation is very similar then as it is now. Very limited
access to gasoline then and very limited access to natural gas as a transportation fuel today. However, the refueling technology for natural gas is
much more advanced today than what it was at the respective time in
gasoline commercialization. Thus, the natural gas refueling infrastructure
will make an even faster penetration in the market, which in turn accelerates the penetration of natural gas powered vehicles.

One possible objection to equating the length of the life cycle of the
substitution of automobiles for horses to the substitution of natural gas
for gasoline is that today there are 189 million motor vehicles on the
roads of the nation, which arguably is a very large number indeed.
Inspection of Figure 8-6(a) indicates that there were some 5 to 6 million
road horses at the turn of the century in the United States. This number
is less by a factor of "thirty to forty" compared to the present number of
vehicles. However, the substitution of natural gas for gasoline entails a
far lesser change to the system than the change that occurred between
1900 and 1930. It is only a relatively minor modification to the vehicle,

rather than the development of a totally new industry as it was the case with the automobile at the turn of the century. Thus, it is not unrealistic to expect that in a period of thirty years, i.e., by the year 2020, almost all of the vehicles on the roads in the US will be running on natural gas.

Assuming a logistic curve of the substitution of natural gas for gasoline with the 12 year life cycle (10% to 90% market saturation) and a 30 year span (1% to 99% market saturation), one can calculate the number of vehicles that will be running on natural gas between 1995 and 2025 or 2000 and 2030 at the latest. The results of this calculation will be shown in a subsequent section of this chapter, where they will be compared to actual numbers of vehicles on the road as well as other studies predicting the penetration of natural gas vehicles into the market. Admittedly the suggested life cycle of the substitution of natural gas for gasoline is one of the shortest on record and it may appear too optimistic to skeptics of the logistic curve notion as well as of the similarity argument of this substitution with that between the automobile and the road horse from 1900 to 1930. A rather critical fact which can make the replacement of gasoline by natural gas feasible in such a time period is the relatively shorter average length of life of the automobile. This average life is on the order of 6 to 10 years and may be about one-half the suggested life cycle length.

THRESHOLD POPULATION OF NATURAL GAS VEHICLES

Another important question for which data are scarce at best is the minimum number of natural gas vehicles on the market that would ensure the viability of the substitution of natural gas for gasoline. In other words, there must be a minimum population of natural gas vehicles on the market so that the process of the additional acquisition of such vehicles becomes self-sustaining. This minimum population requirement may be deduced from the observation of biological systems[3][4].

Obviously, government regulations and tax incentives are allowing alternative fuels into the automobile market place, which is currently dominated by gasoline and diesel fuels. Several fuels are competing for their share of the market including methanol, ethanol, propane, natural gas and electricity. Each of these fuels has its own minimum threshold of becoming self-sustaining. However, this minimum will be different for each fuel and it may be relatively too high for some fuels. The fuel with the lowest minimum threshold, expressed in number of vehicles in the market utilizing that particular fuel, has the chance to emerge as the dominant one. On the other hand, if this threshold is two high for all alternative fuels the substitution may never occur.

The question then becomes: "What is the minimum population of natural gas vehicles that can ensure the ultimate substitution of natural gas for gasoline?" There is very little, if any, information to be used to provide an answer to this question. One general observation of the logistic growth curves is that typically the ratio "$f/f-1$", where f is the market share of a particular technology, spans in a logarithmic scale a range from 10^{-2} to 10^{2} or 1% to 99% saturation, respectively. Thus, it may be that below the 1% saturation level, the contribution of each competing technology is in a chaotic state of evolution or else represents noise, i.e., its further development is a random process with unpredictable results. In the case of the natural gas or any another alternative fuel vehicle, the 1% saturation level or penetration of the gasoline vehicle market represents about 2 million vehicles. Another observation relates to the fact that of the alternative fuels, natural gas, propane and the alcohols may be somewhat similar in that they do not require a complete change of the technology (vehicle itself) unlike the case of electricity. Thus, it may be that the threshold for natural gas or propane or ethanol or methanol vehicles is lower than that for electric vehicles.

One potential source of information dealing with the determination of threshold criteria and from which some parallels may be derived is to be found once again in biology. Specifically, ample modeling has been devoted to the study of the spreading of epidemics and the prediction of threshold values which indicate whether a certain disease will disappear or prevail in any given population[4]. Typically, a population exposed to a disease is divided into three categories for the purposes of the study of the spreading of the disease: those who can catch the disease (susceptibles), those who are infected by the disease and can transmit it, and those who have had the disease and recovered from it or are immune to it or else are isolated from it.

The analogy between the spreading of an epidemic and the substitution of one fuel for another is predicated on the nature of human interactions. An infectious disease is transmitted form an infected person to a susceptible one because people tend to socialize rather than be secluded. Likewise, the ownership of a natural gas fueled vehicle by one person may induce another person, interacting with the first one, to purchase also a similarly fueled vehicle. In the case of epidemics, if one infected individual during the time that the disease is infectious, infects none, one or more than one susceptible persons, then the epidemic will die (none or one infection) or will spread (more than one infections).

In the case of the substitution of natural gas for gasoline, if the ownership of one natural gas fueled vehicle will lead to the purchase of more than one such vehicles by others during the life of the first vehicle then an increased substitution of natural gas for gasoline will ensue. A very simple and intuitively correct expression for the threshold population size may be obtained(*). This threshold population is determined then in the case of natural gas substitution as the ratio of the rate of removal of natural gas vehicles from the market for whatever reason (aging, poor performance, accidents, etc.) to the rate of induced (public appeal, regulatory fiat, economics, etc.) introduction of natural gas vehicles into the market. Both of these numbers are expressed on a per year basis.

The annual removal rate can not exceed the life of the natural gas vehicle. Thus, the longer a vehicle survives the smaller its annual removal rate becomes. Natural gas vehicles have thus an advantage over all other vehicles, including gasoline, propane and alcohols as it has been discussed already — electricity may have the potential for an even lower than natural gas removal rate, but the electric vehicle technology is at the present far from mature for this feature to be of practical value. For example, if the life expectancy of a natural gas vehicle is 8 years its rate of removal will be 0.125 per natural gas vehicle per year. A methanol vehicle, on the other hand, having a life expectancy of 6 years will have a removal rate of 0.166 per methanol vehicle per year. Thus, the threshold of natural gas vehicles may be 33% lower compared to that of methanol vehicles, all else being equal, i.e., same degree of public acceptance (induced introduction rate).

(*). The threshold population size N_c of a specific alternative fuel vehicle, for example natural gas, is given by the expression : $N_c = a/r$, where a is the removal rate (#/natural gas vehicle/year) and r is the induced substitution rate (#/natural gas vehicle/gasoline vehicle/year). If the population N of that specific alternative fuel vehicle is less than N_c then that alternative fuel cannot be self sustaining and will disappear. Only when $N > N_c$ then the alternative fuel under consideration can increase on its own and eventually replace gasoline in part or totally.

The degree of public acceptance or rate of induced substitution expresses the desirability of the public to replace gasoline fueled vehicles with natural gas (or alternative fuel) fueled ones. The numerical value of the induced introduction rate is obviously unknown. However, the larger the numerical value is for a given fuel then the smaller the threshold for that fuel becomes and the more likely it is for that fuel to prevail. It is reasonable to expect that the induced substitution rate is largest for natural gas, compared to gasoline, propane, methanol and ethanol, in light of the facts that natural gas is the least polluting to the environment, is not toxic or harmful to the user, and has the potential for convenient home refueling. However, the lack of knowledge at the present time of the degree of public acceptance or rate of induced introduction for natural gas vehicles versus gasoline and diesel fuel vehicles makes this simple approach to calculate the threshold value for natural gas vehicles not practical. An alternative approach to be presented shortly may then be employed.

The final question to be addressed in this section is whether natural gas vehicles can replace totally gasoline and diesel vehicles. For it is possible for any alternative fuel, depending on the characteristics of that fuel technology in the market place, to penetrate only portion of the market with the remainder of it still occupied by the existing fuel, i.e., gasoline and diesel fuel in this instance. The degree of penetration or substitution is defined as the ratio of the number of vehicles fueled by a particular alternative fuel, e.g., natural gas, to the total number of vehicles in the market (**). The degree of penetration is a function of a

---

(**). The fraction F of susceptible to substitution gasoline and diesel vehicles (GDV) that survives ultimately,i.e., after a time period T, following the introduction of natural gas vehicles (NGV) at time t_0 is defined by the expression: $F = GDV(t_0+T) /GDV_0(t_0)$. It is assumed that all GDVs are susceptible to substitution,i.e., there exist NGVs comparable in function and performance to all the existing GDVs. The NGV penetration or substitution is then (1-F). If c is the number of GDVs that are expected to be converted to, or be replaced by NGVs for each NGV on the road during the lifetime of the latter, then F = exp {-m+c(F-1)} (see Figure 8-7)[4]. Typically, m which describes the ratio of initial NGVs to initial GDVs,i.e., $m = NGV_0(t_0)/GDV_0(t_0)$, is <<1. The threshold value of c for NGVs to replace GDVs is equal to one. If c<1 then NGVs will never be able to represent a significant component of the vehicle population. Thus, the larger the value of c happens to be — as determined by consumer preference — then the smaller F becomes. The number c is calculated from an expression of the form $c = N_0$ r(t) exp(-at) dt, where r(t) is the induced introduction rate weighted with an exponential function which is the probability of an NGV surviving to age t and "a" is the removal rate of natural gas vehicles from the market due to aging and other reasons. The critical population for NGVs is defined as $N_c = \{ N_0 / c \}$. If $N_0 > N_c$, which implies c > 1, then natural gas will be able to penetrate the gasoline market.

threshold parameter signifying the number of alternative fuel vehicles purchased as a result of the presence of each such alternative fuel vehicle in the market.

The threshold parameter, which is essentially a weighted average value of the rate of induced introduction for a specific fuel vehicle, may have a numerical value less or equal to one, in which case the alternative fuel will never penetrate the market. It can also be higher than one in which case there will be a partial penetration or fuel substitution. Figure 8-7 shows the dependence of the degree of market penetration function on the numerical value of the threshold parameter. It is apparent that a numerical value of 3 or higher for the threshold parameter of natural gas will result in the complete substitution of gasoline by natural gas in the automotive market. A numerical value of 2 for the threshold parameter results in a 50% substitution.

However, the most likely value of the threshold parameter of natural gas will be either less than one in which case the *status quo* is maintained or else it will be higher than 3 in which case gasoline and diesel fuel vehicles are totally replaced with natural gas vehicles. This claim is

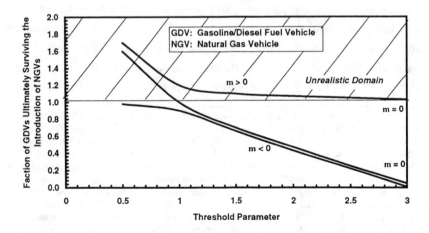

FIGURE 8-7. Dependence of the Degree of Market Penetration "F" or Substitution of Gasoline by an Alternative Fuel (e.g., Natural Gas) on the Threshold Parameter "c" Signifying the Number of Induced Alternative Fuel Vehicle Purchases Due to the Presence of Each Such Alternative Fuel Vehicle in the Market.

based solely on the observation that it will be expensive and inefficient to maintain two different systems motor vehicle fueling infrastructures and motor vehicle technologies simultaneously, if one or other of these systems can perform the task of personal transportation as well.

It is important to note that the numerical value of the threshold parameter is defined over the length of the substitution period, which is essentially the life cycle of the logistic substitution of the particular alternative fuel vehicle, i.e., NGVs for gasoline and diesel fuel vehicles. Obviously, the numerical value of the threshold parameter depends strongly on the utility of NGVs *vis-a-vis* other vehicles in the estimation of the consumers. Lastly, the critical population of vehicles running on a specific alternative fuel is defined as the total vehicle population divided by the threshold parameter for that alternative fuel. The importance of the attainment of the alternative fuel vehicle threshold population is that it signifies the permanent existence of a sizeable representation of the particular alternative fuel vehicles in the overall vehicle population.

The preceding analysis affords a numerical evaluation of the desirable threshold parameter as well as the threshold population for natural gas vehicles. Let us assume that natural gas vehicles have the utility that enables them to replace totally gasoline and diesel fuel vehicles. This would be tantamount to reversing the present state of affairs where gasoline and diesel fuel vehicles represent 99.9% of the total vehicular population. Thus, if natural gas vehicles were to represent ultimately 99.9% of all the vehicles on the road, then one can readily estimate the required threshold value of 7.01 for natural gas vehicles substituting gasoline and diesel vehicles — one can set $F = 0.001$ and assuming that $m = 0.1$ solve the equation to obtain $c = 7.01$. This high threshold parameter for natural gas vehicles indicates that every NGV on the road must induce during its lifetime the purchasing of seven more NGVs to replace existing gasoline and diesel fuel vehicles. In this instance the threshold population for NGVs is about 14% of the total vehicular population at the time.

According to the logistic growth of the gasoline and diesel vehicles to be discussed shortly, the total vehicle population year 2020 will be approaching 95% of its ultimate maximum value. This implies a total population of about 240 million vehicles in the country. The threshold value for self-perpetuating natural gas vehicles is about 34 million units.

It is interesting to note that the decline in the horse drawn carriages began when the automobile had established a 12% market share. This number is not too far off from the 14% number calculated by us here.

THE PENETRATION OF NATURAL GAS AS A MOTOR FUEL

The progress of the natural gas penetration into the transportation sector as a substitute of gasoline is proceeding currently at a slow pace. This may appear as a surprising result given all the advantages of natural gas versus gasoline and other fuels discussed in previous chapters. However, the observed presently slow penetration of natural gas is entirely reasonable in light of the logistic growth patterns. Numerical values of the various parameters discussed in the previous sections will be calculated in this section, notwithstanding the uncertainty of obtaining such numerical values due to the lack of appropriate data.

The number of natural gas fueled vehicles in the world was on the order of 700,000 as of 1992[10]. Table 8-1 summarizes the distribution of these vehicles worldwide. Almost all natural gas vehicles use CNG as the fuel form. For comparison purposes the distribution of LPG vehicles in the world is also included. The CNG vehicle numbers in Table 8-1 reflect the natural gas vehicle population in the US prior to the passage of the 1992 Energy Policy Act which directs the conversion of federal, state, public utility and private business fleets to alternative fuels beginning in 1994 and through 2003. It is important to emphasize that the 35,000 vehicles in the US represent essentially conversions of gasoline vehicles, as the first production CNG vehicles did not become commercially available until 1992 and even then in limited quantities. A more recent publication by the US DOE on the number of alternative fuel vehicles in the country as of 1992 gives a total estimate of no less than 250 thousand[11]. Of these vehicles, some 220,500 are fueled by LPG, about 24,500 by CNG, 2,700 by M-85 and 1,700 by electricity. However, the same report indicátes that the number for LPG vehicles may be underestimated by as much as 50 percent. The current growth rate of CNG vehicles has been estimated at 1,500 to 10,000 per year in the US and 4,000 per year in Canada[10]. As more and more CNG vehicles enter the market the annual growth rate is expected to rise.

TABLE 8-1. Worldwide Distribution of CNG and LPG Vehicles as of 1992

Country	CNG Vehicles	LPG Vehicles
Argentina	15,000	—
Australia	—	200,000
Canada	20,000	140,000
Italy	300,000	—
Korea	—	160,000
Mexico	—	435,000
Netherlands	—	700,000
New Zealand	125,000	50,000
Soviet Union	20,000	—
United States	35,000	500,000
World Total	700,000	2,500,000

TABLE 8-2. Historical and Projected Annual Use of Natural Gas Fuel
as CNG in the United States

Year	1990	1991	1992	2010[1]
Consumption (10^9 scf/yr)	0.270	0.367	0.511	150–485

1. The lower projection is by the US DOE EIA and the higher projection is by GRI.

The consumption of natural gas as an automotive fuel in the United States is given in Table 8-2[11][12][13]. Data have been reported by the Energy Information Administration (EIA) only since 1990. Future consumption projections are also included. Notice that EIA projects a 150 billion scf use by 2010 or less than 1% of the anticipated by then 24 trillion scf consumption, while the Gas Research Institute (GRI) projects a three times higher consumption or about 2% of the natural gas use in the country[12][14]. Both of these predictions are very conservative and indicate an extremely modest growth in the penetration of natural gas vehicles in the market. If the use, for example, per vehicle is 45,000 scf annually (11,000 miles at 27 mpg equivalent), on the average, the EIA and GRI natural gas fuel predictions correspond to 3.3 million and 9.7 million CNG vehicles, respectively. These predictions are indeed very conservative and appear to ignore entirely the logistic growth penetration of natural gas as a fuel in a gasoline dominated transportation system. This will be shown shortly.

In order to begin the examination of the rate of substitution of natural gas for gasoline as a vehicular fuel, one has to establish first the anticipated growth of the automobile population in the United States. The history of the transportation infrastructure substitution in the US, shown in Figure 8-8, clearly indicates that road transport reached the peak of its expansion around 1970 and is now on the decline, while air transport is on the rise[8][9]. This means that fewer people rely on road or automobile transport for longer distances or else that air transport is used more and more for shorter distances that were formerly accommodated by road transport. For example, the number of people travelling by automobile from coast to coast is small compared to those travelling by plane. But fewer people travel even shorter distances by car and more people use the plane. In fact, the growth of airlines in the future will be in the short distance transport[15]. Although the term "short distance" has not been defined, it is likely that the lower limit of the distance to be accommodated by air transport in the future will be on the order of 200 to 300 miles (intercity transport). This estimate is based on the comparison of the amount of time required to travel this distance by private vehicle versus an airplane, including the time required to and from the airport as well as the more rigid departure scheduling of a plane.

It is also interesting to note that the life cycle length of the logistic growth for the various transport modes in Figure 8-8 is 30 years for canals, 50 years for the railways, 90 years for surfaced roads and more than 130 years for the airway routes. The significance of the logistic growth curves of Figure 8-8 is that the present average distance travelled by each automobile of about 11,000 miles per year as well as the saturation of vehicles in the country of 58% for passengers cars and light trucks (144 million vehicles versus 250 million people) or 75% for all vehicles (189 million) will not increase any further, but it would decline in the years to come.

It is also interesting to speculate on the birth and growth of a new transport infrastructure occurring at the present time. This infrastructure is indicated as "telecommuting" in Figure 8-8 and will eventually

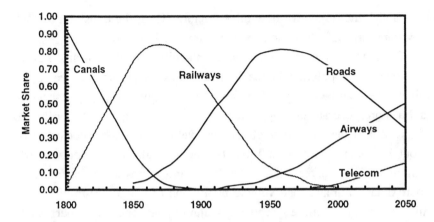

FIGURE 8-8. The History of Transport Infrastructure Substitution in the United States from 1830 to 1982 with Logistic Growth Projection of Market Shares from 1800 to 2050 and Measured as the Fractional Market Share "f" of a Given Transport Length Infrastructure in the Total Length of All Transport Networks.

replace air and land transport[16]. As of 1994, about one third of the work force (43.2 million) worked at least part time at home. In comparison, only 24 million people (21% of the workforce) worked at home in 1988. Telecommuters who work for corporations numbered more than 7.6 million in 1994, up 15.7% from 1993. Ownership of a personal computer approaches almost 60% and of a cellular phone exceeds 70% among homeworkers.

The movement away from the traditional offices is tied to a number of socioeconomic changes (e.g., increasing dual income families, rising real estate costs), demographic changes (e.g., environmental laws like the 1990 Clean Air Act), and technological changes (e.g., lower cost lap top computers, high speed modems, cellular phones). Moreover, many first time telecommuters rely on business center providers and hybrid satellite offices to replace the lost amenities of the traditional office. However, the life cycle length of telecommuting, whose birth may be in the early 1980s, will be longer than that of airways, probably on the order of 200 years. Incidentally, the longer life cycle of each new mode of transport over its predecessor is directly linked to the higher investment required to establish the respective new infrastructure. Thus, the transition to each new transport mode takes longer than the preceding one.

The next question to answer is the magnitude of the ultimate size of the vehicular population in the United States. A preliminary value for this number can be deduced form the data in Figure 8-6(c) by inspection and a more accurate one by fitting the data in Table 1-1. According to Figure 8-6(c) the saturation of all road vehicles in 1990 appears to be about 70% and according to Table 1-1 the vehicular population was 189 million vehicles in the same year. It is straightforward to calculate an approximate ultimate road vehicle population of about 270 million (189 million /0.70). A more precise calculation has been also performed using the data in Table 1-1.

The logistic growth analysis has been performed separately for passenger cars and for trucks/buses. The results of this analysis are given in Table 8-3. According to the more precise calculation the ultimate vehicular population in the United States will reach 255 million, of which 190 million will be passenger cars and 65 million will trucks, buses and other similar vehicles. Thus, the power of the logistic growth substitution allows to predict that number of vehicles in the United States will never exceed 255 million. It is important to appreciate that this prediction is based on the logistic growth which includes implicitly the historical patterns of population growth and of automobile use in the United States and as such it is consistent with the socioeconomic, demographic and technological characteristics of the country.

It should be noted that the 90% saturation level of the road vehicle population will be reached no later than the year 2010, while the 99% saturation will take 30 more years, i.e., the year 2040, to be attained. The implication of this prediction is that even if the population of the country continues to grow other modes of transport such airways and telecommuting will increase their transportation market share to pick up not only the new growth but also the declining share of the automobile mode. It is also important to note that a declining market share by a transportation mode does not imply a reduced absolute size of that mode as the absolute size of the total transportation sector keeps increasing.

The previous conclusions can be used to arrive at certain predictions of the substitution of gasoline for natural gas as vehicular fuel.

TABLE 8-3. Logistic Growth Calculation of the Vehicular Population in the United States with Separate Analyses for Passenger Cars and for Trucks/Buses

Year	Number of Passenger Cars		Number of Trucks/Buses	
	Actual	Predicted[1]	Actual	Predicted[2]
1940	27×10^6	22×10^6	5×10^6	5×10^6
1950	40×10^6	38×10^6	9×10^6	9×10^6
1960	62×10^6	61×10^6	12×10^6	15×10^6
1970	89×10^6	89×10^6	19×10^6	19×10^6
1980	121×10^6	121×10^6	34×10^6	34×10^6
1990	144×10^6	144×10^6	45×10^6	44×10^6
2000		162×10^6		52×10^6
2010		174×10^6		57×10^6
2020		181×10^6		61×10^6
2030		185×10^6		63×10^6
2040		188×10^6		64×10^6

Notes. The equation used here has the form $N(t) = N_0/(1 + e^{a(t-t_0)})$, where t is the time in years and t_0 is the year at which a 50% saturation is attained. The scientific notations $10^3 = 1$ thousand and $10^6 = 1$ million are used occasionally.
1. For passenger cars the constants of the logistic growth equation are: $N_0 = 190$ million, a = - 0.06324 yr^{-1}, and $t_0 = 1972$. The life cycle spans the years 1937 to 2007 and is therefore 70 years long. 2. For trucks/buses the constants of the logistic growth equation are: $N_0 = 65$ million, a = - 0.06324 yr-1, and $t_0 = 1978$. The life cycle spans the years 1943 to 2013 and is also 70 years long.

The logistic growth substitution is implemented with a life cycle of 12 years (10% to 90 % saturation interval) and a 30 year period from the 1% to 99% saturation level. Moreover, it is assumed that the substitution process begins in the window between 1995 and 2000. A crucial characteristic of the calculation is the estimation of the time that it will take for the substitution process to reach the 1% saturation level — some 2.1 to 2.2 million natural gas fueled vehicles on the roads of the country, if it happens sometime between 2000 and 2005. The 1998 to 2003 period of the introduction of ULEVs in California from 3% to 15% of new vehicles sold may be also targeted as the time when natural gas vehicles have reached the point in their evolution where they can be offered at the high compression, high efficiency, very low emission, single fuel substitute to the gasoline alternative.

One possible scenario for the required annual net growth of natural gas vehicles as well as the resulting cumulative growth from now until

TABLE 8-4. Annual Net and Cumulative Growth of Natural Gas Vehicles to Reach the 1% Market Penetration Level by 2002.

Year End	1998[1]	1999	2000	2001	2002
Number of NGVs					
Vehicles (10^3)/Year[2]	100	200	400	600	800
Cum. Vehicles (10^3) [3]	198	395	789	1377	2157

1. It is assumed that some 100 thousand NGVs will be on the road at the beginning of 1998.
2. New and converted NGVs produced in that year. 3. A constant 2.5% removal rate of older NGVs is assumed in each year.

then is given in Table 8-4 — net NGV growth is expected to be very much identical to the number of new NGVs as there will be a very small replacement of such vehicles due to age in the five year period. This proposed scenario requires about 100 thousand new and converted NGVs in 1998 and 800 thousand by the year 2002. However, the California standards account for no more than 60 thousand ULEVs in 1998 and no more than 300 thousand ULEVs in 2003 presumably all NGVs. Consequently, other states must account for the balance of the required number of natural gas vehicles.

There is good reason to believe that this may happen. The Ozone Transport Commission (OTC), which includes twelve northeastern states (ME, VT, NH, MA, RI, CT, NY, NJ, PA, DE, MD, portions of VA) and the District of Columbia have recommended implementation of the Low Emission Vehicle program similar to that of the California — one of the differences is the possible exclusion of ZEVs. The EPA, somewhat reluctantly, approved this recommendation in December of 1994. It is expected that the OTC program will account for a significant number of NGVs in the northeast. Finally, the State of Texas, the largest producer of natural gas in the country, is implementing an aggressive program for NGVs over the next several years. Obviously the longer it takes to reach the 1% penetration level, the longer it will take for natural gas to replace gasoline and diesel as automotive fuels.

The projected number of 800 thousand NGVs sold in the year 2002 will represent some 5% of the total sales of new vehicles in the country.

While prior to 1998 the majority of NGVs will be the result of conversions, the growth in NGV sales thereafter will be primarily due to automotive manufacturers, i.e., OEM, production. Assuming that the 1% penetration level has been reached in a given year, here in 2002, one can then establish with the aid of the logistic substitution the growth in the number of vehicles fueled by natural gas in the following years. If the logistic growth is assumed to have a 12 year life cycle and a 30 year span between the 1% and 99% market penetration levels, then the 50% substitution level will be attained by 2017. Table 8-5 summarizes the assumed levels of NGV substitution in the automotive market. It is important to note that a 50% market penetration or substitution of gasoline and diesel fuel for natural gas is not the same as the 50% NGV penetration of the ultimate automobile market, which will keep growing through 2050, albeit at a very small pace particularly after 2020. This simultaneous growth of the ultimate automobile market with the on-going substitution of the present fuels with natural gas results in a shift of about one year between the two 50% penetration levels, the NGV 50% penetration of the ultimate motor vehicle market occurring in 2018. The results of this logistic growth analysis regarding the substitution of natural gas for gasoline as the vehicular transportation fuel of choice are

TABLE 8-5. Logistic Substitution Analysis of Gasoline and Diesel Fuel for Natural Gas in the United States over a Postulated 30 Year Period of 1% to 99% Market Penetration for NGVs

Year			Total No. of Vehicles (10^6)	Total No. of NGVs (10^6)	NGV Market Penetration (%)
2002	or	2XXX	218	2.2	1
2011		2XXX + 9	233	23.3	10
2017		2XXX + 15	239	119.7	50
2023		2XXX + 21	244	219.8	90
2032		2XXX + 30	249	246.3	99

Notes. The total number of vehicles in the market is calculated from the equations in Table 8-3. The NGV market penetration is assumed and the NGVs are calculated as percent of the total number of vehicles.

TABLE 8-6.   Predicted Logistic Growth and Substitution of Gasoline and Diesel Fuel for Natural Gas and Calculated Natural Gas Fuel Use in the United States from 2002 (or Year of 1% NGV Penetration) to 2050 (or 48 Years after the Year of 1% NGV Penetration)

| Year | Number of NGVs | | Market Penetration (%) | Av. NGV Fuel Use | | NG Fuel Use (10^9 scf/yr) |
	New (10^6/yr)	Total (10^6)		(mpg)	(10^3 scf/yr)	
2002	0.8	2.2	1	23.1	53	0.116
2005	1.7	5.1	2	24.5	50	0.270
2010	5.5	21.2	8	27.3	45	0.954
2015	12.5	73.7	29	30.7	40	2.948
2020	18.5	164.7	64	35.0	35	5.764
2025	23.0	245.9	96	40.9	30	7.375
2030	24.0	248.2	97	42.3	29	7.198
2040	25.0	254.6	99	43.8	28	7.129
2050	25.0	255.0	100	45.4	27	6.885

Notes. The equation $N(t) = N_0/(1 + e^{a(t-t_0)})$ for the total number of NGVs has as parameters a =-0.30 yr^{-1} and t_0 = 2018 the year at which the 50% NGV ultimate market saturation is attained. The N_0 is equal to 255 million vehicles. New NGVs reflect vehicle units required to replace gasoline and diesel vehicles that are removed form service as well as new additions to augment market size. Gasoline and diesel fuel vehicle production ceases after about the year 2020.

given in Table 8-6. The logistic equation for the NGVs of Table 8-6 is the best fit of the data assumed in Table 8-5. In this analysis passenger cars, light trucks, vans, heavy trucks and buses have been lumped together as far as total vehicle numbers are concerned. While this assumption may not be entirely correct, it is adequate for the purpose of demonstrating the logistic type development of the NGV population. An estimate of the annual natural gas vehicle production required to meet the substitution goal is also given. The number of new NGVs required annually is not different than the production rate necessary of the domestic manufactures and imports to replace existing vehicles. An anticipated average fuel consumption per vehicle is also included and the resulting natural gas consumption is therefore calculated.

It is assumed that initially the average fuel consumption per NGV will be 53,000 scf/yr (NGVs predominantly light trucks and vans), which is equivalent to a fuel efficiency of 23.1 gpm gasoline equivalent at 11,000 miles per year. Moreover, it is expected that this fuel efficiency will exceed 40 mpg in a period of 20 years (all vehicles). Passenger cars alone will soon reach the 27 mpg (gasoline) CAFE standard, which equals 45,000 scf/yr for natural gas fuel. A 40 mpg average fuel efficiency for the entire automotive fleet of the country to be attained by 2025 represents a rather conservative expectation, given that as a late as the fall of 1993 GM, Ford and Chrysler reached an understanding with the President of the United States to produce, on a voluntary basis, 80 mpg passenger cars by the end of this decade. Thus, the ultimate consumption of natural gas as transportation fuel will be on the order of 7.0 trillion scf/yr and conceivably significantly less. This consumption of natural gas for transportation is about the same as the current use in the residential and commercial sectors combined.

THE TRANSPORTATION SECTOR AND NATURAL GAS FUEL

The projection of natural gas use as a transportation fuel by GRI as indicated in Table 8-2 is about two times less than the logistic growth and substitution predictions of Table 8-6, both in terms of the number of NGVs as well as the CNG fuel consumption by the year 2010 — 10 million versus 20 million vehicles and 0.45 trillion scf/yr versus 1 trillion scf/yr of natural gas. The GRI prediction, which is three times as large as the DOE prediction, appears to be conservative compared to the logistic growth prediction developed here. The obvious question then is whether the logistic growth employed in this analysis is a more realistic description of the substitution of gasoline and diesel fuel with natural gas as the transportation fuel of choice.

There are two fundamental assumptions in the logistic substitution scenario used in this analysis. These two assumptions are:

I.   The year of attainment of the 1% natural gas market substitution; and

II. The time span between the 1% and 99% natural gas market substitution or alternatively the length of the life cycle (time from the 10% to the 90% substitution).

Of these two assumptions, the answer to the second one can be possibly ascertained on the basis of past history. However, one must be careful in considering only the analogous situations of logistic growth to the present one. Specifically, the substitution of gasoline and diesel fuel for natural gas fuel is not an infrastructure development case analogous to the development of railways, roads, airways (airports) and pipelines (oil or gas). The elements of the infrastructure for natural gas based transportation are already in place, whether they comprise roads or natural gas transport from production sites to consumption sites. The fact that no CNG compressors are available at home or at work presently is in no way different than the situation prevailing between 1900 and 1930 when the automobile replaced the horse as the prime people mover. In fact the situation today is much more favorable than it was then, as local utilities and oil companies are ubiquitous in all metropolitan areas. The installation of CNG compressors for refueling at home, business place and central public locations can develop in parallel with the acquisition of NGVs by the public. Thus, the analogous logistic substitution will be that pertaining to the prime mover change.

There exist at least four examples of such substitution in the United States. The first one has already been mentioned and involves the replacement of the horse by the automobile. The entire process from the 1% to the 99% substitution took 30 years and the life-cycle from 10% to 90% substitution took 12 years.

As a second example, one can invoke the replacement of the piston engine by the jet engine in commercial aviation[8][9]. The 50% market saturation of the piston engine plane occurred in 1936 with the introduction of the DC-3. The 50% market saturation of the jet engine occurred in 1966 with the introduction of the B-747, exactly 30 years later. Incidentally, the measured saturation parameter in this comparison is the engine performance, i.e., maximum horse power for piston engines and maximum take-off thrust for jet engines. The 30 year time lag between the 50% market saturation of the two technologies may be used as an indicator of a potentially similar 50% market saturation lag between gasoline/diesel fuel and natural gas. Unleaded gasoline, which represents the latest major automotive fuel substitution, attained the 50% gasoline market share in 1981 and the 50% market share of the automotive fuel market (gasoline and diesel fuel) in 1984[17]. This implies that a new automotive fuel replacing gasoline and diesel fuel may attain a 50 % automotive fuel market share by 2014. It is also worth noting that the automotive fuel consumption in the US attained its 50% market share, i.e., the 50% level of its ultimate consumption of about 8.5 million bbl/day in the early 1960s[17].

A third example of technology substitution is the replacement of steam for diesel locomotives[9]. The first diesel locomotive was placed in service in 1925, the 1% penetration level was reached in 1938 and the 99% locomotive market share was attained by 1963. The life cycle of the technological substitution (10% to 90% market share) was also 12 years, but the time span of the 1% to 99% market share at about 25 years was even faster than that of the substitution of the horse by the automobile. Incidentally, a few electric locomotives were introduced even before the diesel ones, but they never gained importance in the United States because the long distances involved required expensive, and obviously not cost-effective, infrastructure development (power lines along the railroad lines).

The fourth example, already mentioned here, is the substitution of leaded by unleaded gasoline. The drive for this replacement was environmental in nature. First, there was the concern of lead pollution to the environment and particularly the health effect of it on humans. Second, the implementation of emission control catalysts in cars to reduce air pollution required the simultaneous elimination of lead from gasoline because it poisons the catalysts and renders them ineffective very quickly. The 1% to 99% gasoline market share by unleaded gasoline was attained in about 21 years between 1972 and 1993, while the span of the life cycle of this substitution has been about 15 years from 1975 to 1990[17]. In this instance the federal mandate for cleaner emission vehicles led to the installation of catalysts in new automobiles by the auto manufacturers and the concurrent requisite supply of unleaded gasoline by the oil companies.

The important conclusion from the preceding examples is that technological change takes place very quickly, whenever it occurs. Thus, the next transportation fuel will replace gasoline and diesel fuel in a period of about 30 years. Of course, the previous examples do not tell us what the next transportation fuel will be or when the substitution (1% market share) will begin. It is easy to surmise on the basis of technological development and environmental consequences that natural gas is the only logical next choice to replace gasoline and diesel fuel, if a replacement indeed is going to happen in the near future.

Thus, one can now attempt to re-evaluate the first of the two assumptions above, i.e., when this substitution of gasoline and diesel fuel for natural gas fuel may begin. In the last section, the year 2002 was selected as that time on the basis of clean air legislation going into effect a few years prior to that date. If the unleaded gasoline substitution example is of any value, it supports to certain extent the selection of 2002 as the 1% market share attainment date for natural gas. Obviously, the more states adopt the California ULEV emission requirements by the year 1998 or thereabouts the more likely it becomes for the beginning of the 21st century to mark the inception of the substitution of gasoline and diesel fuel by natural gas.

The year 2002 may then be very close to the correct date marking the beginning of this substitution process. It is legitimate then to ask whether this date, only eight years away, can witness a cumulative number of 2.1 million NGVs on the road. Of course, one-third of these NGVs will be produced in 2002 alone according to the scenario of Table 8-4. While this number can vary by some percentage, it is unlikely that more than 1 million NGVs can be produced that year alone. It is very instructive and useful to examine then, whether from now until the beginning of the next century a million or so NGVs can be put in use across the country.

A study commissioned by the National Gas Vehicle Coalition (NGVC) and funded by NGVC as well as EDO Corporation and the State of New York Department of Economic Development has produced a number of projections to the year 2000 regarding the NGV market[19]. This study targeted the fleets of ten or more vehicles as these fleets are required by the Energy Act of 1992 to switch to alternative fuels beginning as early as 1994[20]. These fleets include the federal, state and local governments as well as all public utilities (electricity, gas, water, telephone) and private business. As of 1991, there were 91,000 fleets in the US with 10 or more vehicles per fleet. These fleets consisted of just about 12 million vehicles, of which 46% were passenger cars, 27% were trucks, 5% were buses and the remainder were tractors and other off-the-road vehicles. More than 50% percent of the fleets have central refueling facilities at the present time, between 80 and 90% of the vehicles in these fleets are driven daily under 200 miles, and two-thirds of the fleets have already access to natural gas.

The aforementioned study found that state (CA and TX) and federal (Energy Policy Act of 92) mandates will result in the adoption of over 0.850 million NGVs from 1994 through the end of 2000. Moreover, the study found that the economic attractiveness of the NGV adoption depended on the payback time of the initially higher NGV cost through fuel cost savings. A 2 year or less payback time guaranteed a 100% conversion of the aforementioned fleets to natural gas, while a 4 year or longer payback virtually eliminated any voluntary conversion. A $0.30 per gallon fuel differential between natural gas and gasoline or diesel fuel could result in the acquisition of an additional 1.7 million NGVs from 1994 through the year 2000 for a total of 2.5 million NGVs on the road. However, a fuel price differential of $0.50 per gallon would result in over 5 million voluntary NGVs on the road, in addition to those mandated by law so that a cumulative number of almost 6 million NGVs may be available on the roads of the country. While, the NGVC study does not provide NGV numbers for 1998, it is clear that a $0.30 per gallon fuel differential and the present legislative mandates will be sufficient to attain the penetration level projected in Table 8-6 for the year 2002. Moreover, a $0.50 per gallon fuel price differential will realize the prediction of Table 8-6 for the year 2005 five years earlier. Since, the current price differential between the price of gasoline or diesel fuel and natural gas is on the order of $0.30 to $0.50 per gallon, the selection of the 2002 date as the 1% penetration attainment of the transportation sector by NGVs constitutes a valid assumption.

The final question to address is whether natural gas will become the fuel of choice in transportation. It has been indicated on several occasions that this appears to be the case on the basis of economic and environmental criteria. Is there any evidence for the logistic growth of natural gas in the energy economy that natural gas will become the next transportation fuel? The answer to this question appears to be on the affirmative. Figure 8-9 shows the competition of the different sectors of the US energy economy for natural gas[7]. The substitution process indicates a continuous and steady trend toward greater use of natural gas in

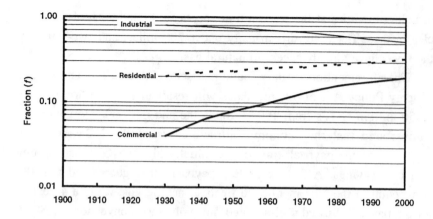

FIGURE 8-9. Actual and Projected Logistic Growth in the Use of Natural Gas by Energy Sector in the United States from 1900 to 2100 with an Implicit Natural Gas Based Transportation Sector Emerging at the Turn of the 21th Century.

the residential and commercial sectors. Moreover, the share of natural gas in the industrial sector, which includes also electric utilities, is decreasing. This result shows that natural gas has the characteristics of a premium fuel.

Industry has more technological opportunities to switch between fuels and to implement pollution controls with less clean fuels. For example, electric utilities have almost doubled the use of coal for the generation of electricity between 1973 and 1991. In the same time period the use of natural gas has declined by 30% while production of electricity has increased by more than 50%[21]. In addition, industry has also the capability to improve process energy efficiency at a much faster pace than the other two sectors. Since 1973 industry has reduced the use of natural by about 20% and total energy use by 6%, while output has more than doubled[22]. On the other hand, the residential and commercial sectors comprise a very large number of small users concentrated in urban areas. Thus, these sectors are expected to use the cleanest available fuels. Next to electricity, natural gas is the cleanest final energy form.

It will be instructive to attempt to derive any trend of future natural gas use for transportation from the logistic curves of Figure 8-9. Using the appropriate equations describing the end use of natural gas in the three energy sectors, namely, industrial, residential and commercial, one can determine their future share of the natural gas market from 1990 through 2030 as shown in Table 8-7. The logistic market share prediction by energy sector for 2030 shows a 40.2% industrial consumption, a 35.7% residential consumption, and a 24.1% consumption for the commercial sector. However, there is no provision for transportation. Does this mean then that natural gas will never become a significant transportation fuel? Not necessarily.

It is possible that the consumption of natural gas as a transportation fuel is imbedded somewhere in the logistic growth and substitution curves of Figure 8-9 and values of Table 8-7. Let us examine the situation a little more in depth. One of the unknown quantities not predicted in either Figure 8-9 or Table 8-7 is the total natural gas consumption by, say, the year 2030. Is it possible for us to establish that number? The answer to some of these questions is developed in the following paragraphs.

Of the three energy sectors, the industrial sector is the one most likely to predict in terms of natural gas use 40 years from now. In 1990, the total natural gas consumption was 18.7 trillion scf, while 16.8 tril-

TABLE 8-7.   Predicted Logistic Market Share for Natural Gas in the
Three Energy Sectors 1990-2030

Year	Residential	Commercial	Industrial
1990	26.1%	15.6%	58.3%
1995	27.2	16.8	56.0
2000	28.4	17.9	53.7
2005	29.5	19.1	51.4
2010	30.7	20.1	49.2
2015	31.9	21.2	46.9
2020	33.1	22.3	44.6
2025	34.4	23.2	42.4
2030	35.7	24.1	40.2

Notes. The equation $\ln\{f/(1-f)\} = a\,(t-t_0) + b$ has as parameters $t_0 = 1930$, $a = +0.0113$, -0.0182 and $b = -1.719$, $+1.424$ for the residential, industrial sectors, respectively and t is the year from 1930 to 2030. The natural gas consumption was 18.7×10^{12} scf in 1990 and the market share is the actual one.

lion scf were delivered to all industrial, residential and commercial consumers — the 1.9 trillion scf difference reflects the amount of natural gas used in its extraction and processing (lease and plant fuel) which amounts to 1.2 trillion scf and the pipeline operation fuel of 0.7 trillion scf. The US DOE natural gas consumption data show that a 20% reduction in use occurred by the industrial sector proper in the 1970s and a 20% lower consumption by the electric utilities in the 1980s[23]. The industrial sector proper was adjusting to the "oil crisis" induced energy price increases in the 1970s, while electric utilities were responding to perceived natural gas scarcity and the ensuing regulation in the first half of the 1980s. Thus, these drastic fuel switching occurrences in the industrial sector from natural gas to other fuels were the result of exceptional conditions.

Assuming that such conditions will not reappear between 1990 and 2030, it is then plausible to infer that the use of natural gas in the industrial sector will decline at the same rate as the total energy use in the that sector. The total energy use in the industrial sector has declined, on the average, about 3% per decade after 1973[23][24]. Hence, one can deduce to a first approximation a 12% reduction in the total industrial energy use from 1990 to 2030 and a similar reduction in the use of natural gas in the industrial sector. Thus, the industrial sector may reduce its use of natural gas from 9.8 trillion scf in 1990 to 8.6 trillion scf in 2030, while industrial output maintains its traditional average annual increase of about 4% per year[24]. However, a 8.6 trillion scf industrial natural gas energy consumption in 2030 implies, on the basis of the results of Table 8-7, a total natural gas delivery to all customers of 21.4 trillion scf during the same year. The total natural gas consumption in 2030 will be almost 23.8 trillion scf, if the standard 10% lease plant and pipeline transportation natural gas use is also included. Table 8-8 summarizes these projections along with other information to be discussed shortly.

Employing once more the estimates of Table 8-7 for the natural gas market share of the residential and commercial sectors as well as the total amount of gas delivered to customers, one can readily calculate the expected absolute delivery of natural gas in these two sectors by 2030. Thus, the natural gas predicted to be delivered is 7.6 trillion scf and 5.2 trillion scf, respectively. However, there exist independent means to esti-

TABLE 8-8. Projected Natural Gas Use by Energy Sector and Calculation of the Implicit Contribution of Natural Gas Use as Transportation Fuel in the Residential and Commercial Sectors from 1990 to 2030 in Trillion scf/yr

Year	Ind. Sec.	Total Use Del.	Total Use Cons.	Res. Sec. A	Res. Sec. B	Com. Sec. A	Com. Sec. B	Imp. Transp. Use Res.	Imp. Transp. Use Com.
1990	9.8	16.8	18.7	4.4	4.4	2.6	2.6	0.0	0.0
2030	8.6	21.4	23.8	7.6	2.9	5.2	2.3	4.7	2.9

Notes. Ind(ustrial) Sec(tor) derived as explained in text. Total Use Del(ivery) and Cons(umption) derived from "Ind. Sec." as explained in text. Res(idential) Sec(tor): "A" derived from "Ind. Sec." and Table 8-7; and "B" calculated from an assumed increase in number of households from 90 million in 1990 to 120 million in 2030 and an average natural gas use per household for domestic purposes (space and water heating, cooking, etc.) of 50% less in 2030 than in 1990. Com(mercial) Sec(tor): "A" derived from "Ind. Sec." and Table 8-7; and "B" calculated from an assumed increase in building floor area from 40 billion ft^2 in 1990 to 70 billion ft^2 in 2030 and building energy per sq. ft. of floor space is reduced by 50% in the same period. Imp(licit) Transp(ortation) Use: Res(idential) and Com(mercial) is the difference of "A-B" in the respective columns.

mate the natural gas delivered to the residential sector and the commercial sector by that year.

In the residential sector, the average increase in the number of households is on the order of 8 million per decade. Thus, it is expected that the total number of households (occupied housing units) will increase by 30 million between 1990 and 2030 for a total of about 120 million. Residential building energy efficiency standards that went into effect in the early 1980s for new houses as well as retrofitting of existing houses because of higher fuel prices in the 1970s as well as utility rebates thereafter have resulted in an average decrease of energy use per household of about 1.75% per year[25]. Thus, the average energy use per household and in particular the use of natural gas for space and water heating, also decreasing at the same rate, will be in 2030 about 50% of what it was in 1990. This calculation gives a residential sector natural gas delivery requirement for the traditional household uses of 2.9 trillion scf by 2030. Comparison of the residential sector natural gas use on the basis of the logistic growth and of the calculated average use of natural gas in the residential sector by taking into account energy efficiency measures already in place for more than ten years now indicates a 4.7 trillion scf/yr excess use between the former and the latter predictions.

Since neither the logistic growth trend nor the energy efficiency trend can change, unless a major catastrophe were to occur, it is apparent that the 4.7 trillion scf/yr by 2030 represent the amount of natural gas used to refuel private vehicles at home.

The increase of floor area in the commercial sector has been on the order of 8 billion square feet per decade since the early 1960s[24]. Thus, the commercial building floor area will increase from 40 billion ft^2 in 1990 to about 70 billion ft^2 in 2030. Incidentally, in the commercial sector the floor area rather than the number of buildings is an appropriate measure of energy use. Federal and state energy efficiency measures already in existence for new buildings and the continued retrofitting of existing commercial buildings with utility support will result in an energy reduction of about 50% per floor area between 1990 and 2030[24]. This reduction applies to natural gas usage as well. The resulting use of natural gas in the commercial sector amounts to 2.3 trillion scf/yr by 2030. Consequently, the excess use of natural gas in the commercial sector predicted by the logistic growth represents the use of natural gas for refueling vehicles at commercial facilities, which may also include public stations.

The preceding analysis indicates that the combined use of natural gas as a transportation fuel, as part of the residential and commercial sectors, will be on the order 7.6 trillion scf/yr in the year 2030. This result is very close to that predicted independently by the earlier advanced substitution scenario of natural gas for gasoline and diesel fuel, which is given in Table 8-6. Moreover, the results of the preceding analysis confirm the thesis put forth earlier that natural gas will be utilized as a transportation fuel both at home and at the work place. Indeed the long term breakdown between home and work refueling will be approximately 2/3 and 1/3 of the fuel, respectively. The implicit nature of a natural gas transportation sector, as part of the residential and commercial sectors, in contrast to the present explicit or independent of the other sectors gasoline and diesel fuel based transportation energy sector, has far reaching implications. It signifies that there will be a very small number of public refueling stations, if any, when natural gas replaces gasoline and diesel fuel as the land transportation fuel. It signifies also that "telecommuting" replaces the traditional work environment. Finally, the analysis places a limit as to the maximum long term total consumption of natural gas in the US at about 24 trillion scf per year.

Another far reaching conclusion is that the US will never be nearly as dependent on natural gas imports as it has been on oil imports even when natural gas fuel replaces totally gasoline and diesel fuel. This result can be deduced from the aforementioned maximum projected consumption of natural gas in the US and the following additional facts. First, the international LNG transport by tanker has already reached a 90% saturation level as the logistic growth curve of Figure 8-10 suggests[5]. Liquefied natural gas represents, of course, the only practical means of importing natural gas to the US from non-neighboring producing countries. Thus, the US will not import significantly more LNG in the long term compared to that imported today. Second, as it will be discussed in the last chapter, some 2 to 4 trillion scf of natural gas may be obtained annually by converting natural gas liquids and other heavier hydrocarbons from the refining of oil. Assuming that the present production of 18 trillion scf per year will not increase, then the maximum level of natural gas imports via pipeline from Canada and Mexico will be on the order of 2 to 4 trillion scf per year or 8 to 16% of the annual natural gas consumption.

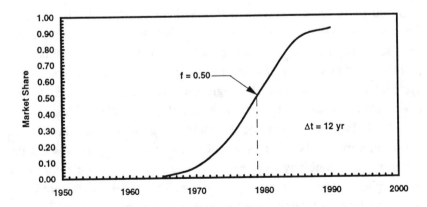

FIGURE 8-10. Logistic growth of world LNG market indicating a 90% saturation attained by 1985 and a 12 year life cycle. The world LNG market saturation represents 2.2 trillion scf of natural gas annually.

Before this chapter is concluded three important remarks are in order with regard to the logistic growth and the technological substitution process. First, it should be noted that in the early stages of the substitution of one technology by another several candidate technologies appear on the horizon, each one competing to dominate the market. Eventually, only one of these technologies becomes the dominant one, while all the others comprise only minute fractions of the market share. Thus, natural gas, propane, methanol, ethanol and electricity will initially compete in the substitution of gasoline and diesel fuel. However, only one of these alternative fuels will succeed in displacing the present fuels and capturing over 90% of the motor vehicle fuel market share. All other fuels will either represent a few percentage points of the market share or else will totally disappear. If this substitution occurs, the thesis here is that natural gas will become the dominant motor vehicle fuel in 35 years very much as gasoline is the dominant fuel today.

Second, there is evidence that technological innovation occurs in waves or cycles in a free market economy. At the beginning of a new cycle, which is typically marked by a stagnant economic activity, mature technologies are being replaced by new ones. These technological replacements or substitutions invigorate gradually the economy which reaches a high level of activity sometime during the mid of the cycle. These cycles have been found to have a constant duration of about 60 years and are known as Kondradief cycles[2][5][6]. The last two Kondradief cycles spanned the time intervals between 1871 to 1930 and 1931 to 1990. The new Kondradief cycle began in 1991 and will take us to 2050. The importance of being at the beginning of a new Kondradief cycle indicates a heighten technological innovation which favors, among others, the large scale introduction of natural gas vehicles.

Third, logistic curves by themselves cannot predict the future. However, they can be used as a tool to recognize the period when the limits of one technology have been reached and a successor technology is emerging or has the potential to emerge. This should be factored into the formulation of business strategies and policy. In short, logistic curves can be useful so long as they are used intelligently. Thus, the reduction of vehicle air emissions by a factor of ten or more from the present level cannot be attained in a practical manner with the continued use of gasoline and diesel fuel but it can be attained with the use of one of three alternative fuels: natural gas, hydrogen and electricity. However, hydrogen and electricity require radical changes in vehicle technology which are currently, i.e., next 15 to 20 years, neither practical nor cost effective. Only natural gas can utilize the present engine and emission catalysts, with minor modifications, to attain this large reduction in emissions.

It is natural, therefore, to consider natural gas as the only viable alternative fuel to substitute gasoline and diesel at the present time and within the foreseeable future. Incidentally, the future of other technologies will be addressed in the next chapter. Likewise, natural gas is the only alternative fuel that has the potential to eliminate in the most efficient and economic manner the dependency of the US on foreign oil. Given then that natural gas is by far the most likely candidate alternative fuel to replace gasoline and diesel as the transportation fuel of choice, the aforementioned logistic substitution curves indicating the substitution time frame can be used for business planning by the entities to be directly affected. These entities include the automobile manufacturers, the new component suppliers (CNG tanks, compressors, etc.), natural gas producers, pipeline companies and utilities. Obviously, a single logistic curve is not as useful for planning purposes as a set of logistic curves with different aspects of the same technology and market. However, such an undertaking is beyond the scope of this work and must be developed by the affected businesses along with their other related, but business specific, characteristics as part of their future strategic planning.

REFERENCES

1. T. H. Lee, B. C. Ball, Jr. and R. D. Tabors, Energy Aftermath, Harvard Business School Press, Boston, MA, 1990.

2. N. Rosenberg, Exploring the Black Box-Technology, Economics, and History, Cambridge University Press, Cambridge, UK, 1994.

3. D. W. Pearce and R. K. Turner, Economics of Natural Resources and the Environment, The Johns Hopkins University Press, Baltimore, MD, 1991.

4. J. D. Murray, <u>Mathematical Biology</u>, Springer-Verlag, Berlin, FRG and New York, NY, 1989.

5. C. Marchetti, "The Future of Natural Gas: A Darwinian Analysis", Ch. 3, pp.45-59, <u>The Methane Age</u>, T. H. Lee, H. R. Linden, D. A. Dreyfous and T. Vasko (eds.), Kluwer Academic Publishers, Boston, MA, 1988.

6. C. Marchetti, "Infrastructures for Movement: Past and Future", Ch. 7, pp. 146-174, <u>Cities and Their Vital Systems: Infrastructure, Past, Present , and Future</u>, J. H. Ausubel and R. Herman (eds.), National Academy of Engineering, National Academy Press, Washington, DC, 1988.

7. A. Gruebler and N. Nakicenovic, "The Dynamic Evolution of Methane Technologies", Ch. 2, pp. 13-44, <u>The Methane Age</u>, T. H. Lee, H. R. Linden, D. A. Dreyfous and T. Vasko (eds.), Kluwer Academic Publishers, Boston, MA, 1988.

8. T. H. Lee and N. Nakicenovic, "Technology Life Cycle and Business Decisions", pp. 411-426, <i>Int. J. Tech. Management,</i> v. 3, no. 4, 1988.

9. N. Nakisenovic, "Dynamics and Replacement of US Transport Infrastructures", Ch. 8, pp. 175-221, <u>Cities and Their Vital Systems: Infrastructure, Past, Present, and Future</u>, J. H. Ausubel and R. Herman (eds.), National Academy of Engineering, National Academy Press, Washington, DC, 1988.

10. B. Willson, "Evaluation of Aftermarket Fuel Delivery Systems for Natural Gas and LPG Vehicles", prepared for National Renewable Energy Laboratory (RT-1-00752) for US Department of Energy, April 1992.

11. Energy Information Administration, "Propane-Provider Fleet Survey 1993" in <u>Monthly Energy Review November 1994</u>, DOE/EIA-0885(94/12), US DOE, Washington, DC, 1994.

12. Energy Information Administration, <u>Natural Gas 1992: Issues and Trends</u>, DOE/EIA-0560(92), US DOE, Washington, DC, 1993.

13. Energy Information Administration, <u>Natural Gas Annual 1991</u>, DOE/EIA-0131(91), US DOE, Washington, DC, 1992.

14. Energy Information Administration, <u>Annual Energy Outlook 1993</u>, DOE/EIA-0383(93), US DOE, Washington, DC, 1993.

15. J. Sanchez, "Upstart Airline Winning the West with Low Fares", p. D1, *The Los Angeles Times*, December 12, 1993.

16. "Teleworking", *Business Facilities*, v. 28, no. 1, pp. 19-22, January 1995.

17. Energy Information Administration, <u>Monthly Energy Review June 1992</u>, p. 57, DOE/EIA-0035(92/06), US DOE, Washington, DC, 1992.

18. Statistical Abstract of the United States 1970, 91st Ed., p. 548, US Department of Commerce, Bureau of Census, Washington, D.C., 1970.

19. "NGV Market Projections to the Year 2000 Based upon Federal and State Legislative Mandates", produced by Market Direction, Fairfield, CT for the Natural Gas Vehicle Coalition, Arlington, VA, June 1993.

20. House of Representatives US Congress, <u>Energy Policy Act of 1992</u>, Report 102-1018, pp. 251-256, US Government Printing Office, Washington, DC, 1992.

21. Energy Information Administration, <u>Monthly Energy Review June 1992</u>, *loc. cit.*, p. 91.

22. Energy Information Administration, <u>Monthly Energy Review June 1992</u>, *loc. cit.*, p. 29.

23. Energy Information Administration, <u>Monthly Energy Review June 1992</u>, *loc. cit.*, p. 73.

24. E. Hirst, R. Marlay, D. Greene and R. Barnes, "Recent Changes in US Energy Consumption: What Happened and Why", <u>Ann. Rev. Energy</u>, v. 8, pp. 193-245, Annual Reviews, Inc., Palo Alto, CA, 1983.

25. R. H. Williams and Gautam S. Dutt, "Future Energy Savings in the US Housing", <u>Ann. Rev. Energy</u>, v. 8, pp. 269-332, Annual Reviews, Inc., Palo Alto, CA, 1983.

Chapter 9

Natural Gas and the Hydrogen Economy

INTRODUCTION

The complete replacement of gasoline and diesel fuel by natural gas as the motor vehicle fuel of choice in the US is projected to occur no later than the year 2030. While this time-frame may appear to most people as remote, it is in fact very close to the present time. Thus, the time that it will take for natural gas to command a 99% share of the vehicular fuel market is no more removed into the future than, for example, is removed into the past the inception of the Apollo program that resulted in the landing of the first man on the moon and later evolved into the on-going space shuttle program[1]. Another way of appreciating the relative shortness of this timespan is to realize that fully two-thirds of the population of the Unites States today will still be alive by the year 2030 to witness the completion of the transition from gasoline and diesel fuel to natural gas[2]. The process of replacing the present transportation fuels with natural gas will be evolutionary in its nature, but it has the potential for revolutionary results on several counts.

First of all, air pollution will be reduced by a factor of "twenty" from its present levels. That is to say, the emitted air pollutants from the tailpipe of all the vehicles in the US will be 5% or less of what they are today. This reduction will be the combination of two results: I. An at least ten-fold decrease in the emissions by switching to natural gas; and

II. A better than two-fold increase in average vehicle fuel efficiency due in part to the natural gas implementation (high compression) and in part to the continuation of on-going improvements in the efficiency of vehicles (weight reduction, system optimization, etc.). Thus, the net result will be the aforementioned reduction in air pollutants even if one takes into account the 25% or so increase of the vehicle population in the country during the same time period.

Second, natural gas as a motor fuel will bring about the improvement in the balance of payments and particularly in the reduction of the trade deficit by avoiding the importation of some 3 billion barrels of crude oil and petroleum products annually, the reduction in military expenditures to guarantee the supply of oil from politically unstable territories, the savings from reduced medical bills and lost work, and the creation of an industry at home to manufacture, sell and maintain the different type of infrastructure (home and work refueling).

Thus, natural gas as a transportation fuel will drastically reduce automotive pollution to a point, undoubtedly, within the so called assimilative capacity of the environment[3]. The term assimilative capacity refers to the ability of the natural environment to take wastes generated either by natural or human processes and convert them into harmless or even ecologically useful products. However, there is an upper limit as to the amount of wastes the environment can assimilate in a continuous fashion. The assimilative capacity of local environments with respect to air pollution has obviously been exceeded in numerous locations in the country as it is evidenced by the presence of visual and other indicators.

A consequence of replacing gasoline and diesel fuel with natural gas with the attendant air quality benefits is that the internal combustion engine gets an extension in life or utilization for at least another fifty or so years. This observation leads immediately to two obvious questions:

I.   Will the introduction of natural gas, which is an extremely clean fuel compared to gasoline and diesel fuel, delay or even eliminate the introduction of other fuels such as electricity or hydrogen, which can in principle at least be even cleaner than natural gas?

II. Should the *status quo* of gasoline and diesel fuel vehicles be maintained for now in the hope that at a later time electric and hydrogen vehicles may become technologically and economically feasible substitutes, rather than replacing the present vehicles with natural gas vehicles in the immediate future?

These questions will be addressed in the following sections of this chapter and examined in detail so as to leave little doubt whether natural gas is indeed the only practical future automotive fuel. At the same time, a number of future technologies pertaining to vehicular transportation will be considered as part of the analysis to answer the two questions posed above.

ELECTRIC VEHICLES

Vehicles powered by electricity or hydrogen are generally considered to represent to cleanest possible vehicle types at the local (vehicular) level. This may or may not be true, however, on a global scale (generation of electricity or hydrogen) depending on vehicle fuel efficiency as well as the method of generating these fuels.

The commercialization of electric vehicles was a widely pursued goal in the early days of the development of the automobile. The lead acid storage battery was invented and perfected in France[4]. In 1859 Gaston Plante devised a practical battery, which was subsequently improved by Camille Faure so that by 1880 sufficiently heavy currents could be generated to power road vehicles by electricity. A little earlier in 1866, the modern DC electric motor and generator were invented by Werner von Siemens and Karl Wilhelm Siemens in Germany[5]. In 1888 Nikola Tesla built the first single-phase induction motor in the USA and in the following year Dolivo von Dobrovolski built the first three-phase squirrel-cage induction motor in Germany.

Electric cars were commercially produced first in France starting in 1894. However, the only significant manufacturer formed in 1895 to produce electric taxicabs went out of business in 1907. If the electric car found little enthusiasm in France, it briefly played a prominent role in the emerging American automotive industry[4]. The first electric vehicle in the US was built by William Morrison of Des Moines, Iowa in 1891 and driven on the streets of Chicago a year later. In 1894, Henry G. Morris and Pedro G. Salom built in Philadelphia another early American electric car, the "Electrobat". They formed later a company, the Electric Carriage and Wagon Company, which began to operate twelve of its electric vehicles as a fleet of taxicabs on the streets of New York in January 1897.

Another early manufacturer of electric vehicles in the US was Andrew L. Riker, who built an electric tricycle in 1884, formed the Riker Electric Motor Company to make electric motors in 1988, and then organized the Riker Motor Vehicle Company in 1898 at Elizabeth, New Jersey, to make electric cars. Riker, who was one of the foremost early automotive engineers, switched over to designing luxurious gasoline powered automobiles in 1902. Later in 1905, he became one of the founders and the first president of the Society of Automotive Engineers (SAE), an influential group of American automobile trade journalists and engineers dedicated to the improvement of the state of automotive technology through the publication of relevant articles.

The most important early manufacturer of electric and all other motor vehicles was the Pope Manufacturing Company of Hartford, Connecticut, one of the nation's leading bicycle manufacturers, which began producing electric automobiles in 1897. By the end of 1898 Pope has made some 500 electric and 40 gasoline automobiles. In 1899 the Pope motor vehicle division was acquired by the Electric Vehicle Company, a New Jersey holding company established in 1897 by Isaac Rice, a manufacturer of lead acid batteries. The Electric Vehicle Company, which had also acquired the Electric Carriage and Wagon Company in 1897 and the Riker Motor Vehicle Company in 1900, represent one of the most notorious examples of misplaced optimism and consequent overcapitalization, combined with poor technological judgement.

The Electric Vehicle Company formed the so-called Lead Cab Trust in 1899, whose objective was to place electric cabs on the streets of major American cities. Operating companies in New York, Boston, Philadelphia and Chicago were formed. The Electric Vehicle Company, for a short time the leading manufacturer of motor vehicles in the United States, produced 2,000 electric cabs and a few electric trucks in 1899. The ultimate plans of the Lead Cab Trust for 12,000 vehicles were, however, squelched because of the failing performance of its electric cabs when put into service. The company progressively declined and eventually went into receivership as a result of the 1907 recession.

The electric car was the most conservative form of the automobile as it bore the closest resemblance to the horse-drawn vehicle in both appearance and performance. Manufacturers of electric cars closely copied fashionable carriage forms. In the city, the electric vehicle offered some advantages over gasoline and steam powered cars as well as the horse. It was silent, odorless, and easy to control. Therefore, it was especially favored by women drivers, who were concerned foremost about comfort, cleanliness and who had a hard time either controlling a spirited horse or starting a gasoline-powered car with a hand crank and learning to shift gears. These advantages, however, were greatly outweighed by the many liabilities of the electric car. It was far more expensive than the gasoline automobile to manufacture and about three times more expensive to operate. As late as 1910, its range was only 50 to 80 miles on a battery charge, charging facilities were virtually non-existent outside large cities, the storage batteries deteriorated rapidly, and its hill-climbing ability was poor because of the excessive weight of the batteries for the horsepower generated.

It is generally agreed that the demise of the electric car came about with the development of the self-starter by Charles F. Kettering in 1911[6]. The rapid acceptance of the self-starter, called the "ladies' aid", after its introduction in the 1912 Cadillac and the development of the closed car in 1919, which eliminated the need to wear special clothes while motoring, put middle-class women drivers in conventional gasoline automobiles by the droves[7]. Electric cars gradually diminished in numbers and by the 1930s were essentially extinct on the roads of America.

A thirty year hiatus ensued in the development of electric vehicles until about the early 1960s when the interest was renewed. This time, however, the interest in the US was driven primarily by environmental reasons and to a lesser extent by concerns of oil availability. Activity in electric car development in Europe and Japan was driven by a different rational. Although concern over air pollution played undoubtedly an important role, the acute need for smaller cars (to which electric propulsion is ideally adapted) and the higher costs of gasoline carried a much greater weight. By the mid 1960s several development programs were underway in the US In addition to several smaller companies, American Motors (acquired since then by Chrysler), Chrysler, Ford, GM, General Electric and Westinghouse were actively engaged in the effort[8].

Most notably General Motors had built by the late 1960s three experimental vehicles: the Electrovair based on a redesigned GM Corvair, the Electrovan based on a converted GM van and the Stir-Lec I based on a converted 1968 Opel Kadett with a small Stirling engine (hybrid vehicle) to charge the batteries. The principal drawbacks of these vehicles other than cost were the limited number of charge-recharge cycles of the battery and the high weight of the inverter (235 pounds) required to convert battery DC current to AC current for the AC induction motor. Some ten years later, in the early 1980s, another temporary revival occurred when GM announced the development of a sodium-chlorine storage battery breakthrough meeting the high energy density and longevity requirements. However, this breakthrough was proved once more himeric as the safety problems associated with chlorine appeared to be insurmountable.

The third postwar revival of electric vehicle interest began in 1989, when the California Air Resources Board (CARB) announced the ZEV requirement set to go into effect in 1998. Since then a very aggressive development program has been pursued by the three major automotive manufacturers, GM in particular, and a large number of small companies and a variety of entrepreneurs. In 1990, GM unveiled the "Impact", shown in Figure 9-1, a sporty, two-seater vehicle with all the performance characteristics of a gasoline passenger vehicle except range. Table 9-1 summarizes the characteristics of the Impact as of early 1994 after the vehicle had undergone several development phases since 1990. Currently, fifty of these vehicles have been produced and become available to the public for evaluation in selected areas of the country during a two year period ('94 and '95).

The initial plans were to begin production of the Impact vehicles in 1995. In late 1992, however, GM announced the postponement of the production plans for further vehicle evaluation by the public. Apparently, the cost of production of the vehicle appears to have been much higher than originally though so that either GM had to subsidize heavily the production cost of the vehicles or else the demand would become

FIGURE 9-1. The GM Impact two-passenger, state-of-the art, producible Electric Vehicle, whose production has been postponed indefinitely because of the high cost.

virtually non-existent. The initial cost of production of the Impact was estimated at about $60,000 to $70,000, although a cost reduction of about a factor of three was deemed feasible through economies of scale[9]. Unfortunately, even at $20,000 per vehicle the market demand was estimated to be on the order of only 10,000 vehicles per year. This rate would translate to several decades of vehicle sales before the cost reduction due to economies of scale would materialize. However, the results of the on-going evaluation by the public of the fifty "Impact" vehicles may alter the last conclusion.

In 1993, Ford unveiled its electric prototype vehicle, the Ecostar, which is a light utility van. Figure 9-2 shows the Ecostar and Table 9-1 summarizes its main performance characteristics. The cost of the Ecostar was reported to be on the order of $100,000[10]. Early in 1994 Ford announced that it was also postponing plans for further develop-ment of electric vehicles after it had spent over one hundred million

FIGURE 9-2. The Ford Ecostar, a producible light utility electric van, whose production has also been postponed because of the high cost entailed.

dollars for engineering development. However, more than 100 Ecostars have been built and are evaluated by the public in a 30 month program.

Chrysler has also been developing an electric van for $100,000 per vehicle. The performance characteristics of the Chrysler electric van, which is based on the minivan chassis, can be compared against the performance of the 19941/2 model year compressed natural gas ULEV Chrysler minivan that went into production in the spring of 1994[11]. The electric minivan weighs 1,000 lb more, attains a 0-50 mph speed in twice as long time (26 sec vs. 11 sec), has a maximum speed of only 65 mph vs. 109 mph for the natural gas minivan and has only half the range (80 miles vs. 150 miles).

One of the major improvements in technology since the late 1960s has been the development of very low weight and low volume power controllers. The 102 kW inverter of the Impact is on the order of 30 lb and about one cubic foot in volume. The heavy and bulky silicon con-

TABLE 9-1. Performance Characteristics of the GM Impact and the
Ford Ecostar Electric Vehicles as of 1994

Characteristics	GM Impact 3	Ford Ecostar
Vehicle Type	Two Passenger Car	Light Utility Van
Motor Type	3-Phase, AC Induction	3-Phase, AC Induction
Motor Size	137 hp	75 hp
Inverter	102 kW	56 kW
Transmission	Single-speed	Single-speed
Steering	Power Electro-Hydraulic	Manual Rack and Pinion
Brakes	Power Electro-Hydraulic Regenerative, ABS	Power Hydraulic Regenerative
Wheels/Tires	Lightweight Aluminum Low Rolling Resistance	Lightweight Aluminum Low Rolling Resistance
Chassis	Aluminum	Steel
Drag Coefficient	0.19	—
Curb Weight	2910 lb	3200 lb
Payload	400 lb	900 lb
Maximum Speed	75 mph	70 mph
Acceleration	8.5 sec, 0-60 mph	12 sec, 0-50 mph
Battery Type	Lead-Acid	Sodium-Sulfur
Energy Storage*	16.8 kWh	30 kWh
Range EPA City/Hwy*	70 mi	100 mi
Charging	220 V, 6.6 kW Inductive	120/240V, 30 A
Charging Time*	2 to 3 hrs	2 to 3 hrs (min)
Climate Control	Electric Driven Heat Pump Solar Reflective Glass	Electric Driven A/C Resistance Heater Solar Ventilation

(*) To 80% depth of discharge.

trolled rectifiers (SCRs) of the 1960s have been replaced by lightweight and compact Insulated Gate Bipolar Transistors (IGBTs) that have been commercialized in the last decade. Thus, current technology has solved one of the problems associated with electric propulsion, namely the motor controller. This development allows for the use of the more efficient, light-weight, high-speed three-phase induction motor versus the heavier, bulkier and less efficient DC motor. A DC motor requires also the use of a two speed ordinary transmission because its power and torque versus speed characteristic are not sufficient to cover the requisite vehicle speed range (0 to 55 or higher mph). However, the sophisticated induction motor inverter constitutes an expensive component of the modern electric vehicle. On the other hand, the AC induction motor can offer an electrical vehicle performance comparable to that of the gasoline vehicle. It should be also mentioned that in recent years another motor has emerged as a competitor to the induction motor. This is the brushless permanent DC motor which is commutated electronically using solid state devices[12]. The high commutation frequency required is obtained by the use of IGBTs as well, which result also in an expensive system.

In general, the high cost of electronic controllers of state-of-the-art electric vehicles is due to the amount of semiconductor silicon present in these devices. This observation then poses the natural question: "What does it take to bring down these costs?". The answer may be obtained by considering computers, whose cost is also a function of the amount of semiconductor silicon in each device.

The dramatic reduction in the cost of computers in the last three decades is not the result of reducing the cost of silicon, but rather the amount of silicon in each unit. This has been attained through the development of the integrated circuit and the evolution of microelectronics, whereby an ever increasing number of functions can be accommodated per unit surface area or unit volume of semiconductor silicon. Thus, a reduction in the cost of electric vehicle controllers implies a reduction in the amount of semiconductor silicon per unit, which in turn can be attained by downsizing the vehicle maximum power requirements.

However, the power requirement of a vehicle is roughly proportional to its weight. For example, let us consider three GM vehicle cases: the subcompact GEO Metro, the compact Chevrolet Corsica, the midsize Chevrolet Lumina and the full size Chevrolet Caprice. Table 9-2 summarizes the weight and engine power characteristics of these vehicles[13]. Moreover, the corresponding parameters for the GM Impact and the experimental lightweight (carbon fiber composite) GM Ultralite powered by a gasoline engine are also included in the Table 9-2[14].

It is apparent that the GM Impact has a higher performance than the bulk of production vehicles, and that the lightweight gasoline vehicle has an even better one. Thus, assuming an electric powered vehicle with the weight of the GM Ultralite and the performance of production gasoline vehicles, the reduction in semiconductor silicon for its controller would

TABLE 9-2. Mass to Power Ratio of Selected GM Gasoline Production Vehicles, the GM Impact and Ultralite and a Hypothetical Light Weight Electric Vehicle

Vehicle	Mass[1]		Power		Mass/Power	
	(lb)	(kg)	(hp)	(kW)	(lb/hp)	(kg/kW)
GEO Metro	1617	735	55	41	29.4	17.9
Chevrolet Corsica	2695	1225	95	71	28.4	17.2
Chevrolet Lumina	3190	1450	110	82	29.0	17.7
Chevrolet Caprice	3927	1785	170	127	23.1	14.1
GM Impact	2910	1323	137	102	21.2	13.0
GM Ultralite	1400	635	111	82	12.6	7.7
{Ultralite Electric}[2]	1400	635	54	40	26.0	16.0

1. Curb weight. 2. Hypothetical with performance of production vehicles.

have been over 60% compared to the Impact. Consequently, the weight in an electric vehicle needs to be reduced in order to bring down the cost of associated electronics and motor by an almost proportional amount.

Weight reduction in an electric vehicle could be the result of employing alternative materials for the vehicle body other than steel and of reducing the weight of batteries. The reduction in chassis weight will be considered in the next section. The reduction in battery weight will be addressed in the remainder of this section. Since the early days of electric vehicles battery weight has always been one of their main drawbacks. Eighty years later the picture has not changed very much despite the progress in materials science and electronics.

An ideal rechargeable battery for electric vehicles would be one that is capable of high energy and high power densities at ambient temperatures, that has a high electrochemical efficiency (low internal losses), and that can utilize inexpensive, safe materials in a simple configuration with a long life. Figure 9-3 shows the specific energy and specific power of battery systems that are viewed as the leading candidates for electric vehicle propulsion for one reason or another. These reasons will be discussed shortly. However, the lead-acid battery, of all these systems, is today the only viable option in terms of technological maturity, performance and cost as it was at the turn of the century.

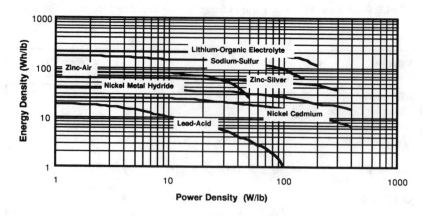

FIGURE 9-3. Specific Energy Storage and Specific Power of Various Battery Types for Vehicular Propulsion.

All the salient properties of the various battery systems considered for electric vehicle propulsion have been qualified and quantified in Table 9-3[15][16][17][18]. Besides the advanced maintenance free (sealed) lead acid (Pb-Acid) battery, the following batteries are considered: Nickel-Cadmium (NiCd), Nickel-Metal Hydride (NiMH), Sodium-Sulfur (NaS), Zinc-Air (Zn-Air) and Lithium-Polymer (Li-Org.). The nickel cadmium battery was invented in Sweden in 1900, but it was not until about 1944 that it was perfected in Germany for starting jet aircraft engines[15][19]. Over the years this application has remained the main use of NiCd batteries. The Boeing 777, for example, to be introduced in 1995 is equipped with four sealed NiCd batteries. Probably the high cost of cadmium and the relative scarcity of it have prevented NiCd batteries from large-scale commercial uses, even though they are the most versatile commercial batteries available today.

In recent years, there has been considerable effort to develop an alternative to the NiCd by replacing the cadmium anode with an alloy of metals (titanium, zirconium, vanadium, etc.) that have the ability to absorb hydrogen. This modification results in the so called nickel-metal hydride battery with somewhat improved performance characteristics over a NiCd battery requiring periodic maintenance (adding water) and a significantly improved performance over a sealed NiCd bat-

TABLE 9-3. Current Characteristics and Ratings (E = Excellent, G = Good, F = Fair and P = Poor) of Selected Battery Systems Considered for Vehicular Propulsion

Characteristic	Pb-Acid	NiCd/NiMH	NaS	Zn-Air	Li-Org.
Specific Energy, Wh/lb	16	29/38	45	45	45
Specific Power, W/lb	110	110/110	50	18	90
Energy Density, Wh/gal	300	380/380	490	320	285
Power Density, kW/gal	2.3	3.0/3.0	0.5	0.2	0.6
Cycle Life, #	500	2000/<500	<500	<500	<500
Cost, $/kWh[1]	100	450/ 250	150	150	150-500
Recharge Time	G	E / E	G	G	E
Servicing	E	G / E	E	F	E
Simplicity	E	E / E	F	F	E
Recycling	F	F / E	E	E	G
Material Availability	E	P / E	E	E	G
Safety	E	G / E	F	G	E

1. This is the estimated long term cost for all batteries except the lead-acid one. Present cost of the nickel batteries is 2.5 times higher, of NaS and Zinc-Air 3 to 4 times higher, and of the lithium polymer probably 10 times higher than the long term cost.

Note. All batteries are sealed except the NiCd and Zn-Air. Sealed NiCd's are available, but their specific energy is then reduced to about 16 Wh/lb.

tery[16][20][21]. Incidentally, in the charging mode of a NiMH battery hydrogen from the splitting of water in the aqueous potassium hydroxide electrolyte is absorbed in the anode forming a metal hydride. During the discharge hydrogen leaves the anode and hydroxyl ions leave the nickel cathode to combine and reconstitute the water. Unfortunately, the cost of the NiMH battery is still high, even though it is lower than that of the NiCd battery. The life of the NiMH battery is also shorter compared to a NiCd. The only two major improvements of the NiMH battery are the replacement of the toxic cadmium metal with others less toxic and the ability to deliver high power and energy density in a maintenance free configuration (sealed battery).

The sodium-sulfur battery was pioneered in the 1960s in the USA by General Electric and the Ford Motor Company[15][18][21]. It is a high temperature battery (550°F) with the electrodes (sodium and sulfur) in the liquid state and a solid electrolyte (beta alumina) that allows the transport of sodium ions only. While the materials are readily available and inexpensive and the performance is good, the major drawbacks of the NaS battery have been the failure of the solid electrolyte limiting its life and the high operational temperature that must be maintained even when the battery is not in use.

The zinc-air battery, which was developed initially by Gulf General Atomic in the 1960s and more recently by the Dreisbach ElectroMotive, has a serious performance drawback (low power density), requires maintenance (replacement of the spent electrolyte) and has a very short life due to the degradation of the cathode by the carbon dioxide in air[15][22]. Other metal-air batteries, notably the aluminum-air one promoted in recent years by ALCOA, have similar drawbacks[15][23].

The battery anode material that is most attractive from an energy standpoint is lithium. However, lithium is a very reactive metal that is incompatible with an aqueous electrolyte. Thus, the electrolyte may be a molten salt of lithium or an organic material. One concept that received a good deal of attention by General Motors several years ago was the lithium-chlorine battery, which uses a molten lithium anode, a molten lithium chloride electrolyte and a chlorine (gas) cathode[15]. While the performance of this battery has been very good, further development was abandoned because of the toxicity problem posed by the chlorine gas in the battery. More recently the attention has been focused on lithium organic electrolyte batteries. In particular, the use of a solid polymer electrolyte is currently investigated as the ultimate vehicular electric energy storage system. The polymer electrolyte, which is conductive to lithium ions only, must have typically a thickness of about 10 micrometers (0.4 thousands of an inch) and must be defect (pinhole) free along with the equally thin lithium anode and metal oxide (e.g., manganese dioxide or vanadium oxides) cathode[18][21]. This is by no means a small materials science task. If a lithium ion conductive polymer electrolyte can be successfully developed, it will then take one to two decades for the battery to be commercialized[24].

It is apparent that the progress in the development of electrochemical storage for vehicular propulsion has been extremely slow and has not been able yet to move away from the lead-acid battery. In fact, recent developments, if proven viable, may further extent the practicality of lead-acid batteries over any emerging competitor systems[18]. The use of fiberglass filaments coated with lead to form a woven lead-acid battery plate grid have resulted in a higher specific energy (19 Wh/lb to 25 Wh/lb) and extension of life (over 900 cycles to over 500 cycles, respectively), albeit at an increased cost ($150/kWh)[25].

In 1991, the US Department of Energy, the Big Three US Automakers and the Electric Power Research Institute (EPRI) formed the United States Advanced Battery Consortium (USABC) to fund the development of several advanced technologies. A total investment of $260 million is slated from 1991 to 1995 and the technical goals for the program are highly ambitious, if not unrealistic[26]. By 1994, USABC wants its subcontractors to demonstrate the feasibility of batteries with double or triple the specific energy of lead-acid batteries. By the end of the decade it wants a battery that can supply a vehicle with range and acceleration equal to that of a gasoline car and last for the lifetime of the vehicle. Needless to say that the 1994 milestone has been missed, although significant progress has been made toward that goal.

Nickel metal hydride and sodium sulfur batteries qualify for the first milestone and lithium polymer electrolyte for the second one. In the United States, the Ovonic Battery Company of Troy, MI and SAFT America are currently developing the NiMH battery under USABC funding. The NaS battery is now solidly a European technology with Asea-Brown-Boveri (ABB) establishing pilot plants in Germany. The lithium-polymer battery development, which is still in the laboratory stage of evolution, is pursued by three teams of companies headed by W. R. Grace, 3M and Delco Remy, respectively and the participation of one of the national laboratories, the Lawrence Berkeley Laboratory (LBL), for basic research.

Another potentially viable option for storing energy for vehicular propulsion is through the exploitation of mechanical storage techniques, of which the high speed rotating flywheel offers perhaps the most convenient method[15][18]. The kinetic energy built up in the wheel is transferred gradually as needed to an electric generator and thence to a motor. The system is regenerated by bringing the flywheel back to maximum speeds during charging with electric power fed to the generator which acts then as a motor. From a vehicular standpoint, an attractive feature of a flywheel is its capacity to give up its energy very rapidly. Moreover, the life of a flywheel can conceivably be made to exceed that of the vehicle it powers. The constraints on a flywheel are the stress limitations of the flywheel itself that place an upper limit to the specific energy that it can store and the gyroscopic effects resulting from the conservation of angular momentum.

A simple analysis shows that in order to store the maximum energy in a given flywheel mass, it makes sense to have several smaller diameter flywheels rather than a single large one. The energy stored in a given geometry flywheel is proportional to its mass, but it increases as the square of its rotational speed. Moreover, the maximum stress of the flywheel occurring at the rim is proportional to the diameter as well as the rotational speed of the wheel. Thus, for a given maximum allowable flywheel material stress, one can meet the stress constraint with a higher rotational speed and a smaller diameter thereby maximizing the energy stored for a given total mass.

The use of composite materials and in particular carbon fibers with a very high tensile strength allow for a much higher specific energy storage than the more traditional steel flywheels. Unfortunately, the use of several smaller flywheels reduces the specific energy and the energy density because of the need for separate housing, motor and controls for each unit. The housing is required for performance as well as safety reasons. At the high rotational velocities envisioned for practical flywheels one has to maintain a vacuum of at least 10^{-6} atm in order to avoid frictional heating of the rotating wheel. Moreover, a catastrophic failure of the wheel has to be also contained, although the use of carbon fiber composites reduce significantly the danger of injury as the latter material, unlike steel, tends to disintegrate into small fibers. The gyroscopic or inertial problem in driving up and down hills or in turning right and left, depending on the orientation of the flywheels, could be eliminated by either using opposed counter-rotating flywheels or gimbals suspension at considerable system weight increase and complexity.

In 1980, Canada initiated a program to design, develop and test several high energy density composite fiber flywheels for vehicular applications. These flywheels stored 1.33 kWh and were rated at 105 kW and 100,000 charge/discharge cycles. The maximum speed was 22,000 rpm and the outer diameter was 24 inches. The hub (12.6 in. OD) and central ring (13.2 in. OD) are made of 7075-T651 aluminum, and the rotor consists of S2-Glass composite internal ring (18 in. OD) and E/XAS Carbon external ring (24 in. OD). A magnetic bearing suspension is utilized to further reduce frictional losses, while the housing vacuum is 10^{-5} Torr (1 atm = 760 Torr). The cycling loading efficiencies are usually 99% or higher. The specific energy is 21.5 Wh/lb. Specific energies up to 36 Wh/lb are deemed feasible in a practical design according to the Canadian program.

In the last several years similar developments are also taking place in the USA. In 1994, American Flywheel Systems unveiled the design of a vehicular carbon fiber flywheel, which was manufactured by Honeywell and was installed in a Chrysler vehicle[28]. No flywheel specifications were released other than a potential maximum speed of 200,000 rpm, and that on an equal mass basis a flywheel electric vehicle could more then triple the range of a lead-acid battery powered one, implying a potential specific energy of over 45 Wh/lb. However, the consensus seems to be that electric cars using the flywheel technology for energy storage will not be ready for the market until well into the next century.

The need of composites and in particular carbon fibers to establish themselves in the engineering consciousness is a prerequisite in order to achieve an economic scale of production. For example, carbon fiber cost $14 per lb in 1988 with a potential price reduction to $5 per lb on a commercial scale using polyacrylonitrite (PAN) as the feedstock material[29]. The present cost of a carbon fiber flywheel storage system is upward of $3,000 per kWh with a potential reduction to $1,000 per kWh. Even the long term cost of flywheel energy storage is at best 10 times as expensive as lead-acid battery energy storage, albeit the life of a flywheel may be several times that of a lead-acid battery. Thus, an initial cost of $15,000 may be required for energy storage alone in a flywheel equipped electric vehicle. This is a prohibitively high incremental cost, even if it provides the range of a present day car.

Other energy storage schemes are possible, besides electrochemical and mechanical storage. Thermal storage is one such possibility. It appears, however, that the use of an on-board chemical fuel (storage) and the use of an appropriate conversion engine into electricity may offer the only viable option for zero emission vehicles with comparable performance characteristics to the present day gasoline ones.

HYDROGEN VEHICLES

Hydrogen, whose properties as automotive fuel have been examined in an earlier chapter, is the most abundant element in the universe comprising some 80% of it with the remainder being mostly helium — all the other heavier elements account for less than 1% of the mass of the universe. The major source of hydrogen on earth is none other than water, which constitutes 2.4% of the mass of the earth or some 3.1×10^{21} lb in total[30]. Water contains about 11% hydrogen with the remainder being oxygen. Hydrogen as a chemical element was discovered in 1766 by H. Cavendish in England[31]. Oxygen was discovered a few years later by the British scientist and preacher Joseph Priestley and the Swiss-German apothecary Carl Wilhelm Scheele, while the French chemist Antoine Laurent Lavoisier was the first to demonstrate in 1785 that hydrogen and oxygen constitute the basic elements of water.

In 1800 two English scientists, William Nicholson and Sir Anthony Carlisle, discovered electrolysis — the breaking down of water into its two constituent elements by passing an electrical current through it. The discovery of electrolysis occurred only a few weeks after the Italian physicist Alessandro Volta built the first electric cell (battery).

The history of hydrogen as motive fuel can be traced as early as 1820, when a clergyman and member of the Philosophical Society, the Reverend William Cecil, presented a lengthy treatise "On the Application of Hydrogen Gas to Produce Moving Power in Machinery" to the dons of Cambridge University in England[31]. However, the discussion of hydrogen as a fuel did not remain the exclusive purview of scientists. Jules Vern, the famous French science fiction author, gives a remarkable prescient description in *The Mysterious Island* written in 1874 of how hydrogen would become the world's chief fuel. Hydrogen would have water as its source by decomposing the latter into its elements with electricity. Of course, Verne did not explain what the primary energy source would be to generate the electricity necessary to decompose water.

The 1920s and 1930s witnessed a flowering of interest, especially in Germany and England, in hydrogen as fuel. On the conceptual side, J. B. S. Haldane, the brilliant Scottish scientist, gave in 1923 a famous lecture at Cambridge University in which he advocated hydrogen as the fuel of the future derived from wind power by electrolysis, liquefied and stored in underground cryogenic reservoirs[31][32]. This view was repeated in more technical detail in 1938 by the American helicopter pioneer Igor Sikorski. On the practical side, F. Lawaczeck, R. Erren, K. Weil, J. E. Noeggerath, H. Honnef and H. Niederreither in Germany were actively pursuing various aspects of hydrogen research and were advocating the use of hydrogen as fuel[31][32]. The best known of all these early hydrogen advocates has been Rudolph Erren whose hydrogen fueled internal combustion engines were powering several thousand vehicles in both Germany and England in the 1930s.

Hydrogen became of interest again in the early 1950s, when F. T. Bacon, a British scientist developed the first practical hydrogen-air fuel cell — the first fuel cell was constructed in 1829 by the Englishman W. Grove, but it produced only water and no electricity[31][32]. The fuel cell was to become later the cornerstone for power generation in the US space program. In 1959, A. M. Weinberg was the first American to propose the use hydrogen as a vehicular fuel[33]. In 1965, E. Justi in Germany proposed the concept of hydrogen from land-based solar farms along the Mediterranean supplying far-off cities in northern Europe. In 1970, the term "hydrogen economy" was first coined by J. O' M. Bockris during a discussion on alternative transportation fuels to eliminate pollution at the General Motors Technical Center in Warren, Michigan[31][32]. Since the beginning of the 1970s, interest in hydrogen began to grow by leaps and bounds[31]. Several programs have been underway in the US, Germany and Japan to produce practical means for the use of hydrogen as an automotive fuel. The most unique of these programs will be reviewed in the remainder of this section.

Starting in the mid 1960s and for the next ten years R. Billings and several others converted and/or modified gasoline powered vehicles to run on hydrogen. These events marked the beginning of hydrogen use as a potential automotive fuel in the Unites States[31][32][34]. These attempts demonstrated the feasibility of burning hydrogen in an internal combustion engine, although initially two serious problems emerged. One problem was that of engine backfiring and the other had to do with reaching a decision as to the best way to meter the fuel flow. The backfiring problem has been resolved by introducing tiny water droplets into the air/fuel charge before the latter enters the combustion chamber. The vaporization of the water following the charge ignition absorbs energy, thereby reducing the peak combustion temperature and quenching all auto-ignition phenomena.

An added benefit of water introduction is the reduction in the formation of NO_x, the only pollutant gas from the vehicle tailpipe. If the water droplet injection rate is adjusted such that the peak combustion temperature falls below 2372°F, then the amount of NO_x emitted from the hydrogen engine may fall below 0.02 gram per mile. The required water to hydrogen mass ratio to attain this NO_x reduction is on the order of about fifteen to one. However, this reduction makes no use of a catalytic converter. Given that the latter can reduce the amount of NO_x form the engine exhaust to the tailpipe exhaust by better then a factor of 50, a water to hydrogen mass ratio of 8 and the use of a catalytic converter may result in the same tailpipe emission of 0.02 gram per mile. It may appear that too much water is required to accomplish the task of reducing NO_x emissions to an ultra low level. However, hydrogen has a very high energy density. Thus, a vehicle with a 40 mpg fuel efficiency would require 8 kg of hydrogen for a 320 mile range. The required 64 kg of water for the reduction of NO_x emissions to an ultra low level is significant, but not excessive.

The metering system of the hydrogen fuel flow may consist of conventional carburation or of fuel injection of a similar nature used with other gaseous fuels such as propane or natural gas. One of the disadvantages of converting a gasoline engine to run on hydrogen is the potential loss of power because during the intake stroke a large percentage of the air-fuel volume is occupied by hydrogen compared to less than 1% in the case of gasoline. Thus, there is not enough oxygen to react with the hydrogen fuel to generate power. The solution to this problem is to have direct hydrogen fuel injection into the engine cylinder[34][35]. This may be accomplished by placing position sensors on the crankshaft to help synchronize the injection with the engine cycles. However, the directly injected hydrogen fuel must be compressed anywhere from 10 to 20 atm in order to reduce its volume, thereby reducing the direct injection port orifice size and also producing a turbo-charging effect. Direct hydrogen

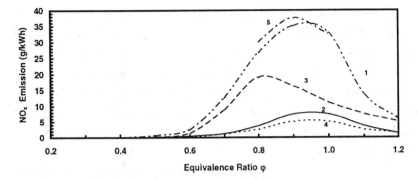

FIGURE 9-4. Typical Values for the NO_x Emission of a Hydrogen Powered Internal Combustion Engine as a Function of the Equivalence Ratio: 1. External Mixture Formation (Carburation)[36]; 2. External Mixture Formation with Water Injection[36]; 3. Direct Fuel Injection[37]; 4. Direct Fuel Injection with Best Obtainable Results[38][39]; and 5. Typical Data for Conventional Gasoline Engines.

injection not only regains the engine power, but it eliminates backfiring as well.

The use of direct injection can also be employed to reduce the NO_x emission without having to resort to water injection. Because hydrogen has a vary wide flammability range in air from 5% to 75% by volume (vs. 2% to 8% by volume for gasoline), an internal combustion engine can operate on hydrogen with high amount of excess air (lean fuel mixture). The optimal efficiency of a hydrogen fueled motor is achieved at an equivalence ratio of about 0.4, which is particularly advantageous for NO_x emission reduction as the data in Figure 9-4 show[35]. Thus, the use of direct injection appears to be the ideal engineering solution with respect to the replacement of gasoline with hydrogen as a fuel in an internal combustion engine.

Hydrogen has a considerably low octane number compared to all other fuels of about 60[35](*). Thus, the ICE compression ratio is typically between 6:1 and 7:1 for hydrogen fuel. However, the much higher hydrogen flame velocity compared to gasoline and the extremely fast

---

(*). The research octane number (RON) of hydrogen is in excess of 130. However, the motor octane number (MON) of hydrogen may be very low. For any fuel the RON is always larger than the MON. Moreover, the octane number of a fuel is defined as the arithmetic mean of its RON and MON ratings. The large difference between the RON and MON for hydrogen is the result of the test procedures by which each of these two numbers are measured. The RON is measured at a low engine speed, a low fuel-air mixture temperature and a fixed spark timing, while the MON is measured at a high engine speed, a high mixture temperature and a variable spark timing.

mixing of hydrogen with air results in a more efficient fuel combustion process. The combustion efficiency is, of course, augmented by the excess air so that the total increase in vehicle fuel efficiency with hydrogen ranges between 25% and 40% over that with gasoline according to a variety of test data in the US and Germany[32][35]. Finally, the wear on a hydrogen powered ICE is virtually nill as there are no solid residues in the cylinders and hydrogen does not cause thinning of the engine oil.

The only technological disadvantage of hydrogen as a vehicular propulsion fuel in conjunction with an internal combustion engine is the problem of the on-board fuel storage for a range comparable to a gasoline fueled vehicle. This issue will be addressed shortly. Hydrogen despite its high specific energy of about 15.2 kWh/lb (52,100 BTU/lb) has an energy density of 320 BTU/scf, which is probably the lowest among all fuels. Thus the volume associated with the on-board the vehicle hydrogen storage is obviously problematical.

There exist several possibilities for hydrogen storage besides the obvious methods of compression or liquefaction. These options include storage in the form of hydrides with suitable materials (metals) as well as storage in chemicals with high hydrogen content. Obviously, in any of these cases means must also be developed to remove or separate the hydrogen from these materials and chemicals. These means comprise invariably some type of chemical reaction. Table 9-4 compares the specific energy and energy density of different types of hydrogen storage excluding the mass and the volume of any containment or other required components[35][40][41]. The comparable energy storage characteristics of traditional automotive fuels are also included.

It is interesting to note that of the various hydrogen storage techniques only liquid hydrogen and the metal hydrides offer a comparable energy density to CNG and LNG. In reality, however, inclusion of a cryogenic tank or the hydride enclosure reduces the theoretical energy density for either one of these two systems. Thus, the specific energy is reduced to about 11,000 BTU/lb for liquid hydrogen and about 2,500 BTU/lb for compressed hydrogen. Finally, the Fe-Ti hydride appears to be the most practical hydride in terms of cost as well as operational temperature ($<100^\circ$C) requirements. All the other hydrogen storage tech-

TABLE 9-4. Comparison of Specific Energy and Specific Volume of Various Alternative Means to Store Hydrogen On-Board a Vehicle and Comparison to Traditional Automotive Fuels

Method/Material	H_2 Storage Capacity (% weight)	Specific[1] Energy (BTU/lb)	Energy[1] Density (BTU/gal)
Hydrogen Fuels			
Compressed H_2 (3000psi)	100	51,570	7,750
Liquid H_2 (-418°F)	100	51,570	29,720
Adsorbed H_2 (-112°F, 750psi)[2]	2	1,030	3,880
Magnesium Hydride	7	3,610	43,950
Magnesium-Nickel Hydride	3	1,550	34,900
Iron-Titanium Hydride (Fe-Ti)	2	1,030	41,350
Methylcyclohexane ($C_6H_{11}CH_3$)	6	3,100	1,300
Methanol (CH_3OH)	12.5	6,450	7,750
Ammonia (NH_3)	17.6	9,070	9,050
Hydrazine(N_2H_4)	12.5	6,450	7,750
CNG (3,000psi)	25	12,890	9,050
LNG (-258°F)	25	12,890	19,400
Traditional Fuels			
Gasoline	N/A	20,130	115,000
Diesel Fuel	N/A	19,820	128,400
CNG (3,000psi)	N/A	23,700	34,900
CNG (3,600psi)	N/A	23,700	41,870
LNG (-258°F)	N/A	23,700	74,950

1. Specific energy refers only to the hydrogen energy contained in a fuel divided by the total mass of the fuel (hydrogen and non-hydrogen components). Energy density refers the hydrogen energy contained in the fuel divided by the total volume of the fuel. All masses and volumes refer to the fuel only and exclude the mass and volume of containers and associated equipment. In the traditional fuels the total energy content is considered.
2. Experimental technique making use of superactivated carbon as a hydrogen adsorber at low temperatures and elevated pressures.

niques require an on-board the vehicle chemical reaction to yield hydrogen and have not received as much attention because the added volume requirements make them rather unrealistic prospects. Even assuming a very efficient internal combustion engine powered vehicle with an average energy use of 2875 BTU/mi (equivalent to a 40 mpg gasoline vehicle), a 320 mile vehicle range requires the on-board storage of about 18 lb of hydrogen with a volume of 80 gal or 8.5 cubic feet either as a liquid or as a hydride. In the latter case, the weight of the Fe-Ti hydride would be more than 1100 lb. Thus, the range of all practical hydrogen powered vehicles developed up to now with an internal combustion engine as a propulsion plant is typically on the order of 100 miles.

Since the early 1970s several types of production vehicles have been converted to run on hydrogen in the US, Germany and Japan[31][32][34][35]. Liquid hydrogen was the favored form of storage in the earlier days, but in more recent times the Fe-Ti hydride appears to have become the more desirable storage technology. While both of these technologies are roughly comparable in terms of energy density, the hydride tanks can be reconfigured easier from a packaging point of view in a vehicle. Moreover, the safety issues associated with the storage of a cryogenic liquid have never been resolved to point that the technology could be employed on a daily basis operation by the average individual — the maintenance of liquid hydrogen storage systems associated with the US space program since the late 1950s as well as with the possible future use in commercial aircraft cannot be exercised by an automobile operator.

The evaporative losses of even a very good, but relatively small, cryogenic tank may amount to 2% per day. Thus, a significant loss of hydrogen fuel will occur amounting to about 10% of each full tank, on the average, depending on driving patterns. Last but not least, liquid hydrogen is a very energy intensive material to obtain. It takes a minimum (theoretical) 6,000 BTU/lb of energy to liquefy hydrogen and 16,700 BTU/lb in actual large scale liquefaction facilities[35]. Thus, it takes 32% of the energy content of hydrogen to liquefy it. The actual liquefaction energy use could be reduced in the future to a potential 10,800 BTU/lb by employing more efficient technologies, but it would still amount to 21% of the fuel energy content. Even if natural gas is used as the hydrogen source, hydrogen liquefaction is a highly energy wasteful process. Consequently, it is impractical to liquefy hydrogen for automotive fuel uses.

Currently, two major automotive manufacturers, Mercedes-Benz in Germany and Mazda in Japan, have developed concept hydrogen powered vehicles based respectively on the 200 Series and RX-7 production vehicles. Both vehicles use a Fe-Ti hydride storage system. Figure 9-5 shows the Mercedes-Benz 230E with the Fe-Ti hydride hydrogen storage and all the other modifications of the internal combustion engine necessary to operate on this fuel. A combination of direct hydrogen injection and water injection into the engine is employed to minimize NO_x emissions. The construction of the Fe-Ti hydride tank is also shown in Figure 9-5. Each of the cylindrical tanks contains hydride powder with a porous central tube supplying and withdrawing hydrogen. Disc-like fins improve heat transfer between the stored hydride and the heating /cooling medium. Typically, hydrogen gas supplied to an empty storage system up to a 750 psi pressure will react with the metal power to form the hydride and will release heat that must be removed to maintain an appropriate for the hydride formation reaction system temperature below $120^{\circ}F$. In order to remove hydrogen from a charged system, heat must be supplied to maintain the temperature above $120^{\circ}F$ and pressure must be reduced so as to lead to the decomposition of the hydride.

The aforementioned limitations of hydrogen storage on-board a vehicle coupled with the low efficiency of an internal combustion engine give hydrogen vehicles a practical range of about 100 to 120 miles. The obvious question is whether one has to develop a more efficient propulsion system or a better hydrogen storage system or both if hydrogen is to become technologically feasible as a transportation fuel - costs will not be of concern until after the strictly technological issues can be advanced.

The development of a radically different hydrogen storage system than any of the present ones would require a technological breakthrough whose occurrence cannot be predicted with any certainty. On the other hand, the possible development of any of the known alternative automotive propulsion systems can proceed in small incremental steps with the potential for eventual success. Consequently, most of the research is currently concentrated on the development of alternative automotive propulsion systems. In particular, two alternative automotive propulsion systems have been pursued by industry, academia and the government with a significant research investment since the early 1960s. These two alternative automotive propulsion systems include the gas turbine and the fuel cell.

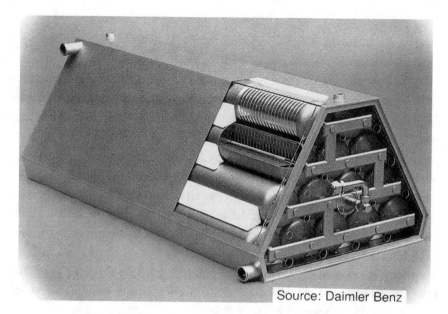

Source: Daimler Benz

Typical Construction of a Fe-Ti Hydride H2 Storage System

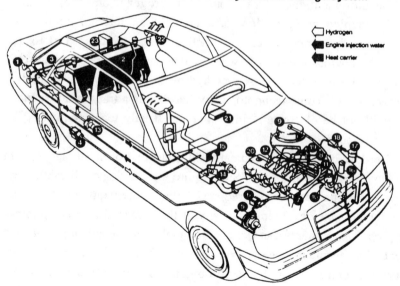

1	Refueling connections	8	Hydrogen metering device	17 Water feed pump
2	Metal hydride hydrogen storage unit	9	Differential pressure regulator	18 Filter
3	Blowoff valve (50 bar)	10	Hydrogen distributor	19 Water metering device
4	Solenoid valve	11	Intake manifold	20 Water injection nozzles
5	Pressure reducing valve	12	Hydrogen injection nozzles	21 Information display
6	Solenoid valve	13	Circulating pump	22 Ventilation outlet for storage system
7	Flow meter	14	Exhaust gas flap (pneum, actuated)	23 Electronic control unit
		15	Exhaust gas/water heat injection system	

FIGURE 9-5. Mercedes-Benz 230E with Hydrogen Fuel Stored in a Fe-Ti Hydride System which is Shown also in Detail (Source: Daimler-Benz).

A gas turbine constitutes the third basic type of an internal combustion engine[8][42]. Unlike, the spark ignition (gasoline) and compression ignition (diesel) engines, however, gas turbines operate in a continuous combustion mode. Similarly to the other two engines, gas turbines have zero torque at zero speed and therefore require a motor/battery ignition system. In a gas turbine the hot gases produced by the burning of the fuel/air mixture are expanded through a turbine to provide power. The basic gas-turbine configuration consists of a turbocompressor, a combustor and a turboexpander. The turbocompressor may in principle be on the same shaft as the expander. A single shaft gas turbine type is appropriate for fixed speed operation such as propelling an aircraft. At low shaft speed the compressor will be inefficient and the output torque very low. Thus, a more practical arrangement for an automotive application, where variable loads and variable speeds are required, is the compound (split shaft) or "free" turbine with a two-stage expander as shown in Figure 9-6[8]. The first stage is simply the power supply for the compressor, which operates at constant speed regardless of load.

An alternative design of a more efficient single shaft turbine under partial loads is the differential turbine shown also in Figure 9-6[8]. In this design a transmission or torque corrector is added so that the compressor fan and turbine are interconnected by means of a differential gear. The compressor is connected to a central sun gear, the turbine to an annular or ring gear, and the power output shaft to the intermediate planetary gears. The objective is to maintain the compressor speed constant while varying the turbine speed from zero to several thousand rpm. The differential gas turbine can provide up to 65% reduction in fuel consumption with decreasing output speed while still providing maximum torque on the output shaft[43].

Some of the main advantages of a gas turbine as an automotive powerplant are its light weight, compactness and reliability. The major disadvantage of a gas turbine, however, is its extremely low efficiency under no load or partial load, which constitute a considerable fraction of the actual operation in an automotive application. Another advantage of a gas turbine engine over the spark ignition and diesel engines is that the latter require fuels with nearly exact composition. Gas turbines can

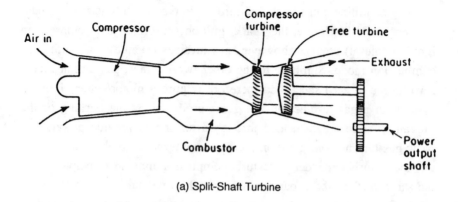

(a) Split-Shaft Turbine

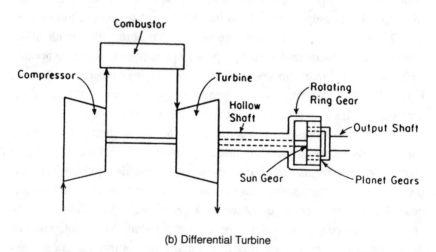

(b) Differential Turbine

FIGURE 9-6. Schematics of Gas Turbines for Automotive Applications: (a) Split-Shaft Turbine; and (b) Differential Single-Shaft Turbine. The Three Fundamental Components of a Gas Turbine, i.e., Compressor, Combustor and Expander (Turbine), are Discernible in both Configurations.

operate satisfactorily with a variety of fuels, including kerosene, diesel fuel, natural gas, hydrogen and others.

Since, the compressor of a gas turbine supplies several times the amount of the theoretically required air for complete fuel combustion, the exhaust gases are relatively free form smoke and have much reduced hydrocarbon and carbon monoxide concentrations compared to the piston engines. However, the emission of nitrous oxides may be significantly higher. A final problem of employing gas turbines in applications where small amount of power is required, under the range of 50 hp to 100 hp, may be that efficiency and weight considerations make them impractical. Also, gas turbines are significantly more expensive than the other two types of internal combustion engines. Typically a jet aircraft turbine costs currently some \$250 per hp, while a mass produced automotive gas turbine may cost \$125 per hp in the future. This latter cost is still five or six times higher than the cost of a good spark ignition engine.

Several attempts in the past by the major automakers to develop automotive gas turbine propulsion systems, in the 200 hp class or higher, have failed to produce viable competitors to the spark ignition and compression ignition engines, although gas turbines have been found to be lighter and more compact than comparable supercharged diesel engines[8][42]. In the last decade or so research on automotive gas turbines has concentrated in raising the operating turbine gas inlet temperature from about 1900°F, which is the limit for today's metal superalloys, to 2450°F in order to increase the thermodynamic and consequently fuel efficiency. However, this higher operating temperature requires the coating and/or replacement of all internal metallic surfaces with heat-resistant ceramic materials such as silicon carbide and silicon nitride. The processes involved are inherently complex, require expensive materials and need further engineering development[42]. Higher temperature gas turbines are developed by several manufacturers. For example, Ford and Garrett are developing the AGT-101 turbine for passenger car use by the mid 1990s under the sponsorship of the US DOE[42]. This is a single-shaft differential turbine to be used in conjunction with a continuously variable transmission for maximum drivetrain efficiency.

The interest in gas turbines has been also revived recently with regard to the hybrid electric vehicle propulsion system. There are two types of a hybrid drivetrain configurations. The first one is the parallel hybrid, which means that the vehicle has two operating systems: an internal combustion engine or other propulsion system and an electric motor. The propulsion system, deriving its energy from fuel stored on-board the vehicle, is used to give the vehicle normal acceleration, maximum speed and operating range. The electric motor, deriving electricity from batteries or flywheels on-board the vehicle, is used for pure electrical operation in instances of lower power needs such as in city traffic at lower speeds.

The second type of hybrid operation is the serial hybrid which consists of only one drivetrain system, namely the electric motor one. Electricity is still stored in batteries or flywheels (technically electricity is converted during storage into chemical or mechanical energy, respectively). In city traffic (intracity traffic) the electric storage makes it possible to operate the vehicle as a pure electric one for the shorter distances and with performance which enables the vehicle to keep up with the rest of the traffic. When the vehicle is driven on the freeway over long distances (intercity traffic), the ICE or other powerplant through a generator is charging continuously the batteries or flywheels, which in turn provide electricity to the electric motor. The ICE is operating at fixed power output for maximum fuel efficiency and reduction in air pollution. The parallel hybrid drive train is easier to implement as it consists of two independent systems, but it is heavier and provides minimal increase in efficiency and air pollution reduction. The series system requires significant engineering sophistication, but results in a lighter system, and obtains the maximum possible fuel efficiency improvement and air pollution reduction.

A few prototype vehicles have been developed in recent years using hybrid drive trains. The CAT (Clean Air Technology) passenger car, developed with support from the City of Los Angeles and local utilities among others, made use of the parallel technology. The electric motor was a DC conventional one, and the internal combustion engine was a spark ignition engine fueled by gasoline. General Motors unveiled in 1991 the Freedom electric hybrid vehicle, which was based on the production Lumina APV van and made use of the series hybrid system. The electric drivetrain consisted of DC brushless motors and the internal combustion engine was a spark ignition engine fueled by gasoline. This vehicle meets the California ULEV standards for NO_x and CO, but not for hydrocarbons. Finally, Volvo unveiled in 1993 the Environmental Concept Car (ECC), based on the 850 passenger production vehicle and consisting of a series hybrid system as well[44]. A DC conventional motor is employed, but the internal combustion engine is comprised of a single shaft gas turbine that can be fueled with diesel fuel, gasoline,

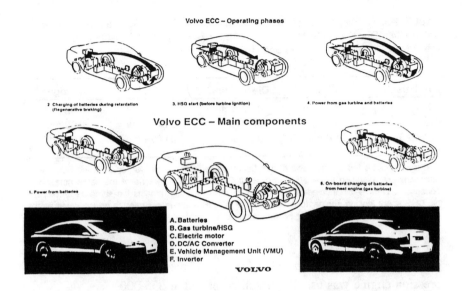

Volvo ECC – Operating phases

2. Charging of batteries during retardation (Regenerative braking)

3. HSG start (before turbine ignition)

4. Power from gas turbine and batteries

Volvo ECC – Main components

1. Power from batteries

5. On-board charging of batteries from heat engine (gas turbine)

A. Batteries
B. Gas turbine/HSG
C. Electric motor
D. DC/AC Converter
E. Vehicle Management Unit (VMU)
F. Inverter

VOLVO

FIGURE 9-7. The Main Components, Operating Phases and Model Photographs of the Gas-Turbine/Electric Drive Volvo Environmental Concept Car (Source: Volvo Car Corporation, Goeteborg, Sweden).

alcohols, natural gas and presumably hydrogen. The Volvo ECC vehicle configuration and operation are shown in Figure 9-7. The powertrain consists of a 41 kW (56 hp) gas turbine, a 39 kW high speed generator (HSG), a 70 kW (95 hp) electric motor, a two-speed automatic transmission and 16.8 kWh of Ni-Cd storage batteries. The 3,410 lb vehicle, which has a maximum speed of 110 mph and a maximum acceleration of 0-60 mph in 13 sec., has a 43 mpg average fuel efficiency (diesel fuel) based on the US Federal Driving Cycle and a driving range of 420 miles on the gas turbine (9.2 gal fuel tank size). The ECC meets the California ULEV emission standards very easily as shown in Table 9-5. The major drawback of the gas turbine technology at this time is the limited availability of small turbines (under 50 to 100 kW) for automotive applications and the high cost of the technology compared to a spark ignition engine. However, Volvo plans to offer a modified version of the ECC in California starting in 1998[69]. A 50 hp spark ignition engine and a 100 hp electric motor will be employed instead. This vehi-

TABLE 9-5. Comparison of Air Emissions of the Volvo ECC Gas Turbine Hybrid Vehicle with Diesel Fuel to the California ULEV Standard and Projected Emissions of the Volvo ECC with Natural Gas and Hydrogen as Fuels

Pollutant	ULEV	Diesel Fuel	CNG[1]	Hydrogen[1]
NO_x	0.20 g/mi	0.17 g/mi	0.01 g/mi	0.02 g/mi
CO	1.70 g/mi	0.13 g/mi	0.04 g/mi	0.00 g/mi
NMOG	0.04 g/mi	0.01 g/mi	0.002 g/mi	0.00 g/mi

1. Emission estimated on the basis of the fuel characteristics as follows: for CNG the CO, NMOG emissions are assumed to be 1/5 that of a CNG spark ignition engine of the same horsepower because of the five-fold increase in air/fuel ratio, while the NO_x remains the same as a comparable CNG spark ignition engine; for Hydrogen the NO_x estimate is assumed to be the same as that of a comparable spark ignition engine with water and direct fuel injections.

cle will get 33 mpg on gasoline (38 mpg if natural gas and a high compression engine was used) and will be priced at $35,000.

An alternative powertrain in the series hybrid configuration is the fuel cell which may be used instead of a spark ignition engine or a gas turbine. A fuel cell is a device that converts a fuel stored on board the vehicle to electricity through an electrochemical process. Present day fuel cells require that this fuel be hydrogen. Thus, if another fuel containing hydrogen must be used, the fuel cell system has to include an additional apparatus that dissociates the on-board fuel into its constituents to obtain the hydrogen. The fuel cell oxidizes hydrogen with oxygen from the air into water. The excess energy of the oxidation reaction is released mostly in the form of electricity, the remainder being low temperature heat. Unlike an internal combustion engine which has an average operating fuel efficiency of under 30% for converting the fuel energy into useful work, a fuel cell can convert more than 60% of the fuel energy content into electricity[45][46].

A variety of fuels can be theoretically employed, such as hydrocarbons, alcohols and hydrides. Gasoline, kerosene, propane, natural gas, and acetylene rank among the most desirable hydrocarbons because of their high energy content and low cost. Methanol is the most desirable alcohol, although it is a more expensive fuel. The two nitrogen hydrides ammonia and hydrazine are also excellent fuels, although hydrazine can be eliminated form consideration because of its extremely high cost.

Since a fuel cell requires hydrogen as a fuel to operate, all the afore-mentioned fuels must be reformed to yield hydrogen either externally or possibly in the future internally to the fuel cell. The first fuel cells to be commercialized were developed for the US space program, have an alkaline electrolyte (potassium hydroxide) and make use of pure hydrogen as fuel and pure oxygen as an oxidizer. The alkaline electrolyte fuel cells (AFC) cannot operate on industrial quality hydrogen and air because any carbonaceous impurities such as CO and CO_2 react with the electrolyte and poison the platinum electrodes. Moreover, AFCs require very high loadings of platinum, which limit their application to specialized space and military uses.

Over the years, fuel cells with other electrolytes such as phosphoric acid (PAFC) operating at $750^\circ F$, molten carbonates of sodium, potassium and lithium (MCFC) operating at $1200^\circ F$ and solid oxide of yttria-stabilized zirconia (SOFC) operating at $1800^\circ F$ have been developed that are tolerant to the carbonaceous contaminants found in the hydrogen fuel and oxidant used in terrestrial applications and require less platinum[45][46][47][48][49]. Natural gas is the fuel of choice for these fuel cells. However, these high temperature fuel cells are more appropriate for stationary applications such as decentralized power generation. Currently, only the PAFC appears to be nearing commercialization that could commence in the mid 1990s, depending on the outcome of extensive trials of 50 to 500 kW units being tested around the world[47][48][49][50].

The most promising fuel cell for automotive propulsion is the one that uses a solid polymer electrolyte (SPE) as shown in Figure 9-8[34][47]. This type of fuel cell (SPFC) was also developed in the early 1960s as part of the space program. The solid electrolyte, which was developed by General Electric under the trade name "nafion", is a perfluorinated polymer that allows hydrogen ions to pass through it, but not electrons, hydrogen and oxygen molecules. Hence, an alternative name of the SPE fuel cell is the proton exchange membrane or PEM fuel cell (PEMFC). The hydrogen required to operate the SPFC may be stored on board the vehicle in the form of compressed gas, liquid at cryogenic temperatures, or be chemically bound in hydride materials (titanium, magnesium, iron, etc.). Natural gas or methanol may also be the fuel stored on board the vehicle, from which then hydrogen is obtained by reformation.

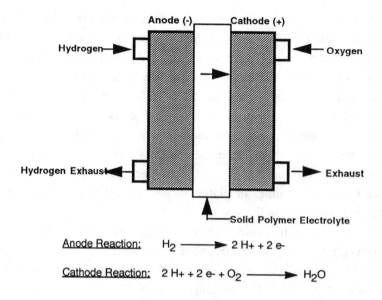

Anode (-)   Cathode (+)

Hydrogen→   ←— Oxygen

Hydrogen Exhaust←   —→ Exhaust

—Solid Polymer Electrolyte

Anode Reaction: $H_2 \longrightarrow 2H+ + 2e-$

Cathode Reaction: $2H+ + 2e- + O_2 \longrightarrow H_2O$

FIGURE 9-8. Schematic and Reactions of a Solid Polymer Electrolyte or Proton Exchange Membrane Fuel Cell with Potential for Vehicular Propulsion.

Alternatively, reformation can be readily employed at a fuel filling facility, where natural gas, for example, is converted to hydrogen, stored under pressure and then transferred to an appropriate hydrogen tank onboard the vehicle. It is also important to mention that the SPFCs operate at temperatures below 200°F, which is a very desirable feature for automotive applications with regard to safety.

While there exist certain technological problems to be resolved with regard the SPFCs such as the drying out of the polymer membrane the major drawback of their use in automotive applications is the high cost. This high cost, which applies to all fuel cells, is due to the need for a significant amount of platinum in the electrodes of the system to catalyze the oxidation of hydrogen and oxygen. Moreover, the polymer electrolyte is even more expensive than the platinum in the SPFCs. The current platinum loadings of an SPFC is typically on the order of 20 g per kW of power generated[50]. At a market price of $390 per troy ounce (31.1 g) for platinum, the previous platinum loading figure translates to

$250 per kW resulting in a final fuel cell cost well in excess of $1,000 per kW ($750 per hp). While fuel cell prices as high as $1100 or $1200/kW may be acceptable for power generation, they are totally unrealistic for automotive propulsion.

Thus, fuel cells cannot become an element of automotive propulsion in the next 15 or 20 years, unless major breakthroughs were to occur reducing significantly the required platinum loading and producing less expensive electrolyte membranes. Nevertheless, several companies including Ballard Power Systems of Vancouver, BC, an SPE fuel cell supplier, General Motors through its Allison Gas Turbine Division, and Mazda are working on prototype SPE fuel cell powered buses and passengers vehicles.

The world's first hydrogen fuel cell powered transit bus, designed by Ballard in conjunction with Science Applications International Corporation (SAIC) and built by National Coach Corporation, was unveiled recently in Vancouver, BC[51]. This bus has a 32 foot long chassis, weighs 22,000 lb and makes use of a 120 kW (169 hp) SPFC system. The fuel is compressed hydrogen in nine fiberglass-wrapped aluminum cylinders and the vehicle has a range of 100 miles. A 60 kW lead-acid battery pack is part of the propulsion system to provide additional power. This bus, shown in Figure 9-9, has a 20 passenger capacity. Three additional development phases are in plans through 1998 at which time this ZEV is expected to have a range in excess of 300 miles and a passenger capacity of over 60 persons. These improvements will come about by increasing the efficiency of fuels cells and decreasing their volume and weight as well as by employing better hydrogen storage techniques.

It should be mentioned parenthetically that fuel cells in general suffer form an inherent low power density, which requires the use of batteries in automotive applications. Moreover, batteries help reduce the size of the fuel cell stack, which invariably results in a reduced propulsion system cost given that batteries will remain less expensive than fuel cells in the foreseeable future. Projected specific power and power density for the SPFC are 300 W/lb and 1.2 kW/l, respectively[47]. The fuel efficiency of the Phase I Ballard hydrogen bus, whose development began in 1990, is about twice that of a similar diesel fuel powered bus.

(a)

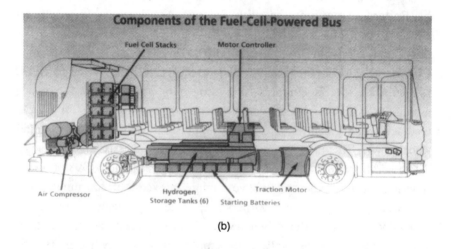

(b)

FIGURE 9-9. The Phase I Proof-of-Concept Hydrogen Solid Polymer Fuel Cell Powered Bus Designed by Ballard and Unveiled in Vancouver, BC in 1993: (a) The Fuel Cell Bus Operated by BC Transit; and (b) Components of the Bus Showing Location of Fuel Cell, Air Compressor to Feed the Fuel Cells with the Oxidant, Hydrogen Storage Tanks, Lead-Acid Batteries, Electric Motor and Motor Controller (Source: American Hydrogen Association).

In late 1993, Ballard entered a joint venture with Dow Chemical to develop inexpensive electrolyte membranes so that by the year 2000 the cost of SPFCs will be on the order of $1000 per kW[52]. However, the intended market for these relative inexpensive SPFCs is power generation. At that price SPFCs are not cost effective even for buses, let alone passenger vehicles. Incidentally, another large market for SPFCs appears to be the world of appliances requiring small power such as laptop computers, movie cameras, sensors and lighted highway signs among others[53]. For these applications the aforementioned target cost of fuel cells may be comparable to the present cost of batteries they may be replacing. The fuel of these SPFCs will be compressed hydrogen gas in small replaceable cartridges.

General Motors is the only major company in the US involved currently in the development of a proof-of-concept fuel cell passenger vehicle. This is not, however, the first attempt ever by GM in the fuel cell automotive propulsion business. As early as 1966, GM developed the ElectroVan, a delivery type van, using a 94 kW Union Carbide hydrogen-oxygen AFC with a power density of 26 Wh/lb, too low for a practical vehicle[8]. Since 1990, GM in conjunction with the Los Alamos National Laboratory (LANL) is developing under the sponsorship of the US DOE a SPFC system for a passenger vehicle that uses methanol as the fuel[50]. Ballard is supplying the fuel cell stacks, while LANL is responsible for the development of an on-board compact methanol steam reformer. The methanol reformer presents a two-fold challenge: it must have a fast response, particularly in a cold start to generate the requisite hydrogen fuel rate, and it must be able to reduce the amount of CO in the hydrogen to a very low level, below 10 ppm, to avoid poisoning the platinum in the electrodes. It is not clear whether these requirements can be met within the volume constrains of a passenger vehicle and without adding significantly more to the cost of an already too expensive propulsion system.

Work on practical fuel cells has been going-on now for more than 40 years. A steady, but slow progress has been occurring during these years with a more renewed interest in the last decade because of air quality problems. It seems that fuel cells may become a commercial reality within another ten years or so, albeit for power generation applications only. It will require a major breakthrough in materials science to reduce the cost of electrolyte and catalysts in a fuel cell before it can become a viable automotive propulsion option. Even then it will take 10 to 15 years before a commercial product becomes available. Thus, the use of fuel cells to replace the internal combustion engine in an automobile cannot happen any earlier than 2010 to 2015 and most likely after the year 2020, if past experience of technological change is any indicator of the time frame of future technological changes.

NATURAL GAS AS A SOURCE OF AUTOMOTIVE HYDROGEN FUEL

Notwithstanding Jules Vern's prediction of hydrogen generated from water by electrolysis with the aid of electricity from an undetermined source, the most likely sources of hydrogen in the foreseeable future are from fossil fuels. Currently, some 2.2 trillion scf of hydrogen are produced in the US alone annually to be used in a multitude of industrial applications[54]. Natural gas is by far the best fossil fuel source of hydrogen in the US and most of the world today because the natural gas to hydrogen conversion is benign to the environment, entails a more convenient process and results in the least expensive hydrogen. Very small amounts of high purity hydrogen (0.01 trillion scf /yr) are produced from the electrolysis of water for specialized applications such as in the manufacture of pharmaceuticals and the hydrogenation of fats and oils in the food industry, where the high cost of electrolytic hydrogen can be readily absorbed in the final price of the product. Large amounts of hydrogen (0.7 trillion scf/yr) are consumed in refineries to improve the quality of liquid fuels such as gasoline through hydrogenation. Hydrogen produced in refineries is also the feedstock material for a large number of industrial chemicals. Ammonia used predominantly in the manufacture of fertilizers constitutes the largest volume such material (1.1 trillion scf hydrogen/yr). The second largest volume chemical derived from hydrogen is methanol (0.2 trillion scf hydrogen/yr). The manufacture of other chemicals such cyclohexane, benzene, oxo-alcohols and aniline make the balance of hydrogen use (0.2 trillion scf hydrogen/yr).

Both ammonia and methanol have been considered as potential sources of hydrogen as automotive fuel. In particular methanol has been promoted for some time now as the likely candidate of the on-board the vehicle fuel because of its liquid nature. Methanol will have to be reformed on-board the vehicle to yield hydrogen which will then be consumed in the fuel cell propulsion system of future automobiles.

Methanol dissociates at the relatively low temperature of 600°F into hydrogen and carbon monoxide according to the reaction[54][55]:

$$CH_3OH \xrightarrow{\quad 600°F \quad} CO + 2\,H_2 - 90.7 \text{ kJ/mol}$$

However, carbon monoxide in these large quantities will poison very quickly the platinum catalysts of a fuel cell, let alone that it will result in a serious air pollution if it were released into the atmosphere. Consequently, a second reaction must be employed to reduce carbon monoxide. This is the well known water shift reaction, in which steam reacts with carbon monoxide at 750°F in the presence of suitable catalysts to oxidize it to carbon dioxide with the release of additional hydrogen as follows:

$$CO + H_2O \xrightarrow{\quad 750°F \quad} CO_2 + H_2 + 41.2 \text{ kJ/mol}$$

In practice the last reaction does not move 100% to the right so that small amounts of carbon monoxide of a few to several percent volume still remain in the gaseous stream consisting ideally of 25% carbon dioxide and 75% hydrogen. Hence, a third step must be employed to further reduce the carbon monoxide content of the CO_2 and H_2 mixture to below the 1% level[45]. A catalytic oxidizer of CO to CO_2 offers a potential solution for the third step of the so called steam reformation of methanol to hydrogen.

The Los Alamos (LANL) team working with GM on a methanol fueled SPFC powered vehicle has developed such a three-stage methanol reformer (primary reformer, water-gas shift reactor, and preferential oxidation reactor) that purports to reduce the CO concentration to below 10 ppm[50]. Besides being able to reduce the CO concentration in the hydrogen stream to very low levels, the methanol reformer has potential problems with delivering the requisite instantaneous rate of hydrogen fuel and the time it takes to be operational from a cold start. It should be noted that an SPFC powered automobile with a methanol reformer on-board and a hydrogen fuel consumption of 1,500 BTU/mi (80 mpg gasoline equivalent) would generate a CO emission of 1.5 g/mi at the 1% CO concentration level in the hydrogen fuel and 0.0015 g/mi at the 10 ppm CO concentration level. Finally, it is worth noting that 1 lb of methanol (0.78 liters) requires 0.56 lb of water (steam) to yield 0.19 lb of hydrogen with a minimum energy input of 1,000 BTU per lb of methanol assuming a 67% thermal efficiency of the reactions of the process.

Ammonia can be cracked on-board a vehicle in a conceptually straightforward manner at 1,300°F to yield a 25% nitrogen and 75% hydrogen gas stream which can then be used to power a fuel cell stack. While ammonia can be readily liquefied under moderate pressure and prevailing ambient temperatures, it is a highly irritating gas if inhaled. Hence, ammonia has been eliminated as a viable candidate source of hydrogen fuel on-board vehicles.

Natural gas and specifically methane is the only other viable candidate source of hydrogen on-board a vehicle. Hydrogen may be obtained from natural gas with either one of two processes[54][55][56][57]:

Steam Reformation
$$CH_4 + H_2O \xrightarrow{1450°F} CO + 3\,H_2 - 206.1 \text{ kJ/mol}$$

$$CO + H_2O \xrightarrow{750°F} CO_2 + H_2 + 41.2 \text{ kJ/mol}$$

and

Pyrolysis
$$CH_4 \xrightarrow{1650°F} C + 2\,H_2 - 87.4 \text{ kJ/mol}$$

in the presence of suitable catalysts. The first of these processes is used in the industrial manufacture of hydrogen from natural gas, while the second process is used in the production of carbon black. In the steam reformation process, 1 lb of methane (24,000 BTU content) requires 2.58 lb of water (steam) and yields 0.5 lb of hydrogen with a minimum energy input of 4,450 BTU per lb of methane. In the pyrolysis process, 1 lb of methane yields 0.75 lb of carbon and 0.25 lb of hydrogen and requires a minimum energy input of 2,370 BTU per lb of methane. The volume of 1 lb of methane is 0.7 gal at a 3000 psi pressure. It should be also pointed out that actual steam reforming efficiencies for methane is on the order of 70%, i.e., input energy 1.43 times higher than the theoretical minimum, and 80% for methane pyrolysis, i.e., input energy 1.25 times higher than the theoretical minimum. Finally, in the steam reforming processes the energy input must be supplied by increasing accordingly the amount of fuel required for the propulsion of the vehicle, while in the pyrolysis process portion of the generated carbon may be oxidized to carbon dioxide to provide the additional energy.

It would appear that methanol is a more desirable storage medium of hydrogen on-board a vehicle than methane or natural gas because of lower input energy requirements and lower operating temperatures of the transformation. It is true that at the vehicular level methanol requires less energy to break down and yield hydrogen. However, hydrogen from methanol is much less efficient to produce from a total energy or global point of view even if natural gas is used as the methanol feedstock. Methanol from natural gas is produced by the steam reformation of it and the subsequent catalytic recombination of carbon monoxide and hydrogen as follows[57]:

$$CH_4 + H_2O \xrightarrow{\text{1450}^{\circ}\text{F}} CO + 3\,H_2 - 206.1 \text{ kJ/mol}$$

$$CO + 3\,H_2 \xrightarrow{\text{500}^{\circ}\text{F}} CH_3OH + H_2 + 128.2 \text{ kJ/mol}$$

Thus, 1 lb of methanol production requires 0.5 lb of methane, a minimum energy input of about 1,050 BTU or 1,660 BTU of actual energy input at the typical 63% industrial conversion efficiency. The production of hydrogen from methanol by reformation takes place at a lower temperature, but it requires as many steps as the reformation of methane and twice as many steps as the pyrolysis of methane. Thus, the potentially lower degree of complexity of the natural gas utilization to produce hydrogen may offset the lower operating temperatures to produce hydrogen from methanol on-board a vehicle. The steam reforming of natural gas can be of course readily employed in a stationary fashion at a public station, home or business, if hydrogen is the fuel stored on-board the vehicle.

No natural gas steam reforming device has ever been built for an on-board the vehicle application. Likewise, the pyrolysis of natural gas is a well established process in a large scale, i.e., at refineries, to produce hydrogen, but no small scale apparatus has ever been built for stationary or mobile applications[58]. It should be also mentioned that for the small scale generation of hydrogen in stationary applications the thermal cracking of ammonia has been the preferred process[55]. An added advantage of the methane pyrolysis process is that no carbon dioxide is emitted into the atmosphere, while the residual carbon has commercial value as carbon black (US consumption 1.5 million tons per year). However, methane pyrolysis will generate vast amounts of carbon as, for example, 1 trillion scf of natural gas contains 14 million tons of carbon. Other uses must be found for this carbon or else it must be landfilled, a process which is considered to be environmentally benign because carbon is a very stable material.

It was assumed in the previous chapter that by the time natural gas replaces totally gasoline as the automotive fuel of choice, the average fuel efficiency of vehicles in the US will have risen to about 40 mpg (all mpg numbers in gasoline equivalent units). This is equivalent to an energy consumption of about 2,875 BTU/mi (0.842 kWh/mi) for the internal combustion engine based propulsion system of the vehicle fueled by natural gas. If the internal combustion engine is replaced by a hybrid SPFC propulsion system with a two times higher average efficiency, the same vehicle will consume 1,440 BTU/mi (0.421 kWh/mi) and obtain a 80 mpg fuel efficiency. The hydrogen fuel requirement on-board the SPFC based vehicle will be 10 lb for a vehicle range of about 360 miles and 6.6 lb for a range of 220 miles. Incidentally, the use of hydrogen with an internal combustion engine may increase the fuel efficiency by as much as 30% so that a 40 mpg CNG vehicle may become a 52 mpg hydrogen vehicle with a 2,210 Btu/mi (0.648 kWh/mi) fuel consumption. The corresponding hydrogen requirements are then 9.4 lb for a 220 mi range and 15.3 lb for a 360 mi range.

The average fuel efficiency of a motor vehicle with a hybrid propulsion system based on an internal combustion engine and using GNG as fuel with a small hydrogen fuel content, i.e., up to 5%, can be also increased to about 80 mpg, as it will be discussed in the next chapter. This fuel efficiency corresponds to an energy use of about 1,400 Btu/mi (0.42 kWh/mi). Table 9-6 summarizes the mass and volume require-

TABLE 9-6. Mass and Volume of Vehicle Fuel Tank for a 40 mpg CNG Vehicle to be Operated on Hydrogen with Either the Same ICE Propulsion System or with a Hybrid ICE Propulsion or a Hybrid Solid Polymer Electrolyte Fuel Cell Propulsion and a Constant Vehicle Range of 220 Miles

Fuel Type & Fuel Storage	ICE 50 mpg H_2	Hybrid SPFC 80 mpg H_2	Hybrid ICE 80 mpg CNG/H_2
CNG (3000 psi)			
Mass (lb)	122	77	43
Volume (gal)	26	17	10
CH_2 (3000 psi)			
Mass (lb)	201	126	N/A
Volume (gal)	61	40	N/A
LH_2 Mass (lb)	57	35	N/A
Volume (gal)	43	28	N/A
Fe-Ti Hydride			
Mass (lb)	549	341	N/A
Volume (gal)	12	8	N/A

Notes. Mass includes that of the tank made of composite materials as well as that of the fuel. The fuel mass and volume of a 40 mpg CNG vehicle with ICE propulsion are 82 lb and 17.75 gal. Vehicle range is assumed to be 220 mi. The CNG fuel is catalytically converted (pyrolysis) to carbon and hydrogen on-board the vehicle. The CNG fuel numbers do not include the mass and volume of the pyrolysis device, but include the additional fuel necessary to supply the pyrolysis energy. The Hybrid-ICE and Hybrid-SPFC fuel numbers do not include any of the electrical (battery) or mechanical (flywheel) energy storage on-board the vehicle. The CNG/H2 fuel composition is assumed to be 95% and 5% per volume, respectively (see next chapter).

ments of the vehicle fuel tank for all these three cases. The 220 mile vehicle range has been selected as illustrative of the range of home or business refueled vehicles expected to be the norm at that time as it has been discussed earlier.

The results in Table 9-6 are very instructive in terms of future technology development. The compressed hydrogen option can be eliminated altogether for any propulsion system. Liquid hydrogen may be practical for the hybrid SPFC propulsion system, but its two drawbacks of being cryogenic and requiring significant amounts of energy to be liquefied very much eliminate any universal applicability. The iron-titanium hydride has excellent volume characteristics, but relatively poor weight properties even for the hybrid SPFC propulsion system. The CNG on-board hydrogen fuel generation option has good volume and excellent weight characteristics compared to the other options, although it requires the development of a compact pyrolysis device.

Two general observations, however, emerge from the results of Table 9-6. First, it is very unlikely that hydrogen will become an automotive fuel until the average vehicle fuel efficiency reaches or exceeds the 40 mpg level. Second, the necessity of a fuel cell propulsion system, which by nature is a hybrid system, is not the only alternative propulsion system as a very high efficiency hybrid ICE system can be also as good. Finally, the use of CNG with some hydrogen content in a hybrid ICE configuration is a far more practical option than any one based on pure hydrogen as a fuel. This issue will be discussed at length in the next chapter.

METHANE AND WATER AS LONG TERM SOURCES OF HYDROGEN

The adoption of natural gas as the new transportation fuel is entirely compatible with, and may become the forerunner of the implementation of the hydrogen economy sometime in the next century. No one doubts that hydrogen is the ultimate clean fuel in transportation as it produces virtually no pollutants with the proper propulsion system. However, hydrogen has to be manufactured from another energy source. The two long term potential sources of hydrogen are natural gas or methane and water. Incidentally, the terms natural gas and methane will be used interchangeably in this section as natural gas is essentially methane.

While other fossil fuels such as coal and oil may be used in the interim period to produce hydrogen through the well established process of steam reformation, natural gas is the only long term choice for hydrogen production for a number of reasons[40][57]. First, natural gas can be converted to hydrogen in a more straightforward fashion than other fossil fuels, thereby keeping the cost of hydrogen low. Second, the conversion of natural gas to hydrogen generates the least amount of air pollution to the environment, which essentially consists of carbon dioxide and traces of carbon monoxide. Third, natural gas can be readily converted to hydrogen through pyrolysis to eliminate entirely the carbon dioxide problem (greenhouse gas). Fourth, natural gas or more accurately methane can be produced from biological sources, if and when methane from fossil sources is no longer feasible, thereby eliminating once more the carbon dioxide contribution to the greenhouse effect. The methane-biomass option will be discussed shortly.

The electrolysis of water to generate hydrogen, besides relying on abundant water, is very electricity intensive. It requires about 46 lb of water to produce 1,000 scf of hydrogen via electrolysis consuming 135 kWh of electricity[40]. Taking as an example an annual production of 3 trillion scf of hydrogen with an energy content of about 1 trillion scf of natural gas, it would take 16.5 billion gal of water and 405 billion kWh of electricity. While this water requirements can be easily met in the US (200 gal daily per capita water use), the electricity demand is much too high (the current annual production of electricity in the US is 2,700 billion kWh).

Two long term alternative sources of hydrogen are possible, if the fossil methane is no longer available. Incidentally, non-availability of fossil methane or natural gas for hydrogen will be the result of source depletion and not of greenhouse emission restrictions as it has already been explained. These two hydrogen sources consist of :

I.   Methane produced from the anaerobic digestion of biomass and steam reforming to produce hydrogen;

and

II. Water electrolysis with electricity supplied by renewable resources such as solar or wind energy.

In either case, the use of fossil fuels to supply methane or generate electricity is not considered a viable long term option as it would defy the essence of using hydrogen as an ultra clean fuel on a global sense. The current cost of hydrogen produced from natural gas and the electrolysis of water is shown in Table 9-7, where both the cost due to the plant as well as the cost of the input fuel are included[40]. Other sources of hydrogen such as coal and naphtha are also included. Several observations can be made on the basis of the information in Table 9-7. First, it is instructive to note that the renewable electricity costs are currently on the order of $0.08 to $0.11 kWh from wind and solar thermal and at

TABLE 9-7. Comparison of Costs of Hydrogen Production from Natural Gas, Coal and Oil Reforming and Water Electrolysis in the US for 1990 Prices

Process/ Raw Material	Thermal Efficiency	Raw Material Price	Plant Cost $/10^6$ BTU	Total Cost $/10^6$ BTU
Natural Gas	0.74	$6/1,000 scf	2.1	10.9
		$3/1,000 scf	2.1	7.0
Coal	0.52	$23/ton	5.5	13.4
Naphtha	0.73	$300/ton	2.2	18.2
Electrolysis	0.75	$0.08/kWh	11.0	39.7
		$0.05/kWh	11.0	28.9

Notes. Two natural gas prices are considered typically representing current average residential and industrial prices. Coal prices refer to the average of bituminous, subbituminous and lignite price per metric ton at the mine. The naphtha price is $0.91/gal ($38.2/bbl) and excludes any taxes. Two electricity prices are considered reflecting the national average residential/commercial and industrial prices.

least twice as much from solar electric (photovoltaic) facilities[59][60][61]. These renewable electricity costs, however, have never been demonstrated in a large scale, longtime (30 year), utility type generation environment. On the positive side, significant cost reductions have been attained in all these types of renewable electricity generation in the last ten years or so to justify the optimistic ultimate generation forecasts at $0.08/kWh (in 1990 dollars) of wind, solar thermal and solar electric[60][62][63]. Inspection of Table 9-7 reveals that a natural gas price of $27 per 1,000 scf or higher (in 1990 dollars) would be required for hydrogen from electrolysis to become more cost effective than hydrogen from natural gas. This natural gas or methane price range between the $6/1,000 scf and $27/1,000 scf leaves a large window of opportunity to produce this fuel from biomass.

The use of biomass in the US is significant amounting to 3 quads annually (3 x10^15 BTU/yr)[63]. Thus, biomass accounts for almost 4.5% of the energy produced and about 3.7% of the energy consumed in the US on an annual basis. This biomass consists predominantly of wood (83%), waste including solid municipal wastes, manufacturing wastes and landfill methane (14%) and ethanol (3%). The national energy policy act of 1992 gives a $0.01/kWh credit to the electricity generated from biomass wastes. This credit has already resulted in the establishment of industries collecting agricultural wastes to produce fuel for power plants rather than letting farmers continue the traditional burning of such wastes to clear the fields before each year's planting of a crop.

Some 2 billion kWh of electricity are generated annually from biomass by utilities compared to 3 million (!) from wind and solar and 250 billion from hydropower. However, most of the biomass is used to generate steam and electricity by the industries that produce it thereby reducing their purchasing of energy from utilities. About 2/3 of the wood biomass is used by industries such as the Paper and Allied Products and the Lumber and Wood Products and 1/3 by the residential sector as heating fuel. Wastes biomass on an energy content basis is comprised of the following: 73% solid municipal waste; 19% manufacturing waste consumed almost exclusively by the industries that generate it such as Food and Kindred Products, Paper and Allied Products, Furniture and Fixtures, Petroleum and Coal Products and Electric and Electric Equipment; and 8% landfill gas. During 1990, some 31 billion scf of methane (55 billion scf of landfill gas) were captured and used to generate electricity in 86 landfill gas facilities across the country, while an additional 68 facilities are in various stages of development. Incidentally, the landfill gas consists typically of 60% methane and 40% carbon dioxide and can be converted into high heating value gas (synthetic natural gas) by removing the carbon dioxide or more commonly is burned directly to generate electricity.

The direct combustion of biomass practiced currently in the US and most of the world is not the most effective way to utilize it in a large scale. While electricity is a very versatile form of energy, it is not rational to replace coal with biomass in its generation. Biomass may be utilized more effectively in the generation of transportation fuels such as methane that command a premium value because of environmental considerations. To be sure, coal can be used also to produce synthetic natural gas. Some 53 billion scf of synthetic natural gas are produced annually in the US in one facility, the Great Plains Synfuels Plant in Beulah, ND, since the early 1980s[65]. Moreover, the current trend in coal combustion for electricity generation is coal gasification in order to reduce the combustion pollutants released to the atmosphere and improve energy efficiency[66]. The gasification takes place at the power plant and results in the destruction and/or removal from coal of all major pollutants such as sulfur. The combustion of the resulting gas (syngas) to generate electricity is more efficient and results in reduced air emissions. Increased efficiency can improve the economics of the process known as Integrated Gasification Combined Cycle (IGCC), while reduced emissions are sufficient to meet the new more stringent environmental laws for power generation.

Thermal processes may be employed with biomass to yield synthetic natural gas. These processes include pyrolysis, gasification with air and gasification with steam[67]. However, these processes require extensive modification and several steps to obtain the final product. While biomass may be more desirable as a gasification feedstock than coal, because it contains more oxygen and hydrogen relative to carbon, it also contains excessive amount of water that makes the conversion process inefficient. On the other hand, the liability of the biomass water content for thermal conversion processes becomes an advantage if biological conversion processes are employed instead.

The best known biological fuel conversion process is that of yeast fermentation which has been employed since antiquity to convert sugars into ethanol or more appropriately alcoholic liquors. Fuel ethanol from the fermentation of sugars (sugar cane, root beet) in Brazil and starches (corn) in the US is a very recent idea, although ethanol has been produced by fermentation as a chemical, as a medicinal spirit and as a solvent for more than a hundred years (after World War II the fermentation process for ethanol production was abandoned in the US and the rest of the industrialized world in favor of using ethylene derived from natural gas and petroleum as the feedstock).

Another biological process that may become even better known in the future because it converts certain types of biomass to methane is the anaerobic digestion. It consists of the breakdown of biomass by the so called "methanogenic bacteria" in the absence of oxygen (air) that evolves methane gas together with some carbon dioxide, while leaving non-digestible residues in the form of a slurry. This process has been known for centuries and is currently applied in most major cities in the treatment of sewage wastes in order to decompose the organic component for easier disposal, while the generate methane is used to generate electricity to operate the facility. Landfills, marshes and rice fields are places where anaerobic digestion takes place in a natural manner.

The desirable biomass feedstock for anaerobic digestion consists of polysaccharides (cellulose and hemicellulose, especially xylose), proteins, non-protein nitrogenous compounds and lipids. Some cellulose is, however, difficult to degrade, especially if the fibers are lignified, such as in wood. On the other hand, livestock waste, grass, leaves, and the bulk of agricultural residues (cereal straw, sugar beet tops, potato stems and reject tubers, beans and peas stems, vegetable wastes, and fruit wastes) are ideal for anaerobic digestion. Table 9-8 shows the methane yields from selected biomass sources via anaerobic digestion[68]. The output products of the anaerobic digestion are methane, carbon dioxide and a slurry of undigested organic material. The carbon dioxide and possibly small traces of hydrogen sulfide are removed from the gas by scrubbing in a manner akin to that already utilized in the natural gas industry. The effluent slurry contains water and organic matter. If the biomass feedstock is agricultural residues, the solid portion of the slurry after separation from the water may be sold as fertilizer or fertilizer supplement as it is very rich in nitrogen and minerals.

TABLE 9-8. Methane Gas Yields from the Anaerobic Digestion of Selected Biomass and Solid Wastes per Unit Dry Mass

Source	Total Gas Yield (10^3 scf/ton)	Methane in Gas (%)	Methane Yield (10^3 scf/ton)	Half-Digestion Period (days)
Waste Paper	8.2	63	5.2	8
Dairy Wastes	34.9	75	26.1	4
Cattle Manure	8.5	80	6.8	20
Municipal Sewage	15.3	78	11.9	8
Wheat Straw	12.5	78	9.7	12
Potato Tops	18.9	75	14.2	3
Maize Tops	17.4	83	14.5	5
Beet Leaves	16.4	85	13.9	2
Grass	17.8	84	15.0	4

Notes. The gas and methane yields are expressed in scf per metric ton (2,200 lb) of dry biomass or waste solids. The gas consists of carbon dioxide and methane.

Anaerobic digestion is an extremely versatile, well developed and comparatively uncomplicated technology suitable for a wide range of biomass inputs. However, maximum yields are obtained when the biomass input has a consistent composition and the process is controlled for temperature, pressure, pH and water content. The process takes place on an industrial basis in a digestion vessel, where all the critical parameters are continuously monitored. The energy inputs for the anaerobic digestion process of biomass appear to be on the order of 20% to 25% of the energy output in methane and consist of steam (process heat) and electricity in roughly equal amounts[68]. This energy input may be provided by other sources such as the wastes themselves or residual wastes rather than the produced methane which is a premium fuel.

The cost of methane obtained from biomass via anaerobic digestion has been estimated through numerous studies in the mid 1970s[68]. The costs given in these studies have been increased by a factor of 2.5 to reflect the ratio of the consumer price index between 1974/75 and 1990. The final cost consists of three major components: (a) the cost of cultivation of a crop; (b) the cost of collection and/or transportation of appropriate biomass; and (c) the cost of the anaerobic conversion process.

The cost of cultivating a biomass crop such as grass (rye, bermuda, elephant, napier) is on the order of $50 per dry ton (1990 dollars). The cost of collecting and transporting the biomass is on the order of $50 to $100 per dry ton and obviously displays a significant variability. The cost of anaerobic digestion of appropriately grown biomass rather than wastes appears to be on the order of $9 per 1,000 scf of methane. Since one metric ton of dry biomass yields on the average 15,000 scf of methane according to Table 9-8, the contribution of the cultivation of biomass to the total methane cost is $3 per 1,000 scf. Moreover, the contribution of biomass collection and transportation to the total methane cost may range from $3 to $6 per 1,000 scf of methane. Thus, the total cost of methane production from biomass may range from $15 to $18 per 1,000 scf of methane. Consequently, the cost of bio methane is almost an order of magnitude higher than the cost of fossil methane. Nevertheless the cost of bio methane is still a factor of two less than the breakeven price for natural gas of $27 per 1,000 scf above which hydrogen from water via electrolysis utilizing renewable resources becomes more cost effective than hydrogen from methane reforming.

It is instructive to discuss briefly the size of agricultural residues and other wastes in the United States that can be used in an anaerobic process to yield methane. The annual production of corn (maize) is on the order of 200 million tons, soy beans 50 million tons, wheat 50 million tons, sugar beets 25 million tons and potatoes 20 million tons. Moreover, the production of paper and paperboard is on the order of 75 million tons per year. The ratio of grain to straw is 1.25 for wheat and 1.00 for corn, while the yield of sugar beets to the beet tops is about 1.05 and the yield of potatoes to potato tops is 5.68[67]. Assuming a 50% moisture content in the residues of these crops and a 50% ability to collect the residues, one obtains a 75 million ton dry agricultural residue yield from the aforementioned crops. Moreover, a 50% or so recycling of paper will yield another 35 million tons of dry waste paper. Using the methane yields of Table 9-8, the 75 million tons of collected agricultural residue will generate over 1 trillion scf of methane. Paper wastes will generate another 0.2 trillion scf of methane.

Municipal wastes collected in the US amount to about 350 million tons per year. A modular system developed in the last decade can be employed by municipalities across the country to obtain another 1 trillion scf of methane annually[70].

Alternatively, grass may be used as a source of methane. Typical yields of temperate grass such as rye grass and bermuda grass are on the order of 10 tons of dry matter per acre per year, while sub-tropical grasses such as elephant grass and napier grass have yields of 25 tons of dry matter per acre per year[68]. Temperate grass may be grown in areas with abundant rainfall such as the southern states in the US, while sub-tropical grasses may be grown in Florida, Louisiana, Puerto Rico and parts of Texas. The temperate grass yield translates to 150 thousand scf of methane per acre per year. Thus, a 10 million acre grass land will yield 1.5 trillion scf of methane annually. Since the cropland in the US is about 350 million acres, it is reasonable to assume that no more than 35 million acres or 10% of the cropland could ever be dedicated to bio-fuel production. This implies a bio-methane production of about 5.25 trillion scf per year.

In a previous chapter, it was determined that a 40 mpg average fuel efficiency of vehicle by 2030 would require no more than 7.5 trillion scf of natural gas annually. If the average fuel efficiency of CNG powered vehicles were to increase to 80 mpg, then less than 4 trillion scf/yr of methane would be required. Thus, the 35 million acres dedicated to the production of bio-methane plus agricultural and municipal wastes would suffice to meet all the needs of the entire US land transportation utilizing essentially natural gas as its fuel.

The pyrolysis of 4.5 trillion scf methane will produce 9 trillion scf of hydrogen, while the steam reformation of it will yield 18 trillion scf of hydrogen. These hydrogen yields may be reduced by 15% if the energy required for the methane to hydrogen conversion process is derived from the methane fuel itself, although it is more sensible to use less valuable energy inputs for that task. The fuel needs of a 260 million hybrid-SPFC vehicles running on hydrogen with an average fuel efficiency of 80 mpg gasoline equivalent and an average driving distance of 10,000 miles per year will be about 12 trillion scf of hydrogen. In this instance 30 million acres of land dedicated to bio-methane production are more than sufficient to meet the country's long term land transportation energy needs.

While the preceding numbers are only illustrative of the various long term possibilities to derive methane and hydrogen from renewable resources, they point out to two crucial facts. Hydrogen as a transportation fuel is far more likely to come from biomass rather than electrolysis of water powered from solar or wind electricity. Even then, hydrogen will be only feasible if the average fuel efficiency of the vehicles in the US or anywhere else for that matter exceeds significantly the 40 mpg level and most likely approaches the 80 mpg level. The inescapable conclusion is that hydrogen has a chance as a transportation fuel only if, and when the vehicular fuel efficiencies rise dramatically not only from their present day levels but also from the levels expected to be realized in the next several decades as CNG becomes the motor fuel of choice.

REFERENCES

1. W. Von Braun, F. I. Ordway, III and D. Dooling, <u>Space Travel: A History</u>, Harper and Row Publishers, New York, NY, 1985.

2. <u>Britannica Book of the Year 1993</u>, Nations of the World: United States, p. 741, Encyclopeadia Britannica, Inc., Chicago, IL, 1993.

3. D. W. Pearce and R. K. Turner, <u>Economics of Natural Resources and the Environment</u>, The Johns Hopkins University, Baltimore, MD, 1990.

4. J. J. Flink, <u>The Automobile Age</u>, pp. 8-10, The MIT Press, Cambridge, MA, 1990.

5. T. Kenjo, <u>Electric Motors and their Controls</u>, pp. 172-173, Oxford University Press, Oxford, UK, 1991.

6. J. J. Flink, <u>The Automobile Age</u>, *loc. cit.*, pp. 212-213.

7. J. J. Flink, <u>The Automobile Age</u>, *loc. cit.*, pp. 162-163.

8. R. U. Ayers and R. P. McKenna, <u>Alternatives to the Internal Combustion Engine</u>, pp. 206-229, pub. for Resources for the Future, Inc. by The Johns Hopkins University Press, Baltimore, MD, 1972.

9. J. Ellis, GM Electric Vehicles, private communication, 1993.

10. M. Parrish, "Driving Force Behind Electric – Utilities Take on Detroit in Defending Green Rules", *Los Angeles Times*, p. D1, November 24, 1994.

11. H. McCann, "NGV's: Natural Gas Nears Lead in Alternative Fuel Race", *WARD'S Auto World*, v. 29, no. 6, pp. 32- 37, June 1993.

12. W. M. Anderson and C. S. Cambler, "Integrated Electric Vehicle Drive", SAE Paper 910246, Society of Automotive Engineers, Warendale, PA, 1991.

13. Hallwag's Automobil Revue, <u>Cars International 1990</u>, Hallwag AG, Bern, CH, 1990; English edition, PRS Publishing Ltd, London, UK, 1990.

14. C. A. Sawyer, "Carbon Fiber 101", pp. 20-24, *Chilton's Automotive Industries*, v. 172, No. 3, March 1992.

15. R. U. Ayres and R. P. McKenna, <u>Alternatives to the Internal Combustion Engine</u>, pp. 86-112, published for Resources for the Future, Inc. by Johns Hopkins University Press, Baltimore, MD, 1972.

16. D. Linden, <u>Handbook of Batteries and Fuel Cells</u>, McGraw-Hill Book Co., New York, NY, 1984.

17. Technical Marketing Staff of Gates Energy Products, Inc., <u>Rechargable Batteries Applications Handbook</u>, Butterworth-Heinemann, Boston, MA, 1992.

18. M. J. Riezenman, "The Great Battery Barrier" in "Electric Vehicles", v. 29, no. 11, pp. 97-101, *IEEE Spectrum*, November 1992.

19. A. Fleischer, "Sintered-Plate Nickel-Cadmium Batteries", Proc. Fourth Annual Battery Research and Development Conference, United States Army Signal Engineering Laboratories, Fort Monmouth, NJ, 23-24 May, 1950

20. J. P. Cornu, "The NiCd Battery: The Actual Best Electrochemical Generator for Electric Vehicles", SAFT Industrial Battery Division, Romainville, France, 1992 (available from SAFT America, Inc., Cockeysville, MD).

21. L. O'Connor, "Energizing the Batteries for Electric Cars", v. 115, No. 7, pp. 73-75, *Mechanical Engineering, ASME,* New York, NY, July 1993.

22. M. C. Cheiky, L. G. Danczyk and M. C. Wehrey, "Second Generation Zinc-Air Powered Electric Minivans", pp. 79-86, <u>Electric and Hybrid Vehicle Technology</u>, SP-915, Society of Automotive Engineers, Inc., Warrendale, PA, 1992.

23. J. H. Stanard, Alupower Canada Ltd., private communication, Kingston, OT, 1990.

24. M. Ingram, "More Flexibility for Batteries", *Nature,* v. 362, pp. 112-113, 1993.

25. C. J. Coe, Electrosource, Inc., private communication, Austin, TX, 1993.

26. G. Stix, "Electric Car Pool", v. 266, no. 5, pp. 126-127, *Scientific American*, May 1992.

27. R. C. Flanagan, "Design, Manufacture and Test Results for Four High Energy Density Fibre Composite Rotors", pp. 901-907, Proceedings IECEC '86, San Diego, CA, August, 1986.

28. M. Parrish, D. W. Nauss, "The Spin Doctors: Flyweels Seen as Key to a Practical Electric Vehicle", pp. D1-D4, *Los Angeles Times*, January 5, 1994.

29. P. J. Mills and P. A. Smith, "Carbon-Fiber Reinforced Plastics", pp. 39-47, Concise Encyclopeadia of Composite Materials, A. Kelly (ed.), Pergamon Press, Oxford, UK and The MIT Press, Cambridge, MA, 1989.

30. M. Taube, Evolution of Matter and Energy, Springer-Verlag, New York, NY, 1985.

31. P. Hoffmann, The Forever Fuel: The Story of Hydrogen, Westview Press, Boulder, CO, 1981.

32. J. O'M. Bockris, Energy Options: Real Economics and the Solar-Hydrogen System, John Wiley & Sons, New York, NY, 1980.

33. A. M. Weinberg, *Physics Today,* p. 18, 1959.

34. R. E. Billings, The Hydrogen World View, American Academy of Science, Independence, MO, 1991.

35. W. Peschka, Liquid Hydrogen – Fuel of the Future, Springer-Verlag, New York, NY, 1992.

36. R. R. Adt, Jr., M. R. Swain, J. M. Pappas, Hydrogen Engine Performance Project, (a) US DOE, Second Annual Report, Contr. No. EC-77C03-1212, Washington, DC, 1980 and (b) Report DOE/CS/31212-1, Washington, DC, May 1983.

37. P. C. T. De Boer, W. J. McLean, H. S. Homman, "The Performance and Emissions of Hydrogen-Fueled Internal Combustion Engines", *Int. J. Hydrogen Energy*, v. 1, p. 153, 1976.

38. S. Furuhama, Y. Kobayashi, "Development of Hot-Surface-Ignition Hydrogen Injection Two Stroke Engine", *Proc. 4th World Hydrogen Energy Conf.*, v. 3, pp. 1009-1020, Pergamon Press, New York, NY, 1982.

39. H. S. Homman, P. C. T. De Boer, W. J. McLean, "The Effect of Fuel Injection on NO_X-Emissions and Undesirable Combustion for Hydrogen Fueled Piston Engines", *Int. J. Hydrogen Energy*, v. 8, pp. 131-146, 1983.

40. C. J. Winter, J. Nitsch (eds.), Hydrogen as an Energy Carrier, Springer-Verlag, New York, NY, 1988.

41. K. A. G. Amankwah and J. A. Schwarz, " Assessment of the Effect of Impurity Gases on the Storage Capacity of Hydrogen on Activated Carbon Using the Concept of Effective Adsorbed Phase Molar Volume", *Int. J. Hydrogen Energy*, v. 16, no. 5, pp. 339-344, 1991.

42. U. Seifert and P. Walzer, Automobile Technology of the Future, Society of automotive Engineers, Inc., Warrendale, PA, 1991.

43. A. W. Judge, Small Gas Turbines, Macmillan Co., New York, NY, 1960.

44. Volvo Car Corporation, "Environmental Concept Car", Press Information, Public Relations and Public Affairs, Goeteborg, SW, 1993.

45. A. J. Appleby, "Advanced Fuel Cells and Their Future Market", v. 13, pp. 267-316, Ann. Rev. Energy, Annual Reviews Inc., Palo Alto, CA, 1988.

46. B. Stoddard, "Fuel Cell Update: Coming to Market", pp. 16-19, *American Gas J.*, June 1993.

47. D. G. Lovering, "The Grove Fuel Cell Symposium", v. 33, no. 4, pp. 169-177, *Platinum Metals Rev.*, 1989.

48. D. G. Lovering, "Second Grove Fuel Cell Symposium", v. 35, no. 4, pp. 209-221, *Platinum Metals Rev.*, 1991.

49. D. G. Lovering, "Third Grove Fuel Cell Symposium", v. 37, no. 4, pp. 197-209, *Platinum Metals Rev.*, 1993.

50. G. A. H., "Realizing the Potential of Fuel Cells", v. 37, no. 1, pp. 24-25, *Platinum Metals Rev.*, 1993.

51. M. Presley, "First Hydrogen Fuel Cell Powered Bus", *Hydrogen Today*, v. 5, no. 1, pp. 1-3, American Hydrogen Association, Tempe, AZ, 1994.

52. R. Lipkin, "Firing- Up Fuel Cells: Has a Space-Age Technology Finally Come of Age for Civilians?", v. 114, n. 20, pp. 314-318, *Science News*, 1993.

53. M. Parrish, "Fuel Cells Coming to Life", *Los Angeles Times*, p. D1, February 26, 1994.

54. B. D. Mandelik and D. S. Newsome, "Hydrogen" in Encyclopeadia of Chemical Technology, Kirk-Othmer (eds.), 3rd ed., v. 12, pp. 938-982, John Wiley & Sons, New York, NY, 1980.

55. W. L. Faith, D. B. Keyes, R. L. Clark, Industrial Chemicals, 3rd ed., John Wiley & Sons, New York, NY, 1965.

56. G. J. MacDonald, "The Future of Methane as an Energy Source", Ann. Rev. Energy, v. 15, pp. 53-83, Annual Reviews Inc., Palo Alto, CA, 1990.

57. R. F. Probstein, R. E. Hicks, Synthetic Fuels, McGraw-Hill Book Company, New York, NY, 1982.

58. J. B. Pohlenz and L. O. Stine, "New Process Promises Low-Cost Hydrogen", *The Oil and Gas Journal*, pp. 82-85, April 23, 1962.

59. C. J. Weinberg and R. H. Williams, "Energy from the Sun", Energy for Planer Earth : Readings from Scientific American, pp. 106-118, W. H. Freeman and Co., New York, NY, 1991.

60. G. W. Braun and D. R. Smith, "Commercial Wind Power: Recent Experience In the United States", v. 17, *Ann. Rev. Energy Environ.*, pp. 97-121, Annual Reviews Inc., Palo Alto, CA, 1992.

61. "The Quixotic Technology: Is Wind Energy an Impossible Dream?", *The Economist,* pp. 99-100, November 14, 1992.

62. D. Jaffe and R. E. Herbster, "SEGS VIII Solar-Power Project: Apply Latest Technology at Solar-Powered Generating Plant", *Power,* v. 134, no. 4, pp. 19-23, 1990.

63. D. E. Carlson, "Photovoltaic Technologies for Commercial Power Generation", *Ann. Rev. Energy,* pp. 85-98, Annual Reviews Inc., Palo Alto, CA, 1990.

64. Energy Information Administration, "Estimates of US Biofuels Consumption 1990", DOE/EIA-0548(90), US DOE, Washington, DC, 1991.

65. Energy Information Administration, "Energy Information Sheets", DOE/EIA-0578(91), US DOE, Washington, DC, 1993.

66. M. Valenti, "Coal Gasification: An Alternative Energy Source is Coming of Age", *Mech. Eng.*, v. 114, no. 1, pp. 39-43, 1992.

67. L. P. White and L. G. Plaskett, <u>Biomass as Fuel</u>, Academic Press, New York, NY, 1981.

68. M. Slesser and C. Lewis, <u>Biological Energy Resources</u>, E & F N Spon Ltd, London, UK and Halsted Press, John Wiley & Sons, New York, NY, 1979.

69. S.F.B., "Gasoline-Electric Volvo", p. 30, *Popular Science,* v. 247, no. 1, July 1995.

70. Organization for Economic Co-operation and Development, <u>Biotechnology for a Clean Environment</u>, p. 47, OECD, Paris, FR, 1994.

Chapter 10

Strategies to Implement Natural Gas as a Vehicular Fuel

INTRODUCTION

Natural gas is the most versatile and most valuable fossil fuel available today both in the US and the rest of the world. Let us summarize once more its present use in the country. The current consumption of natural gas in the US is on the order of 20 trillion scf per year. Of this amount, 4.8 trillion scf/y or 24% are consumed in the residential sector, 2.8 trillion scf/y or 14% are consumed in the commercial sector and 7.6 trillion scf/y or 38% are employed in the industrial sector. In addition, the electric utilities utilize 2.9 trillion scf annually or 14.5% of the total for the generation of 275 billion kWh/y of electricity. The remainder 1.9 trillion scf/y or 9.5% are used as either lease and plant fuel (1.3 trillion scf/y) or pipeline fuel (0.6 trillion scf/y). Lease and plant fuel comprises the natural gas used in the production and processing of natural gas. Pipeline fuel is the natural gas consumed in the transportation of natural gas form the processing plants to the consumers.

The uses of natural gas in the residential and commercial sectors encompass space heating, domestic water heating, cooking and clothes drying. On the other hand, natural gas is used in the industrial sector as the feedstock for the manufacturing of a variety of chemicals such as ethylene for most plastics, ammonia for fertilizers, methanol and ethanol for plastics and solvents, and hydrogen used in oil refining. In the future, the motor gasoline and diesel fuel presently used to power passenger cars, light trucks, vans, heavy trucks and buses will be replaced with natural gas. This fuel switching for transportation will require ultimately some 8 trillion scf/y including the lease, plant and pipeline losses — possibly as low as 4 trillion scf/yr depending on whether the average vehicle fuel efficiency can be raised to 80 mpg gasoline equivalent.

Some of the 4 to 8 trillion scf/y may come from increased natural gas production. However, the majority of the increase in demand for natural gas must be met by reducing the current use of natural gas through increased efficiency. Natural gas is obviously a versatile fuel because of the multitude of uses it can accommodate. The natural gas resource has a finite magnitude, although biomass derived natural gas can be produced at a much higher cost and lower rate than fossil natural gas. The maximum annual production of fossil natural gas that can be sustained in the US may on the order of 25 trillion scf/y on the basis of past history[1].

It is instructive, therefore, to examine the efficiency with which natural gas can be used in a variety of applications including automotive propulsion. The purpose for this examination is to establish a hierarchical ordering of the use of natural gas in the economy of the country. This ordering based on efficiency will then serve as a guide to allocate natural gas use to higher efficiency tasks and use alternate fuels, not as versatile and therefore not as valuable, for the lower efficiency tasks. It is important to appreciate the fact that while the general concept of efficiency has a physical and a technological basis, the implementation of efficiency has also an economic basis that needs to be addressed as well. As is was made clear in an earlier chapter, technological change always intertwines technology and economics.

PHYSICAL EFFICIENCY IN THE USE OF NATURAL GAS

The physical efficiency in the use of natural gas as well as any other fuel has to be established with the aid of the laws of thermodynamics applied to a particular task or process[2][3]. The first law efficiency measures the relationship between total energy inputs and useful energy outputs. The second law efficiency relates to a more subtle concept, one that defines the optimal efficiency as the minimum energy input required to perform a given task.

The First Law states that energy (chemical, electrical, mechanical, heat, etc.) can only be transformed from one form to another, but cannot be created or destroyed. The corresponding efficiency of an energy using process may be defined as:

$$e_1 = \{useful\ energy\ output\}/\{energy\ actually\ input\}$$

Application of the first law efficiency requires definition of the boundaries of the system within which the process occurs, and the determination of energy flows across these boundaries, including input, output and losses[*]. For example, energy losses in a residential forced-air furnace consist of the heat carried-off in the flue gases and the heat transmitted to the environment through conduction, convection and radiation rather than heating the air stream. Typical first law efficiencies of residential natural gas forced-air furnaces are 0.85 and can be as high as 0.96 for the so called pulsed combustion furnace[4].

The Second Law seeks to distinguish between energy that is available and unavailable for doing useful work. The concept of entropy is introduced to describe the state of order of the system. In the residential forced-air furnace example, the entropy of natural gas plus that of cold air is lower than the entropy of hot air plus the entropy of the combustion products. The capability of extracting useful work from the natural gas/cold air system is much higher than that of hot-air/combustion products after the combustion of natural gas in the furnace. The second law efficiency relates the minimum input required to perform a given task to the maximum useful work that could have been extracted from the fuel used. It may be defined as:

---

[*] In a heat device such as a forced-air furnace or an internal combustion engine, the chemical energy content E_i of the fuel burned (e.g., natural gas) produces an output E_o (warm air or kinetic energy), then $e_1 = E_o/E_i = 1-(E_l/E_i)$ with E_l the energy losses during the conversion (combustion in this instance) process and $E_i = E_l + E_o$ according to the first law. In a fuel cell the first law efficiency is equal to the ratio of actual (operating or closed circuit) device voltage V to the electromotive or open circuit voltage E so that $e_1 = V/E$.

e_2 ={theoretical minimum energy required}/
{maximum useful work available from actual energy input}

In the simple case of a heat device with heat transfer from a hot source to a cold reservoir which is to be heated, the theoretical minimum energy required is defined with respect to the ideal Carnot energy cycle between the same two temperatures[*]. If the temperature of the cold reservoir is zero (absolute zero temperature) then the second law efficiency is 100 percent ($e_2$max = 1.00). However, the Third Law of thermodynamics states that the absolute zero temperature cannot be attained. If the process of converting one form of energy into another entails the direct conversion of chemical energy into electricity as in a fuel cell, the second law efficiency, defined by the same equation as before, is given as ratio of the electrical work done by the cell (Gibbs free energy) to the energy available in the combination of the reactants under constant pressure (enthalpy)[**][6]. It should be noted that contrary to claims in the popular press that the second law efficiency of fuel cells is 100%, there is a finite increase in entropy in converting chemical energy to electricity. Thus, the theoretical second law efficiency of hydrogen and oxygen combining in a fuel cell is 94% at 77°F (298 K).

In the example of the residential natural gas furnace, one may use 32°F (273 K) for the ambient air temperature and 77°F (298 K) for the temperature of the hot air delivered into the house. Then, one obtains e_{2max} = 0.084 or 8.4 percent and e_2 = 0.08 or 8% as the second law efficiency. It is apparent that for the residential forced-air furnace the first law efficiency is very high, but the second law efficiency is quite low.

The second law efficiency may be increased in any of three ways:

- Improve the Device
- Change the Device in Use
- Change the Process

---

[*]. The theoretical minimum energy required $E_w = E_o \{(T_h - T_a)/T_h\}$, where E_o is the thermal energy transferred, T_h is the absolute temperature of the hot reservoir and T_a is the absolute temperature of the cold reservoir. Thus, the maximum value of e_2 for a process operating between two temperature reservoirs, i.e., involving the transfer of heat, is the Carnot cycle efficiency $e_{2max} = (T_h - T_a)/T_h$.

[**]. The second law efficiency of an electrochemical conversion is given by the expression e_{2max} = DG/DH = 1 - (T DS)/DH, where DG is the Gibbs free energy, DH is the enthalpy, T is the absolute temperature of the reaction and DS is the entropy change of the reactants before and after the reaction. In general, whether a heat engine or an electrochemical device is involved, it is true that (energy output) = e_1 x (maximum useful work available) so that e_2 = $e_1 \cdot e_{2max}$.

Following the example of the forced-air furnace, one may improve this system by preheating the exterior air with indoor return air (implemented already in the high first law efficiency of a natural gas forced-air furnace). One may also change the device from a forced-air furnace to a heat pump with a first law efficiency higher than one. Finally, one may change the process by heating people directly rather than the air surrounding them. Three cases of the use of natural gas are considered with respect to efficient resource utilization and certain conclusions are derived regarding the emphasis for future product development.

Natural Gas Space Heating. Three devices or systems are considered here. Two of these devices have been used traditionally in the US for residential space heating, while a third device may become available in the future. These devices or systems are: the natural gas forced-air furnace, the electric vapor-compression cycle heat pump and the natural gas proton membrane fuel cell[4][5][7]. The first and second law efficiencies of a natural gas forced air furnace have already been described. As it has already been mentioned, the first law efficiency is 0.85 to 0.96 for present day natural gas forced-air furnaces, whereas the calculated second law efficiency ranges from 0.07 to 0.08 for the same device. The first law efficiency of the heat pump is none other than the coefficient of performance (COP) of the heat pump[*]. Typically, the seasonal COP for a residential heat pump may very from 2.0 to 2.5. The operational temperatures are assumed to be the same as for the natural gas furnace. One important consideration for heat pumps is that the COP depends very strongly on the ambient temperature. The lower the ambient temperature is the lower the COP becomes. If an operational COP of 2 is assumed, a value of 0.16 is obtained for the second law efficiency. The residential fuel cell is envisioned to be a 5 kW device producing electricity at a 40% efficiency and low temperature heat at a 45% efficiency[7]. The fuel will be natural gas which will be steam reformed to hydrogen to power the proton exchange membrane fuel cell. The low temperature

---

[*] In the case of a heat pump, the respective efficiencies are defined as follows: $e_1 = Q_o/W_i$ and $e_2 = e_1 \{(T_h - T_a)/T_h\}$, where Q_o is the heat removed from the environment and W_i is the electric energy used to drive the heat pump compressor.

heat is a by-product of the fuel cell electricity generation and can be conveniently utilized for space heating as well as domestic water heating — for this device one has $e_1 = E_o/E_i$ and $e_2 = 0.94 \, e_1$. The residential proton membrane fuel cell has values of 0.40 and 0.38 for the first and second law efficiencies, respectively. It should be noted that the aforementioned efficiencies include the reformation efficiency from natural gas to hydrogen. Thus, the utilization of a fuel cell at home powered by natural gas can generate not only electricity at much higher efficiency than that of the utility (40% at home vs. less than 30% delivered by the utility), but it is also several times more effective in using a high quality fuel as natural gas to heat space and water than a forced air furnace or a heat pump which also uses premium energy, i.e., electricity, for the same purpose.

Natural Gas Power Generation. Natural gas is being used and will continue to be used in the generation of electricity. Two devices are considered here for the conversion of natural gas to electricity. The first device is the aeroderivative gas turbine which is currently used widely either as a peaking system or as baseload system in areas with severe air pollution where no other fuel may be employed. The second device is the phosphoric acid fuel cell which is rapidly reaching the commercialization status. The aeroderivative gas turbine system includes a second stage steam turbine to increase both first law and second law efficiencies[8][9]. The exhaust gases from the gas turbine are used to generate steam which in turn powers a steam turbine for additional electricity generation[*]. The maximum operational temperature of the gas turbine combined system is currently 2300°F (1550 K). Hence, one obtains 0.81 for the maximum Carnot efficiency of the system at an ambient temperature of 81°F (300 K). Practical first law efficiencies for electricity generation have already reached 58 percent[9][42]. Thus, the first and second law efficiencies for the current combined cycle gas turbine are 0.58 and 0.47, respectively. The phosphoric acid fuel cell uti-

---

[*]. The first and second law efficiencies of the gas turbine combined system are given by $e_1 = E_o/E_i$ and $e_2 = e_1 \{(T_h - T_a)/T_h\}$, where E_o is the generated electricity by the two stage system and E_i is the input to the system natural gas energy.

lizes natural gas as a fuel. The natural gas reformation to hydrogen by steam takes place externally to the system. This is again a direct conversion system from fuel to electricity. Hence, the first law efficiency includes the efficiency of reforming natural gas to hydrogen. Typical performance characteristics of phosphoric acid fuel cells are 40 % electricity generation and 45% heat generation in the form of hot water[10]. Thus, one obtains 40% (electricity) and 45% (heat) for the first law efficiency and 38% (electricity) and 42% (heat) for the second law efficiency. Under development natural gas fuel cells such as the molten carbonate and solid oxide ones will reform internally the natural gas (at the electrodes) thereby increasing significantly the first and second law efficiencies for electricity generation, while the heat generation efficiency will diminish accordingly. Thus, future natural gas fuel cells for stationary applications may have first and second law efficiencies in the vicinity of 55% for electricity and 25% percent for heat.

Natural Gas Vehicle Propulsion. Natural gas will be used to fuel vehicles of any type. The efficiencies of three propulsion systems are considered. The first propulsion system consists of an internal combustion engine (ICE) and represents current technology. The second power train consists of a hybrid electric-ICE system. The third power train is also a hybrid system with a solid electrolyte (proton exchange membrane) fuel cell replacing the internal combustion engine. The internal combustion engine considered is the four stroke motor represented theoretically by the Otto cycle. The first law efficiency of the Otto cycle is well known and is a function of the engine compression ratio as well as the physical properties of the working fluid (air-fuel mixture)[2][*]. The allowable engine compression ratio is a function of the octane rating of the fuel. The compression ratio must be such that it will not lead to spontaneous ignition of the fuel before the advent of the spark. Thus, the higher the octane rating of the fuel is, the higher the compression ratio can be. For a gasoline

---

[*]. The first law efficiency of the otto cycle engine is given by the expression $_e 1 = 1 - 1/\{(r)^{g-1}\}$, where r is the engine compression ratio and g is the ratio of heat capacities under constant pressure and constant volume of the working fluid (air-fuel mixture). The value of g for stoichiometric composition of the air-fuel mixture is 1.373 for gasoline, 1.394 for natural gas and 1.399 for hydrogen.

engine the compression ratio is typically nowadays about 8.9:1 using unleaded gasoline with an octane rating from 87 to 92, while the ideal compression ratio for the same engine with natural gas fuel (octane rating 128 to 130) is 14:1, even though it can be even higher. The theoretical first law efficiency of an internal combustion engine using either motor gasoline or natural gas is given in Table 10-1. The practical first law efficiency of an internal combustion engine is significantly lower, irrespectively of whether motor gasoline or natural gas is used as a fuel. Factors such as friction, acceleration, accessories, turbulence, and heat losses to the environment are responsible for the much lower practical efficiencies shown in Table 10-1. The maximum second law efficiency of an internal combustion engine is given by the Carnot cycle expression. Assuming a maximum working fluid temperature in the engine cylinders of 2300°F (1550 K) and an ambient temperature of 81°F (300 K), the maximum second law efficiency (practical Otto Cycle) of 0.806 is calculated (Carnot cycle efficiency). Significant amount of research is being car-

TABLE 10-1. First and Second Law Efficiency of an Internal Combustion Engine (ICE), a Hybrid Electric-ICE and a Hybrid Electric-Fuel Cell (Solid Polymer Electrolyte) Power Trains for Gasoline and Natural Gas Fuels

Parameter	ICE	Hybrid-ICE	Hybrid-SPE FC
First Law Efficiency			
Theoretical			
Gasoline (CR = 8.9:1)	0.558	0.558	N/A
Natural Gas (CR = 14:1)	0.646	0.646	0.675[1]
Practical			
Gasoline (CR = 8.9:1)	0.200	0.300	N/A
Natural Gas (CR = 14:1)	0.230	0.350	0.405[2]
Second Law Max Efficiency			
Any Fuel	0.806	0.806	0.940
Second Law Practical Efficiency			
Gasoline (CR = 8.9:1)	0.161	0.242	N/A
Natural Gas (CR = 14:1)	0.185	0.282	0.387

1. It is assumed that the hydrogen to electricity conversion efficiency is 90%, while the efficiency of reforming natural gas to hydrogen is 75 percent. 2. A 90% inverter/electric motor efficiency is assumed in converting electrical energy from DC to AC and that into mechanical energy.

ried out to increase the second law maximum efficiency by increasing the operating temperature of the internal combustion engine. To this end, the development of ceramic coatings for the interior of the cylinders and in particular the surface of the pistons may allow a higher operating temperature by a few hundred degrees thereby increasing the Carnot Cycle efficiency by as many as 10% points and the second law efficiency by 1 or 2 percentage points. The hybrid-ICE system is assumed to have a minimum 50% increase in fuel efficiency from an identical ICE system even after one accounts for the possible incremental vehicle weight due to electrochemical or other storage. This hybrid-ICE performance is also reflected in Table 10-1. The utilization of a proton exchange membrane or a solid polymer electrolyte fuel cell (SPFC) as a vehicular propulsion system requires the presence of an additional component such as electrochemical batteries or flywheels. Moreover, the use of low temperature fuel cells, inherently appropriate for mobile applications, requires that the natural gas fuel is reformed externally to the fuel cell to produce hydrogen which is in turn oxidized in the fuel cell to generate electricity. An electric motor completes the power train of a fuel cell powered vehicle. Besides the proton membrane fuel cell efficiency of converting hydrogen to electricity at about 60 percent, one must account for the steam reforming of natural gas to hydrogen with an efficiency of 75 percent and the conversion of electricity to mechanical energy by the motor/inverter with an efficiency of about 90 to 95 percent. First law, second law and total efficiencies for the hybrid fuel cell system are summarized in Table 10-1 as well.

Conclusions. The consideration of the first law efficiency only in the utilization of natural gas in a variety of energy related applications gives an incomplete picture regarding the proper use of a high quality fuel. In other words a high quality fuel such as natural gas may be used for low quality applications, albeit with great efficiency. High quality is here synonymous to the low entropy content of the fuel or in more practical terms the notion of the ability of the fuel to power a high temperature thermal engine. The purpose of calculating the second law efficiency for the same applications is to establish a better match between energy sources and end uses so that a high quality energy source, which may be scarce, is not used to perform low quality work.

The first observation along the second law efficiency argument is with regard of the use of natural gas for space and water heating. About 50 percent of the natural gas consumed annually in the commercial and residential sectors or some 3.8 trillion scf/y are used for space heating. This is a task with a first law efficiency of over 80 percent, but a second law efficiency of only 8 percent. Space heating using a natural gas forced air furnace is obviously a case of a high quality fuel used for a low quality task. On the other hand, the use of natural gas as a fuel for the internal combustion engine of a vehicle has roughly twice the second law efficiency as for space heating. Thus, natural gas is utilized much more effectively, one hundred percent to be specific, when used to propel a vehicle rather than to heat space. It is worth noting that the last statement is true for presently available technology, i.e., the internal combustion engine and the forced air furnace. The advent of the fuel cell technology for space heating and vehicle propulsion results in a second law efficiency comparable for both applications. Moreover, the utilization of fuel cells for space heating increases the second law efficiency by almost 5 times compared to the forced air furnace and 2.5 times compared to the electric heat pump. On the other hand, the utilization of fuel cells for vehicular propulsion, although the most efficient from the second law perspective, is only 25% more efficient than the utilization of a hybrid ICE propulsion system fueled with natural gas. Thus, it is fair to conclude that on the basis of the second law of thermodynamics current technology favors the switching of the use of natural gas from space heating to vehicle propulsion. In addition and even more important, the development of proton exchange membrane fuel cells at the 5 kW level for residential applications constitutes a superior objective compared to the application of the same type fuel cells for vehicular propulsion.

The second observation concerns the use of natural gas for centralized electricity generation. The second law efficiency of electricity generation by a gas turbine with a combined cycle is very close to that of a solid polymer electrolyte or phosphoric acid fuel cell, albeit slightly higher. On the other hand, the solid polymer electrolyte or phosphoric acid fuel cell generates an even higher amount of low temperature (160°F) thermal energy than even its electricity output. This indicates that utilization of natural gas by a solid polymer or a phosphoric acid fuel cell is ideal (more efficient) for decentralized electricity generation associated with the use of thermal energy in single-family and multi-family residential buildings, in commercial buildings and in industrial facilities. Moreover, the use of natural gas as a fuel of a gas turbine combined cycle in base load and intermediate load power plants for electricity generation should be replaced with combined cycle clean coal technologies. These technologies, which display high thermal efficiencies alongside emission levels that approach those of natural gas fueled power generation, include the commercially available integrated coal gasification combined cycle (IGCC)[10][11][12]. These processes make use of a gas turbine topping cycle and a steam turbine bottoming cycle with efficiencies in the range of 45%-48% and ultimately as high as 52% with the use of a 60% efficient gas turbine[43]. Coal is gasified, while it is also desulfurized, and the resulting gases are combusted in low emission NO_x burners and then fed into a gas turbine. In a variant of the IGCC process some natural gas is mixed with the coal gases to boost the temperature and increase efficiency. The implementation of the IGCC and other combined cycle technologies to all base and intermediate load power plants will not only allow better utilization of coal for a cleaner electric power generation, but it will also eliminate the need to burn natural gas in base load and intermediate load power plants.

Incidentally, the trend of coal gasification rather than direct coal burning for power generation may be evident from the logistic curves of primary energy sources substitution in the US (Figure 8.3). The contribution of coal appears to remain constant at about 25% of the total rather than becoming only a few percent, while natural gas appears to increase to capture more than 50% of the market share. One plausible explanation is that coal retains its present level of production, but the market share of coal burned directly for power generation eventually diminishes to a few percent point, while the coal gasification process becomes dominant. The market share of coal used in coal gasification is then counted as part of the natural gas market share to result in the very large future contribution of natural gas as an energy source in this country.

It should be noted that during the last 20 years there has been a significant improvement in the use of natural gas for space and water heating, while the same degree of improvement has not been witnessed in the use of electricity. Thus, the use of natural gas in the residential and commercial sectors during this period has remained unchanged at about 7.5 trillion scf per year. During the same 20 years the electricity consumption in the residential and commercial sectors combined has increased from about 1025 billion kWh/y to 1850 billion kWh/y with a corresponding energy input of 12 quads and 20 quads, respectively. During the last twenty years the first law efficiency of forced air furnaces, for example, has increased from 50% to over 90%, while the second law efficiency has remained the same. Now, the second law of thermodynamics dictates the course of action with regard to the utilization of natural gas in building applications. Thus, the stage is being set for the next step in efficiency increase, which entails the development of fuel cells for decentralized power and heat generation in buildings with natural gas as the input fuel.

However, the implementation of fuel cells for automotive propulsion is a much more difficult proposition to attain. This difficulty is due in part to the fact that the internal combustion engine has almost as good a second law efficiency as a fuel cell, while the first law efficiency of the former can be also improved to approach that of the latter. Thus, another criterion besides physical efficiency should determine the viability of an internal combustion engine versus a fuel cell as well as the selection of the fuel of choice in the area of land transportation.

ECONOMIC EFFICIENCY IN THE USE OF NATURAL GAS

Considerations of first and second law efficiencies in substituting a fuel or a technology for another are necessary, but not sufficient conditions for their implementation. The economic justification of the substitute fuels and technologies must be also addressed and be part of the implementation process. However, the laws of thermodynamics and economic processes are nor unrelated in the context of utilizing our natural resources to sustain and improve our standard of living[13][14][15]. The higher first and second law efficiencies in the implementation of an alternative fuel with the associated technologies or devices will reduce the consumption of the fuel, which will in turn reduce the rate of depletion of the natural resource. The use of the alternative fuel may also improve the environmental quality not only because of the reduced use of the fuel, but even more so because of the inherent qualities in the alternative fuel chosen to replace an existing one. Natural gas is in fact a case in point with respect to automotive applications. Its gaseous nature combined with its chemical constitution allow for a more efficient utilization and a much lower environmental impact compared to any other fossil fuel and even energy carriers such as electricity and hydrogen depending on the mode of their generation.

The environment in its most global sense consists of the planet Earth and is essentially a closed economic system with one external source of energy — solar energy. The economy and the environment are characterized by a circular relationship rather than linear interactions. Thus, everything is an input into everything else. Consequently, the creation of utility for an individual, a community or a country, which is the purpose of economic activity or the economy in general, will be determined by the limits or boundaries set by the closed system within which all these entities function. The relevance of the First and Second Laws of thermodynamics in the economic activity and the environment is inescapable. Any economic activity uses up natural resources and generates wastes. The first law essentially states that energy and matter cannot be destroyed. Hence, the amount of resources used up in any period is equal to the amount of resources embodied in capital equipment plus the waste generated during the formation of new capital as well as the wearing out of existing capital. The economy and the environment are interlinked through a circular relationship, i.e., everything depends on everything else aboard the closed economic system of "Spaceship Earth"[13].

The notion of recycling waste to convert it back to resource becomes then a relevant economic activity in the light of the circular relationship between economy and the environment. The recycling of paper, glass, steel, aluminum, plastics and a multitude of other materials is a natural and inevitable consequence of the aforementioned circular relationship, rather than an imposition of the will of a small group of

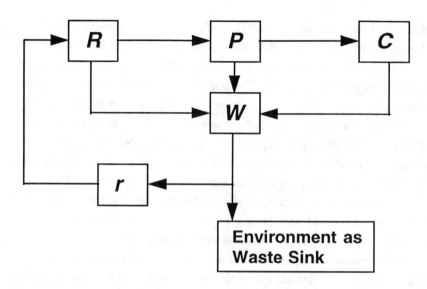

FIGURE 10-1. The Circular Economy Making Use of Resources "R" Resulting in the production "P" of consumer items "C", while it Generates Wastes "W" that are Disposed in the Environment with a Fraction "r" Being Recycled.

activists and government officials. So is the development of clean air laws requiring the reduction in pollution generated, for instance, by automobiles to mention an example relevant to the subject of natural gas as a transportation fuel. Figure 10-1 shows in a schematic form the circular relationship between the economy and the environment.

The natural observation is that if all waste were to be recycled then the economy would become a closed system. Unfortunately, the second law of thermodynamics becomes relevant in the context of a closed economic system in that it places a limit to the extent of recycling waste[14]. There is a basic or fundamental reason for the lack of complete recycling of waste generated by economic activity. The resources that get used in the economy tend to be used entropically, i.e., they get dissipated within the economic system. For example, it is very unrealistic to recycle every material used in the manufacturing of an automobile. Such recycling is unrealistic not so much from a physical point as it is from an economic point of view. That is to say, it would be prohibitively expensive to contemplate recycling all materials in a car. However, the

degree of recycling in a vehicle can be optimized (increased) by designing the automobile in such a way so as to be more conducive to recycling. As another example, let us consider the combustion of a fossil
fuel in the engine of an automobile. The combustion process in the
engine converts the chemical energy of the fuel into vehicular kinetic
energy (useful work) along with heat energy rejected to the environment
and the air emissions (material) to the atmosphere. One could in principle collect the exhaust gases, which are mainly carbon dioxide and
water vapor, and combine them through a series of chemical reactions
with the input of free solar energy to recreate the already consumed
fuel. Such a process makes undoubtedly no economic sense whatsoever.

What makes sense, on the other hand, is to select a fuel that burns
more efficiently and generates less waste. Thus, selecting natural gas as
the next transportation fuel may be the optimal choice in the circular
economy. The meaning of an optimal choice here is with regard to the
maximum reduction in waste sank into the environment from the present fuel (gasoline) per unit of added monetary investment of the alternative fuel vehicle over the present one. Table 10-2 shows clearly that
natural gas represents the optimal choice over all other alternative transportation fuels. The analysis in Table 10-2 is rather simplified in nature,
but nevertheless conveys the economic efficiency of using natural gas as
a transportation fuel. It is worth noting that natural gas offers by far the
most cost effective reduction in air pollution compared to other alternative fuels such as methanol and electricity. In fact, methanol is worse
than electricity, if the long term incremental cost of an electric vehicle
can be maintained around $10,000 over its gasoline counterpart.

Thus, the application of the first and second laws of thermodynamics to economic activity indicates that the use of natural gas as a transportation fuel is a far better choice than all the other major alternatives.
The obvious question to ask then is whether there is a need to replace
gasoline vehicles with natural gas vehicles. After all the numbers in
Table 10-2 seem to indicate that gasoline requires no additional cost
compared to all other fuels, if the current level of air pollution is acceptable. Unfortunately, a lot of people are misled in answering this question because they only consider the first law of thermodynamics applied
to economics. The first law would probably indicate that the economic

TABLE 10-2. Comparison of Relative Changes in Environmental Waste Generation and Attendant Economic Investment of Gasoline, Methanol, Natural Gas and Electricity as Land Transportation Fuels

Fuel	Level of Pollution[1]	Incremental Cost[2]	Pollution Reduction per Unit of Investment[3]
Gasoline	100%	$ 0	—
Reform. Gasoline	90%	$2,000 ($0)	5% / $1,000
Methanol	80%	$4,000 ($1,000)	5% / $1,000
Natural Gas	15%	$1,400 ($3,000)	60% / $1,000
Electricity	0%	$10,000 ($11,500)	10% / $1,000

1. Relative levels with respect to gasoline representing the base case. A very conservative estimate has been used for natural gas and an extremely favorable one for electricity. 2. Total of added vehicle cost, shown in parenthesis, and differential fuel cost with respect to the gasoline alternative vehicle and fuel; 4000 gal gasoline equivalent fuel use per vehicle (10 years at 400 gal/yr) with a $0.50/gal higher fuel cost for reformulated gasoline, a $0.75/gal higher fuel cost for methanol and $0.40/gal less fuel cost for natural gas; 25,000 kWh fuel use for electric vehicle (2,500 kWh/yr for 10 years) at a price of $0.10/kWh versus 4,000 gal gasoline at $1.00 per gallon. 3. Ratio of relative decrease in pollution per $1,000 of total incremental cost.

benefits from the added efficiency of natural gas vehicles (increased fuel efficiency, longer vehicle life, lower fuel price, etc.) may not be higher than the economic costs of replacing gasoline vehicles (new infrastructure cost, higher vehicle costs, etc.) even in the long run. The answer to the question whether gasoline vehicles should be replaced by natural gas vehicles becomes, however, a resounding "yes" on the basis of the second law of thermodynamics applied to economic activity.

There is a limit to the amount of waste that can be released into the environment without ultimately adversely affecting it. It is true that the environment has the capability to take wastes and to convert them into harmless or ecologically useful products with the aid of the solar energy that represents the only external flow into the closed system of planet Earth. This capability is the environment's assimilative capacity[15]. It is apparent that the economic activity, which encompasses transportation and much more, generates more waste in certain areas of the country than the assimilative capacity of the local environment. Hence, it becomes necessary that measures be taken to reduce the waste from economic activity and bring it within the assimilative capacity of the environment. Transportation plays a major role in the economic activity of the US and the industrialized world today and eventually will become a major player in the economies of the entire world. Moreover, it is apparent that the present transportation sector in the US based primarily on the gasoline vehicle is producing wastes at a rate well above the assimilative capacity of the environment. The replacement of gasoline and diesel vehicles by natural gas vehicles in land transportation presents the most economically efficient solution from among all alternative fuels. As it will be shown in a subsequent section, the replacement of gasoline vehicles by natural gas vehicles represents also a choice with the ability to reduce waste generation well below the assimilative capacity of the environment.

Natural gas as a transportation fuel and the replacement of gasoline and diesel vehicles by natural gas vehicles in the US through 2030 and the world during the first half of the 21st century constitutes, in the opinion of this author, part of what has been described in recent years as sustainable development[16]. Economic development without paying attention to the environment cannot last. It is not sustainable in that it reduces eventually human welfare. The air pollution in most of the metropolitan areas in the US with its impact on humans is an example of reduced welfare. Other parts of the world with an even lesser level of economic activity than the US face an even more serious problem of lost welfare due to air pollution. Sustainable development does not imply, however, zero or negative economic growth as some environmental advocates will have us believe. Economic growth is necessary for the continuous improvement of the human welfare here and abroad. Thus, sustainable development requires an economic growth which is optimal not from the point of view of the first law of thermodynamics alone, but rather from the inclusion of the second law as well. Sustainable development in the transportation sector consists of the continuous reduction in air pollution while the welfare of individuals increases. Technology and economics point clearly to natural gas vehicles as the way to attain sustainable growth in the transportation sector.

GASOLINE TAXATION VS. NATURAL GAS FUEL SUBSTITUTION

An alternative title of this section, indicative of its context, could have been " Can Higher Gasoline Prices Alone Reduce Air Pollution in the US?". It has been argued by several individuals, organizations and others concerned with environmental quality that gasoline is too cheap in the US so that it encourages a wasteful use. The comparison is often made with water leading to the apparent truism that "gasoline is cheaper than water in the US". The same argument then continues by saying that if gasoline prices in the US were similar to those in Europe and elsewhere ($4/gal vs $1.2/gal), people would espouse again public transportation that they abandoned in favor of the private automobile decades ago. Moreover, high gasoline prices will make electric vehicles an instant success despite their high initial cost because of very much reduced fuel costs. While such arguments make a lot of sense on the surface, a closer examination reveals that they are fraught with serious fallacies.

First, one must appreciate the fact that the prevailing present transportation system including fuel prices has evolved slowly over several decades. Nobody has decreed low gasoline prices. Instead the need for higher productivity and efficiency in the economy have lead to the present state of affairs. Likewise the level of European and Japanese gasoline prices reflect the historical evolution in these areas and reflect the realities of their economies. Secondly, an increase in gasoline prices by government fiat cannot and will not function in a linear fashion. As it has been stated numerous times, the economy represents a circular system with everything depending on everything else. Thus, higher gasoline prices will increase all other fuel prices as it became abundantly clear during the energy crises of the 1970s. In addition, higher gasoline prices of the proposed level will send the economy into a tailspin by triggering inflation, reducing productivity, and increasing unemployment to mention only just a few consequences. Finally, people will resist abandoning their private vehicles for other modes of transportation which are no longer popular with the public because they do not offer the same degree of amenity and efficiency as the private automobile. Amenity and efficiency have, of course, economic value or utility in that they increase the productivity of the economy.

Economists have develop a term to quantify the change in consumption of a commodity when its price changes[17]. This term is the so called elasticity of demand. It describes essentially the aforementioned facts of the interlinkage of the various activities within the economy as well as the resistance of the consumer to reduce his or her standards by abandoning the utility of a product because of increased price. An elasticity of demand equal to zero means than no matter what the price of a product becomes the rate of consumption remains unchanged. An elasticity of demand equal to one implies a linear relationship between a price change and the consumption change. Generally, a product has a highly elastic demand if its elasticity of demand value is equal to one or greater than one. Similarly, an elasticity of demand less than one describes an inelastic product particularly if the value is closer to zero. For example, the value of the elasticity of demand for gasoline is less than one[*].

An important consideration regarding the value of the elasticity of demand of a commodity such as gasoline is not a constant. It depends on the value of the commodity itself. Thus, the elasticity of demand for gasoline decreases as the price of gasoline increases. A typical value for the elasticity of demand for gasoline at the prices prevailing in recent times appears to be on the order of 0.5 to 0.6[18][19][20]. However, values as low as 0.15 and as high as 0.85 have been quoted in a variety of studies performed in the 1970s. This is indicative of the uncertainty of econometric models to predict the outcome of large price changes from the present price. It is interesting to note that the price of gasoline has remained essentially unchanged in constant dollars since 1930 even though occasionally brief fluctuations occur such as those in 1974 and 1979 following the two energy crises[18].

The preceding discussion indicates that higher gasoline prices will not automatically result in a significant improvement in air pollution

---

(*). The price elasticity of demand E for a commodity such as gasoline is defined as $E_{av} = -\{DQ/Q_{av}\}/(Dp/p_{av})$, where DQ is the change in the demand of a commodity with an average demand Q_{av} over the interval of change and Dp is the price change of the commodity with an average price p_{av} over the interval of change. The point or instantaneous price elasticity of demand at price p_0 and consumption Q_0 is given by $E = -\{dQ/dp\}/\{p_0/Q_0\}$, where dQ/dp is the instantaneous rate of change (first derivative) of Q with respect to p at the point (p_0, Q_0).

through reduced use of the private automobile and the increase in mass transit — which is, of course, assumed to be less polluting. In fact, if higher gasoline prices constituted a sufficient condition for reduced private vehicle ownership, it would have happened long time ago in Europe and Japan. Historical evidence, however, suggests otherwise. Thus, the private vehicle ownership has been constantly increasing in Europe and Japan as these regions become more prosperous. Moreover, intercity public transportation, i.e., trains, is being abandoned in favor of the automobile. Even intracity private vehicle transportation has increased to its capacity determined by the limited of parking space in most European and Japanese cities.

Finally, pollution control laws were enacted in the US more than twenty years ago, much later in Japan and only recently in Europe. The much more intense use of the private automobile in land transport in the US necessitated the introduction of air pollution controls through standards in the early 1970s. However, the several times higher price of gasoline in Europe and Japan has not been adequate to protect the environment by discouraging the use of the private automobile. Japan and most of Europe have instituted now air pollution control standards similar to those in US as the only means to abate further deterioration of air quality. What this occurrence implies is that high prices alone cannot guarantee a clean environment. Technology has to play also a very important role toward attaining that goal. This is clearly a reverse example of the interplay of technology and economics. Economic measures alone without technological content cannot bring about technological innovation.

The significance of adopting low-polluting technologies in land transportation in order to improve air quality has been demonstrated recently through a series of case studies by the World Bank[21]. These studies were prepared for the 1992 World Development Report on Development and the Environment and compare the impact of price controls vis-a-vis low-polluting technologies and practices in land transportation. The results of these case studies are perhaps surprising to the individual with no-economic background in energy and environmental matters. Specifically, this study examined the vehicular emissions in developing countries for a forty-year period from 1990 to 2030 for a

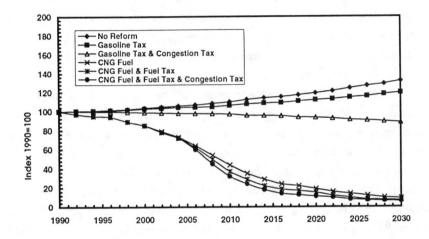

FIGURE 10-2. Relative Air Pollution Emissions from Land Transport Over a Forty Year Period with a Gradual Application of a Variety of Scenarios: I. No Change either in Vehicular Technology (Emissions, Fuel Efficiency) or Gasoline Price ($1/gal); II. Imposition of a $2/gal Gasoline Tax; III. Imposition of a $2/gal Gasoline Tax and a $4/gal Congestion Tax; IV. Replacement of Gasoline with CNG Fuel (90% Reduction in CO, NMOG and NOx Emissions) and a 40 mpg Average New Vehicle Fuel Efficiency by 2005; V. GNG Fuel plus a $2/gge Fuel Tax; VI. CNG Fuel plus a $2/gge Fuel Tax and a $4/gge Congestion Tax.

variety of scenarios. Figure 10-2 summarizes these findings for three different scenarios adapted by the author to the US conditions.

The first scenario, which also serves as the base case, consists of no new fuel price changes or additional pollution control mechanisms beyond the ones already in place, while the number of vehicles increases. The gasoline price is assumed to be $1 per gal (1990 $). It is also assumed that the average vehicle fuel efficiency rises by 2% per year. This implies an average fuel efficiency of about 30 mpg by 2010 from the 20 mpg in 1990 (no further increases in the CAFE standard takes place). The second scenario consists of gradually rising fuel taxes. The gasoline tax is assumed to rise 3% per year until it reaches about $2 per gal (in 1990 $) by 2030. The third scenario assumes the previous fuel tax plus the imposition of congestion taxes. A congestion tax of $2 per vehicle is imposed for vehicles entering the central business district of a city during business hours. This congestion tax is equivalent to $4 per gal, assuming a 30 mile roundtrip to the city and a 15 mpg city fuel efficiency (1990 $). The congestion tax is assumed to rise by 4% per year until it attains its maximum value by 2030.

To each of these three scenarios two technological solutions are added: air emission reductions of 90% for each of carbon monoxide, hydrocarbons and nitrous oxides become possible with the substitution of gasoline with natural gas. Moreover, average new vehicle fuel efficiency increases from 27.5 mpg to 40 mpg by 2005 (new CAFE standard). The cost of these two added technological developments is calculated to be equivalent to an increased CNG fuel price of $1.15/gge from its actual price of $0.65/gge (the total cost is the $0.50/gge fuel price increase times the number of gge of CNG consumed during the life of the vehicle).

The results of Figure 10-2 are extremely informative. Without any additional pollution controls, all forms of pollution rise as one would expect due to increased automobile population as well as driving. A fuel tax of $2/gal reduces gasoline consumption almost to the point to offset increases in automobile population. Only the addition of the $4/gal congestion tax succeeds to bring pollution levels slightly below the present level. The low elasticity of demand for gasoline and the growth in the income of the population essentially more than offset the high gasoline prices of 3 to 5 times the present price.

The substitution of clean fuel technologies, on the other hand, has a decisive effect in reducing pollution well below its present level in spite of population growth in numbers as well as in wealth. It is indeed remarkable that the technological solution of clean fuels can reduce air pollution to between 5 and 10% of the present level even as consumption is rising. It is interesting to note also that the technological solution, namely, the substitution of gasoline for natural gas, gives very similar ultimate pollution results whether there are no new taxes or there is an imposition of a $2/gal fuel tax and/or an imposition of a $4/gal congestion tax.

Obviously, the technological solution of substituting gasoline for natural gas is not free of cost. The important question is to determine how these costs compare to the various tax schemes suggested above. Assuming a 300 to 400 gal gasoline consumption annually, the fuel tax cost alone can be $600 to $800 per year or $6,000 to $8,000 during the life of the vehicle. This cost is two to three times higher than the long term incremental cost of an average natural gas vehicle. Moreover, the natural gas alternative transportation fuel results in 10 times less pollution than that of a $2/gal gasoline tax. Thus, the technological solution of substituting gasoline for natural gas compared to the $2/gal to $4/gal gasoline tax alternatives reduces air pollution by more than 10 times at less than 1/3rd the cost.

The preceding results clearly show what many economists have concluded already. Indirect taxes on gasoline can be an exceedingly blunt instrument for reducing air pollution, and a relatively ineffective one, when compared to the technological solution of substituting gasoline and diesel fuel vehicles with natural gas vehicles.

ULEV VERSUS ZEV: IS THERE A NEED FOR BOTH?

The relevance of the first and second law of thermodynamics to economic activity cannot and must not be overlooked in the consideration of our interaction as living human beings to the natural environment. The notions of the circular economy and of the entropic or waste generating use of natural resources are the consequences of that relevance. While there is little doubt that the validity of these two notions is intuitively apparent to most people, it requires somewhat more reflection to associate them with the laws of thermodynamics. The notions of the circular economy and the entropic use of resources are intimately associated with three economic functions that pertain to the natural environment. It is important to emphasize once more that the economy, any economy, operates within the context of the natural environment. The supply of all resources but one (solar energy) of the economy originates from the natural environment, i.e., the earth. The environment has a capability to take wastes, manmade or otherwise, and to convert them to harmless or ecologically useful products up to a limit. This capability is described as the assimilative capacity of the natural environment.

Finally, the environment possess and supplies certain direct utility to people in the form of aesthetic enjoyment. Notice that if wastes in excess of the assimilative capacity are disposed of in the environment, the aesthetic enjoyment is reduced. Polluted air, for example, is not as pleasing to the eye as clean air. These three economic functions, resource supply, waste assimilation and aesthetic commodity may be regarded as components of a general function of the natural environment, namely, the sustainance of life.

The realization that the environment possesses a finite assimilative capacity is of paramount significance in chartering a desirable course of economic activities. In the past, the economy of industrialized countries has developed without consideration of the consequences to the environment. In recent times, however, the visible damage to the environment has forced the public and governments to take appropriate decisions to reduce or minimize further damage. Unfortunately, there are several instances where such decisions are void of common or economic sense and become counterproductive. Let us consider, for example, the case of air pollution caused by the operation of motor vehicles. There is no doubt that in several parts of the US the combined emissions of mobile (automobiles) and stationary (power plants, industrial facilities, etc.) sources generate more pollutants, i.e., waste, than the local environment can handle.

The use of emission controls in vehicles has been one measure to reduce automobile pollution generation. In the last twenty years substantial reduction in the emissions of new automobiles has been attained approaching almost an order of magnitude reduction (factor of ten) from the precontrol levels. However, the number of automobiles has been steadily increasing as the population increases, as the need for efficient transportation rises, and as the higher disposable income affords more vehicles per household. Moreover, emission control devices have a useful life of only one-half that of the vehicle life because of the gasoline fuel used. Finally, the use of gasoline places also certain limitations as to the minimum attainable level of emissions with a reasonable investment, which in an automobile cannot be more than about 10% of the cost of the vehicle.

Another proposition, favored mainly by the academia and other theoretical proponents, is the notion of abandoning the private automobile and returning to public transportation. However, the proponents of this scenario ignore consistently the dynamics that led to the substitution of public transportation by the private automobile. The flexibility of the private automobile, which essentially reduces the time it takes for an individual to move form one intracity point to another, cannot be matched by any present public transportation system even in the face of traffic jams and congested streets. Technological developments in the future may revive public transport in the form of the so called smart shuttle vehicles. These are low occupancy vehicles that can be dispatched via phone on demand and have variable routes to accommodate the passengers. More likely, however, the same technological developments will reduce the need of commuting altogether thereby eliminating the number of vehicles on the road (telecommuting).

A very recent development that began in California and may be spreading to other states is the mandate of zero emission vehicles as it was discussed in an earlier chapter. On the face of it, a zero emission vehicle is the ultimate in private transportation as it guarantees no emissions of any kind during its entire lifetime. However, the present type of ZEV can only be an electric vehicle. Electricity generated by power plants results of course in the emission of pollutants which are by no means negligible. In fact, as it was discussed in an earlier chapter, the pollutants from an electric utility powered ZEV may be comparable in magnitude to, or even higher than, the pollutants generated by a compressed natural gas vehicle, albeit the former are emitted in remote areas while the latter are still released in and near urban areas.

While this question of the relative pollution generation of an electric vehicle versus a natural gas vehicle has been debated for some time now with no resolution in sight, the even more crucial discussion of the respective costs involved is rarely being addressed. As it was demonstrated in a previous section, the cost of reducing the release of pollutants to the environment from an electric vehicle is more than five times higher than that from a natural gas vehicle. Hence, the cost required to reduce the release of NO_x, CO and NMOG per unit mass by operating an electric vehicle is more than three times higher than the cost resulting by operating a natural gas vehicle. In other words, the natural gas vehicle option removes pollutants from the atmosphere in a much more efficient or economical manner than the option of a comparable electric vehicle. Nevertheless, one may argue than no pollution locally is preferable than some pollution locally no matter how small the latter is.

It is here then that the notion of the assimilative capacity of the environment becomes very important. So long as the amount of pollutants by natural gas vehicles remains within the assimilative capacity of the local environment, the issue of zero versus finite emissions from vehicles becomes irrelevant. As far as the environment is concerned both an electric vehicle (ZEV) and a natural gas vehicle (ULEV) become identical with regard to air emissions. Consequently, one must ascertain the range of the assimilative capacity of different local environments and then build vehicles powered by natural gas with emissions falling within this assimilative capacity range. It should be emphasized that of all the alternative liquid or gaseous chemical fuels, with the possible exception of hydrogen, natural gas is the only one that has shown the potential for extremely low emissions when burned in an internal combustion engine. Fuel cells are not considered as practical automotive propulsion systems because of high cost. Even then, however, a natural gas fuel will be less polluting than any other chemical fuel with the exception of hydrogen.

The first consideration is the estimate of the possible reduction in automotive emissions assuming a variety of different scenarios. The results are summarized in Table 10-3. The current US emission standards assumed to be representative of the long term emissions of gasoline vehicles form the base case scenario. The California ULEV emission standards form the basis of the medium term (year 2000) natural gas vehicle scenario. The emissions of presently available natural gas vehicles such as the Chrysler full size and minivan are also included[20]. The long term scenarios include high fuel efficiency vehicles as well as hybrid vehicles using natural gas as a fuel[23][24].

Improved fuel efficiency implies proportional reduction in the power output of the engine and therefore of the emissions of the vehicle. This can be deduced form the performance points of four typical engines plotted in Figure 10-3. Significantly improved efficiency will result in the

TABLE 10-3. Comparison of the Potential Reductions in the Emissions of Natural Gas Fueled Passenger Cars and Light Trucks Under Different Scenarios

Vehicle/Fuel Description	Emissions (g/mi)		
	CO	NMOG	NO_x
1994 US Standard, Any Fuel, All Veh.	3.40	0.250	0.40
1996 US Standard, Any Fuel, All Veh.[1]	3.40	0.125	0.40
2001 US Standard, Any Fuel, All Veh.[1]	3.40	0.075	0.20
1997 CA ULEV, Any Fuel, 15% Veh.[2]	1.70	0.040	0.20
1992 GM Freedom Hybrid Van, Gasoline[3]	0.90	0.200	0.15
1992 GM Freedom Hybrid Van, CNG[4]	0.30	0.010	0.01
2.8 L GM Engine, CNG, US FTP Cycle[5]	0.22	0.010	0.011
1993 Volvo ECC Hybrid Car, Diesel[6]	0.13	0.01	0.17
1993 Volvo ECC Hybrid Car, CNG[7]	0.06	0.001	0.10
1995 Chrysler Ram Van/Wagon, CNG[8]	1.70	0.020	0.08
1995 Chrysler Mini Van/Wagon, CNG[9]	0.30	0.004	0.04

1. These are the 50k-mile numbers. At 100k-miles emissions are allowed to increase as follows (year in parenthesis): CO 4.2 g/mi; NMOG 0.156 g/mi (96) and 0.09 g/mi (01); and NOx 0.6 g/mi (96) and 0.3 g/mi (01). 2. The penetration of ULEV begins at 2% in 1997 and reaches 15% in 2003. 3. Lumina APV van with a 1 liter engine, 43 kW (Geo Metro), DC brushless motor, lead-acid batteries. 4. Projected emissions by author. 5. Test results on the 90 kW engine with a 14:1 compression ratio. 6. Measured data, 41 kW gas turbine. 7. Projected emissions by author. 8. LEV certified, 5.2 liter engine, 149 kW. 9. ULEV certified, 3.3 liter engine, 112 kW.

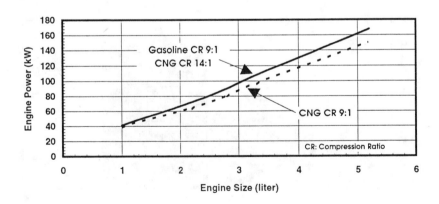

FIGURE 10-3. Power Output and Displacement Correlation of Typical Production Automobile Engines that Operate or Could Operate on Natural Gas Fuel.

utilization of smaller engines for all vehicles. For example, if the fuel efficiency of the Chrysler mini van were to be raised from 20 mpg to 30 mpg, the 112 kW engine power output might be reduced to about 85 kW for the same vehicle performance. Likewise a vehicle such as the Chevrolet Corsica with a current 71 kW engine and a fuel efficiency of about 24 mpg would need a 52 kW engine if the fuel efficiency rose to 40 mpg, which is approximately the engine of the 1995 Geo Metro sedan. The feasibility of attaining the aforementioned fuel efficiencies for full and mid-size cars will be examined in the following section.

An important consideration with respect to emissions as well as fuel efficiency and noise is the influence of stop-and-go traffic. Significant reduction in the emissions occurs when the engine is operated at a constant speed. Figure 10-4 shows data from European tests comparing the emissions, among others, at a constant speed and at the "ECE Cycle" — counterpart of the US FTP Cycle[25]. The constant speed case would be representative of the emissions of a hybrid vehicle employing the same engine. It is worth noting that CO emissions are reduced by a factor of three, HC emissions are reduced by a factor of five and NO_x emissions by a factor of more than six. Incidentally, the emissions shown in Figure 10-4 represent engine-out emissions and are comparable to the respec-

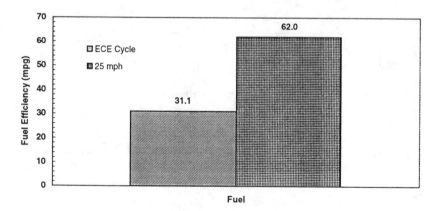

FIGURE 10-4. Comparison of the Fuel Consumption, Engine-Out Emissions and Noise of a Fixed Speed (25 mph) versus a Variable Speed (ECE Driving Cycle) ICE Fueled by Gasoline — Engine-Out and Tailpipe Emissions of the 2.8 L GM Engine are also Given for Gasoline and CNG Fuels based on the US FTP Driving Cycle.

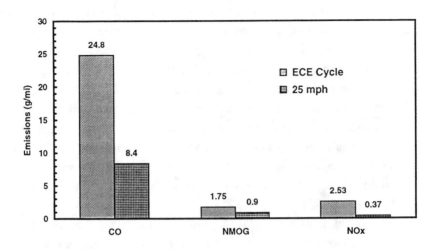

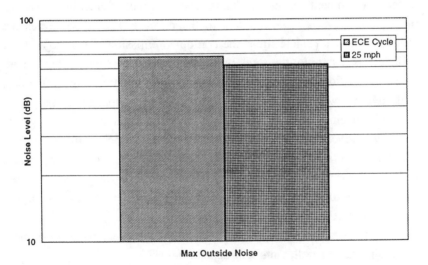

<u>2.8 L Engine / FTP Cycle</u>

	Gas.	CNG		Gas.	CNG		Gas.	CNG
<u>CO (g/mi)</u>			<u>NMOG</u>			<u>NOx</u>		
Engine-Out	18.6	11.7	Engine-Out	3.04	0.56	Engine-Out	2.58	1.40
Tailpipe	0.53	0.22	Tailpipe	0.19	0.01	Tailpipe	0.12	0.01

FIGURE 10-4. (Continued)

tive emissions of the 2.8 L, 90 kW GM engine of Figure 10-3 operating on gasoline. The use of a catalytic converter reduces engine-out emissions by about 95% as indicated in Figure 10-4. However, the ratio of emissions between a regular vehicle and a hybrid one ought to remain roughly the same as those shown in Figure 10-4. The results of Table 10-3 point to the fact that combined emissions (all three pollutants) of new passenger vehicles and light trucks can be reduced from the present level of 4.05 g/mi with gasoline to under 0.30 g/mi with CNG in a spark ignition engine and 0.15 g/mi in a gas turbine. These are the potential low limits of emissions of internal combustion engines with natural gas as a fuel.

The limit of 0.30 g/mi to 0.15 g/mi per vehicle of the combined vehicular emissions must be compared against the assimilative capacity of the environment for air pollutants. The total daily vehicular emissions in a given location will be equal to the number of vehicles times the miles driven per vehicle times the combined emissions per mile and per vehicle. For example, the total emissions in the Los Angeles basin with some 11 million vehicles, each driven daily for an average 30 miles, will have a lower combined emission of 100 tons (spark ignition) to 50 tons (gas turbine) daily. If the daily assimilative capacity of the environment in a given location is higher than the total local daily emissions (mobile and stationary sources), then air pollution disappears. Otherwise, air pollution remains, albeit at reduced rates. The question then is how to estimate or calculate the assimilative capacity of the environment at a given location.

The factors that determine locally how effectively the environment can assimilate air pollutants will depend on[26][27]:

(a) The total amount of emissions emitted within the given area;

(b) The meteorological conditions within that area comprising the local microclimate; and

(c) The configuration, i.e., intensity and distribution, of the individual sources.

The assimilative capacity of the local environment with respect to air pollution is expected to fluctuate from day to day, month to month and even year to year as it must depend on weather effects that show similar fluctuations. Obviously, the fluctuations will be at a maximum from day to day, will vary less on a monthly basis and will show the least variability on an annual time frame. Thus, the long term assimilative capacity of air pollutants of a particular geographical location must attain a stable value. The general meteorological conditions that affect pollution locally consist of the stability of the air as determined by the vertical variation of temperature and the direction and strength of the wind. Ultimately, the air movement disperses the pollutants from the concentrated sources to larger areas so that natural occurring processes in the air, water and soil (chemical and biological reactions) eliminate these pollutants.

It should be mentioned that not all mechanisms of pollutant removal from the atmosphere are known or understood. For example, carbon monoxide may be oxidized in the air with the aid of solar radiation to carbon dioxide, which in turn is absorbed in the oceans or by the biomass. Carbon monoxide is also rapidly depleted from the air near the ground surface by acidic soils high in organic matter content[28]. Hydrocarbons get oxidized to carbon dioxide, carbon monoxide and water by the action of solar radiation. The nitrogen oxide (NO) component of the NO_x emissions is also oxidized to nitrogen dioxide (NO_2), which is the other component in the NO_x emissions. The soil is possibly acting as a sink of NO_2 where microbial and chemical reactions can immobilize it[29].

The intensity of pollutant emissions from automobiles is relatively small compared to other sources such as factories and powerplants. Moreover, the distribution of pollutants emitted from automobiles is much more uniform over a given area compared to stationary sources. Thus, the configuration of automobile emissions is one of low intensity and high expansion in any given location. Obviously, there will be distribution peaks in areas where a lot of vehicles converge such as the center of a city. However, the typical profile of the distribution of automobile pollutants with a lower intensity and a higher spread is advantageous with respect to their assimilation by the environment compared to much stronger and highly localized sources of the same total emissions. Thus, if the low intensity per unit area of automotive pollutants can be further reduced below a threshold value, it may be easier for the local environment to assimilate these pollutants versus those emitted by fewer but much more intense stationary sources.

Unfortunately, the present state of our scientific understanding of the meteorological processes at the microclimactic or local level is too limited to enable us to calculate this threshold value. Moreover, this lack of scientific understanding may take several decades to resolve. Mankind does not have the luxury of waiting for another half-century before a decision can be taken, because of the potentially accelerated degradation of the environment as more and more pollution sources are introduced not only in the US but everywhere around the globe. The apparent way out is to demand zero emissions from vehicles to ensure no emissions locally. Nevertheless, pollution of much higher intensity is generated in this instance away from urban centers. It is not clear or obvious, however, that this is a better solution than having instead extremely low intensity emissions within urban and sub-urban areas. This may be demonstrated by the following example dealing with NO_x emissions.

The NO_x emissions from ULEVs occur very near the ground and are of very low density per unit surface area. The air movement disperses then the NO_x over larger areas but still near the ground. Depending on the amount of vegetation in the soil and the acidity of it, most or all of this NO_x may end up being immobilized in the soil. The extremely high NO_x emissions by a powerplant supplying electricity for ZEVs is normally rejected in the atmosphere through a stack at some high point above ground. The objective is to disperse quickly these emissions into higher layers of the atmosphere so that they can be transported over long areas. However, it is reasonable to assume that because of the very high concentration of NO_x and depending on the air movement some small fraction of it may eventually end up in the higher level of the atmosphere, where it will act as an ozone destructive compound. If this situation were to occur, then the second (ZEV) solution is exceedingly more harmful to the environment, including the population, than the first (ULEV) solution. Hence, the zero emission solution may not be desirable not only because of the economic considerations presented in an previous section, but also on technical grounds. Thus, it behooves us to attempt to determine a finite limit of extremely low automotive emission levels that it may be in the best interest of both the environment (assimilation) and the people (health, pocketbook, aesthetic utility).

The most reasonable way to determine an assimilative limit of local environments for specific pollutants such as automotive emissions is to combine technological information with historical data. Let us begin with the historical data. Los Angeles has the worst air quality problem in the US and has had this distinction since the mid or late 1940s when smog began manifesting itself in a visible manner. The fact that Los Angeles has a severe air pollution problem is not an accident. The presence of a large number of mobile and stationary sources exacerbates the problem, but the prevailing meteorological conditions have a lot to do with it. From the standpoint of air pollution potential, Los Angeles and Southern California in general is one of the worst possible locations of a city in the US. Places like Casablanca, Morocco, Cape Town, South Africa and Santiago, Chile are among the worst city locations in the world with regard to potential air pollution problems.

The high air pollution potential in Los Angeles and other locations is the result of the confluence of well understood meteorological conditions[25]. Essentially the presence of a high pressure center (anticyclone) over the area most of the time results in light winds and inversions (stable vertical air masses) in addition to clear skies and reduced rainfall. An inversion is characterized by an increasing air temperature with height instead of the normal decrease. Thus, vertical motion of air is effectively prevented because air at a lower height has a higher density than the air above. Moreover, the winds are very light to effect any significant horizontal motion destabilizing the system. Only during the winter months the occasional invasion of storms, fronts, and cold unstable air masses interrupt the anticyclonic influence.

The high pressure center in the Southern California region is typical of the ones existing over the subtropical oceans (latitude below 45°) and the adjoining coasts as a result of the trade wind movement in the atmosphere. A typical inversion pattern over Southern California is shown in Figure 10-5. The inversion layer extends between 1000 ft and 3000 ft height above ground level. Vertical air movement is thus allowed between the surface and about 1000 ft elevation diluting any pollutants. Light winds may also transport pollutants across the surface

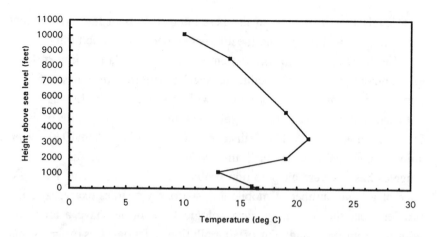

FIGURE 10-5. Typical Atmospheric Temperature Profile as a Function of Height above Sea Level at Southern California Coast in the Summer (Santa Monica, CA, July 1, 1957).

and within the 1000 ft band for further mixing. This situation prevails both during day time and at night for most of the year with the exception of the winter, when storms may occur that temporarily disrupt the inversion layer. Since Los Angeles presents the worst location in the US with respect to air pollution, it can be used to establish the upper bound of automotive emission levels that if met, would fall within the assimilative capacity of the environment anywhere in the country.

The pollution potential C of a geographical region (city, etc.) can be estimated in terms of its physical expansion area A, the height above ground level H within which air pollutants mix, the distance of downwind pollutant movement, the local automobile air pollution emission rate Q_{ms} assumed to be uniform and the wind speed V[25]. Thus, one obtains:

$$C = Q_{ms} (A)^{1/2} / V H$$

where $\{(A)^{1/2}\}$ represents the average linear expansion of area A. In order that C remains below the assimilative capacity C_{ac} of a given location the rate of emissions Q_{ms} must not exceed the value:

$$Q_{ms} < r_{ms} C_{ac} (V H / (A)^{1/2})$$

where r_{ms} is the percentage of all air pollution in the location under consideration due to mobile sources and in particular motor vehicles.

It is interesting to note that in the preceding equations the term (V H / (A)$^{1/2}$)) is a function of the physical and meteorological characteristics of the location. For the Los Angeles area, for example, the numerical values of these parameters in the preceding equation are: H = 0.2 mi, (A)$^{1/2}$ = 60 mi and V = 11 mph so that (A)$^{1/2}$ / V H is equal to 27.2 h(ours)/mi(le). Values of the parameter C/Q = (A)$^{1/2}$ / V H have been calculated for the US from small cities (6 mi linear expansion) to very large cities (60 mi linear expansion)[25]. Figure 10-6 gives the annual median value of C/Q and Figure 10-7 gives the values of C/Q exceeded 10% of the days annually. The calculations have been performed for meteorological data at 10 AM, when typically the wind has its lowest value and the height above which an inversion layer begins is also smaller than later in the day. Thus, the majority of primary pollutants have their diurnal maximum concentration a few hours after sunrise. The effects of pollution on health are typically dependent on the concentration multiplied by the duration of exposure (dosage).

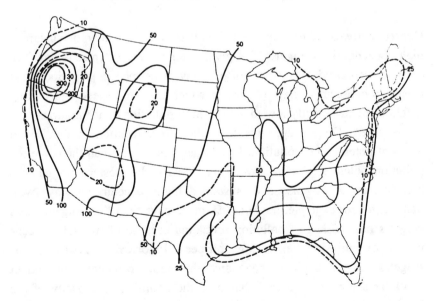

FIGURE 10-6. Values of the Median of the Annual Concentration Ratio { C/Q = (A)$^{1/2}$ / V H } in Units of s/m (1 second/meter = 0.447 hours/mile) Calculated in the Morning for Cities of 6 mi (Dashed Lines) and 60 mi (Solid Lines) Linear Expansion.

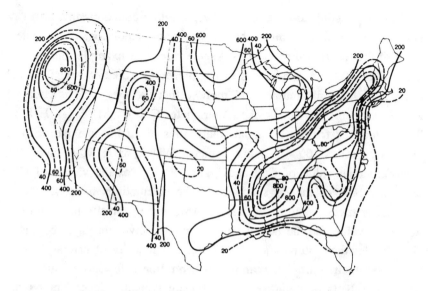

FIGURE 10-7. Values of the Highest 10% of the Annual Concentration Ratio { C/Q = (A)$^{1/2}$ / V H } in Units of s/m (1 second/meter = 0.447 hours/mile) Calculated in the Morning for Cities of 6 mi (Dashed Lines) and 60 mi (Solid Lines) Linear Expansion.

Consequently, another important factor is the frequency of sustained high concentrations. Figure 10-8 gives the number of "episode days" in a five year period, where an episode day is defined as a period of at least two consecutive days (48 hr) in which the wind speed and mixing height were sufficiently low to lead to high pollution concentrations.

Southern Oregon appears to be the worst location in the US in terms of potential air pollution. Los Angeles has more than the twice the pollution potential of New York City. Finally, the western US has the highest number of episode or sustained high concentration days with San Diego, for example, having 50% more days than Los Angeles. Los Angeles has the largest pollution problems because of its high concentration of emission generating sources. Historically, however, Los Angeles did not begin to have any air quality problems until about 1940. This implies that until that time the assimilative capacity of the local environment was adequate to eliminate all pollutants as they were generated on an instantaneous manner. This observation will enable us to evaluate a value for the quantity C_{ac} in the equation which gives Q_{ms} under very conservative assumptions.

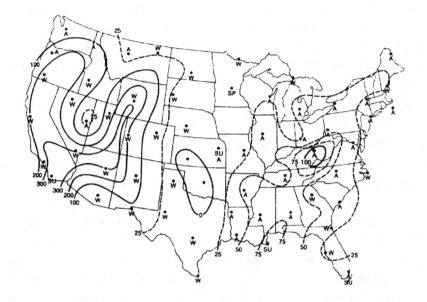

FIGURE 10-8. Number of Days in a Five Year Period for which Conditions favored reduced Dispersion of Air Pollution Continuously for at Least 48 Hours and Season in which Most of These Days Occurred (W:Winter, SP:Spring, SU:Summer, A:Autumn).

The number of motor vehicles in Los Angeles were on the order of 0.8 million in 1940. Moreover, the combined emissions of these vehicles were on the order of 110 g/mi (76% CO, 22.5% NMHC and 1.5% NO_x) with some 25 miles driven per day per vehicle, on the average. The combined emission of new vehicles today is less than 5 g/mi and the daily average distance traveled per vehicle is about 30 miles. Since the efficacy of catalytic converters may last for half of the life of the vehicle (50,000 mi), then the emissions may revert to the pre control level (1970) of about 40 g/mi. Thus, the average emission number of present day cars over their lifetime (100,000 mi) may be on the order of 20 g/mi.

There is evidence that this conclusion may not be far from the actual state of affairs[30]. Between 1955 and 1990 the peak ozone levels in Los Angeles were reduced from about 680 ppb to 300 ppb or a factor of

2.27. Ozone is a secondary pollutant generated from the oxidation of hydrocarbons. In 1955 the HC emissions were 24.8 g/mi and by 1970 they were reduced to 4.1 g/mi following the introduction of the crankcase blow-by control. Since 1980 the standard of HC emissions is 0.41 g/mi following the introduction of catalytic converters. Thus, there has been a reduction in HC emission of a factor of 60 between 1955 and 1990. At the same time the population of vehicles in the Los Angeles area has increased by a factor of 4.6 (2.3 million versus 10.6 million). Thus, the ozone level ought to have been reduced by a factor of 60/5 = 13. Yet, this is not what has been observed.

However, if the lack of effectiveness of the catalytic converter in gasoline vehicles during the second half of their existence is taken into account, the average vehicle lifetime HC emissions will increase to about 2.25 g/mi. Thus, the average improvement in ozone generation between 1955 and 1990 should be (24.8)/(2.25 x 4.6) = 2.39, which is virtually identical to the observed reduction. The assimilation area over which pollutants are emitted is assumed to be 60 mi x 60 mi = 3,600 square miles. Finally, it is assumed that in 1940 mobile sources account-ed for 50% of air pollutants, the same as today[30]. Thus, $r_{ms} = 0.5$ and the value for $\{(A)^{1/2} / V H\}$ is 400 s/m = 179 h/mi from Figure 10-7. The value of Q_{ms} for 1940 is equal to $(0.8 \times 10^6$ vehicles)x $(100g/mi)x(25mi/d/vehicle)/(3,600$ $mi^2)= 0.555$ $g/mi^2/d$. Hence, one obtains: $C_{ac} = 0.0062$ g/mi^3 as a value for the assimilative capacity of the environment near the surface of the earth.

Between 1940 and 1990 the number of vehicles in Southern California has increased by more than 13 times, while the average com-bined automobile emission has been reduced by about 4.6 times, if the increase in driving distance is taken also into account ((110/20)x(25/30)=4.58). Thus, it appears that automobiles in Southern California generate nowadays almost three times (13/4.6 = 2.8) as much air pollutants as they did 50 years ago. Moreover, the combined air pol-lutants emitted today from mobile and stationary sources exceed by a factor of five or six the amount that the environment can assimilate.

It is interesting to note that the 1996 standards and beyond require a total emission of a little under 5 g/mi during 100,000 miles of vehicle operation. Assuming that this is feasible with gasoline vehicles and taking into account a 35% increase in the vehicle population, then the total automobile emissions will be reduced by almost a factor of 3 from the present level. This will bring us to the 1940 mobile source levels, but allows for no margin of safety whatsoever. It does not guarantee a clean environment also on account of the fact that stationary sources must also reduce their emissions by a factor of three or better at the same time.

On the other hand, the 100,000 mi emission of ULEVs fueled with natural gas appears to be capable of remaining well below 1 g/mi and even under 0.5 g/mi for the average, mid-size vehicle as the numbers in Table 10-3 indicate. The attainment of the 1 g/mi emission level by natural gas vehicles over a 100,000 mi operation is significant in another way. If this emission level reflects the average emission of all vehicles on the road, which is certain to be the case on account of the Chrysler mini van certification, then air pollution due to transportation will represent as little as 10% and no more than 20% of the assimilative capacity of the environment. Thus, natural gas as a universal transportation fuel allows for a relatively larger contribution of emissions from stationary sources, if it turns out that it is more difficult or expensive to reduce the level of the latter by the same degree. Finally, the long term use of hybrid vehicles fueled by natural gas with a combined emission not to exceed 0.25 g/mi after 100,000 mi of operation will result in a motor vehicle air pollution representing only 5% of the assimilative capacity of the environment.

Up to this point all three major automobile air pollutants (CO, NMOG, NO_x) have been lumped together as one emission. The same analysis can be performed based on either non-methane organic gases or nitrous oxides or both combined, but without the inclusion of carbon monoxide. This may be justified on the basis that NMOG and NO_x are more damaging pollutants than carbon monoxide. However, it is obvious form the numbers in Table 10-3 that consideration of NMOG or NO_x only favors even more the use of natural gas as a fuel compared to electricity. In fact, the advantage is roughly a factor of ten as of the 1 g/mi or 0.5 g/mi or 0.25 g/mi combined emission less than 10% will be NMOG and NO_x emissions. In this case, the emissions of natural gas fueled ULEVs will represent only a few percent of the assimilative capacity of the environment.

It is apparent that natural gas vehicles in the ULEV category have the potential to reduce the air pollution burden to the environment to represent only a fraction of its assimilative capacity even in the most highly congested areas such as Southern California. The alternative choice of ZEVs will place no environmental burden locally, although there will be some such burden in another location. However, the cost to the consumer of a ZEV to attain the zero local environmental burden is significantly higher than the cost of a natural gas ULEV which essentially places no perceptible burden to the environment either. There should be no doubt at this point that if the entire motor vehicle fleet of the US were to consist of natural gas fueled ULEVs with an average combined emission over all vehicles during their lifetime of less than 1 g/mi, of which 10% or less comprise the NMOG and NO_x components, then these ULEVs will be "practically" as benign to the environment as any ZEVs. Consequently, the development emphasis and financial resources on controlling motor vehicle air pollution should be solidly placed on ULEVs with the aforementioned emission characteristics that can only be realized with the use of natural gas as a fuel. In fact the ULEV standard, in addition to being adopted across the country, ought to become more stringent in the future in order to reflect the true air pollution reduction capability of natural gas vehicles.

ULTRA EFFICIENT MOTOR VEHICLES

The first oil crisis of 1973 moved the fuel consumption of automobiles to the center of the attention worldwide. This attention, which lasted throughout the 1970s, resulted in a major technological thrust to improve fuel efficiency. In the US particularly, the technological thrust for increased fuel economy was given additional impetus by the implementation of legislative actions that included the CAFE (Corporate Average Fuel Economy) standards and the "Gas Guzzler Tax." By the time of the second oil crisis in 1979, the average fuel efficiency of new passenger cars sold in the US had risen by almost 50% compared to their pre 1973 values. Figure 10-9 shows the actual CAFE values from 1978 to 1990 and a forecast of the range of a possible average fuel efficiency increase after 1990. The discussions in the US Senate of these fuel efficiency increases, including a possible raise of the CAFE stan-

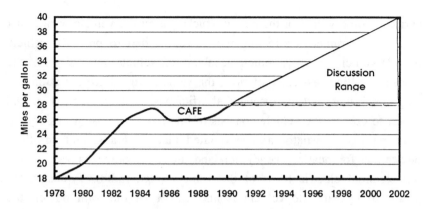

FIGURE 10-9. Actual Values of the CAFE Standard (27.5 mpg maximum) in the US from 1978 to 1990 and Projected Fuel Economy Values through the Year 2000 based on Discussions in the US Senate.

dard to 40 mpg, have been temporarily halted as the "Big Three" promised the President of the United States late in 1993 that they would voluntarily attempt to develop vehicles with an 80 mpg fuel efficiency by the end of this decade.

There are two major benefits to be derived from increased automobile fuel efficiency. The first benefit is a proportional reduction in the demand for fuel. The second benefit is the reduction of the impact of air pollution at an even more pronounced reduction rate due to the finite assimilative capacity of the environment. Thus, a fuel economy increase is extremely desirable.

The fuel use by a vehicle is a function of both its make-up as well as its pattern of use. While each vehicle owner uses his or her vehicle differently, certain general patterns have been established over the years that are amenable to a statistical representation. Thus, an average driving pattern may be established that is representative of the typical use of a vehicle. This is essentially the basis of the derivation of the US FTP Cycle since 1975, which is used to simulate fuel efficiency and emissions of all new vehicles. Having thus eliminated the variability of the human factor in automotive fuel consumption, one can concentrate on the vehicle make-up in order to improve fuel efficiency.

To propel and operate a motor vehicle, the engine must be able to generate certain amount of power. The integration of this power over a period of time will give the energy (fuel) use by the vehicle during that time. The parameters affecting the power needed to propel a vehicle include vehicle velocity, vehicle acceleration, vehicle mass, slope of the road, the rolling resistance of tires, the vehicle frontal cross section and drag coefficient, and the mechanical efficiency of the transmission. The power to operate the vehicle consists of internal power use necessary for fans, pumps, alternator and associated electric loads, and auxiliary power use for heating, ventilation and air-conditioning as well as the non-essential electric loads of the vehicle (e.g., radio). Typically, the power to operate the vehicle is about 50% of the total power, the remainder being used to propel the vehicle. Furthermore, the auxiliary power is about 10% of the total power. It is important to note that a smaller power required to propel the vehicle implies a proportionally smaller internal power use.

The mass of the vehicle is a large contributor to the power required to propel the vehicle[*]. This is shown clearly in Figure 10-10 for two different vehicle masses. The rolling resistance is the second major factor in power use by a vehicle. The rolling resistance is a function of the tire pressure, as is shown in Figure 10-11. The tire design and materials used are critical in obtaining a low rolling resistance. The final factor affecting power use is the vehicle drag coefficient and vehicle frontal area. This factor starts to become important at speeds above 30 mph only. The power required to accelerate a vehicle as well as to enable it to climb a hill is in excess of the power required for cruising. Figure 10-10 shows the power required to accelerate a 2,000 lb vehicle at three different acceleration rates, which represent a medium accelerating capability (0 to 60 mph in 13 to 14 sec).

Since 1973 several improvements have taken place to reduce the power requirements in order to increase fuel efficiency. Reduction in mass has been most probably the largest single factor of improvement. Full and mid size vehicles are now 25% to 30% lighter than their earlier

---

[*]. The instantaneous vehicle power requirement P as a function of velocity v, acceleration a, mass M and frontal area A is given by $P = (C/e)[(r + s + (a/g)) M v + c_d A v^2]$, where e is the mechanical efficiency of the transmission, r is the tire rolling resistance, s is the road slope, g is the gravitational acceleration, c_d is the drag coefficient and C is a constant.

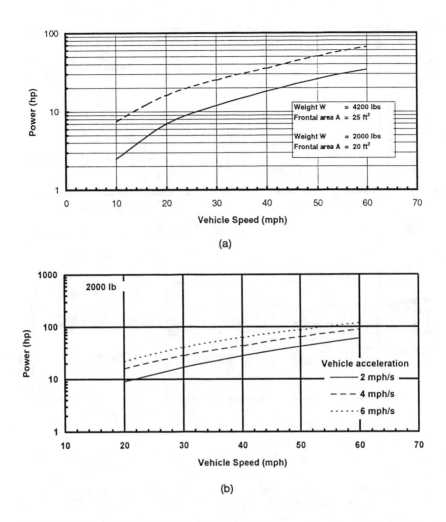

FIGURE 10-10. Power Required to Propel a Vehicle as a Function of : (a) Mass and Frontal Area; and (b) Different Acceleration Rates for a 2,000 lb Vehicle Mass. (0.1 g = 2.2 mph/s).

counterparts. Sub-compact and compact vehicles have been reduced in mass by a lesser amount (15%). In all vehicle categories safety and comfort features have increased despite reduction in mass and physical size. This has been accomplished through better engineering (improved structural design, effective space utilization) and the implementation of new technologies (air bags, etc.). The reduction in physical size and the

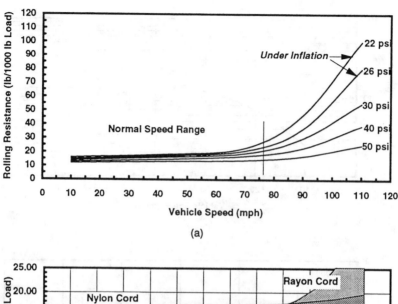

(a)

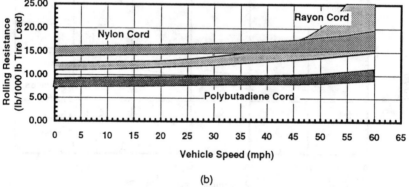

(b)

FIGURE 10-11. Rolling Resistance versus Vehicle Speed as a Function of:
(a) Tire Pressure; and (b) Different Tire Design and Materials.

use of more aluminum and plastics have resulted in the aforementioned
mass savings. The continued use of lightweight materials, particularly
plastics, along with other technological developments will easily reduce
the weight of most vehicles by another 10 to 15% in the future[25].

Assuming identical vehicle performance, i.e., acceleration, uphill
driving ability and top speed, a mass reduction of 10% reduces the fuel
consumption of a 2,200 lb vehicle by a little over 5% for the average
city/freeway US driving schedule. Drastic reductions in vehicle mass
can only be attained through the use of composite materials such as car-

bon fiber for the body and chassis construction. The 1991 GM Ultralite prototype vehicle is an example of such construction[31]. This vehicle has the dimensions of a mid-size car such as the GM Corsica, but only 53% the mass of the latter vehicle (1400 lb for the Ultralite vs. 2650 for the Corsica). The average city/freeway fuel efficiency of the Ultralite is 61 mpg versus 24 mpg for the Corsica. Obviously such a drastic reduction in mass is not foreseeable for production cars in the near future given the high prices of composite materials. The carbon fiber content of the Ultralite has been on the order of $13,000 (1991 prices). However, a 10% to 20% mass reduction on the average, more for larger vehicles and less for smaller ones, appears to be feasible and cost effective within the next decade or so.

Tires fulfill several functions: safe road contact, low rolling resistance, high vibration damping and low noise generation. From a fuel economy consideration low rolling resistance is of paramount importance. The introduction of radial tires in the last 20 years has resulted in higher tire pressures and reduction in the friction coefficient. Currently, a tire pressure of 44 psi is becoming more common up from the earlier 32 psi pressure. An increase to 56 psi in the future is well within the realm of possibility. In fact all prototype vehicles, where efficiency is very crucial, such as electric vehicles (GM Impact and others) or the Ultralite, make use of high pressure (over 50 psi) tires. As Figure 10-11 shows, a 75% increase in tire pressure from 32 psi to 56 psi would reduce the rolling resistance by 50% across the driving speed spectrum.

Technological advances already under development will allow in the future the continuous monitoring of tires for underinflation and would automatically compensate or else warn the driver. Improvement in the tire design and in particular the tread has the potential to reduce the rolling resistance coefficient to at least 50% of the present value which is about 0.010 (10 lb/1000 lb vehicle mass)[25]. Thus, the rolling resistance coefficient of future tires can be as low 0.005 (5 lb/1000 lb vehicle weight). In fact, the 175/65R-18 Goodyear special tires used on the GM Impact and GM Ultralite have a rolling resistance coefficient of less than 0.003 even at highway speeds[31]. The decrease in fuel consumption due to reduced tire rolling resistance is on the order of 10% for every 30% reduction in the value of the rolling resistance coefficien assuming that the vehicle mass, drag coefficient and front area remain unchanged.

The drag coefficient of production vehicles has been steadily declining since the mid 1970s. Most production vehicles have today a drag coefficient of about 0.25 to 0.30 compared to one ranging from 0.40 to 0.45 in the early 1970s[25]. This represents an almost 35% reduction in the drag coefficient of production vehicles. The frontal cross sectional area has been also diminishing, particularly for larger vehicles. An average reduction of the frontal area by 15% has been also attained during the same period. The average fuel consumption of a mid-size vehicle is reduced approximately by 10% for every 30% reduction in the product value of the drag coefficient times the frontal cross sectional area. In the GM Ultralite example the drag coefficient is 0.192 and the frontal cross sectional area is 18.5 ft^2. The corresponding numbers for the GM Corsica are approximately 0.28 and 25.9 ft^2. Thus, the potential exists for a mid-size car reduction of over 50% in the value of the drag coefficient-frontal area product for current production vehicles.

Even a less stringent 25% reduction in the drag coefficient-frontal area product will still yield a 20% improvement in fuel economy for a mid-size vehicle. Figure 10-12 shows the incremental contributions of a variety of aerodynamic features resulting in a 25% reduction of the drag coefficient[25]. Further reductions in the drag coefficient-frontal area product become more difficult to attain for values below 0.25 for the drag coefficient so that the frontal area must also be reduced. Optimization of the exterior vehicle shape and interior vehicle volume with the aid of extensive computational analyses are necessary in order to design for reduced drag coefficient and frontal area. Moreover, the utilization of state-of-the-art laser beam based doppler-effect techniques rather than the classic use of dynamic pressure probes, which disturbs the flow field, will be employed for the air flow field surveillance and the development of optimal frontal areas.

The calculated incremental contributions of the various discussed measures in reducing the fuel consumption of a present mid-size vehicle (GM Chevrolet Corsica) as it transitions to a future mid-size vehicle (GM Ultralite) are shown in Table 10-4. The calculations are based on the US average city/freeway driving schedule. It is instructive to note

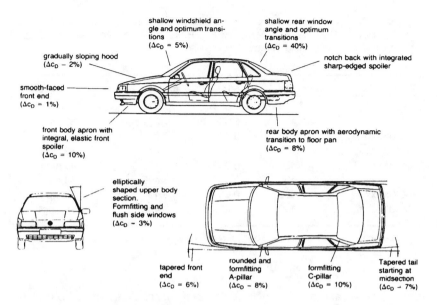

FIGURE 10-12. Incremental Contributions of Each Aerodynamic Feature to the Total 25% Reduction in the Drag Coefficient Value (Source: VW-Audi Group).

the contribution of the three different vehicle parameter changes either alone or in pairs or all combined. Given the practical limitations in the reduction of the vehicle mass, tire rolling resistance, and aerodynamic drag, one must determine an optimal reduction level of all three parameters such that the maximum increase in fuel economy occurs per dollar of incremental cost. The other important observation is that a significant reduction of the rolling resistance and aerodynamic drag combined obviate the need for a large mass reduction, which may be more difficult (i.e., expensive) to attain.

Engine efficiency may also be improved in a number of ways. These include: a higher compression ratio, stratified charging, use of hydrogen as a fuel additive, and engine operation at a constant speed. Other options are also possible such as a variable engine compression, a lean burning engine and new materials for engine parts.

The impact of increased compression ratio is quite significant in engine performance. However, there is a limit to the allowable compression ratio depending on the fuel type because of the engine knocking

TABLE 10-4. Calculated Incremental Contributions in Average City/Hwy Fuel Economy Due to Reductions in Mass, Rolling Resistance and Aerodynamic Drag of the GM Corsica Transitioning into the GM Ultralite

Vehicle Name	m (lb)	r(#)	c_d A (ft^2)	Fuel Economy
GM Corsica	2,650	0.009	7.271	24 mpg*
XX Xxxxxx	1,400	0.009	7.271	33 mpg
XX Xxxxxx	2,650	0.003	7.271	36 mpg
XX Xxxxxx	1,400	0.003	7.271	39 mpg
XX Xxxxxx	2,650	0.009	3.495	45 mpg
XX Xxxxxx	1,400	0.009	3.495	54 mpg
XX Xxxxxx	2,650	0.003	3.495	58 mpg
GM Ultralite	1,400	0.003	3.495	61 mpg*

Note. Fuel economy numbers followed by "*" represent measured data.

effect. The octane number of a fuel is a measure of the threshold of the engine knocking effect. Motor gasoline has today an octane number in the range of 86 to 93, while natural gas has an average octane number of 128 to 130 depending on its composition. Thus, a natural gas fueled engine can accommodate a much higher compression ratio. Table 10-5 shows the theoretical improvement in efficiency of a spark ignition engine at different compression ratios.

The improvement in efficiency of a spark ignition engine from the current 8.9:1 compression ratio and gasoline as fuel to a compression ratio of 14:1 and natural gas as fuel is about 15% (0.558 vs. 0.646). Thus, the increment in fuel efficiency by increasing the engine compression ratio is one of the largest ones compared to all other measures to improve fuel economy. Higher compression ratios present no technological challenge — diesel engines have ratios of 20:1 or higher. However, there is an economic cost as higher compression ratio engines must be sturdier and heavier to accommodate the higher operating pressure.

In a conventional ICE the load is varied by changing the quantity of the fuel-air mixture, while the ratio of air to fuel remains constant. The efficiency of fuel utilization, particularly under partial load conditions, could be considerably improved if the ratio of fuel to air could be varied such that a constant amount of air is used with a variable amount of

TABLE 10-5. Comparison of Theoretical Efficiency of the Spark Ignition Engine at Different Compression Ratios and Different Fuels with a Stoichiometric Fuel-Air Composition

Compression Ratio	Gasoline	CNG	Hydrogen
8.9:1	0.558 (1.00)	0.577 (1.03)	0.582 (1.04)
10.0:1	0.576 (1.03)	0.596 (1.07)	0.601 (1.08)
14.0:1	N/A	0.646 (1.15)	0.651 (1.17)

Note. Numbers in parenthesis indicate relative efficiency with respect to the base case of 8.9:1 compression ratio and gasoline as fuel.

fuel. Unfortunately, the resulting lean burning engine under part load suffers from a few major drawbacks. Emissions of hydrocarbons increase significantly. Moreover, the ignition of a lean fuel-air mixture becomes unreliable so that a torque unsteadiness and rough engine running result. It is the purpose of the stratified charge injection system to produce a "rich" mixture in the immediate vicinity of the spark plug. The lean mixture elsewhere in the cylinder is then consumed by the resulting flame.

There are many possible design techniques by which the desired stratification effect can be attained. In a typical stratified engine a high velocity swirl is imparted to the intake air through proper design of the air-intake port. The fuel is injected during compression at an angle back toward the swirl of the air, where it is entrained and carried toward the spark plug in the center of the cylinder so that the fuel is concentrated at the ignition point. When ignition occurs, the flame spreads outward in a concentric manner toward the cylinder walls. Under condition of partial load, combustion will not spread to the outer areas of the cylinder because only air will be present there. As an additional bonus, the stratification technique eliminates the danger of auto-ignition and the sensitivity of the combustion to the fuel octane number is reduced. The control of hydrocarbon emissions can be attained by utilizing an oxidation catalyst (platinum and palladium only) rather than the three way catalyst. The technology today makes it feasible to inject directly fuel into the cylinder after the intake valve has been closed[25]. The advantages of the stratified charge approach are:

(a) The compression ratio can be increased without regard to the fuel octane number.

(b) The lean overall fuel mixture ratios result in more favorable part-load fuel economy and reduced emissions.

(c) The ability to control the engine load by air-fuel mixture ratio alone makes the stratified charge technique especially adaptable to the two-stroke engine cycle.

In general the stratified charge principle allows a 10-20% more efficient fuel combustion and combines many of the better features of the Otto and Diesel cycles: it has a higher fuel efficiency than the first, a lighter, less expensive structure than the second, and less rigid fuel requirements than either of them. However, the stratified charged engine will probably be heavier and more expensive than the conventional spark ignition engine.

It was mentioned in the last chapter that the use of hydrogen as fuel in spark ignition engines has shown to increase the average fuel economy of the vehicle by 25 to 50%, depending on the engine modification and performance optimization applied. Unfortunately, the use of hydrogen as an automotive fuel is not likely to occur in the foreseeable future for the reasons given in the last chapter. Fortunately, there is evidence that mixing small amounts of hydrogen with hydrocarbon fuels may also have a positive impact on the average fuel economy of the vehicle and emissions[32]. However, the engine type as well as the type of hydrocarbon fuel appear to have a very strong influence on the magnitude of the fuel efficiency increase.

Specifically, use of 5% to 30% hydrogen mixed with gaseous fuel mixtures such as coal gas rather than gasoline and increased compression ratios resulted in an increased efficiency of about 15% as shown in Table 10-6. Other tests with compression ratios as high as 16:1 did not result in any preignition problems. Moreover, all the aforementioned tests were carried out with diesel engines rather spark ignition ones. While these data are old and not systematic, the conclusion is that mixing some amount of hydrogen with a gaseous fuel may increase vehicle fuel economy. The fuel economy increase that may be attributed to a 5% hydrogen fuel content at a compression ratio of 14:1, if the higher

TABLE 10-6. Influence of Increased Compression Ratio on Fuel Economy as Heat Energy Input per Mechanical Output of ICEs with a 5%-30% by Volume Hydrogen Booster Fuel

Fuel	Compression Ratio				
Type (Units)	6.08:1	6.60:1	8.00:1	10.00:1	16.00:1
Liquid (BTU/hp.h)[1]	8730				
(%)[2]	100				
Gaseous (BTU/hp.h)[1]		7,965	7,020	6,545	5,215
(%)[2]		91	80	75	68

1. The absolute unit is BTU per h(orse)p(ower).h(our). 2. Gaseous fuel efficiency with respect to the liquid fuel at lowest compression ratio.

compression ratio effect is removed, is on the order of 15% for a gaseous fuel such as natural gas. This result is derived by analyzing the limited data and needs obviously further corroboration.

The mixing of small amounts of hydrogen (less than 5%) with natural gas has the potential to reduce significantly emissions of NO_x as well as of CO and HC in a lean burning engine[33]. While a lean high compression engine fueled by CNG shows an almost 20% increase in fuel efficiency from its gasoline counterpart, it also generates much higher NO_x and HC emissions than a stoichiometric engine.

In summary, the proper injection of the high pressure CNG fuel containing a relatively small amount of hydrogen into the air intake of an internal combustion engine, may result in:

(a) Stratified hydrogen charge at time of combustion and continued combustion at lean local mixture conditions.

(b) Increase in volumetric efficiency due to supercharging effect and control of power by quality only.

(c) Much better combustion of gaseous hydrocarbons (methane and ethane) with higher output and lower specific fuel consumption.

(d) Reduction in the emissions of CO, NMOG and NO_x.

The appropriate storage of hydrogen either separately on-board a vehicle or in the natural gas fuel and the proper injection scheme must be investigated and the most effective solutions be found in terms of fuel efficiency and cost.

A significant energy loss in a motor vehicle occurs in the transmission of power from the engine to the wheels. An engine can produce a given power most economically at high torque and low speed. In most instances, however, the vehicle operating points are removed from the regions of maximum engine efficiency. The most economical operating points can be realized through a continuously variable transmission. Such a transmission enables the engine to run independently of driving speed at optimal operating points. A continuously variable transmission is equivalent to having an infinite number of gears. Alternatively, an electronically controlled transmission can be employed whereby a computer switches gears to the optimal engine regimes most of the time. Electronically controlled or shifted transmissions have become already available in the more expensive vehicles. These transmissions, which are by nature automatic, have been able to outperform on occasion five speed manual transmissions in terms of efficiency. Continuous variable transmissions, which create also the possibility of operating the engine at full load independent of driving speed — except for starting, have become available in recent years as well. However, they can be only used in small cars (power 50 kW or less). Several automotive companies are exploring ways to employ them to large vehicles as well.

One obvious way to improve fuel efficiency and reduce emissions is to run the engine of the vehicle only when power is needed. A variety of ways can be conceived to accomplish this task through an appropriate engine-transmission management system[25]. This idea of the so called "start-stop" system has shown 20% fuel savings in the European urban driving cycle. Fuel savings as high as 30% can be apparently reached in practical driving situations.

Another possibility in remedying the significantly higher inefficiency of an internal combustion engine (ICE) under part load is to eliminate the need of part load operation alltogether. This is the situation with a series hybrid propulsion system. An electric motor propels the vehicle drawing electricity from on-board storage (batteries, flywheels) and a generator driven by an ICE, which is operated either at a constant speed only or else is in the off mode. Despite the increased mass of the vehicle propulsion system, the performance of an ICE at constant speed improves dramatically. Both fuel efficiency and emissions attain large improvements in a hybrid vehicle vs. a similar gasoline one. The use of CNG rather than gasoline in a hybrid vehicle can further improve both of these parameters.

Figure 10-4 gives an example of the potential in increasing fuel efficiency along with reducing emissions of a fixed vs. a variable load engine. Another example of the improvements in fuel efficiency and emissions is summarized in Table 10-7[25]. The production vehicle is a VW Golf with a curb mass of 2,000 lb and a 40 kW diesel engine. The hybrid vehicle consists of a 6 kW electric motor used for up to speeds of 35 mph and 13% grade and the same 40 kW diesel engine used for acceleration, speeds above 35 mph and any other condition requiring more than 6 kW of power. This is a series hybrid vehicle. Emissions of all three primary pollutants, i.e., CO, HC and NO_x, indicate a reduction of about 50% for each one of them between the production model and the hybrid model. Moreover, the fuel consumption of the hybrid version has been reduced by 35% so that average city-highway fuel efficiency has increased form 45 mpg to over 60 mpg. Other series hybrid vehicles have resulted in an increase of fuel efficiency of over 50% as are the cases of the GM Lumina Van/Freedom Hybrid and the Volvo 850 example of the previous chapter indicates — the production 850 vehicle has a 25 mpg city/hwy average fuel efficiency, while the ECR version of the 850 attains a 38 mpg (gasoline equivalent) city/hwy average fuel efficiency. It would appear that the impact of a hybrid drivetrain in improving fuel efficiency is proportionally less for a standard vehicle with a

TABLE 10-7. Measured Exhaust Emissions and Fuel Efficiency of a VW Golf Hybrid Vehicle with a 40 kW Diesel Engine and a 6 kW Electric Motor and Percent Reduction of these Quantities from those of the Production VW Golf Diesel Vehicle with a 40 kW Engine for the US 75-FTP Driving Schedule

| Exhaust Emissions | | | | | | | | Consumption | |
| CO | | HC | | NO_x | | Particles | | Diesel Fuel | |
g/mi	%	g/mi	%	g/mi	%	g/mi	%	gpm	%
0.37	58	0.16	54	0.46	47	0.10	47	60.7	35

Note. The emissions of both production and hybrid vehicles are essentially engine out emissions as no catalytic converter is utilized in either vehicle. If CNG fuel were used instead and a catalytic converter with a typical 90% efficiency were employed, the resulting tail-pipe out emission would have been approximately on the order of: 0.04 g/mi for CO, 0.01 g/mi for NMOG, 0.05 g/mi for NO_x and 0.00 g/mi for particles.

higher fuel efficiency, but in that case a higher absolute fuel consumption reduction may also result.

The combination of the various fuel consumption reducing measures and their contribution to an increased fuel efficiency are summarized in Table 10-8. The estimates for each measure are conservative in nature and account also for any reduction in total benefit due to overlapping contributions. The measures are presented in a hierarchical sequence of increasing cost. That is to say, measures that appear to require less expenses for their implementation are assumed to be implemented first. However, several measures may have a similar expense in which case the order is not relevant. An estimate of the cost associated with the particular measure is also included as well as a description of the applicable technology. Finally, the base case vehicle which serves as the launching platform is a 2,600 lb, 26 mpg city/fwy, five-passenger mid-size sedan that is the most preferred passenger vehicle in the United States (e.g., Chevrolet Corsica, Ford Taurus, Honda Accord).

The results of the Table 10-8 indicate that an 80 mpg mid-size vehicle is possible with presently available technology. The big question, of course, is the economics associated with such technological accomplishment. The associated cost of about $5,000 per vehicle represents roughly 1/3 of the present price of a mid-size production vehicle. Economies of scale, on-going implementation of certain of the required measures (e.g. active suspension, etc.) and optimal introduction of the proposed measures over a period of ten or so years will diminish the impact of this incremental cost. Moreover, the savings associated with less fuel use will further diminish the incremental cost. Incidentally, the benefit associated with fuel savings is on the order of about $300 per year or $3,000 during the lifetime of the vehicle. Finally, the emissions of an 80 mpg hybrid vehicle fueled by natural gas can be estimated on the basis of the Volvo ECC and the VW Golf vehicles and are given in Table 10-9. It is interesting to note that these emissions represent less than 10% of the ULEV standard and they are truly insignificant compared to either the utility power emissions for electric ZEVs or the assimilative capacity of the environment. Thus, an 80 mpg mid-size automobile based on natural gas fuel and the proven technology of an internal combustion engine is the ultimate rational private transportation system.

TABLE 10-8. Incremental Contribution and Cost of Measures to Increase Fuel Efficiency of a Present Mid-Side Passenger Vehicle Without Reducing its Performance, Safety, Utility and Comfort Characteristics.

Measure/Description		Fuel Eff.	Cost
I.	Base Case Vehicle Fuel Efficiency	26 mpg	N/A
II.	Mass, Drag and Friction Reduction Measures		
IIA.	Mass reduction 20% using lightweight alloys of aluminum and magnesium in lieu of steel[1].	3 mpg	$200
IIB.	Drag coefficient reduction by 25%, including reduction in frontal cross sectional area[2].	7 mpg	$350
IIC.	Tire rolling resistance reduction by 60% with appropriate improvements in suspension and traction control[3].	7 mpg	$450
	Base Case Vehicle Plus Set II of Measures	43 mpg	$1,000
III.	High Compression Stratified Charge Engine Measures		
IIIA.	CNG fuel only at a CR of 14:1[4].	7 mpg	$500
IIIB.	CNG fuel with 5% H_2 boost and an even higher CR of 16:1[5].	7 mpg	$500
IIIC.	Stratified charged ignition engine[6].	7 mpg	$500
	Base Case Vehicle Plus Set II and III of Measures	64 mpg	$2,500
IV.	Hybrid Propulsion Measures		
IVA.	Electric drive with small battery or flywheel storage and a high compression, stratified charged ICE on CNG fuel[7].	16 mpg	$2,500
	Base Case Vehicle Plus Set of II, II and IV Measures	80 mpg	$5,000

1. It is assumed that magnesium and aluminum at $0.7/lb will replace steel at $0.5/lb partially in the chassis/body of the vehicle. 2. Optimized shape reducing drag coefficient and frontal cross sectional area requires additional components such as an underbody pan, front and rear spoilers and cross wind stabilizers. 3. Requires more expensive high pressure, low rolling resistance tires along with active suspension elements for handling and traction. 4. It is assumed that engine is modified to run on CNG only from a previous dual fuel operation (gasoline and natural gas) and composite tanks are used to reduce vehicle mass. 5. Requires means to generate and inject hydrogen in the CNG fuel either on board the vehicle or during refueling. 6. Successful implementation of stratified charging has to follow the use of a gaseous fuel only (CNG) and better yet the inclusion of H2 boost fuel in the CNG fuel. 7. It is assumed that the electric motor, inverter, batteries will be small (10 kW motor/inverter, 4 kWh storage) akin to the VW Golf example.

TABLE 10-9. Projected Tail Pipe Emissions of the 80 mpg Vehicle with a Hybrid Propulsion Drivetrain and Natural Gas as Fuel

Emissions (g/mi)	CO	NMOG	NO_x	CO_2[1]
80 mpg CNG Hybrid	0.06	0.005	0.04	86
ULEV	1.70	0.04	0.20	N/A

1. The CO_2 emission includes the methane contribution in the exhaust. By comparison the CO_2 emission of a 26 mpg gasoline vehicle is 350 g/mi.

NATURAL GAS AS AN INTERNATIONAL AUTOMOTIVE FUEL

Currently there exist over 550 million motor vehicles around the world with the US accounting for slightly less than one-third of these vehicles[34]. Table 10-10 shows the countries with the largest vehicular population as of 1990. Only thirty years ago the US automobile population accounted for more than 80 percent of the world's total. In the future, more and more vehicles will be acquired by nations other than the US, the European countries and Japan. For example, China today has a total vehicle population of 6 million. This vehicle number could increase to 600 million, if China were to have the same number of vehicles per capita as Japan has today. Indeed the vehicle population of the world could increase to 1.5 billion units, if most of the world were to attain moderate living standards. Such a huge number of vehicles would impose a severe strain on the environmental and the world resources unless these vehicles can be fuel efficient and low polluting.

Fortunately, most of the world does not have the affinity of America for bigger cars, which has evolved historically because of the relatively lower cost of vehicles and fuel in this country. Thus, a sub-compact vehicle is much more acceptable in most of the world. Consequently, an average 80 mpg fuel efficiency can be attained in most of the developing world. For example, a 1994 GEO Metro size vehicle with a present city/hwy fuel efficiency of 55 mpg can readily reach the 80 mpg mark through mass, drag and rolling friction reductions as well as the use of a high compression engine running on natural gas. A 20% mass reduction of the base 1600 lb vehicle may increase fuel efficiency by 5 mpg. Reduction in the drag coefficient may add another 5 mpg and higher

TABLE 10-10. Number of Vehicles in Descending Order in the Twelve
Top Countries in the World as of 1990

Country	Pass. Cars	Trucks and Buses	Total Vehicles
USA	143×10^6	46×10^6	189×10^6
Japan	37×10^6	23×10^6	60×10^6
Germany	36×10^6	4×10^6	40×10^6
Italy	28×10^6	3×10^6	31×10^6
France	24×10^6	5×10^6	29×10^6
United Kingdom	20×10^6	3×10^6	23×10^6
Canada	13×10^6	4×10^6	17×10^6
Spain	12×10^6	3×10^6	15×10^6
Brazil	12×10^6	1×10^6	13×10^6
Australia	8×10^6	2×10^6	10×10^6
Mexico	7×10^6	3×10^6	10×10^6
Russia	9×10^6	1×10^6	10×10^6
12-Country Total			447×10^6
World Total			565×10^6

pressure, low rolling resistance tires may also add 5 more mpg to the fuel efficiency, bringing the vehicle total to 70 mpg. Finally, a high compression ratio engine (14:1) may augment the fuel efficiency the vehicle by 10 mpg for a total of 80 mpg.

The use of natural gas as a fuel becomes important for two different reasons: First, to attain the higher fuel efficiency of the vehicles; and Second, to obtain very low emissions per vehicle that are even more imperative given the projected large number of vehicles on the roads of the developed and developing countries.

The world has sufficient proved reserves of conventional natural gas to last 60 years at current consumption rate[35][36]. New natural gas resources are discovered continually. Moreover, increase in natural gas use for current and new applications, including transportation, can be offset in part or even wholly through increased efficiency in current and new uses. Global natural gas reserves stand currently (1993) at about 4,885 trillion scf and are distributed widely across the world in 85 countries covering a much wider part of the world compared to oil[35]. This

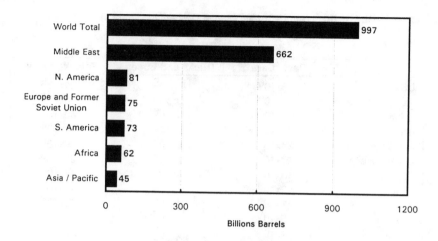

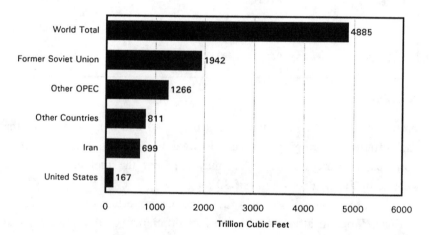

FIGURE 10-13. World Natural Gas and Crude Oil Reserves as of 1 January 1993 (Source: Oil and Gas Journal, December 28, 1992).

is shown clearly in Figure 10-13, where the world's oil and natural gas reserves are compared[34].

The present world natural gas reserves are equivalent to 900 billion bbl of oil or more than 90% of the world's total oil reserves. As late as 1990 natural gas reserves were 4,625 trillion scf and were equivalent to 85% of the world's oil reserves. Table 10-11 summarizes the top countries in the world with respect to proven reserves, production and consumption as of 1990. While natural gas consumption is expected to

TABLE 10-11. Top Countries in the World for Natural Gas Reserves, Production and Consumption as of 1990

Proven Reserves			Gross Production			Consumption		
Country	Natural Gas		Country	Natural Gas		Country	Natural Gas	
	Tscf	%		Tscf	%		Tscf	%
FSU	1850	40	FSU	29.4	34	FSU	25.0	34
Iran	605	13	USA	21.2	24	USA	18.7	26
Abu Dabi	185	4	Canada	4.9	5	Germany	4.5	6
Saudi Arabia	185	4	Algeria	4.3	5	UK	2.7	3
USA	167	4	Netherlands	2.7	3	Canada	2.4	3
Qatar	164	3	Indonesia	2.0	2	Japan	2.0	3
Venezuela	121	3	UK	1.9	2	Italy	1.8	2
Algeria	113	3	Saudi Arabia	1.7	2	Netherlands	1.5	2
Iraq	110	2	Iran	1.5	2	Saudi Arabia	1.3	2
Nigeria	100	2	Venezuela	1.3	2	France	1.3	2
Canada	96	2	Mexico	1.3	2	Rumania	1.1	1
Indonesia	92	2	Norway	1.3	2	Norway	0.9	1
Norway	82	2	Rumania	1.1	1	Mexico	0.9	1
Australia	75	2	Nigeria	0.9	1	Venezuela	0.8	1
Mexico	75	2	Argentina	0.9	1	Iran	0.8	1
70 Others	627	13	55 Others	11.5	13	57 Others	9.8	13
World	4625	100	World	87.8	100	World	74.7	100

Notes. 1 Tscf = 1 trillion scf. FSU : Former Soviet Union. Other major consumers include: United Arab Emirates : 0.7 Tscf; Australia : 0.6 Tscf; China 0.5 Tscf; Indonesia : 0.5 Tscf; Denmark : 0. 5 Tscf; Belgium : 0. 4 Tscf; Algeria : 0.4 Tscf; and India : 0.4 Tscf.

increase by 2.2% per year worldwide in the next 20 years, the rate of new discoveries has been and continues to be even higher (2.7% in the last few years).

The "Former Soviet Union" (FSU) has the largest reserves, the largest production and the largest consumption of natural gas in the world. European countries can be further supplied with natural gas via pipeline from the FSU (already in existence) to augment the localized production in the Netherlands, UK, Norway, Italy and a few central European countries. Africa has an abundance of natural gas that can be transported via pipeline anywhere in that continent. India and China can augment their apparently limited conventional reserves with supplies via pipeline from the former Soviet Union, Iran, and Indonesia. China and other Asian countries may have significant undiscovered natural gas resources as evidenced by recent off-shore conventional findings as well as large non-conventional resources, i.e., coal field methane. Japan is the only major consumer in the world which may have to import natural gas in the form of LNG, although it is feasible to bring natural gas from Siberia via a short pipeline under the Sea of Japan.

As an example of comparing available natural gas resources vs. potential use in the transportation sector, let us examine Australia and Africa[32][35]. The continent of Australia has an automobile population of about 10 million and a per capita automobile ownership slightly lower than that of Japan. Even if the ultimate vehicle population in Australia were to double, while fuel efficiency reached the 80 mpg (gasoline equivalent) target level, the annual use of natural gas to operate these vehicles would be on the order of 0.3 trillion scf. The added consumption for transportation is very small compared to the current reserves. Africa has presently some 12 million vehicles and an automobile ownership ratio of 55 persons per vehicle. Assuming that the ultimate population of Africa reaches 1 billion and that the automobile ownership ratio declines to about 2, i.e., becomes equal to that of Japan or Germany, the natural gas fuel consumption for all these automobiles at an 80 mpg (gasoline equivalent) fuel efficiency is on the order of 7.5 trillion scf per year. Once again it is interesting to note that the natural gas reserves of Africa are sufficient to meet the additional use of natural gas for transportation from indigenous sources.

It becomes apparent that the increase in consumption of natural gas due to the use of it as an automotive fuel with vehicles approaching an 80 mpg fuel efficiency can be met in all continents by local natural gas reserves only. Moreover, the proven world reserves in Table 10-11 do not include those from non-conventional sources. Indeed natural gas is such an ubiquitous fuel that it could become available in just about every country in the world[38]. The crucial element is the availability of high efficiency vehicles throughout the word that not only stretch the life of natural gas as fuel, but they also result in very minimal emissions due to the use of much less of an inherently clean fuel. The complete transition of the US from gasoline to natural gas around 2030 is likely to be followed by the rest of the world with a 20 year timelag.

STRATEGY FOR THE FUTURE

The preceding presentation must have shed ample light on the pros and cons of alternative transportation fuels. It ought to have also clarified the pertinent issues regarding the introduction of alternative automotive fuels to the transportation sector of the United States. It is apparent that natural gas is the fuel of choice for the transportation sector in the 21st century. This is evident form the results of Table 10-12, where the various fuels are compared with regard to a variety of critical factors. These factors include infrastructure development, fuel characteristics, and vehicle attributes that are affected by each particular fuel.

TABLE 10-12. Qualitative Comparison of Various Automotive Fuels with respect to Critical Characteristics in Order to Establish the Most Desirable Fuel for Transportation in the United States

Characteristic	Fuel				
	Gasoline	Natural Gas	Methanol	Ethanol	Electricity
Infrastructure					
Central	+++	+	0	0	0
Home	0	(+++)	0	0	(+++)
Fuel					
Availability	++	+++	0	+	++
Cost	++	+++	+	+	+
Toxicity	++	+++	+	++	++
Vehicle					
Cost	+++	++	++	++	+
Emissions	+	+++	+	+	+++
Efficiency	+	++	+	+	+++
Reliability	++	+++	+	++	++
Cum. Score	++	+++	+	++	++

Note. The scale is 0, +, ++, and +++ from the lowest to the highest score. A zero score indicates a very low or negligible representation at the present time. A score in a parenthesis indicates future potential rather than currently available representation. The cumulative score has been derived by taking an arithmetic average of the values of all the scores for each fuel.

The obvious question is then how to effect the switch of automotive fuels from gasoline to natural gas in an expedient and cost effective manner. Given the superiority of natural gas *vis-a-vis* all other transportation fuels, including gasoline, one is tempted to conclude that the switch is inevitable. This may be true in general. However, market distortions, imperfections, biases as well as the general political climate do not allow for an entirely free competition. Thus, it becomes necessary to device a certain strategy that will not only facilitate the switch to natural gas, but it will also ensure that less desirable fuels do not gain a foothold in the market, thereby displacing good ones and at the same time using up ineffectively financial resources to delay full implementation of more desirable fuels.

There exist three major collective players that will play important roles in this transition from gasoline to natural gas. These players are:

I.   The federal, state and local governments, who are the policy setters;

II. The automotive manufacturers and their component suppliers who must provide the appropriate vehicles and technology;

III. The fuel and infrastructure suppliers, who must deliver to the customers the requisite fuel for vehicular propulsion from the fuel production sites.

There is also a fourth collective player, the consumer public or customers, who will eventually purchase natural gas vehicles and fuel. However, the function of the consumer public is not to promote one fuel over another, but rather accept the one fuel, fuel system and vehicle type that makes the most sense. Hence, the contribution of the public must be in the arena of feedback regarding the vehicle type, fuel type and infrastructure that offers the most utility. This is an excellent use of the input of the consumer to guide the decision makers in the first three groups of players to move in the most desirable direction. Thus, the role of the consumer public appears to be more diffuse in nature compared to the well focused roles of the other three players even though the role of the public is the most critical one. After all without the consumer, government policy, automotive technologies and alternative fuels cannot function in a free market economy. Thus, consumer education with respect to the new transportation fuel and the consumer feedback to various alternative fuel developments are crucial to the introduction of natural gas as the new transportation fuel.

Federal, State and Local Governments. The role of the federal, state and local governments is primarily one of policy making. A secondary function may be that of funding the promotion of selected activities with respect to the introduction of alternative fuels. The federal government has already established the desirability for cleaner air and alternative fuels through three pieces of legislation enacted between 1990 and 1992. These pieces of legislation consist of :

a. The 1990 Clean Air Act Amendments (CAAA) emphasizing the placement of low emission vehicles (LEV) in certain non-attainment areas of the country;

b. The 1991 Intermodal Surface Transportation Efficiency Act (ISTEA) designed to assist States implement their transportation/air quality plans;

c. The 1992 Energy Policy Act (EPACT) requiring the purchase of alternative fuel vehicles by government and private fleet operators over a period of time.

Both ISTEA and EPACT have provisions for financial assistance to offset the cost of implementing alternative fuel vehicles that improve air quality. In particular the EPCAT will affect more the 10 million vehicles between its initial implementation in 1993 and its conclusion in the year 2005. The ISTEA allocates some $1 billion annually for 6 years (1992-1997). The EPACT provides a tax deduction of $2,000 per passenger vehicle and up to $50,000 for a heavy duty truck. The EPACT also provides a tax deduction for refueling installations of up to $100,000 per facility. More than $60 billion in federal tax deductions will become available through the EPACT resulting in a net federal tax reduction (30% tax bracket) for individuals and business of $20 billion through 2005.

The $6 billion grants of the ISTEA and the $20 billion of tax reduction of the EPACT may be viewed as a fund supplied by the federal government and available to everyone to utilize in order to offset the initial costs of alternative fuel vehicles. However, the EPACT does not make a choice for a particular fuel. Rather, it leaves up to the individuals and businesses to utilize these funds for whatever fuel they choose. This is somewhat unfortunate as emissions are not tied into the alternative fuel selected. In other words, the three aforementioned acts address the emissions problem (CAAA, ISTEA) or the dependency on imported petroleum problem (EPACT), but do not attempt to optimize the expenditure of funds to improve both problems simultaneously. Thus, there is a good chance that a good portion of the more than $26 billion available by the ISTEA and EPACT will be used to promote fuels that are either technically (methanol) or economically (electricity) non-competitive.

It is imperative that these funds be utilized to augment the number of natural vehicles on the road. As it was mentioned in an earlier chapter, even if there is no competition from other fuels, there is still a need for a critical number of natural gas vehicles on the road before their increase in number becomes self-sustaining. Thus, an amendment to these acts or additional legislation must be enacted to require a cost-benefit analysis to establish the cost of each pound of pollutants removed by employing alternative fuels. The fuel with the least cost or the most benefit ought to be then selected. On the other hand, it appears that natural gas vehicles are pulling ahead of the competition. This indicates that the consumers are realizing the advantage of natural gas fuel. Depending on whether this trend continues and accelerates there may be no need for amending the present legislation because the market is providing a solution to the problem as the legislators intended.

Various states with California in the leadership are in the process of adopting a variety of emission standards, particularly ZEVs, and also supply tax incentives to alternative fuel vehicles. The extent of these programs as of 1994 is shown in Figure 10-14. Once more, the current state legislation does not address the issue of a cost-benefit analysis to determine which fuel offers the most effective means to reduce pollutants form the atmosphere. Tax credits by state governments to subsidize alternative fuels must be also allocated in the most efficient way.

Local governments have much less resources to promote alternative fuels, yet they may be the most influential ones in bringing about change. One approach is for a local government to select one particular fuel and proceed to convert its vehicles to that fuel as well as promote that fuel type throughout its territory. It is thus very important that local

STATES WITH MANDATED FLEET CONVERSIONS AND/OR CONVERSION INCENTIVES IN PLACE

States with both mandated fleet conversions and conversion incentives.
States with mandated fleet conversions.
States with conversion incentives.

Source: The Clean Fuels Report, January 1994

FIGURE 10-14.   The Status of Mandates and/or Tax Incentives for the Acquisition of Alternative Fuel Vehicles at the State Government Level as of 1994.

governments are well informed of the pros and cons of different fuels in order to make the right choice. As more local governments discover the advantages of natural gas fuel, other local governments will be induced to follow. Moreover, limited funds may become available through the federal government (ISTEA) or the appropriate state government.

The Clean Cities program established by the US DOE in 1993 aims at facilitating cities around the country to develop plans to improve air quality and reduce dependency on foreign oil through the use of domestic alternative fuels. These plans, which must be administered by a designated city entity (e.g., city energy and environmental office), must be developed with the collaboration and participation of local utilities, local fleet owners and operators, and others such as major automotive manufacturers, suppliers of conversion equipment, the appropriate state energy and environmental office and the representatives of the nearest DOE office.

Some of the measures that should be taken by local governments should include the following actions:

a. Designation of natural gas as the alternative fuel of choice for that city or locality;

b. Conversion of existing city vehicles and purchase of new ones to operate on natural gas;

c. Coordination of the acquisition of natural gas vehicles by federal agencies located in the city, primarily the post-office;

d. Development of strategically located central CNG refueling stations throughout the city;

e. Encouragement to fleet owners and operators within the city limits to convert their vehicles into natural gas;

f. Advertisement of the benefits of the natural gas fuel (air quality, non-dependency on foreign oil) to enhance the awareness and educate the local public;

g. Passage of local building code ordinances to require establishment of hook-ups for CNG fueling at all new residential and commercial buildings;

i. Promotion of the conversion and the purchase of private natural gas vehicles throughout the city.

Thus, the local governments should take the lead in establishing natural gas as the alternative transportation fuel of choice. Even though state governments and the federal government have more authority and a wider jurisdiction to implement change, it is the local government that appears to have ultimately more control as to what happens. Consequently, the role of local governments may be much more profound in bringing about the switch from gasoline to natural gas.

Two other areas where federal and state governments can make a difference in promoting the sale of natural gas vehicles are fuel efficiency and emission standards. For example, the federal government can increase the CAFE standard from the present 27.5 mpg to 40 mpg sometime around the year 2000. Dedicated natural gas vehicles (high compression) will have a 5 mpg advantage over other alternative or gasoline fueled vehicles (15% higher fuel efficiency). This 5 mpg advantage of natural gas vehicles will reduce the incremental cost of such vehicles versus gasoline vehicles because it would require additional technologies in a gasoline vehicle to attain the extra 5 mpg fuel efficiency. Thus, high fuel efficiency natural gas vehicles may be comparable in price to gasoline vehicles of the same fuel efficiency.

States with non-attainment areas, which include all the most populous states of the Union, should adopt air emission standards of the California ULEV level or even more stringent ones. These standards can only be met with dedicated natural gas vehicles. In conclusion , the federal, state and local laws must reflect the economic efficiency, fuel efficiency, and air quality level that can be obtained with natural gas. For natural gas, among all fuels including gasoline, offers the most utility to the consumer and the country in terms of air pollution reduction and balance of payments.

It should be pointed out that different levels of government are most appropriate for specific policies. In the broadest term, the appropriate level of government must be chosen such that it: a. can assess external costs and benefits of energy security, air quality, balance of payments and so on; and b. is best able to internalize those external costs and benefits in order to maximize the well being of society. Ultimately, the successful type and magnitude of government policies for the replacement of gasoline and diesel fuel vehicles with natural gas vehicles will be the result of intergovernmental relations or federalism, to use an older term, whereby each level of government has a particular set of responsibilities independent of the other levels.

Automotive Manufacturers and Suppliers. The obvious function of automotive manufacturers and automotive component suppliers is to engineer, build and sell natural gas vehicles. However, automobile manufacturers do not operate in a vacuum. That is to say, there must exist a market for natural gas vehicles in order for GM, Ford, Chrysler and others to manufacture them. Since at the present time the laws of the federal and state governments do not give a preferential position to any of the alternative fuel vehicles, with the possible exception of electric vehicles, alternative fuel vehicles are sold on as needed basis.

Typically, the US Government through its General Accounting Office (GAO) procures a portion of the new vehicle purchases for government needs to be alternative fuel vehicles, i.e., natural gas or methanol, in accordance with EPACT. These vehicles may be passenger cars, vans and trucks and may be on the order of several thousand every year. Unfortunately, all the different branches of the federal government own and operate only 1/2 million vehicles of which the Post Office accounts for 45% and the Department of Defense for 30% (non-military vehicles). Moreover, the federal government cannot claim any tax deduction so that alternative fuel vehicles cost more than regular gasoline ones.

State and local governments may also purchase a small number of alternative fuel vehicles annually. They, too, suffer form the tax deduction ineligibility problem as well. Finally, utility companies (power, water, telephone, etc.) have ownership of a few million vehicles and they too are required to purchase alternative fuel vehicles under EPACT. However, most power utilities generate and sell electricity either exclusively or in conjunction with selling natural gas. Thus, the first priority of most power utilities seems to be the promotion of more electricity sales and consequently of electric vehicle sales. Furthermore, the incremental cost of an electric vehicle is several times the incremental cost of a natural gas vehicle. Thus, if both types of vehicles are purchased by utilities fewer alternative fuel vehicles will be acquired annually compared to the purchase of only natural gas vehicles. Under these circumstances the major automotive manufacturers are faced with a totally fragmented market and cannot plan major vehicle production. Since the private sector reflects ultimately the mass automobile market, manufacturers must be able to attract the public in order to sell natural gas vehicles. Another major concern of the automobile manufacturers is the present lack of infrastructure for CNG refueling.

The preceding observations imply that from a marketing point of view natural gas vehicles must be initially both dedicated and bi-fuel vehicles. Bi-fuel natural gas vehicles should be capable to operate on either CNG or another fuel such as a gasoline. Moreover, bi-fuel CNG vehicles must be designed with both of the following features. The vehicle: a. uses-up the natural gas fuel before the gasoline fuel is employed;

and b. becomes inoperable after continuous use of gasoline fuel for more than a fixed number of miles, say 500, unless CNG fuel is used again. The need for such measures is due to the fact that bi-fuel vehicle operators, particularly in fleets, will tend to revert to gasoline because of habit and convenience.

Dedicated CNG vehicles along with some bi-fuel CNG/gasoline vehicles may be used by governments, public utilities and large private fleets. However, the bi-fuel CNG/gasoline vehicle may be more appropriate for the individual consumer or smaller fleet operator. The bi-fuel CNG vehicles will expose the public to, and familiarize it with natural gas as a transportation fuel. The major incentive of the public to purchase bi-fuel CNG vehicles will be the reduced cost of natural gas versus gasoline and other alternative fuels so long as the vehicle incremental cost can be covered by the federal tax deduction, state tax credit and utility rebate, if any. This bi-fuel scenario may last for up to ten years at which point dedicated only CNG vehicles are marketed. By that time the CNG infrastructure will be well under way to support the further expansion of natural gas as a transportation fuel. This introduction of dedicated CNG vehicles may coincide roughly with the time at which tax credits expire, and potentially higher fuel efficiency standards as well as more stringent air emissions standards go into effect.

At a minimum the 8 to 10 year period from now through 2005 of dedicated and bi-fuel CNG passenger cars, trucks, vans and buses will witness acceptance of the new fuel by the public as well as a substantial reduction of the added initial costs for such vehicles. It is important for automotive manufacturers, however, to interact closely with the natural gas vehicle owners during the initial several years of introduction to obtain valuable feedback in terms of vehicle performance characteristics in order to: a. adjust any problematic areas; and b. identify all the major advantages of the CNG fuel that can be used as a selling tool to attract more buyers.

Manufacturers of dedicated CNG specialty vehicles, such as municipal buses, refuge trucks, dump trucks, street sweepers, and a multitude of others, must expand their designs to accommodate different types of medium and heavy duty natural gas engines replacing the current diesel engines. There is a continuous and predictable demand for these types of vehicles by private companies as well as cities, counties, state government agencies and others. That is to say, the market for heavier vehicles is better defined than that for lighter vehicles. Also, the heavier vehicles tend to consume much more fuel which is advantageous from a vehicle incremental cost pay-back period.

Fuel and Infrastructure Suppliers. Traditionally, the majority of the fuel suppliers as well as marketing agents for gasoline have been the oil companies. While the production of crude oil is almost entirely in the hands of the oil companies, significant portion of the refining of it into products, including gasoline, is performed by independent refinery owners. Likewise some of the gasoline marketing is carried out by independent stations not franchised by the oil companies. This picture is going to change drastically with the introduction of natural gas as a transportation fuel. Unlike gasoline that has to be trucked into the consumption centers from the refineries, natural gas is already piped into the consumption areas from the natural gas processing plants. Moreover, the production of natural gas is not dominated as much by the oil companies as the production of crude oil.

The marketing of natural gas as a transportation fuel will be the responsibility of other entities besides the oil companies. These entities may include local natural gas public utilities as well as independent companies. Obviously, the oil companies that have significant natural gas reserves will enter the market selling natural gas by itself or alongside gasoline in central refueling stations. Likewise natural gas utilities and independents will set natural gas central refueling stations. Both of these types of activities are already taking place and comprise the bulk of the more than 1000 refueling stations operational across the US by the end of 1994.

Another type of refueling station, the home or business CNG fueling facility, will become ultimately more prominent than the central refueling stations. The ownership and maintenance of the home and small business CNG refueling station will not be the purview of either the oil companies or even the local natural gas utilities. The most likely scenario is that independent companies will be established to own and/or operate such facilities. This is entirely feasible from a regulatory point of view as anybody can purchase natural gas and have it delivered to any destination for a fee over pipelines owned and operated by other companies. These independent companies, covering large customer areas, will have a much lower cost of doing business than utilities or oil companies. However, natural gas utilities may also sell natural gas directly to residential customers for transportation use.

Utilities will continue to supply natural gas for all other purposes outside of transportation. A separate meter will be required at that time to measure the consumption of natural gas as transportation fuel. If the present state of affairs is an indication of future developments, there will be a federal and state tax on natural gas used as an automotive fuel. However, this tax will not reach the level of the present gasoline and diesel fuel taxes until after the special tax treatment for alternative fuels expires. One major cost in the price of natural gas delivered to a small user (residential) is the high cost of measuring meters every month or every other month by a utility personnel. The independent companies selling the transportation fuel portion of natural gas will have to use automatic meter reading and recording equipment that are less expensive than utilizing company personnel.

In the next 8 to 10 years a sufficiently large number of residential CNG refueling units must be sold to bring the price of the system to a more reasonable level through economies of scale. During the same time automatic metering and recording techniques will be further perfected and be also reduced in cost. Rebates by natural gas utilities to the public to acquire natural gas vehicles is another means to promote sales. Ideally, these rebates will be sufficient to cover the remainder of the vehicle incremental cost, if any, after federal tax deductions and state tax credits have been claimed.

An important consideration is that of the future of the oil companies and refineries that currently produce gasoline as part of their normal operation. While the need for gasoline and diesel fuel diminishes, the need for other fuels such as jet fuel will increase. A use for the surplus gasoline must be found, if natural gas is going to replace it as an automotive fuel. A barrel of oil yields currently 19 gal of gasoline, 9 gal of distillate (diesel) fuel, 5 gal of jet fuel, 2 gal of liquefied petroleum gas (LPG) and 9 gal of other miscellaneous products (a 42 US gal barrel crude oil yields slightly more than 44 gal of petroleum products due to the reduction in the density of the crude oil during the refining process).

Current trends indicate that the crude oil production in the US may drop to 4 million bbl/d in the next two decades, while production of natural gas liquids will be about 2 million bbl/d — production of natural gas is projected to remain constant between 1990 and 2010[39]. Given the increase in air travel, it is very reasonable to expect that in the same time period the demand for jet fuel will rise to 2 million bbl/d[40]. This implies that the present refining processes must be modified to increase the production of jet fuel, while reducing the production of gasoline and distillate fuel. This modification is technologically feasible through polymerization of lighter products (gasoline and LPG) and cracking of heavier ones (distillate fuels) to shift the process such that it produces more jet fuel[41]. Obviously, these new processes may increase the price of jet fuel depending on their complexity and the final energy efficiency of conversion.

Alternatively, jet fuel may be imported and gasoline exported for a more economical process. Table 10-13 presents a scenario of petroleum products use sometime beyond 2030, when the bulk of automobiles in the US will be fueled by natural gas and the demand for gasoline and diesel fuel will be significantly reduced. There will be no longer importation of crude oil from abroad. The domestic production of crude oil at 4 million bbl/d will be used to supply all the remaining needs for gasoline, diesel fuel, distillate, residual and heavy fuels. In that case, surplus gasoline of up to 2 million bbl/d may have to be exported or else converted to natural gas (95% methane, 5 % ethane)*. The methane will be obtained from the steam reforming of gasoline or other hydrocarbons, while sufficient ethane is found in the natural gas liquids. The surplus of about 3 quads/y of natural gas liquids and/or gasoline can be thus converted to natural gas and petrochemical feedstocks. Depending on the source of the energy input for the conversion process some 2 to 3 tril-

---

[*]. Any hydrocarbon can be converted to methane via: steam reforming, $C_nH_m + n\,H_2O \longrightarrow n\,CO + (0.5m+n)\,H_2$ (30 atm, 700-900°C); water shifting, $CO + H_2O \longrightarrow CO_2 + H_2$; and methanation, $CO + 3\,H_2 \longrightarrow CH_4 + H_2O$.

TABLE 10-13. Projected Liquid Hydrocarbon Production and Use Beyond 2030

Product	Supply/Consumption	Energy Content	Origin
Crude Oil	4.0 million bbl/d	8.5 quad/y	Domestic
Natural Gas Liquids	2.5 million bbl/d	3.5 quad/y	Domestic
Gasoline[1]	0.5 million bbl/d	1.0 quad/y	Domestic
Distillate Fuel[2]		1.0 quad/d	Domestic
Jet Fuel[3]	2.0 million bbl/d	4.0 quad/y	Dom./Imp.
Residual Fuel[4]		2.0 quad/y	Domestic
Petrochemicals		1.5 quad/y	Domestic
LPG[5]		2.5 quad/y	Domestic

1. Over 95% of vehicular transportation is assumed to be using natural gas as a fuel by 2030. Any surplus gasoline produced by refineries is either exported or converted to other products. 2. It is assumed that diesel fuel or distillate fuel is no longer used in the commercial sector and by electric utilities. Some 0.50 quad/y of distillate fuel is used in the industrial sector and another 0.50 quad/y in the transportation sector. Diesel fuel has been replaced by natural gas in most all of the transportation sector. Surplus distillate fuel from refineries is converted to jet fuel. 3. If not sufficient jet fuel can be produced in the modified refining process of domestic crude oil, it must be imported. Thus, 2 to 3 quad/y of jet fuel may be imported. 4. Residual fuel is assumed to be used in the industrial sector (0.50 quad/y), transportation sector (0.75 quad/y) and by electric utilities (0.50 quad/y). 5. Most of the LPG is used in the industrial sector (2.25 quad/y) and the remainder is used in the transportation sector.

lion scf/y of natural gas fuel may be obtained. However, a significant amount of jet fuel may have to be imported, if it cannot be obtained efficiently from the conversion (refining) of the domestic crude oil.

The approach outlined above provides a reasonable course of action for the replacement of gasoline with natural gas as the fuel of choice in the land transportation arena over the next several decades. The following action items summarize the conclusions and recommendations suggested so far. These major action items or steps are as follows:

Step 1. Federal government mandates higher CAFE standards for passengers cars from 27 mpg to 40 mpg and increase accordingly fuel efficiency of light trucks and vans from a present of about 20 mpg to 30 mpg.

Step 2. Federal government establishes a cost-benefit requirement for the application of EPACT funds to purchase alternative fuel vehicles (i.e., CNG vehicles) or convert gasoline vehicles to AFVs through the year 2005.

Step 3.   State governments promulgate very stringent emission standards such as the California ULEV or even more stringent ones and establish tax credits on a cost-benefit analysis to reduce air pollution.

Step 4.   Local and City governments develop initiatives with local utilities and business for natural gas vehicle purchases and conversions as well as public education within their boundaries.

Step 5.   Automobile manufacturers market initially both dedicated CNG vehicles and bi-fuel CNG/gasoline vehicles, depending on the application or end user, and after a decade dedicated CNG vehicles only.

Step 6.   Automobile manufacturers and their suppliers develop technology for super fuel efficient vehicles.

Step 7.   Utilities, oil companies and private businesses develop refueling CNG public stations both central as well as residential ones.

Step 8.   Utilities provide rebates for the purchase of either CNG vehicles as well as home and business CNG refueling facilities to augment federal tax deductions and state tax credits.

Step 9.   Utilities and appropriate technology businesses develop more efficient means of natural gas use in residential and commercial buildings for space conditioning and water heating through the implementation of fuel cells.

Step 10.   Oil companies and refineries shift gradually the prevailing processes to obtain less gasoline and diesel fuel and more natural gas and jet fuel from the refining of the diminishing supply of crude oil, which eventually will be all domestic. Moreover, natural gas liquids are converted to natural gas.

In conclusion, natural gas is unquestionably the fuel of choice among the various alternatives to replace gasoline in terms of efficiency and air pollution reduction. It is abundant domestically and its widespread use as an automobile fuel will virtually eliminate the dependency of the US on foreign oil. The natural gas technology as a transportation fuel is already developed. The lower cost of natural gas along with government and utility incentives offsets the higher cost of implementing a new modality in its early phases. What is required at this time is a concerted effort between government, federal, state, local and the private sector to accelerate the pace of the introduction of natural gas as the next transportation fuel and the replacement of all gasoline and diesel fuel vehicles with natural gas vehicles in the next three decades.

REFERENCES

1. Energy Information Administration, Energy Information Sheets, DOE/EIA-0578(91), p. 19, US DOE, Washington, DC, 1993.

2. M. W. Zemansky, Heat and Thermodynamics, 3rd ed., McGraw-Hill Book Company, New York, NY, 1951.

3. M. Munasinghe, Energy Analysis and Policy, pp. 107-139, Butterworths, London, UK, 1990.

4. Lennox Heating-Air Conditioning, "Lennox Home Comfort Systems", Lennox Industries, Dallas, TX, 1992.

5. United Technologies Carrier, "Carrier Products and Systems – Mini Catalog 1993", Syracuse, NY, 1993.

6. D. W. Devins, Energy: Its Physical Impact on the Environment, John Wiley & Sons, New York, NY, 1982.

7. Technology Advancement Office, 1992 TAO Progress Report, Volume II: Project and Technology Status, "Residential Proton Exchange Membrane Fuel Cell", pp. 91-92, South Coast Air Quality Management District, Diamond Bar, CA, October 1992.

8. R. Boardman, A. White, M. Wusterbarth, "The Most Efficient Combined Cycle Power Plant in the World", GE Industrial and Power Systems, Schnectady, NY, 1993.

9. ABB Technology Update, "How GT24 Technology Achieves 58% Efficiency Without Increasing Emissions and Inlet Temperatures", *Power Engineering,* v. 98, no. 3, p. 6, March 1994.

10. M. Valenti, "Coal Gasification: An Alternative Energy Source is Coming of Age", *Mechanical Engineering,* v. 114, no. 1, pp. 39-43, January 1992.

42. General Electric has announced the introduction of a 60% net efficiency combined cycle gas turbine operating at 2600°F – *Power Engineering*, v. 99, no. 6, pp. 33-36, June 1995.

11. J. M. Klara, "HIPPS:Beyond State-of-the-Art, Part I, DOE's Combustion 2000 Program is Bringing Commercial Reality to Advanced Coal Burning Technology", *Power Engineering*, v. 97, no. 12, pp. 37-39, December 1993.

12. Coal Industry Advisory Board, Industry Attitudes to Combined Cycle Clean Coal Technologies, International Energy Agency, Organization of Economic Co-operation and Development, Paris, FR, 1994.

13. K. Boulding, "The Economics of the Coming Spaceship Earth", in H. Jarret (ed.), Environmental Quality in a Growing Economy, Johns Hopkins University Press, Baltimore, MD, 1966.

14. N. Georgescu-Roegen, The Entropy Law and the Economic Process, Harvard University press, Cambridge, MA, 1971.

15. D. W. Pearce and R. K. Turner, Economics of Natural Resources and the Environment, Johns Hopkins University Press, Baltimore, MD, 1990.

16. D. W. Pearce and J. J. Warford, World Without End: Economics, Environment and Sustainable Development, published for the World Bank by Oxford University Press, New York, NY, 1993.

17. S. Kaplan, Energy Economics: Quantitative Methods for Energy and Environmental Decisions, McGraw-Hill Book Company, New York, NY, 1983.

18. R. Stobaugh and D. Yergin, Energy Future: Report of the Harvard Business School, Random House, New York, NY, 1979.

19. S. H. Schur, J. Darmstadter, H. Perry, W. Ramsey, M. Russel, Energy in America's Future: The Choices Before Us, published for Resources for the Future by The Johns Hopkins University Press, Baltimore, MD, 1979.

20. National Academy of Sciences, Energy in Transition 1985-2000, Final Report of the Committee on Nuclear and Alternative Energy Systems, W. H. Freeman and Company, San Francisco, CA, 1980.

21. D. Anderson, W. Cavendish, "Efficiency and Substitution in Pollution Abatement: Three Case Studies", World Bank Discussion Papers No. 186, The World Bank, Washington, DC, December 1992.

22. R. O. Geiss, W. M. Burkmyre, J. W. Lanigan, "Technical Highlights of the Dodge Compressed Natural Gas Ram Van/Wagon", pp. 9-20, Natural Gas: Fuel and Fueling, SP-927, Society of Automotive Engineers, Warrendale, PA, 1992.

23. R. M. Siewert, P. J. Mitchell, P. A. Mulawa, "Environmental Potential of Natural Gas Fuel for Light-Duty Vehicles: An Engine-Dynamometer Study of Exhaust-Emission-Control Strategies and Fuel Consumption", SAE Paper 932744, Society of Automotive Engineers, Warrendale, PA, 1993.

24. L. W. Huellmantel, M. G. Reynolds, R. A. McCormick, "Emissions and Fuel Economy for the Freedom Hybrid Vehicle - Phase I Results", Research Report No. VS-184, General Motors Research and Environmental Staff, Warren, MI, 1992.

25. U. Seifert, P. Walzer, Automobile Technology of the Future, Society of Automotive Engineers, Warrendale, PA, 1991.

26. M. Neiburger, J. G. Edinger, W. D. Bonner, Understanding our Atmospheric Environment, W. H. Freeman and Co., San Francisco, CA, 1973.

27. N. J. Rosenberg, B. L. Blad, S. B. Verma, Microclimate: The Biological Environment, 2nd ed., John Wiley & Sons, New York, NY, 1983.

28. R. E. Inman, R. B. Ingersoll, and E. A. Levy, "Soil: A natural sink for carbon monoxide", Science, v. 172, pp. 1229-1231, 1971.

29. N. B. Freney, O.T.Denmead, and J. R. Simpson, "Soil as a source or sink of atmospheric nitrous oxide", Nature, v. 272, pp. 530-532, 1978.

30. J. M. Lents and W. J. Kelly, "Clearing the Air in Los Angeles", Scientific American, v. 269, No. 4, pp. 32-39, 1993.

31. C. A. Sawyer, "GM's Ultralite: Is It For Real?", Automotive Industries, pp. 19-24, March 1992.

32. W. Peschka, <u>Liquid Hydrogen : Fuel of the Future</u>, Springer-Verlag, New York, NY, 1992.

33. J. Salva and G. Lopez, "Effects of Hydrogen Addition on Pollutant Emissions in a Gas Turbine Combustor", *proc.* AGARD Meeting on Fuels and Combustion Technology for Advanced Aircraft Engines, Paris, FR, May 1993.

34. "Comparative National Statistics – Transportation", pp. 834-839,<u>1994 Britannica Book of the Year</u>, Encyclopeadia Britannica Inc., Chicago, IL, 1994.

35. J. Homer, "Natural Gas in Developing Countries: Evaluating the Benefits to the Environment", World Bank Discussion Paper 190, The World Bank, Washington, DC, 1993.

36. "International Energy Outlook 1993", DOE/EIA-0484(93), Energy Information Administration, US DOE, Washington, DC, 1993.

37. "Comparative National Statistics – World and Regional Summaries", pp. 756-757, <u>1994 Britannica Book of the Year</u>, Encyclopeadia Britannica Inc., Chicago, IL, 1994.

38. T. H. Lee, H. R. Linden, D. A. Dreyfus and T. Vasko (eds.), <u>The Methane Age</u>, Kluwer Academic Publishers, Dodrecht, NL, 1988.

39. "Annual Energy Outlook with Projections to 2010", DOE/EIA-038(92), p. 27, Energy Information Administration, US DOE, Washington, DC, 1992.

40. "Annual Energy Outlook with Projections to 2010", DOE/EIA-038(92), loc. cit., p. 110.

41. "Petroleum Refinery Processes, Survey" in Kirk-Othmer, <u>Encyclopedia of Chemical Technology</u>, 3rd ed., v. 17, pp. 183-256, Wiley-Interscience, New York, NY, 1982.

42. (see p. 440)

43. S. E. Kuehn, "Combined Cycle Leads Efficiency Race – Top to Bottom, the Gas Turbine Combined Cycle is the Present and Future Choice for New Generation", *Power Engineering*, v. 99, no. 5, pp. 30-31, May 1995.

Appendix A

Selected Suppliers of Natural Gas Vehicles, Components and Fueling Equipment

A partial list of major suppliers of different types of natural gas vehicles, natural gas vehicle components and natural gas refueling equipment is supplied in order to facilitate the identification of desired products by a prospective NGV user. This list cannot be all inclusive as the NGV market is evolving very rapidly at the present time. For more up to date information potential NGV technology users may contact the national Natural Gas Vehicle Coalition (NGVC) in Arlington, VA (703-527-3022). Interested parties may also contact their local natural gas utilities for regional information regarding qualified suppliers of vehicles as well as approved local conversion facilities.

The following list is organized in a functional form beginning with OEM vehicles and continuing with vehicle and infrastructure component suppliers. Since the demand for NGVs is relatively limited at the present time, OEMs accept only orders through their local dealers or offices. Whenever appropriate a central OEM address and phone number is also included.

Passenger Cars

Ford Crown Victoria (Engine 4.6L V8)

(Contact fleet manager at local Ford dealership who will arrange vehicle order and delivery through respective Zone Fleet Manager, or call 1-800-ACT-FUEL)

Light Duty Trucks and Vans

GMC Truck/Chevrolet

Full Size Pickup Truck 1/2, 3/4 &1 ton (Engine 5.7L V8)
Full Size Van (Engine 5.7L V8)
P-Chassis Delivery Truck (Engine 5.7L V8)

(Contact fleet manager at local GMC Truck or Chevrolet dealership who will arrange prep vehicle order and delivery. Requires availability of approved conversion kit.)

Chrysler

Dakota (Engine 5.2L V8)
Ram Truck (Engine 5.2L V8)
Ram Van/Wagon (Engine 5.2L V8)
Caravan/Voyager Minivan (Engine 3.3L V6)

(Contact fleet manager at local Chrysler/Plymouth or Dodge dealership or Chrysler Zone Fleet Manager or call the Chrysler Fleet Operations Hotline at 1-800-255-2616)

Ford

F-Series Pickup Truck, F-150, F-250 (Engine 4.9L V8)
E-Series Van (Engine 4.9L V8)

Medium Duty Trucks

GMC Truck/Chevrolet (Engine 7.0L)

TopKick/Kodiak Truck
School Bus Chassis

(Offered only as an aftermarket conversion kit)

School Buses
Blue Bird Company (Fort Valley, GA, 912-825-2021)

Carpenter Manufacturing (Mitchell, IN, 812-849-3131)

Thomas Built Buses (High Point, NC, 910-889-4871)

Refuse Haulers and Recycle Chassis
Crane Carrier (Tulsa, OK, 918-836-1651)

Street Sweepers
Athey Products Corp. (Raleigh, NC, 919-556-5171)

    Mobile Sweeper M-9 CNG (Santa Fe Springs, CA, 310-944-8061)

Lift Trucks (Off-Road Vehicles)
    Clark Material Handling Co. (Lexington, KY, 606-288-1299)

    Yale Materials Handling Corp. (Flemington, NJ, 1-800-233-YALE)

    Caterpillar Lift Trucks (Mentor, OH, 1-800-CAT-LIFT)

Locomotive
MK Rail Corporation (Oakbrook Terrace, IL, 708-691-7770)

    MK1200G Locomotive, Engine Caterpillar G3516 V16, LNG

GNG Engines

Cummins Engine Co (Columbus, IN, 812-377-5000)	L10-240G Heavy Duty B5.9 Series Medium Duty
Detroit Diesel Corp (Detroit, MI, 313-592-5292)	Series 50 Heavy Duty Series 30 Medium Duty
Caterpillar (Mentor, OH, 1-800-CAT-LIFT)	3306G Heavy Duty
Hercules Engine Co (Canton, OH, 216-428-1038)	GTA 5.7L Medium Duty GTA 3.7L Medium Duty
Tecogen (Waltham, MA, 617-622-1070)	Tecodrive 7000 Medium Duty

CNG Tanks

Brunswick Corporation   All Carbon
(Lake Forest, IL, 708-735-4861)

Comdyne Cylinder Corp   Aluminum/Fiberglass
(West Liberty, OH, 918-838-8948)

EDO Energy Division   All Carbon
(College Point, NY, 718-321-4000)

NGV Systems   Aluminum/Fiberglass
(Long Beach, CA, 310-630-5768)

Norris Cylinder Co.   Aluminum, Steel/ Fiberglass
(Longview, TX, 1-800-527-8418)

Pressed Steel Tank Co.   Steel/Fiberglass
(Milwaukee, WI, 1-800-826-5778)

LNG Tanks

Liquid Carbonic (Oak Brook, IL, 708-572-7294)
M.V.E. Cryogenics (Bloomington, MN, 612-853-9666)

Fuel Control/Engine Conversion Equipment

ANGI (Milton, WI, 608-868-4626)
Essex Cryogenics (St. Louis, MO, 314-8328077)
GFI Control Systems (Commerce City, CO, 303-287-7441)
IMPCO Technology (Cerritos, CA, 310-860-6666)
MESA Environmental (Ft. Worth, TX, 817-924-2353)
Vinyard Energy Systems (San Antonio, TX, 210-520-7924)

Fueling/Compressors/ Equipment

Citizens Gas   Public and Private CNG Stations
(Indianapolis, IN, 317-927-4432)

CVI   LNG/CNG Central
(Columbus, OH, 614-876-7381)   Fueling Stations

Marcum Fuel Systems
(Longmont, CO, 303-651-1895)

Turnkey Public CNG Stations

ECOGAS Corp
(Austin, TX, 512-338-9874)

LNG/CNG Central Fueling Stations

Fuel Maker Corp
(Salt Lake City, UT, 801-328-0670)

Home, Business CNG Refueling

Hansen Coupling Division
(Berea, OH, 216-826-1115)

CNG Nozzles and Receptacles

GassWagen
(Annville, PA, 717-867-1527)

CNG Station Access and Billing

Ingersoll-Rand
(Davidson, NC, 1-800-922-3838)

CNG Compressors

Lectrodryer
(Richmond, KY, 606-624-2091)

CNG Dryers and Filters

Micro Motion
(Boulder, CO, 303-530-8231)

CNG Mass Flowmeters

Parker Hannifan Corp
(Cleveland, OH, 216-531-3000)

CNG/LNG Nozzles and Receptacles

Rix Industries
(Oakland, CA, 510-658-5275)

CNG Compressors

Sherex Industries
(Burlington, ON, 905-639-7701)

CNG Nozzles and Receptacles

Stäubli
(Duncan, SC, 1-800-845-9193)

CNG Nozzles

Only a small percentage of national suppliers of CNG/LNG fueling systems and fueling equipment has been listed above. The local natural gas utility can supply information on regional companies involved in CNG fueling station design and equipment packaging.

Appendix B

States/Areas Affected by the 1990 CAAA

Since the Clean Air Act Amendment (CAAA) was enacted into law on November 15, 1990, the Environmental Protection Agency has been developing regulations to implement the programs mandated by Congress in that Act. One of those programs is the Clean-Fuel Vehicle Fleet program. This program affects certain state and local governments as well as fleet owners because it requires that, beginning in 1998, a portion of the new vehicles purchased annually in ozone and carbon monoxide air problem areas be clean-fuel vehicles.

The EPA has two major roles in this program. First, it must promulgate regulations regarding specified components of the clean-fuel vehicles, including general provisions, emission standards, vehicle conversion rules and exemptions from regulations. Second, it must approve or disapprove revisions to State Implementation Plans (SIPs) incorporating the clean-fuel vehicle fleet program.

The affected states have also two roles in the program. First, they must revise their SIPs by May 1994 to establish clean-fuel vehicle fleet programs for their state. Second, they must enforce these programs once the revised SIPs have been approved by the EPA.

Finally, the affected fleet owners must comply with the state and federal regulations relevant to their fleets as they purchase new vehicles. According to the CAAA, fleets of ten or more vehicles that are owned or operated, leased or otherwise controlled by one entity and are centrally fueled or capable of being centrally fueled must comply with the clean-fuel vehicle fleet program. Private sector fleets as well as federal, state and local government fleets are included.

Certain vehicles are exempt from fleet regulations, including public rental vehicles, law enforcement and emergency vehicles, non-road vehicles, vehicles garaged at a personal residence when not in use, vehicles held for sale by dealers, manufacturers test vehicles, and heavy duty vehicles (over 26,000 lb gross vehicle weight). Moreover, exempt vehicles are not to be considered when determining if a fleet has ten or more vehicles covered by the Act.

The CAAA prescribes purchase requirements in terms of percentage of the total number of new vehicles acquired each year. These requirements are phased-in over a three-year period and are categorized by vehicle type or weight. For light duty vehicles and trucks, the phase-in rate increases from 30% of new vehicle purchases in 1998 to 50% in 1999 and then to 70% in 2000 and beyond. For heavy-duty vehicles, the acquisition requirement is 50% in 1998 and all subsequent years.

The requirements for clean-fuel vehicle fleets can be met in one of three ways: First, acquisition of the appropriate number of vehicles which meet the clean-fuel vehicle emission standards and which consist of LEVs, ULEVs and ZEVs with comparable emission levels to those of the California standards; Second, redemption of credits that can be either generated by the fleet operators or be purchased from other fleet operators; and Third, conversion of conventional existing or new vehicles to clean fuel vehicles in accordance with regulations to be issued by EPA.

The aforementioned credit redemption program provides fleet owners flexibility in meeting vehicle purchase requirements. Credits can be obtained in four ways as follows: I. Early acquisition of clean fuel vehicles; II. Extra acquisitions of clean fuel vehicles; III. Acquisition of

ULEVs and ZEVs; and IV. Acquisition of vehicles in categories not covered. Credits may be traded for use within the same or contiguous non-attainment areas. Credits may also be banked for unlimited amounts of time and with no depreciation in value. However, credits for light duty vehicles and trucks may not be redeemed against heavy-duty vehicle acquisition requirements. Credits are weighted to reflect the level of emission reduction expected to be achieved by the vehicle generating the credit.

As noted above, only fleets operating in certain ozone and carbon monoxide non-attainment air quality areas are required to comply. These areas are defined in the CAAA as having a 1980 population of 250,000 or more and either a serious, severe, or extreme ozone non-attainment or a carbon monoxide non-attainment with a 1989-90 value in excess of 16.0 ppm. There are currently twenty-one ozone and one carbon monoxide non-attainment areas affected by the CAAA. The affected areas as of now and the respective states in which they are located are listed below in alphabetical order.

No.	Affected Area	State
1	Atlanta	GA
2	Baltimore	MD
3	Baton Rouge	LA
4	Beaumont-Port Arthur	TX
5	Boston-Lawrence-Worcester	MA, NH
6	Chicago-Gary-Lake County	IL, IN
7	Denver-Boulder	CO
8	El Paso	TX
9	Greater Connecticut	CT
10	Houston-Galveston-Brazoria	TX
11	Los Angeles-South Coast Air Basin	CA
12	Milwaukee-Racine	WI
13	New York-Northern New Jersey-Long Island	NY, NJ, CT
14	Philadelphia-Willmington-Trenton	PA, DE, MD, NJ
15	Providence	RI
16	Sacramento Metro	CA
17	San Diego	CA
18	San Joaquin Valley	CA
19	Southern Desert Modified AQMA	CA
20	Springfield	MA

21	Ventura County	CA
22	Washington, DC	MD, VA

Other areas may be addded to the present twenty-two areas, if they become reclassified as non-attainment areas by the EPA in the future thereby falling under the provisions of the 1990 CAAA.

Appendix C

Conversion to Metric Units

Throughout the main body of this text the engineering system of units has been employed. This decision was based on the fact that in most engineering and industrial circles this is still the preferred unit system. However, the metric or SI system is gaining more and more acceptance in other circles. To meet the needs of those more familiar with the metric system as well as of readers in other countries the following collection of conversion factors from the engineering to the SI system and vice versa has been compiled for the most commonly encountered units in this work.

Prefixes are used in the SI system to express multiples or fractions of ten of a fundamental unit. The most commonly used prefixes are as follows:

m	(milli)		0.001 or 1/1000
c	(centi)		0.01 or 1/100
k	(kilo)	1,000	
M	(mega)	1,000,000	
G	(giga)	1,000,000,000	

Thus, 1 kg (kilogram) is 1000 g and 1 mm (millimeter) is 0.001 m. In the engineering system of units no prefixes are employed with the possible exception of the symbol "M" used to indicate a factor of 1,000 and occasionally "MM" to indicate a factor of 1,000,000. As an example, 1 Mscf = 1,000 scf and 1 MMscf = 1,000,000 scf. In some instances SI prefixes may also be borrowed. For example, 100k miles =

100,000 miles. Care has been taken in this text to spell out unambiguously any prefixes employed.

The volume of a gas is a function of its temperature and pressure. Thus, the volume of a gas such as natural gas is normally given under specified conditions of temperature and pressure or more commonly under the so called standard conditions. These conditions are 32°F (0°C) temperature and 1 atm = 14.7 psi pressure. The term "standard cubic foot" or "scf" in short is used in this text to express natural gas volume under the standard conditions.

Acceleration
1 ft/s^2 = 0.3048 m/s^2
gravity (g) = 32.17405 ft/s^2 = 9.80655 m/s^2

Area
1 ft^2 = 0.0929 m^2
1 acre = 4,046.9 m^2
1 hectare = 10,000 m^2

Density
1 lb/ft^3 = 16.018 kg/m^3
1 lb/gal(U.S.) = 119.83 kg/m^3
Air = 0.07407 lb/ft^3 = 1.1864 kg/m^3; Water = 62.249 lb/ft^3 = 997.1 kg/m^3

Energy
1 BTU = 1,054.7 J(oule)
1 calorie = 4.1858 J
1 kWh = 3,413 BTU = 3.6 x 10^6 J
1 foot-pound (ft.lbf) = 1.3558 J
1 therm = 1.0551 x 10^8 J
1 ton (equivalent TNT) = 4.184 x 10^9 J
1 quad = 10^{15} BTU

1 quad per year = 0.472 million bbl of oil per day

      = 1 trillion scf of natural gas

      = 44.4 million tons of coal per year

      = 293 billion kWh of electricity per year (100% eff. or 3,413 BTU/kWh)

      = 90.8 billion kWh of electricity per year (31% eff. or 11,000 BTU/kWh)

Force

1 lbf (pound-force) = 4.4482 N(ewton)

1 kgf = 9.80665 N

Length

1 ft = 0.3048 m(eter)

1 in = 0.0254 m

1 mile = 1,609.3 m = 1.6093 km

1 nautical mile = 1,852 m

Mass

1 lb (avoirdupois) = 16 oz = 0.45359 kg

1 oz (avoirdupois) = 2.835×10^{-2} kg = 28.35 g(ram)

1 lb (troy) = 12 oz = 0.37324 kg

1 oz (troy) = 31.103 g

1 ton(long) = 2,240 lb = 1,016.0 kg

1 ton (short) = 2,000 lb = 907.18 kg

1 ton (metric) = 1,000 kg

Power

1 hp = 745.7 W = 0.7457 kW

1 BTU/h = 0.29307 W

1 ft.lbf/h = 3.76662×10^{-4} W

Pressure

1 atmosphere = 101,325 Pa(scal) = 14.7 psi
1 bar = 100,000 Pa
1 in of water = 249.06 Pa
1 in of mercury (Hg) = 3,386.4 Pa
1 psi (lbf/in^2) = 6,894.8 Pa
1 Torr (mm Hg) = 133.32 Pa

Temperature

Degree Celcius (^{O}C) $t_c = (t_F - 32)/1.8$
Degree Kelvin (K) $T_K = t_c + 273.15$
Degree Rankine (R) $T_R = t_F + 459.67$, $T_R = 1.8\ T_K$
Degree Farenheit (^{O}F) $t_F = 1.8\ (t_c + 32)$

Time

1 min = 60 s(econd)
1 h(our) = 3,600 s
1 d(ay) = 24 h = 86,400 s
1 y(ear) = 365 d = 31,536,000 s

Torque

1 lbf·ft = 1.3558 N·m
1 lbf·in = 0.11298 N·m
1 lbf·oz = 0.0070616 N·m
1 kgf·m = 9.80665 N·m

Velocity

1 ft/s = 0.3048 m/s
1 km/h = 0.27778 m/s
1 mi/h = 0.44704 m/s
1 knot = 0.51444 m/s

Viscosity

1 centipoise = 0.001 Pa·s
1 centistokes = 0.000001 m^2/s
1 lb/ft s = 1.48882 P·s

Volume

1 acre-foot = 1233.5 m^3

1 bbl (barrel petroleum) = 42 gal = 0.15899 m^3

1 m^3 = 1,000 l(iter)

1 ft^3 = 0.028317 m^3 = 28.317 l(iter)

1 gal (U.S. liquid) = 231 in^3 = 0.0037855 m^3 = 3.7855 l(iter)

1 gal (U.K. liquid) = 277.418 in^3 = 4.5461 l(iter)

1 quart = 0.94635 l(iter)

1 bu(shel) = 2150.42 in^3 = 0.035239 m^3

1 cd (cord firewood) = 128 ft^3

1 board foot = 2.3597 l(iter)

1 registry ton = 100 ft^3 = 2.8317 m^3

The following mathematical notation may be used to describe large numbers: thousand = 10^3; million = 10^6; billion = 10^9; trillion = 10^{12}.

Index